You Can't

Always

Get What

You Want

MIKE MILLER

Foreword

On March 28, 2020, I began a journal as my wife Rea, was nearing a pivotal point in her journey to uncover the underlying cause of some increasingly problematic medical issues.

For the most part the text of this book comes directly from that journal. It has been edited as little as possible, mostly to correct typos, improve clarity, make the formatting consistent and remove some items which were copyrighted by people other than me.

This account is raw and unfiltered.

Rea-pronounced like "area" without the first 'A'-was my soulmate and inseparable partner for almost 27 years. She stood just under 5 feet tall. As her hair greyed in later years she took to highlighting the ends in a dark shade of purple. She was kind, inquisitive, and hard working. She smiled frequently, and cared deeply about her friends, family and the world around her. She loved music, especially live music and until very near the end, all I had to do was play Phish or the Grateful Dead and she would smile and start moving to the music.

Her unique name came from her mother who combined a blend of family initials-Roy, her dad, and Ernest and Albert, her maternal uncles.

I always believed Rea was one in a million. Tragically, I was right, but not in the way I ever would have chosen.

Chapter 1
(March 2020)

28 March 2020

It's weird how fast things can change. It's not like there weren't hints even a couple of months ago. But I don't think it's possible to conceive of this kind of change until it happens.

The thing that scares me a bit is that COVID-19 isn't really all that deadly for most of us, but it's still more than enough to bring the world to its knees.

So much that we take for granted is temporarily gone now and it will likely be months before we get back to anything close to normal.

Much of the world is under a relaxed form of house arrest and the numbers of infected and dead are steadily escalating each day.

Oddly there are still people claiming it's all overblown.

Not that being cautious is any sort of guarantee, of course. Really there is no guarantee. You can tilt the odds in your favor but short of starting out healthy and finding a very isolated location with a large stockpile of uncontaminated food, there really is no way to be 100% sure you avoid infection.

Of course many have already had the virus. How many remains a mystery and likely will for some time to come.

It's hard not to be a little depressed about the whole situation even if the ultimate outcome is likely to be positive for most people.

I worry about a lot of things right now. Most of all I worry about my frail 87- year-old mother. I last saw her about a month ago. The nursing homes are all closed down now and I couldn't get in even if I weren't 700 miles away. I did talk to her on the phone a few days back. She's nearly deaf, though, so that wasn't very satisfying.

There are other signs of trouble on the horizon, but those are in my personal realm. I'm not going to talk about that now. I'm just going to hope for the best.

Figure 1 Out for a walk. 19 March, 2020.

29 March 2020

Another thing that scares me is the fact that I nearly died of pneumonia twice before I was three years old. I had it again when I was 14 or so and it hit me fast and hard. Thankfully it also receded quickly once I got treated.

Then again, maybe I've already had it? Rea and I were in New York city for a couple of weeks spanning new year's. We were then in the Seattle area in late February and have been in the San Francisco Bay area for most of March. So basically, we've managed to hit all the hot spots. Yay us?

On a more macro level the number of deaths attributed to the virus in the US doubled over the past few days. This might finally shut up some of the people who've been insisting that this is no big deal.

Recently I read that John Prine, a legendary songwriter, is deathly ill with COVID-19-like symptoms. He's 73 and has had a number of health issues over the years so this is very scary.

Prine is a master of the craft. Rea and I saw him a couple of times around 2000, both before and after this cancer surgery and he was incredible. He has so many great songs, and is very well liked and respected. I hope he makes it.

Of course, Prine isn't the only person sick right now and while the worldwide numbers are still small relative to the billions of people who populate the planet, they have been escalating in spite of the fact that this thing isn't all that widespread in a lot of places.

30 March 2020

Rea has a doctor's appointment first thing today so we're going to be up and out early. The standard protocol right now seems to be that only the person with the appointment comes in, so I'll be waiting out in the car. It's one of those fasting appointments, and my main duty will be to find some place we can get takeout after she is done.

Nothing new on John Prine.

It's interesting to watch the evolution of people's reactions. There are more masks in evidence and fewer people seem to be out and about. It's ironic but typically human that this response would have been more productive initially, but it's good regardless, so I guess I shouldn't complain.

An update on John Prine. He is apparently now stable. Fingers crossed.

Worldwide, the numbers are trending mildly positively. In the US the picture isn't as good.

31 March 2020

Rea had another appointment this morning. I went and hung out in the parking lot again. I probably should have walked but my various electronic devices kept me entertained.

The numbers for projected deaths in the US that are being quoted in the press continue to seem absurdly low to me. The White House Task Force did just announce estimates in the 100–240K range. I think the high end of that is low, but at least it's getting within an order of magnitude of the likely upper boundary.

In theory, warmer weather should help, but that assumes that this virus behaves the same way as other viruses like the flu. Not an absurd assumption but it still feels a bit like magic thinking to me.

Don't get me wrong, it would be nice if the low estimates were correct. Very nice, in fact.

As a species we're really horrible at dealing with things that make us uncomfortable. Scientists are better about that than the rest of us, but I don't think they are immune.

There may also be an element of fear. Who wants to be the bearer of bad news? I'm a little broken in that I want to know the truth no matter how unpleasant. I'm not saying that makes me right all the time, but I do think it gives me a tiny bit clearer picture of what is really happening around me. This makes me uncomfortable at times. Anxiety is my near constant companion.

We went for a hike out at Brushy Peak Regional preserve today. Amazingly awesome place. Lots of plants and wildlife including this Western Meadowlark.

He stayed on this post for several minutes as I walked around and took pictures of him from various angles.

I've never seen a more relaxed bird. I was using my Canon EOS 90D and my ultra-wide range (18-300mm) Sigma zoom lens. The pictures didn't turn out as well as I'd hoped but a few were decent with a bit of processing.

Ultra-wide range zoom lenses are naturally mediocre, but they sure are convenient. There is no way my iPhone 6S would have done this well.

Chapter 2

(April 2020)

1 April 2020

April Fool's Day. As the saying goes, the joke is on us. I woke up to find that the fatality numbers for the US had been revised by the site I use to track. I don't have any trust in the CDC. They have their backsides to cover and the President to fear.

The US is increasingly skewing the worldwide numbers which are flattening otherwise.

We should start to see a flattening as well, assuming the various state-instituted "shelter in place" mandates have been followed with any sort of discipline. Here in the San Francisco Bay area, we were the first in the country to go that route. California's numbers are looking very good compared to New York right now and I suspect that is why.

Once this thing makes it someplace it appears to spread like fire on gasoline. We're very, very lucky the mortality numbers are relatively modest, though how modest is still up for debate. Somewhere in the range of 1–4% seems likely.

2 April 2020

Rea had a doctor's appointment to discuss the results of the EEG and MRI she'd had over the previous couple of days. The outcome being there is certainly something wrong, but they don't know what yet. This would be stressful under the best of circumstances but clearly that doesn't describe what is going on right now.

Thankfully we live in a state that was aggressive in the response to the virus, so the healthcare system is still mostly functional, though there have been some canceled and delayed tests. That situation is likely to worsen.

The changes in Rea's cognitive abilities are minor so far but noticeable. They started in January and have so far as I can tell remained roughly the same since. I say they are noticeable but it's actually fairly subtle if you aren't around her a lot or don't know her as well as I do.

Her mother died from complications of Alzheimer's but didn't start exhibiting symptoms until her early seventies. Rea is only 61. We haven't actually talked about that possibility directly, though it has been hinted at. I don't think either of us wants to acknowledge that yet.

It's kinda funny that her doctor has mentioned a couple of times that it's not a tumor, as if that is a good thing. I think both of us would take a tumor over Alzheimer's. Even a 1% chance of survival is better than nothing.

Rea's illness is the real reason we're staying at our small apartment here in California right now rather than heading north to our home in Washington state. Her doctors are all here and until we have a better idea of what is going on it just doesn't make sense to be 700 miles away, especially given the pandemic.

Speaking of the pandemic, yesterday was the first day the US exceeded 1000 fatalities. Math says it won't be the last.

At least the weather is nice.

3 April 2020

The US numbers were a bit better yesterday. Hopefully that is a trend.

Rea started taking a new medication last night. It's an anti-seizure drug apparently. She hasn't had any seizure-like symptoms, but given the EEG results, her doctor thinks it's a good move.

In theory, the dose is small enough that it shouldn't cause any issues, but the possible side effects include dizziness which is something she's been struggling with for a few months now.

I've been taking a lot of pictures on our daily sanity walks. It helps more than a bit to have a distraction. My phone is old at this point, but it still takes a decent picture and some of the software available now does a pretty amazing job of enhancing even mediocre images.

Today is sunny, but the forecast for the next several days indicates rain. We need to get out for an extended walk if Rea is feeling up to it. The new medication seems to have thrown her for a bit of a loop despite the fact that the dose is small.

We both had a bit of a meltdown today. It was mostly my fault. We were going to listen to Trey and Page of Phish talk about their new album on their satellite radio station, but we hadn't signed up for the streaming option yet even though we have the radios in our cars and subscribe that way. Let's just say that the user experience on enabling that was lacking. This sort of thing causes me a lot of anxiety.

It's my observation that there are two different ways that people deal with anxiety. Some panic. I'm not that type. I get angry. Not violent thankfully but I'm not pleasant to be around. I hate that part of me.

I eventually got everything set up and we started listening but a little later I bugged Rea about not taking a couple of her supplements the day before. I think it was the combination of that and my earlier ranting at the computer that pushed her over the edge and she started to cry. She's clearly terrified by this whole thing but neither one of us is very good at talking about it.

I occasionally tell myself that I've had a very privileged life and mostly I believe it. At times, though, it's hard not to be bitter. Rea retired a year and a half ago. Originally, I was going to retire in April of 2019 but decided I wanted to work part-time for another year.

In part I wanted to ease into things and in part I was fearful of being overwhelmed by the amount of travel Rea was going to want to do. Extending my work also helped us pay off a few more bills and pad the retirement savings some more. Neither one of us expected a pandemic or her health problems.

Well, that isn't entirely true. Rea has had a lot of health issues over the years and one of the reasons she wanted to retire at 60 was to maximize the amount of time we had to travel and enjoy ourselves. And now it looks like I screwed that up royally.

So yeah, regrets? I have them. This particular one is currently vying for number one on my lifetime list and it's got a bit of competition.

Our supply of hand sanitizer is declining. I think we may have some up north as well but that's a bit far to drive. At this point we still have about a month's supply so hopefully we'll be OK.

In my weaker moments I kind of wish I'd get the virus. Not a good place to be head space wise but I doubt I'm unique in this.

We have four face masks I bought years ago for woodworking projects. We haven't been wearing them so far, but more and more people have some sort of mask on every time we go out.

I'm thinking of trying to convince Rea to take a short trip up north. We could do our laundry and pick up a few things that will hopefully make our lives a bit easier. Plus, it would be something to do.

4 April 2020

Well, we discussed it and decided we're going to make a short trip up to Washington. We're planning on leaving early tomorrow morning and heading back early Wednesday or Thursday. Tomorrow is Sunday and it's an 11–12-hour drive with brief stops.

It'll be good for both of us to have something to do from a mental health perspective. It's a bit of a risk virus wise but everything is these days. We don't have a washer and dryer in our apartment and the pair here in the four plex are old and not very well maintained. So doing laundry is one part of why we're doing this.

It's also the case that we hadn't planned on staying here long term when we last came down four weeks ago. This will give us an opportunity to be better prepared.

It's supposed to rain today and the next several days. We'll mostly be prepping for an early departure tomorrow morning.

Masks are now recommended, and it seems like more people are finally understanding how serious the situation is.

I cried a little this morning in the kitchen. Rea wasn't awake yet, so it was fine.

We've spent a chunk of the day getting ready to leave tomorrow. We're hoping to be out of here at the crack of dawn but if past experience is any indication, we'll be a bit later. There is always some detail that needs to be taken care of at the last minute.

One of my challenges is keeping my hands away from my face. It's like asking a cat not to lick its ... Well, you get the picture. I've never been very good at similes.

There are a lot of likely half-baked stories circulating about the virus. One is that an early sign of onset is the loss of smell and taste. Another is that different blood types have varying incidents of developing severe symptoms. In the second case, O is the best and A is the worst with B shading a bit towards A in terms of who is most likely.

5 April 2020

We were awake around 4am. We were also in bed at a bit after 8pm, so not too brutal.

It is raining outside and we're eating breakfast and making final preparations for our drive north.

I've been tracking the virus closely. I'm very data focused. In so far as I can, I try not to care about being "right". I'm a lot more interested in what is true. Which doesn't make me very popular in some circles.

Despite my anxiety, I've always had a tendency to say what I think needs to be said. This came at a fairly high personal cost, particularly when I was younger. I was seldom thanked or appreciated for those efforts.

To be fair, I wasn't always right and there were times where I wasn't willing to put my money where my mouth was, so to speak. I eventually figured out a couple of things. First, it went better for me when I asked forgiveness rather than permission. Often, in fact, I found that I didn't have to ask forgiveness if I was subtle enough in my approach.

The second thing I learned is often it doesn't really matter. The thing I was obsessing about turned out to be entirely or mostly a non-issue. Anxiety tends to magnify in my mind's eye what is happening around me. This can make me a tiny bit bipolar while tending toward the downside of the spectrum.

Getting back to the data, it's a bit of a kick in the teeth to look at the numbers and it makes it hard to get away from what is happening but it also helps me feel like I have some measure of control. I don't know if that makes sense. I think it's because understanding a situation helps me to cope. The big challenge here is that I'm not confident in any of the data, but even mediocre data is better than nothing.

Breakfast is about done, time to finish the packing and loading.

Lots of rain during the loading process. We were on the road by 6:45am, though, which is pretty impressive for us.

It's Sunday. I'm not conventionally religious. I consider myself a Christian but I'm not interested in any church. From my perspective churches have too much of humans in them and not enough of Jesus. I know not everyone agrees with me on that and I don't have an issue with it for the most part. I'm sure there are good churches out there and for some people it's the right place to be.

But I've seen too much evil done by people who claim to be Christians yet seem to have absolutely no clue what Jesus said or represented. Hate was clearly not his thing. When people hate it's 100% on them and has nothing to do with Jesus.

None of us is without sin. That's kinda fundamental to the faith – accepting Christ doesn't magically make any of us perfect. Too many people like to pretend it does.

Speaking of not being without sin ... We stopped at the Trader Joe's in Eugene to pick up some essentials like eggs and milk. It was impressive how organized the staff were. They were limiting the number of people who could enter and there was an orderly line outside with wide spacing. We got everything we wanted and headed out to the CR-V. Grocery loading went fine but we already had a lot of stuff in back and I didn't get a couple of the bins in all the way. The rear hatch started to open again, and I lost it a bit and knocked it out of alignment. Remember what I said earlier about anxiety causing me to get angry? Thankfully that doesn't extend to physically attacking people but inanimate objects don't always fare so well. :-(

I managed to get the hatch to close after a bit of fiddling, but I might have caused real damage. Time will tell. Oh yeah, I'm a dumb ass.

Earlier we stopped at a truck stop in northern California to get gas and grab some snacks. It was amazing how clueless everyone was. No masks, walking around without a care in the world.

I get that many rural Americans are generally pissed off about the way this country has been going and until recently I even sympathized on some issues, but this kind of behavior is asinine. Living in a fantasy world only works so long as there aren't significant negative repercussions. Low population density and an aggressive approach to discouraging mobility have saved them until now, but that is no guarantee and that truck stop was exactly the place to be paranoid around. A high density of people and lots of travelers. What can you do, though?

As I was about to fall asleep a lyric idea came to me ...

Jesus do you love us all the same?
Even those who spread hate in your name?

I wonder if I'll have the courage and ability to run with that idea and turn it into a song at some point?

6 April 2020

We got to our place in Washington a bit after 7pm, so it was still mostly light. I got the car unloaded and we were able to relax a bit.

It's obvious that the whole illness thing is getting to Rea and by that I don't mean the virus. I think it's the uncertainty of her situation.

I'm feeling productive. Hopefully that will last. We have plenty of toilet paper and paper towels here and an okay supply of hand sanitizer.

Yesterday I was coughing and my throat felt scratchy, but today I feel better. It's hard to be sure what was going on there. I really wish they had an antibody test. This virus is insidious. Short of a mass extinction event, I can't conceive of anything much worse.

When Rea's mom got sick we were surprised initially, but when we thought about it, we realized there had been signs. Jean had always had a book in her hand for the first several years I knew her, often a horror story. She apparently found them amusing, something I never really understood. I think for some people there is a thrill in being scared or anxious. I'll never understand that. She stopped carrying those books maybe two or three years before she accidentally overdosed on her prescription medication and ended up in the hospital. She moved in with us right after that, as it was then obvious she was having cognitive issues.

There were other things like the time she became upset when she misplaced her scheduling book. In retrospect it had become a crutch that helped her continue doing all the volunteer work she was fond of.

So now I'm asking myself if there have been changes in Rea over the past few years. The answer now that I think about it is yes. The big downturn was sometime in January, but there have been signs for a while now which I just hadn't noticed.

She used to do a lot of selling on eBay but a few years back that stopped, ostensibly because we were in the process of moving from California to Washington. Now I wonder if part of it was that she just didn't feel up to it. The eBay stuff required a lot of bookkeeping and that is something she is increasingly uncomfortable with now.

At times, though, she seems entirely normal and her memory seems fine. Then she'll get confused over which computer she's been using or where she's kept a particular electronic document. It's depressing and maddening. I'm getting better at staying calm and patient, at least outwardly, but it's not easy.

7 April 2020

Second and final full day here in Washington. We'll finish up what we need to get done and head out early tomorrow.

One of the things this trip has done is firm up the idea of where home is. Sadly, given the circumstances, it has also firmed up that being home kinda sucks, particularly for Rea. All the people she wants to see and talk to and all the places she wants to go are off limits to one degree or another.

The same is true for me to a degree, but being an introverted social misfit it's not nearly as big a deal. Not being able to see my mom sucks, but it's just one more bit of suck in a seemingly endless sea right now.

While memory seems to be an issue for Rea at times, the majority of the problems seem to be more "processing" related. For example, last night we were doing laundry and she got confused as to whether the dryer was on the left or the right in the laundry room and even immediately after I clarified this for her, she was momentarily confused.

This morning when I woke up, I asked her if she had turned the heat down last night. This is something she normally does during the colder months. She asked me something along the lines of "Do I do that?". Freaking horrible way to start the day.

Rea's mom and I didn't get along all that well until near the end when I think she had me confabulated with her son. One of the brutalities of dementia-style diseases is not being recognized by your loved ones who are suffering. Rea's younger brother got to experience this on his last trip to visit his mom. I'm a wee bit terrified that I'll be experiencing this with Rea someday.

I'd thought we might extend our stay a day, but Rea is complaining about being bored. I suspect it's a combination of depression over her illness, the world at large, and not being able to do what she wants to do.

The coronavirus numbers have been trending in a positive direction worldwide and in the US over the past few days. I don't understand why, though, and that bugs me. Sheltering in place may be playing a part, but there are a lot of places both in the US and worldwide where that either has not happened or started recently enough that the impact would likely be minimal.

Good news is great, but I don't like it when things appear to magically get better. It generally means one of two things: either the data being reported is bad due to some combination of politics and collection issues; or there are one or more underlying factors at work that we don't yet understand. I guess it could be a combination of those.

Not being good at picking up social cues is awkward. My general anxiety ranges from mildly agitated to angry and freaked out most of the time. Every once in a while, I seem to find my happy place but that is rare. As I shade further to the bad end of the spectrum, I get really bad at processing what is going on in the world around me. I also get bad at reacting naturally. It can start this whole feedback loop that keeps making things worse.

In small groups I'm generally okay. If I think I have something important to say I can speak out in larger groups. I do alright if I have a lot of time to prepare as well, assuming nothing unexpected happens.

Unexpected changes throw me for a loop, and it takes me time to adjust. I've gotten better at this over the years, but my first reaction still tends to be to freak out because all the mental preparation and stress management I've been doing throughout the day/week/month is suddenly thrown out.

I spend some part of my brain power constantly managing my anxiety. I'm thinking about how I'm feeling, what is coming up, and how I can keep on a reasonably even keel.

I haven't talked a lot about what Rea looks like. She's 4'10, though I've been known to exaggerate and say she's 4'11 and a half. I'm 6'2, so we're a bit of a mismatched pair.

We met when I did a site visit to Lawrence Livermore National Laboratory in Livermore California circa 1994. I had friends who worked there as computer support people and she and they were part of a then informal group trying to standardize the way things were done. We were dating/living together within a few months. In early 1999 we snuck off to Hawaii and got married. That was around the time we bought our first house.

Pretty much everyone loves Rea. I say this because it is true. She's outgoing, friendly, and she works hard to make things better around her. She has always been focused on the greater good. A bit too much sometimes, if I'm going to be totally honest, and it has caused some friction between the two of us at times.

She is a beautiful person. Which isn't to say she's perfect. None of us are. Still, I know I won the lottery when she and I got together.

———————

Just heard that John Prine has passed away from complications stemming from the coronavirus.

Nearly 2000 people have died in the US today and I didn't know him personally, but this hit pretty hard. Rea and I saw him live a couple of times and his songs have been part of my personal soundtrack for many years. He was very well regarded and revered in the industry.

I know this year is only a bit more than four months old but at this point even if it ended today, it's pretty much sealed up the top spot in my personal worst years ever list. I'm sure a lot of people are feeling the same way.

Dammit, I'm teary eyed again. Normally I can go years without getting this upset even once.

Muck this virus.

8 April 2020

It's a new day. Hoping for a better one than yesterday, at least on a personal front. Just before bed last night we decided to stay an extra day. My current work responsibilities can be carried out from pretty much any place that has internet. We have a video call with a specialist on Friday that may shed some light on Rea's situation. So we'll either need to leave tomorrow or stay until Saturday.

———————

For the past few weeks, I've been posting pictures of flowers Rea and I see on our sanity walks to Facebook. Social distancing is important, but staying inside all the time is a recipe for disaster. We keep our distance from others and are careful about what we touch, and make sure our hands are sanitized.

This morning's flower was a dandelion.

Dandelions have long had a part in folklore. You can make wine out of them, they can be eaten, and they are even believed to have medicinal properties in some parts of the world. We could all use a lot of healing right now, so it seems like an appropriate choice.

Hmm, turns out that might not be a dandelion. At least it's not the common lawn variety. I got some feedback on Facebook about this. I guess I can say that I'm learning a lot during this whole ordeal.

Rea is smart. Not only book smart, but people smart as well. I envy her that. On the book smart side of things, she has a bachelor's degree in electrical engineering and a master's degree in computer science. When we met, I had 3/4th of a computer science degree. I had taken many of the first- and second-year requirements for a computer science degree and some of the third year as well, but I had zero college math before I dropped out.

In 2007 I decided I wanted to get an MBA. This despite the fact that I didn't even have a bachelor's degree in anything. To apply to business school I had to take the GMAT. Rea tutored me for three weeks and I barely managed to get an average score on the math portion of the test. Luckily I scored very well on the qualitative portion and managed to get into a much better school than I deserved.

Rea is still smart, but I notice differences. I can beat her much more easily and consistently at cribbage and have to help her score most of the time. Her reluctance to work on the spreadsheet we use to track our finances the past couple of months is another.

I'm reduced to hoping this is some sort of weird stroke thing and that she won't get worse. Sometimes I think she's a bit better, sometimes I think she's a bit worse, and still other times I think she's the same. On a day-to-day basis it's hard to tell any difference.

I'm hoping for some good news on Friday but I'm too much of a realist to get a lot of comfort from that thought. Which sucks in this particular case. God I hope I'm wrong about how serious this is.

I got to drive downtown to pick something up. This is highly unusual. Rea loves to go places and because she easily gets car sick, she always wants to drive. This time she chose to stay at home and let me make the trip.

The anti-seizure medication her doctor put her on recently doesn't seem to be doing anything positive. She'd had zero seizures, but apparently the EEG she had last week indicated an abnormal pattern that could lead to future incidents.

The first time she took it was in the evening and she slept for nine or ten hours straight. Before we came down on Sunday she got permission to cut the dose in half while we're away, but she says it's still making things worse. Maybe that's true, but I'm not sure.

A loss of confidence is the other big thing I'm noticing. Rea had me sit in for two calls today regarding that Friday video appointment I mentioned earlier. Not totally unusual given the circumstances but it felt like she wanted me there mostly to pick up any slack and at one point I had to do that.

We made it out at 8:45am or so. Not great but we should make it back to our apartment in Livermore before it gets too late. With no sit-down restaurants open, it isn't like we have much to do other than stop for gas, the bathroom, and a quick bite to eat.

Rea is very methodical when it comes to packing. This has always been the case. I didn't really notice any difference this morning. It always takes two or three times longer than I'd prefer, even when we spend a fair chunk of time beforehand getting ready. To be fair, when I'm traveling alone for some reason I frequently forget something, but I'm mighty speedy at failing.

One thing I realized is that I'm managing to be more patient when things don't go right. That's good but it also bugs me in a way because it means I could have been doing better before this. What's past is past, I guess, but in a sense that is a cop out.

I get to type because I'm the designated navigator. I think I mentioned before that Rea gets car sick. This means the only time I get to drive is when she can't for some reason. I can say without reservation that those rare exceptions were some of the most unenjoyable times in my life. Both because of the circumstances that surrounded them and because of the stress of trying not to make Rea sick. She REALLY hates getting nauseous. There is a story behind that, but I won't get into it here.

———

My throat feels a bit sore again. It seems like this is an every-few-days kind of thing. Normally I'd chalk it up to a persistent mild cold. Odds are that is what it is. Or maybe just stress. COVID-19 has so many ways of making life extra interesting.

———

Public restrooms are getting really hard to find, as businesses either close down or restrict customers to picking stuff up in front of the store.

———

Gotta rant a bit about people in general and a lot of younger people specifically. It's crazy how ignorant some people are. All you have to do is look at what is happening in New York to know how bad things can get once the virus is loose. And they've been sheltering in place for the better part of a month now.

It's been a fairly good trip so far. There was a bit of tension when we stopped for lunch. Rea is generally really good at spatial stuff but that hasn't been true for a few months now.

With so many restaurants closed, it was challenging finding food. Dinner will no doubt be the same, but we'll manage. She tends to get upset when she's confused. Totally understandable and I dealt with it fairly well.

It's bug splatter season. Another sign the weather is warming. Dinner went fine but I think we're both tired of Burger King at this point.

10 April 2020

We got home a bit before 11 last night. I mostly unpacked the truck and we passed out not that long after. This morning we have a video call with a specialist doctor at Stanford. First attempt to log in to the healthcare app was not a success but we have time. Rea is a bit fuzzy this morning.

Well we just finished talking to the doctors via video chat and the preliminary prognosis is pretty much as bad as we'd feared. Creutzfeldt–Jakob disease (**CJD**) is a rapidly degenerative disease of the brain. This sounds and looks a lot like what was referred to as Mad Cow disease several years ago. It has to have been inherited, I think, since we've both been semi vegetarians for decades now.

The initial MRI report mentioned this as a possibility, so we're not completely shocked but we're both devastated. My decision to hold off on retiring for a year is looking worse and worse.

Bad things happen to good people. I've always known this to be true. I'm not sure I'm a particularly good person. I certainly try, but I have nothing on Rea. The only thing one can hope for at this point is a miracle. I'm a believer and I sure would love a miracle right about now, but I know those don't happen very often. I guess we'll just have to try to make our own miracle happen.

The odds of getting CJD are something like one in a million. One in a freaking million.

At some point very soon Rea may stop being Rea. As things stand now, I get to live through that. It beats the alternative but not by a whole bunch. I am so freaking tired.

Let's throw in sad. Duh, right?

Rea just went for a walk so I got to cry a little. It's such a strange mechanism. I have no clue from an evolutionary perspective why we can do it. I have to say I'm glad, though. I always feel a tiny bit better right after.

At some point real soon we're going to have to figure out what and when to tell people. To say this will be devastating to her friends and family is a bit of an understatement. With everything else that is going on right now it's so hard to know what makes sense.

I'm not going to try to make the decision for her. She's still more than capable of figuring this out right now.

Rea just asked me how I was doing. That's a pretty good indicator of what kind of person she is. I told her I was doing okay all things considered. Did I ask her how she was doing? No. That's a pretty good indicator of who I am.

I will ask that question but right now it's just too painful to contemplate.

11 April 2020
We cuddled, talked, and cried a bit once we went to bed last night.

At one point Rea talked about how ironic it was that she'd been worried about becoming friends with our older neighbors up north, many of whom are in their eighties. CJD has a two- or three-year life expectancy once it manifests and we're probably a year-plus into it at this point based on what we've learned about the symptoms.

Looking back to the fall of 2018, Rea was planning on retiring in early December. We'd initially planned for me to work until April of 2019, but I started to get cold feet.

I was enjoying my job and the thought of the near-constant traveling that I knew Rea would want to do was causing my anxiety to spike. Ratcheting down to 60% time at work for a year seemed like a good solution and compromise.

In November of 2018 we bought a house in White Salmon, Washington. It was a bit of an impulse purchase, but we've had no regrets. White Salmon is in the beautiful Columbia River Gorge just across the river from Oregon. I have family nearby which was another attraction.

We'd been negotiating for a few years at that point over where we would land after retirement. Rea favored dry and arid; I favored forested and moist.

White Salmon was a decent compromise. It gets substantially less rain/snowfall than Portland but is much more forested than just a dozen or so miles further east.

Two and a half years later the move is mostly done. I negotiated with my workplace to do two weeks on and two weeks mostly off so long as on my on weeks I was on site. Rent in Livermore at the time was exorbitant so we ended up with an older 500 or so square foot apartment for when I had to be in Livermore.

Initially the plan was that Rea would spend most of her time in Washington when we weren't traveling. It didn't work out that way. Now I wonder if that was another early sign of CJD.

I'll admit I was a bit frustrated about this. I've been writing and recording songs for about five years now. I'd done a bit of that before, but I got serious when I was a couple of years short of my 50th birthday.

I'd tried to get serious about music a couple of times prior to that but something always seemed to happen that would torpedo my efforts. This time turned out to be about the same, as part way into the project my mother got very ill. But I managed to more or less meet my goal which was to record and release a CD's worth of original songs by my 50th birthday. Actually I was a couple of months late but it was close enough.

So in my mind the two weeks in Livermore would be partially for me to get serious about both my songwriting as well as writing fiction and nonfiction.

Every time, though, Rea wanted to come with me for the full two weeks. This led to a bit of tension at times. Now of course I feel guilty about the whole thing.

I also tried to get her to find doctors and other related services in Washington and she just never seemed to get around to it. In part this was because we were seldom there for the first year. Either I was working and so we were in Livermore, or we were traveling and not in Washington.

Rea has never liked being alone but in retrospect that has gotten worse over the past year or so.

I'm not really in the mood to write more about this right now.

For the first time in my life I wish I drank alcohol.

I can honestly say that I don't think I've ever been in this much non-physical pain. Between Rea, my mom, and the virus, I'm pretty sure I'm at my limit. Maybe a refill on that Xanax prescription isn't a good idea.

Thinking about it I should amend what I said before. I've been in this much nonphysical pain before, at least for brief periods of time. When my dad died very suddenly for one. When my mom first got seriously ill about five years ago for another.

Rea is different though. I've spent nearly half my life with her at this point and having experienced her mother's decline I know what I'm in for. The fact that her decline is likely going to be very rapid is a little comforting because she'll lose track of what is happening much more rapidly than her mother did and hopefully suffer less.

Anyone who has experienced a loved one's decline due to any form of dementia will understand what I'm talking about. At some point they stop having the ability to know what is happening to them. Those around them not so much. Those they are in the process of leaving behind suffer for the entirety of the disease but there is some solace in knowing that is a one-sided thing. She even alluded to this last night just before we went to sleep. God I'm going to miss her.

I don't want to pretend our relationship has always been perfect. I've talked about some of my flaws already and Rea has a few of her own as well. Those I'm not going to talk about. I'm fairly confident she forgives me for mine and I know I forgive her for hers.

I'll also say that we could have had a better life if I'd gained this level of clarity and understanding a whole lot sooner.

Reading has always been a refuge to me. I've gotten really bad, though, about not wanting to read books where one or more of the primary characters are obviously evil or unpleasant.

Human flaws are fine. None of us are perfect. I just don't have any desire to hear the villain's side of a story. This is particularly true in fantasy.

I'm okay with being considered superficial because of this. Nuance is fine, and I know not everything is black-and-white but I don't need to have my nose rubbed in that. I read to escape, not to be reminded of the things I'm escaping from.

Currently I'm reading a book that contains the words *"That which is precious to you cannot be seen"*. That really resonates with me right now.

12 April 2020

Today is Easter. I'm enough of a historian to know that the religious significance is overlaid on older pagan ceremonies centered on the spring equinox. As a Christian I've always felt that what Jesus said and did was what mattered. All the stuff layered on beyond that just feels forced and more of man than of Christ to me.

On a much less divine front, the toilet seat in our bathroom cracked yesterday. I talked to the property management company and they gave us permission to buy a new one. They'll compensate us later.

I'm still posting flowers to Facebook each day. I feel a bit dead inside from pretending to be upbeat, but I don't think it's much different from the way most people live their lives.

I'm not saying everyone is normally depressed and pretending to be happy, though there is a lot of that going on right now. I am saying that even before social media the life we presented to the outside world was often an idealized one.

As a species we're not very good at being honest with others. Often that lack of honesty extends to ourselves.

So yeah, I'm putting up a positive front but obviously this is not a good time on any level.

I'm starting to get into a mode of doing projects around the apartment. Organizing things, putting stuff together, cleaning up.

I'm very sensitive to what I view as criticism. This can be a big de-motivator for me when Rea makes a suggestion on how to do something better. This is because her suggestions often cause me anxiety. So since a lot of my life is about minimizing anxiety, I shut down.

It's kind of stupid in a way but if you haven't lived with anxiety don't pretend like you understand.

I'll add that mostly her suggestions are sound. Between her decline, depression, and loss of confidence, she's less likely to interject herself now. It's one of those horrible silver lining kind of things for me. It also means my safety net is vanishing.

Anyone who knows me can tell you that my attention to detail is sub optimal a lot of the time. Again I'll blame this on my near-constant anxiety.

Often I just want to get things done as quickly as possible so I can go find my "happy place".

I spend some portion of my time constantly thinking about what I want to do, what others need me to do, and what my current level of anxiety/stress is. I then plan the near future in detail and stuff further out in less depth. When something new comes up I tend to go a bit off the rails. Particularly when I'm not confident in my ability to handle whatever that new thing is.

All this recent activity is an effort to stay distracted of course. It's good that we have so many coping mechanisms.

The rarity of Rea's disease does seem to be making us popular. Not meaning to sound catty here but given what is going on in the world right now it's fairly impressive when very senior doctors are communicating on the weekend. UCSF is interested in enrolling Rea in a study. Unfortunately that study isn't for a potential cure but anything she and we can do to help in some small way to find a cure for this is a blessing.

I am so effing tired of being on (and sometimes over) the edge of crying. It's likely going to be a month or more before things start to settle down with the virus and I'm really worried about how much Rea will have declined by then. Right now she's fairly normal, and it would be a perfect time for her to hang out with friends and enjoy herself. But she can't do that.

Then throw in the fact that this situation is horrible period and the thought of burdening others with what she and I are going through is just devastating.

I feel like I mostly have to hold it together for her sake. Thankfully the apartment has a separate bedroom where I likely spend too much time. If I were a stronger person I'd be spending more time with her.

So yeah, time to get my shit together and be supportive.

Our friend Debbie just called to say hello and Rea decided to tell her what is going on.

I think this is going to spread. Which is okay if that is what she wants. I feel horrible for the people who are going to find out and be sad but maybe they would prefer to know now. It was going to come out at some point and giving them the opportunity to spend time with her before she's too far gone is probably the right thing to do.

After Rea was done talking to Debbie, we had a good cry and talk. I know I've said it before but Rea is more worried about me than she is about herself. That is so her. Both because she's a good person and because she knows how socially awkward I am. I like people, I want to make the world a better place, but frankly I'm not that good at socializing.

It's funny, on Facebook people who don't know me well probably think I'm a gregarious extrovert. Or maybe not.

When I think back to my youngest days I actually was an extroverted, imaginative, and goofy kid. My family wasn't exactly rich at that point, but we were solidly working class. Things went badly off the rails a bit after I started school for reasons I won't go into here.

Did I suffer from anxiety back then? I'm not sure. I was a fairly sensitive kid, though, and when I got picked on I didn't deal with it well. Which only invited more bullying.

We often say that children are innocent and while it's true, that innocence also has a dark side. Children can be casually cruel to each other without having the slightest idea how hurtful their actions are.

Tomorrow I'm going to try for a bit less of the negative. Today was tough.

On the positive side the virus has been leveling off both worldwide and in the US. I'm not sure I 100% trust the statistics but good news on that front is welcome. I just hope too many stupid decisions don't follow.

13 April 2020

The meaning of life has been debated for a long time now. If it were a profession, it would probably be the second oldest one. My faith comforts me, but it isn't a 100% effective salve and I've always acknowledged that faith and science exist on two different planes. Neither contradicts the other, nor do they need to support each other.

To me faith answers the question of what exists outside the "box" that is the universe we live in. Science is concerned with answering questions about what exists inside that "box".

I think it's a fairly easy and reasonable distinction to make but I'll acknowledge that not everyone agrees.

Last night wasn't a good one sleep wise for Rea. I think the conversation with Debbie and our talk afterwards are weighing on her. We all know we are going to die someday but having a definite cause and a short timeline has to be horrible. I suspect she's awake right now beside me as I quietly type this in bed.

There's a meme on Facebook that encourages us to post our senior pictures in support of this year's high school seniors who have gotten the short end of the stick big time. My yearbook is packed away some place but it's available online in scanned format so I was able to track it down. I ended up looking through the pages a bit and was amazed by how many of the people I didn't remember or recognize from my class. I'd also forgotten how bad my haircut was in that picture. We were poor – really poor most of the time – and my mom always cut my hair. At that point she'd been doing it for a decade-plus and hadn't managed to learn a thing. The sides aren't even at all with each other. You can see most of my ear on one side and none of the other one.

It's kinda dumb to be mildly obsessing over this thirty-five years later but it's an okay distraction I guess.

Rea and I are not big on selfies. When we post pictures to social media they are almost always of the places we're visiting.

Here's an exception from February of last year. This was taken at our house in Washington. I love this picture.

Me on the left obviously and Rea on the right. We got a lot of snow around that time. This year was wet, but not as much of the white stuff.

——————————

I kind of have a plan that says I have to have days where I'm only a little sad. Today is one of those days. It's not like I can really dictate that, but I need to pace myself and try not to wallow both for my sake and for Rea's.

I don't suppose any of this sounds particularly macho. I do not care. Integrity and honesty matter. Taking responsibility matters. What gender you are while doing these things is completely irrelevant.

Which isn't to say that I believe men and women are the same. We are not. There are physical and psychological differences, and failing to acknowledge that makes no sense to me.

Neither Rea nor I have any hang-ups about whom somebody should love.

It's been clear to me since a very young age that gender identity and sexual preference are not simple or one dimensional.

None of us are without sin and we are taught that Jesus loves us all. Why is it so hard for some people to understand this?

I really need to shave soon. My beard is getting a bit out of hand. It is curly so it doesn't get long, but it keeps getting denser and denser if I don't trim it once a month or so.

Ten am appointment somewhere down in the south bay for another EEG; this one will last four hours. We're a bit fuzzy on the details but they are supposed to be sending us information shortly.

Normally making it from Livermore to the south bay by 10am would require leaving around 7am to be certain of making it on time. Traffic right now is a lot lighter due to the virus. I guess that is a very tiny silver lining.

Speaking of the virus, New York continues to have more fatalities every day than California has had for the entire duration of this crisis. It seems clear that shelter in place works since California was a bit more proactive on that front, but it will take time for all the data to be tabulated and conclusions to be drawn. Even then there will likely be a lot of debate.

Overall things are trending in a positive direction, but we're not out of the woods and there are plenty of cautionary tales if one looks around a bit.

Turns out damming things up doesn't work. The emotion wants to overflow eventually. New plan: strategic sadness and keeping busy.

Rea was talking to her friend Andrea who is one of three people who knows about her situation. Andrea convinced Rea to start writing a journal. We'll see where that goes. She's never been much for writing but I think it would do her good to go through the exercise.

———————

I know I end up talking a lot about myself. It's much easier than talking about Rea. I don't think I'm narcissistic but I'd clearly be a poor judge given my obvious bias.

Rea was born in October of 1958 in upstate New York. Her mother Jean was 27 years old at the time and her father Roy was 48. Rea grew up in Adams, New York where her father owned his own business and was for many years the mayor. Her mother was a school teacher, principal, and later the assistant superintendent of the district. Rea has an older half-brother and a younger full brother.

Rea achieved excellent grades through high school and then attended Clarkson University where she continued to excel and completed a BS in Electrical Engineering.

After working for a few years in her field she went to work at Lawrence Livermore National Laboratory in 1983 where she later attained a master's degree in computer science through an extension program that was available at that time in cooperation with UC Davis.

Rea worked for the next 36 years at Lawrence Livermore, initially as a programmer before moving into IT where she fulfilled many different technical roles before transitioning into technical management. She retired in December of 2018.

14 April 2020

It's 5:15am. I'll be waking Rea up in about 15 minutes so we can get ready to head down Palo Alto way for her four-hour EEG appointment. It's at 10am if I haven't already mentioned that.

———————

Wow, I've never seen the commute to Palo Alto be this quick on a weekday. Just about an hour door to door. At least the people who are working don't have to deal with a horrible commute right now.

———————

As I kind of expected I'm not allowed to accompany Rea into her appointment. We could probably have pushed it given her situation, but she's capable of being fairly independent right now and it's never a good plan to piss other people off when it isn't necessary.

Which puts me out in our truck for five to six hours with no nearby bathroom. I could drive home but even with the insanely light traffic that is about a two-hour round trip. Always having a bathroom available nearby is one of those things we take for granted. The virus has turned that whole concept on its ear.

I hear semi drivers are having a major issue with this as well. A lot of restaurants are open for takeout but the bathrooms are almost always closed it seems. I understand that, but it's just adding to the pain.

———————

Last night we watched the first episode of Ken Burns history of country music series. We both enjoyed it, but two hours was a bit of a slog given our general mood.

———————

Okay, waiting in the truck for five or six hours hasn't been so bad. I'm roughly at the halfway point. It helped that I did an hour and a half round trip to the nearby Trader Joe's to use the bathroom and get some more to eat and drink. There was about a 10- to 15-minute wait outside before I could get in as they were metering the number of people in the store.

———————

Got a text from Rea. Looks like she might be done a bit early. Time will tell. In a way being done later might be better though if it means they are seeing stuff they don't expect on the EEG.

———————

Okay, new insight. Living in the moment is better. By that I mean not spending too much time thinking about the past and spending as little time as possible thinking about the future because as of now the future sucks.

15 April 2020

I have a call with my primary care doctor today about my request to refill my Xanax prescription. Have I talked about this before? I'm not sure.

I've always avoided taking it regularly. In theory it helps with anxiety but it's also highly addictive and other than caffeine I have zero interest in being addicted to anything. Mostly it seems to help me sleep and it suppresses the symptoms of my sleep disorder.

It's been a couple of years since my last refill so I guess he wants to talk. Not a big deal I guess but still another bit of stress.

Rea and I had a really good late afternoon/evening yesterday. Phish, a band she really likes, is doing "Dinner and a Movie" every Tuesday night. It's a virus-related effort by the band to help people cope. Each week they put up a full two-set live show from some point in the past. Last night was actually three sets so it started a bit earlier than normal. The show was from their 2015 Magnaball music festivals.

Great show and really good vibe. Getting out and doing something yesterday helped both of our moods, and lounging around watching Phish was a great experience. Rea seemed pretty much normal which didn't hurt my mood any.

Live in the moment, cherish the memories.

Have I mentioned that I've always wanted to be a writer? I have zero desire to go back and read any of this so I'm not sure. I've been paid a few times to write technical articles over the years so I can legitimately say I am a professional writer. I also write songs and have dabbled in the area of fiction.

When I'm in a better frame of mind I want to write stories that are funny, light, and enjoyable. I know that statement would get me mocked in sophisticated circles but so be it. Anyone who romanticizes and glorifies anguish and pain has most likely never experienced either in any depth.

There is an author I really like by the name of E.M. Foner who writes light science fiction which borders on fantasy. The stories are a bit whimsical, caring, and hopeful. They are so good to read. It's like medicine.

I understand that you need conflict to make a good story, but that conflict doesn't have to be on the level of a zombie apocalypse. A lot of really good storytelling exists well short of that line.

———

I'm writing this journal for a couple of reasons. The first is to help me process what is going on. It's painful, but I think it will help in the long run. The second is as practice. Writing is like any other skill: the more you do of it the better you get. At least that is the hope.

The word processor I'm using to create this keeps giving me helpful grammar suggestions. Some of them are useful but about two thirds feel like attempts to make me sound like everyone else. Part of being a writer of any sort is to develop your own voice. It's hard to do that when your word processor is trying to turn your mint chocolate into vanilla.

And finally, to be honest, I'm thinking this is a story that deserves to be told. I'm doing a poor job on the pandemic because I'm distracted by the Rea situation. I'm doing a bad job on the Rea situation because I'm finding it hard to tell her story now that it's likely coming to an end.

I don't know, hopefully something good will come out of this; The rough plan we had for the next 20 years has been totally blown out of the water and I'm badly in need of a bit of structure and distraction.

———

My doctor is nearly 30 minutes late calling. He's one of those people who will take as much time as he needs with a patient so I'm not surprised; it's happened before when I've had an appointment.

———

Talked to my doctor. It's all good, though I'm going to need to do blood work when the lab reopens. Apparently, the government has a fear that some people are getting fake prescriptions, then selling the pills, so I'll need to take one the night before. For now I only get 15 pills. That's typically a couple-year supply for me.

Generally speaking, there have always been two scenarios when it comes to somebody leaving the house (excluding work): Rea goes out to do something she wants/needs to do; or both of us go out together. It's been rare for me to go out by myself.

Twice recently Rea has encouraged me to go take care of some errands by myself. I don't think it's because she doesn't want to go out; I think it's because she's trying to get me used to the idea that the way things currently stand, I'm going to be on my own in the not overly distant future.

It looks like there may be word soon on our medical-related schedule next week, along with information on the extended EEG from yesterday. Looking forward to that. In the immortal words of the late great Tom Petty, "*The waiting is the hardest part.*" This is true on so many different levels right now.

News on the virus could be better, though it could be a lot worse. The places that failed to take early precautions are starting to blow up a bit and NY is still experiencing 700 or more deaths a day. Intellectually I know it could be a lot worse and likely will be in some places for a while.

We have a tentative schedule now. Two days of testing at UCSF on the 20th and 21st which are this coming Monday and Tuesday. I spent an hour or two gathering information and sending and receiving emails related to this. It's good to have something to do.

In the last four days we've gone from needing to have the heat on for some portion of the day to needing the air conditioning on to cool the place off in the evening. It's fairly typical for Livermore to go from too cold to too hot in a very short period of time in the spring. It's also not unusual for the evenings to get chilly into early July. On more than one occasion I've felt like

I was going to get frostbite while watching 4th of July fireworks.

16 April 2020

Thursday.

In a way the days are passing very quickly.

We didn't go out for our sanity walk yesterday. For Rea that was the second day in a row of no appreciable exercise. I'm going to have to encourage her today. God knows she's had to encourage me many times in the past.

Social media continues to be a mixed bag distraction wise. I can't stop myself from occasionally shooting holes in the absurd conspiracy theories that are starting to circulate. This doesn't help my anxiety at all, but poor impulse control isn't a new thing with me.

One of the crazy stories going around is that C-19 actually made it to California in the fall of 2019 and that is why the fatality numbers are so low.

The obvious problem with that? Millions of people travel to and from California from other parts of the country. In particular, travel between New York City and the larger cities in California is very common. I might have mentioned before that Rea and I spent two-plus weeks in Manhattan around New Year. We'd also spent a lot of time in the San Francisco Bay area in the fall and early winter at that point. Our situation is far from unique, particularly with the big ball drop at midnight on New Year's Eve.

With all those people from California in NY City, doesn't it seem likely that C-19 would have conferred the same level of immunity to NY as California appears to be enjoying?

I believe the truth is that population density and when people were asked to shelter in place are the real factors here. If you look at California county level data, you'll see that most of the fatalities are in the southern part of the state where the shelter in place orders came later.

Yes, there are population differences, but I don't think that fully accounts for this.

I just noticed Rea writing in her journal.

Rea's short-term memory is more of a problem than the long-term currently. Especially details.

She was on an anti-seizure medication that is no longer needed based on the current diagnosis. She has to taper off it, though. Last night I described the plan I received from the doctor. She's remembered there is a plan but has had to be reminded what that plan is a few times.

The whole living in the present thing mostly works. Would be nice if the present in the world at large were nicer.

We didn't end up going for a walk. This was mostly on me.

Tomorrow we have some things we need to do in preparation for the appointments Monday and Tuesday for the study enrollment at UCSF. The main one is tracking down the MRI's Rea has already had done.

UCSF pointed me to the website of the CJD foundation. It looks like there are a lot of good resources available there. I think this may be one of the least desirable sites to need to make use of on the internet but it's good to have a resource.

The iPhone SE 2 comes out tomorrow for pre-order. I mentioned it to Rea a couple of times today. Once via email and once pointing out the email later in the day. She hasn't responded.

My phone is about dead, so I really need a new one. I didn't feel like I could just buy it without running things by her, but it's really awkward given the situation. I think I'll just order one for me tomorrow.

When my mom got sick and nearly died about five years back, I spent a couple of weeks in the hospital with her. They were ready to send her to a care facility about a week after her surgery, but it took me another week to talk her into it.

Prior to now that was the most stressful time of my life and it only lasted two weeks. This is going to last months at least. I have so much respect for people who have gone through this kind of thing before and made it through. I'll be lucky if an ulcer is the only health issue I end up having.

Even when I haven't done much physically, I end up exhausted by the end of the day, so at least I'm sleeping most nights.

Sorry, I'm repeating myself here, but I seriously had no clue why anyone would want to drink themselves into oblivion before and now it makes total sense to me.

I always thought I had kind of a crappy childhood but at this point I'm fairly clear on the concept that it could have been a whole lot worse. I was never physically or sexually abused and the emotional abuse was pretty typical for what non-cool kids went through. Without the anxiety it would have been almost idyllic.

A change in perspective, yay?

17 April 2020

Friday. It's payday as well. I suspect I won't be having many more of those, at least in the sense I've been used to until now. My vacation and sick leave will run out in about three more weeks. I didn't have a huge amount on hand, as dealing with my mother's illness and all the vacationing we've done over the past year or so pretty much ran it down.

The vacation part was intentional given our plans. The sick leave part was outside of my control.

It's not like we're about to be destitute. Rea is old enough to have a good pension and I have a modest one as well. We also have good medical insurance and a long-term care plan. In short, we are very fortunate. Still, I'm worried a bit about the finances. That's the nature of healthcare in this time and place.

I ordered the phone. Now I'm feeling bad that I didn't order Rea one.

I kind of feel sorry for anyone who might someday end up reading this. It's the kind of thing that I would never be able to get through. Yet I have to. Well played, universe, well played.

Rea is writing in her journal again. I hope it's providing some comfort/ closure/clarity.

We picked up the second MRI DVD this morning and I'm in the process of copying it now. I was able to zip it into an archive and send a share notice to our contact at UCSF. I wanted to just upload it but their email system won't take large attachments.

A couple of days ago we walked over to one of the local sandwich shops and grabbed some takeout. There is a very small park along the route with a statue of three children playing. We noticed they all had knitted masks on …

I guess you could interpret this act in a lot of different ways, but I'm going to focus on the apparent (to me) whimsy of the action.

New York has had shelter in place going for around a month now and with the new reporting guidelines is seeing over 1000 deaths a day still.

Meanwhile Texas is talking about relaxing their stance on the virus and the president is encouraging people to rebel and "get the economy going" again.

Being kidnapped by space aliens has never sounded this good before. Though I'd prefer to avoid being anal probed in the process if possible.

Rea and I went for an hour-plus walk this afternoon and she asked about the phone out of the blue. I fessed up to having already ordered one and we're going to order another for her.

Her memory is a bit iffy at times but it's more general confusion that is the problem currently. Like not being sure whether she should use her iPad or her Windows laptop for a particular thing or confusing the two. She also almost drove by the turn to our apartment on the way back. We don't generally come from that direction, so it wasn't a huge error.

We're one day away from having her completely off the anti-seizure medication and her balance is fairly good.

She'll be getting another head MRI on Monday or Tuesday, so they'll be able to compare the one taken a few weeks back. We should have a better idea how fast the disease is progressing at that point.

18 April 2020

The problem with me not bringing up the whole phone thing is that the ETA on Rea's is about three weeks out while mine is only one. Hers will be going up north as we're hoping to be up there in a bit more than a week. It's almost identical to the iPhone 6S so I'm hoping she won't be confused by it.

I need to keep in mind how very lucky Rea and I are. Financially we're as well prepared as we could be. We have long-term care insurance, good medical insurance, and a decent nest egg. No guarantees, of course, which is terrifying. I've probably said all of this before.

We drove by that statue of three children I posted a picture of a few pages ago earlier today. Two of the three masks were gone. I hope whoever took them needed them. Though, given how porous they were, I'm thinking they won't work. Maybe one person took both and combined them?

I was just going through the initial MRI report. We got it on March 17 which was just a week or two before I started this journal. I suspect news like this is not supposed to go directly to patients:

Evidence of extensive cortical restricted diffusion that is predominantly seen in the bilateral occipital lobes, left frontal lobe, as well as the posterior thalami (left greater than right). Constellation of findings are most concerning for possible Creutzfeldt Jakob disease, with the differential also including other forms of encephalopathy (limbic, toxic / metabolic eghyperammonemia), recent generalized ictal state, or even paraneoplastic syndrome if there is history of underlying malignancy. Recommend clinical correlation, which may include CSF sampling, as well as post contrast and ASL imaging on future studies for further evaluation.

Imagine reading that out of the blue. At the time I'd started to suspect something serious was wrong but nearly every word in the above paragraph is a short-term death sentence.

To be clear, I'm not mad at the hospital. Humans make mistakes in times of stress. We were both a little freaked out, but it wouldn't be until a week or two later that we started to suspect this was "real". Honestly, we're still not 100% sure. The tests Rea is going to take on Monday and Tuesday will likely seal the deal one way or the other.

I think she's writing in her journal again. I honestly never thought she would spend much time if any on it. She's never been big on writing of any sort. I think she prefers to communicate verbally and visually. We're very opposite in this area. I prefer the written word because it gives me time to think and carefully evaluate what I want to say.

Today we signed up for Disney+. We actually had a free one-year subscription through Verizon, so it doesn't cost us a cent in the short term.

I suspect we'll be spending more time watching streaming services. It's not all bad. We'd planned on doing this when I was fully retired anyway.

I'm noticing a reduced ability to multitask in Rea. I don't think it's recent.

One of the things I struggle with is not over- or under-estimating what is going on with her mentally.

In an alternate reality we're in Berkeley at a venue called The Freight & Salvage seeing an Australian band known as "The Waifs". Thank you Google Calendar for reminding us that we're missing that show. It's not the calendar's fault, of course; it's just doing its job.

19 April 2020

Sunday. Today we need to get prepped for the trip to San Francisco tomorrow for the lab work and testing.

I was thinking about how I've been able to be a better person recently because of Rea's illness. I find myself making the effort not to be visibly impatient or let out my sarcastic side. Her illness was obviously my wakeup call because of the likelihood she doesn't have a lot of time left. But then it occurred to me that we're all on a limited timeline. In fact we or somebody we love could be gone or at death's door at any time.

Intellectually I think most of us know this, but it's just not real until we actually experience it. No matter how this works out I hope I can keep that insight in mind going forward.

Rea is writing in her journal again. For the record I don't plan on looking at it any time soon. I'm not sure I ever will. I'm going to have to be in a very different place mentally. It'll depend on her wishes as well, of course.

20 April 2020

I'll be waking up Rea at 5:30am so we can eat and start heading to San Francisco. Her first day of tests starts at 9am. In pre COVID times we'd need to be leaving earlier to be sure we made it.

I think we both view this as the final chance for this thing to turn out to be less serious than it currently appears. The odds are against that, but we'll hold onto whatever we can find. I never thought I'd find myself in a situation where permanent mild brain damage for Rea would sound like a wonderful option.

Day 1 (4/20)
9–10am – Sign Enrollment Documents
10–11:30am – Cognitive Testing
11:30am–12:30pm – Lunch Break
12:30–2:30pm – History and Physical
2:30–3:30pm – MRI

We had a good experience today, though we didn't get done until about 5:30 as various things ran long. UCSF was a bit of a ghost town. Rea and I are both exhausted this evening.

I've had surprisingly little trouble sleeping. I think it's because I'm emotionally exhausted by the end of the day.

We don't start until 10am tomorrow so we'll be able to sleep in a bit. Plus we now have a better idea of current traffic patterns into the city and how to get where we need to go.

21 April 2020

Day 2 (4/21)
10–11am – Motor Testing
11am–12pm – Genetic Counseling
12–12:15pm – Blood Draw
12:15–2pm– Lunch Break
2–3pm – Conference
3–4pm – Lumbar Puncture

Today we'll likely get a near final diagnosis. The analysis of the fluid from the lumbar puncture results will be the final word I think but getting those back will take a while.

The analytical part of me is not optimistic. The human part of me is praying and begging that this turns out to be something that won't take Rea away from me in the not-too-distant future.

I'll wake her up around 7am (it's six now) and we'll get this show on the road.

––––––––––

Rea woke up just before seven and we got out of the house at about the time I'd wanted. I know I've talked about how light the traffic is right now, but it just keeps surprising me. We're talking 3am levels of traffic at 6:30pm.

Things ran a little long again at UCSF. Given the situation, the staff there have been amazing, so again I'm not complaining.

The diagnosis hasn't changed based on the latest round of testing. The only potential silver lining is it appears Rea has a slower acting variant.

We've talked a bit about when we make this whole situation more public. I don't think it will happen until we're back up in Washington. I'm so not looking forward to that. I think in part because it will make it more real. It's plenty real right now.

Rea is in good spirits given the situation. For her I think it's a relief to be fairly certain we know what's going on. She's lived such a good life, too. Maybe that helps?

One thing we got told today is it would be a very bad idea for Rea to drive. So our trip to San Francisco was her last time driving. This was less about diminished capacity and more about the potential liability if there were an accident. With the virus shutdown I've hardly driven the past couple of months. Luckily, I guess you never forget. The light traffic helped.

I'm exhausted again.

22 April 2020

A good night's sleep helps. I ended up taking the last Xanax from my previous prescription and fell asleep around 9:30. Sleeping until 5:30 is good, at least for me.

One of the things that's freaking me out a bit is I barely managed to take care of myself before Rea and I met. I'm a heck of a lot better at "adulting" now then I was then, but being increasingly responsible for her as well as myself …

I think I need to not think about that right now.

––––––––––

On the C-19 front things are starting to go downhill. Not so much the fatality numbers, which are increasing, but modestly compared to what they could have been. The real problem is that everyone is tired of the social distancing and the impact it has on the economy and people's own well-being. Many have lost their jobs. Others have lost or are in danger of losing their small businesses.

Enter the foreign and domestic trolls to stir the pot and further undermine things.

I've often seen the WWII generation referred to as "The greatest generation". I think that is a fair description. I don't think it is any coincidence that when they started retiring, things began to go south in this country. They are essentially all gone now. Surviving the depression and helping to win WWII gave them a perspective and depth of experience that is lacking in most of us today.

Maybe I'm just an old guy standing on my porch waving my cane at some kids and telling them to get off the lawn. Not that kids went outside much even before the virus. Well, not in the high population areas anyway.

––––––––––

Now we're thinking about renting an RV and touring the country. Honestly, we'd be gone in a heartbeat if not for the virus. Driving around without a bathroom seems like a bad bet with so many places having the restaurants shut down and public restrooms being rare in rural areas.

––––––––––

We finally talked a bit about yesterday and making plans going forward. Rea has agreed to write down what she wants both now and leading up to the end. One thing she made clear is that she wants to be at home at the end, if possible.

I guess I'll mention here that I'm really bad at saying "I love you". I know, it's a guy thing. Rea and I have never been prone to exchanging even more esoteric terms of endearment like "honey" or "dear".

If there were ever any doubt, the way the two of us are reacting to this whole thing makes it very clear how deeply we feel for each other.

―――――――――

The conversation has started about how we want to publicize Rea's illness. In the age of social media, it's both easier and more complicated. Rea would like to control the flow of information so that close family members and friends find out about this before it hits social media.

23 April 2020

I sent an email to the CJD foundation introducing myself, and Rea and my situation. I may or may not hear back. It's okay either way. Just having the potential to hear back from people with first-hand experience is good.

I'm not sure if it's because I'm paying more attention or if there has in fact been a cognitive decline over the past week. It's painful to sit with her working on a puzzle because I'm constantly reminded of how much more capable she used to be at doing them. On the one hand, she wants and needs the companionship, while on the other hand, being with her and seeing that decline is kinda killing me.

I'm struck by how much I stopped seeing Rea before this thing started. By that I mean I think I had a picture of who she was in my mind and I was seeing that picture rather than the real her. The her who was increasingly showing signs of having a debilitating disease.

Maybe that is normal when you're in a long-term relationship.

So much of the "software" that comes with being human is just broken.

The reason I'm mentioning this is that it was very hard to answer some of the interview questions on Tuesday as to when things started going wrong.

Rea's been writing down her wishes. Kind of a will in a sense. I think I'll ask her to let me read it by myself first and comment since she's mentioned there are a number of items she wants to get my opinion on. To belabor the point, I'm not ready to do that with her in the room.

It's not like she hasn't seen me cry recently but: A, I'm a guy; and B, I don't want to increase the burden on her. I already feel like I'm doing a piss poor job.

The afternoon and early evening have been better. I took a short nap which helped. My current epiphany is I need to keep my shit together both for Rea and me. I can't think too much about what is going on because it is going to color my memories of what little time we have left together in ways that aren't going to help me in the long run. I need to work at being grateful for what I still have.

Once word spreads, I'm going to need to stay away from social media for a while, I suspect.

24 April 2020

We'll start packing up to head north today. Rea seems to be in a good mood. I'm never sure how much of that is her natural optimism or her faking it. Maybe a bit of the disease as well? It's good that she seems to be doing okay.

I'm doing better than yesterday. We'll see how it goes.

I probably talked about this before, but I'm so glad we extended our NYE trip to NY City an extra week. We made some great memories there and it was the last trip we took where Rea was more or less normal.

Once the word gets out next week I'm going to need to contact and set up home nursing and hospice in Washington. I go back and forth in terms of how fast I think the disease is progressing. The truth is probably some place in between the two extremes.

We've had a pretty good morning. Take out from Black Bear diner in Pleasanton and we've made some progress on the puzzle we're working on. My new phone has arrived at the UPS store and we'll likely go pick it up in a couple of hours. The value of a mundane day is much higher right now.

The apartment in Livermore is small but there is a decent amount of storage space up high, as the ceiling is an inverted V that is 10 feet or more at the lowest and a good 15 feet at the highest point. So there is space above the cabinets and closets to leave stuff. We have several bins we use to haul things back and forth. I need to pull some of them down so we can start preparing for our return to Washington. It looks like we'll be heading back early Sunday.

We stopped at Target after eating our takeout in the car and picked up a few things.

"Words", a song from the 1980s band Missing Persons was playing quietly on the store PA system: *"What are words for when no one listens any more"*. Kind of a perfect soundtrack for current times. They also had a minor hit "Destination Unknown", which would also fit well on a soundtrack for this point in time.

The new phone is here and taking forever to activate.

We stopped briefly at Safeway to get some things we couldn't find at Target and I chastised some guy for going the wrong way. The narrow aisles in Safeway are one way right now as part of the C-19 mitigation effort. He ignored me. Ironically, I nearly went the wrong way in a different aisle soon after that.

She's been doing so well, but tonight she is clearly depressed. It probably didn't help that I've been a bit on edge. My new phone experience has not been good so far and the overall situation is, well ... mucked up. We're going to go for a walk and work on the puzzle a bit.

A couple of National Geographic dog documentaries helped improve her mood.

25 April 2020

We're working on the "magic" puzzle. I think Rea wants to have it done before we leave. Not sure we can do that today and still leave first thing tomorrow so we may be delayed a bit.

I think she's getting worse. She didn't know what her iPhone was called when she first woke up and has struggled with a word or two since then.

We'll leave when the puzzle is done. I think I'll be spending most of the day helping her with it as she's starting to struggle even with easier-to-place pieces.

I'm feeling a bit numb today. That's probably for the best.

I emailed a longtime friend of mine today with details on what is going on. The circle is slowly expanding. He's not on social media so the risk is low of things getting out before we have a chance to manage the information spread. He wouldn't blab in any case.

Rea got notification of an impending prescription refill earlier. She was able to figure out it was for the anti-seizure medication she'd been taking for a while (Kepra), and talked to the pharmacy and got it canceled.

We had a good afternoon and evening. Didn't go for a walk, which was bad, but we made a lot of progress on the puzzle. I think we'll get it done tomorrow and also have time to finish packing.

26 April 2020

We talked for 45 minutes or so last night once we were in bed. We've gotten to the point where we can talk without breaking down most of the time, but it's hard. It will be until we get to the point where Rea is no longer enough of herself for us to have these kinds of discussions.

We talked about how we're going to tell people a bit and she also told me she is working on a plan for what she wants to do with her remaining time.

The virus complicates that but we'll do what we can. It really is about living in the moment as much as possible.

This morning she seems to be in good spirits and I've noticed little if any impact from the disease. We can still joke around, and the part of her mind that enjoys music hasn't been impacted yet. That is a blessing.

Today has been a good day. We got most of the puzzle done but decided to focus on getting packed. Although Rea had a bit of anxiety, she is doing well. With a few minor exceptions, this was a very good day for her mentally.

27 April 2020

I've often woken up to find Rea awake in the middle of the night reading on her phone recently. In retrospect I think that is her time to deal with what is going on. I'm close by but asleep so she can let her feelings out without feeling guilty for impacting me. This morning when I woke up, she said she was scared and cried a bit. We didn't talk much but we did cuddle. I think she felt better after that.

We are nearly ready to head north to our place in Washington. I likely won't have much time to write today since I'll be driving.

28 April 2020

We did okay yesterday. The drive started out badly with me getting pissed at somebody driving behind us while we were three quarters of the way out of our parking spot after eating breakfast via takeout at Noah's Bagels, and then got worse when someone pulled over at the last minute when we were about to get onto the on ramp to 580 Westbound.

There were two cars in front of us and the idiot in front pretty much slammed on their brakes just before the turn onto the ramp. My plan had been to have most of the bins we were using to take our stuff north in the bed of our truck but the forecast ended up calling for rain so I had to wedge most of the stuff into the back seat area. The sudden braking to avoid a collision caused a paper bag full of snacks to fall forward and hit the shifter which put the truck in neutral. I was hitting the accelerator and nothing was happening. This in turn freaked me out and pissed me off, and then Rea got upset and started to cry. It was horrible. She said something about being upset because she didn't understand what was happening at the time.

There was one more minor incident along the way where I got annoyed at somebody for bad road etiquette, but I just refused to let them in and then let them pass us on the left a bit later.

Before Rea's illness I seldom drove, especially recently since I'm not working. A 600-plus mile drive after having to shoehorn stuff into the truck put me over the edge. Thankfully we made it intact.

We talked about starting to communicate what is going on to more of our friends and family today on the drive. Rea is still asleep. Hopefully we can make progress on that today and put it behind us.

She was in a fairly good mood first thing this morning. She's writing the letter right now to tell people about her situation. I had to remind her, and I feel one part awful and one part okay about that. Awful because she's sad right now but okay because it'll be done and she's likely never going to be as capable as she is today of saying what she wants to say.

The large windows in the living room have a partially tree-obscured view of Mt Hood. Is it odd to find a dormant volcano soothing?

It's much brighter here than in the tiny apartment down south. I think it's a better environment. We're also further away from our longtime friends which is a mixed blessing. Rea has quickly made friends with a handful of people in our new neighborhood. I'm not nearly as good with people. She's told one couple. We're debating whether to spread the news here.

Weird thing, I think I might have almost had a panic attack just now. I did not like that feeling at all. Is it possible to be too sad to be angry?

Rea's across the street talking to our neighbors who know about her situation. In theory I should be with her, but I can barely be strong for just her. Adding other people to the mix kinda terrifies me right now. Especially when I think about the probable near term. Every time she has the smallest lapse it kills me. It could be forgetting the name of a tree or a person or some minor thing that happened within the past hour or two. Maybe I'm blowing things out of proportion. I don't know. It's just so hard to tell.

To try to generate some sort of positive focus I've started thinking about setting up a charitable foundation in Rea's name.

I eventually went across the street and got in on the end of the discussion. It was a good talk, if a bit emotional. The anticipation is sometimes worse than the experience. In part because it hits all at once while the experience ebbs and flows

---

Phish has a song called "The Wedge". We heard "The Wedge" twice yesterday on our drive. Rea just mentioned that.

29 April 2020

Not a bad day so far. We're moving forward on the notification plan. That won't be fun but it needs to be done and just knowing it will happen soon takes a little weight off of both of us.

And now I'm feeling down.

She is very easily confused about timing as we try to coordinate the announcement of her illness. Is this new or just being exposed by the circumstances? I don't know.

I guess I'm still not good at avoiding the roller coaster emotional swings. :-(

We've decided to do all the communication tomorrow. It will be a very long and difficult day, I suspect, but also cleansing?

30 April 2020

For the record Xanax takes the edge off a bit but it's not a miracle drug.

Today we tell everyone. God give me strength to help Rea see this through.

We've told a lot of people but haven't done the big push. That will happen early this afternoon, I think. It's about 11:30am now.

All that is left is to post on Facebook. At this point I think we may wait until tomorrow morning. No use ruining people's sleep.

I haven't said much about C-19 recently. Obviously other things have been top of mind. I do still keep close track of what is going on. NY is trending down, which is good, but other states are trending up – New Jersey and Pennsylvania to name two.

I find it odd that states that were slow to issue shelter-in-place orders like Florida are doing relatively well. I wonder what their death numbers would look like for the past couple of months if compared to the same period last year? It's hard not to be suspicious.

California continues to have very modest numbers given the population of the state, but that is largely attributable to quick action. Even so, southern California is seeing the bulk of the infections and deaths, possibly because they waited a couple of extra weeks to issue shelter in place.

I'm not alone in being ready for this to be over. It would be nice if Rea and I could get in a bit more living while there is time. Having said that, we're not interested in having that happen before it makes sense.

Chapter 3
(May 2020)

1 May 2020

I went to Safeway and the postal annex over in Hood River today to get some groceries and pick up a few packages. Almost all the customers in Safeway were wearing masks. Maybe a new rule went into effect?

If everyone would wear masks and be smart about distancing, we could probably start to open up more stuff.

2 May 2020

We started the day by playing cribbage after breakfast. The last time we did this was probably in March some time. At that point Rea was having a lot of trouble with the scoring. She was arguably a bit better today and no worse. She did get confused a couple of times but hadn't been awake long. Yes, I'm making excuses. Still, it was encouraging.

Late yesterday afternoon I made the "let everyone know" post to Facebook. I used this picture, which was taken a month or so back on one of our sanity walks in Livermore.

People have been very supportive and obviously hurt by this. This leaves me both saddened and a little happy. Saddened because I hate causing good people pain, and happy because it means that Rea's life has not been wasted. She's touched so many over the years and that is a good thing.

———————————

The C-19 thing continues to be frustrating. Listening to the parroting of "Live free or die" bullshit gets on my nerves. Freedom comes with responsibility. That responsibility extends in a lot of different directions including into the community.

It's funny that the same people who will parrot "Freedom isn't free" around the 4th of July apparently have no recollection of this concept when they are asked to do anything that mildly inconveniences them.

Go back two or three generations and our ancestors were living through WWII. They had rationing of every sort, a draft that took most of the able-bodied males away from their families (many never to return), and numerous other hardships. All this came after nearly a decade of devastating economic hardship for most of the country.

Go back 50 years and the draft was still in effect and many young men were being conscripted and sent overseas to potentially die.

We will fail as a country because we've grown soft. External forces are exploiting our failures, but you can't widen cracks that don't already exist.

Once again I struggle with how quickly the disease is progressing. These past few days have been challenging. Is it exposing things that have been there for a while, or are some of the deficits I'm noticing relatively new?

On the plus side, I'm only mildly freaking out when she says or does something that she wouldn't have before CJD.

3 May 2020

Rea wants to visit NY and see her family and friends there one more time. This has me freaking out big time. Mostly because it's becoming obvious that she really wants me to come.

Anxiety is evil. I'm barely managing to hold things together a lot of the time. When she talks to people on the phone, I really need to be someplace else as hearing her talk about her condition pushes me over the edge. Truth is, I'm handling this very badly. Not news based on what I've been saying here, I guess.

Yesterday when she brought NY up I mildly freaked out. I told her it would be cool if she wanted to go by herself but I really didn't want to go. I am a total ass. Then a bit later she wanted to go for a walk and I told her I didn't want to. After she left, I had a short crying jag (I swear to God I have never cried so much in my life) and ran out after her. We walked for a bit in a light rain before heading back home.

Today I'm pricing motor home rentals. We have the money and, not surprisingly, there are some fairly good deals right now. I'm thinking of suggesting that we head out after her next UCSF appointment. What terrifies me is the speed of the progression. I just don't trust myself at this point to know how quickly she is declining. We'll know a lot more after the UCSF appointment as they'll do another MRI along with the other testing. My fear is that if we wait too long she'll be unable to make the trip.

It's clear that she doesn't want to go to NY alone.

We've reserved the motor home. It turns out it is much cheaper to pick one up in the SF Bay area than Portland right now. That includes paying around 10% sales tax in California.

Strange days indeed. Pickup is scheduled for May 23, drop off for July 2. We'll wend our way across to New York. Otherwise no real plans besides Yellowstone. We'd been scheduled to go there at least a couple of times but plans always fell through. Rea has been there once before, a long time ago for a single day. The park may not be open, but we should be able to get close. We'll play it by ear.

Having this in progress is making Rea happy. I'm happy too. It's nice to have something to look forward to. I pray that it goes well. We can't always get what we want or deserve, but Rea deserves to have this trip be perfect. I'll settle for good though.

4 May 2020

Monday. We'll likely head south a week from this coming Thursday or Friday. We won't be back for about a month and a half based on current plans.

The Disney/Pixar movie *Up* opens with the back story of Carl, the crotchety old fellow who is the protagonist. We find out that he lived in the home that is currently surrounded by skyscrapers with his wife Ellie for many years. She is gone now and he is a sad, stubborn, bitter and lonely old man. We also learn that Carl and Ellie tried but were unable to have children. Rea and I decided early on not to have children.

Why do I bring this up? We're currently working on a two-sided puzzle that has a young Carl and Ellie on one side and the old version of them on the back. When it came time to choose which side to do, I suggested the young version. The old version hits far too close to home right now.

Rea suggested the puzzle and we didn't discuss the similarities between ourselves and Carl & Ellie. Maybe she didn't realize, maybe she did. I sometimes think we're talking to each other in code a bit.

It's not that we haven't discussed the current situation, though arguably we don't discuss it enough. Or maybe we do. Humans, at least modern humans, aren't well equipped for this kind of thing. Go back just three or four generations or travel to less developed parts of the world though and things quickly get a lot more grim.

We are blessed in so many ways. This world is neither heaven nor hell though it can sometimes feel like either. What we experience is a combination of our own thoughts and actions, our interactions with others and random chance.

———————————

Sometimes it feels like I'm losing my mind. I think it's just the stress. Case in point, I spent 30 minutes looking for my wallet today. It turned out it was under a piece of paper on the couch where I'd sat a couple of times to take a break while searching.

I do worry a bit about the possibility that Rea got CJD from something she ate. She and I seldom have the same thing whether we're at home or eating out. Neither of us eats Beef either so I think that's unlikely. Bottom line, I'd be lying if I said that the thought hadn't occurred to me that I might have somehow gotten CJD as well.

5 May 2020

Okay, so maybe I'm getting sick. Hopefully not with the dreaded C-19. I'm a little congested and really tired and fuzzy headed. We did see our friend Debbie last Friday and I've been out for groceries and to pick up mail a couple of times in the past week. I always wore a mask when close to other people and used hand sanitizer and soap so in theory I was safe.

Rea is doing reasonably well today. We played some cribbage at breakfast and her scoring and play were decent. She's beaten me the past two games we've played and I haven't been holding back.

———————————

Lunch time cribbage wasn't quite as good.

She'd been hanging out with some of our neighbors for a couple of hours so was likely tired.

Still overall a good day so far. Weather turned out much better than we expected. It's really beautiful outside. Inside my head is not so good but that's going to be my life for a while.

6 May 2020

Decent day so far. Played some more cribbage and while she struggles a bit with the scoring, she was still less confused than a while ago.

7 May 2020

I haven't been feeling very verbose the past day or so. It's not a depression thing. I just don't seem to have much to say right now that isn't repetitive. The world is a major downer, as is our personal situation.

One new thing is I think we're going to plan on being in California for Rea's final days. We have a much better safety net down there and once the C-19 stuff starts to recede a bit it's much easier to get in and out of there for people coming to visit from far away. Flight wise, that is. Let's ignore the traffic issues for now.

We don't want to stay in the current apartment, though. It's dark and run down. It was perfect for what we needed when we rented it but it is the wrong place for Rea to spend her final days.

Rents are coming down, but are still outrageous but thankfully we can afford it. I'd make it work even if we couldn't.

———————

Today hasn't been great for Rea, but it's been fairly horrible for me for reasons that aren't entirely clear. On the plus side I did start a group on Facebook that has the goal of keeping people informed and asking for non-monetary help for the two of us. It's up to 23 members already.

I go from terrified, to deeply depressed to in denial constantly. I keep thinking I'm getting better at this and I am, but it sure is a slow process.

I've started corresponding with a fellow who went through the same experience a couple of years ago. His story is eerily similar to the one Rea and I are going through. The first several months in particular were nearly identical including the time of year. There were some deviations after that, mostly in our favor for which I am grateful. Rea seems to be progressing more slowly being the biggest one.

At least two more decent months Lord. Can we get that please?

———————

I think today is the day I finally accepted that this is happening. I hope it gets easier from here.

8 May 2020

Social media sure can kill my sense of calm quickly. Time to cut back on that I think.

―――――――――――

We're spending some of today packing. This always stresses Rea. I've seen a bit of that today. Nothing too horrible.

She likes to have lots of options in the morning when she gets dressed. I've pretty much settled on jeans and cheap T-shirts of various colors so we're pretty far apart on that front. Having to narrow things down doesn't make her happy.

The motor home we're renting is 25 feet long. It has a decent amount of storage space, but we can only carry so much. I'm going to do my best to be accommodating, though.

―――――――――――

I'd say I'm feeling about 50% as bad as I have the past several days. Accepting this new reality is going to be an ongoing process, but I really feel like I made a huge step yesterday. I'm still not sure I'm strong enough to get through this, although I'm feeling much better about it now.

―――――――――――

I'm still arguing with people on Facebook but dealing with it a bit better this afternoon.

―――――――――――

Looks like we'll be leaving a week from today since stuff I ordered from Amazon that was supposed to be here earlier will now not make it until Thursday. Lots of things are slipping schedule wise. Given the times I understand it on a rational level, but it is frustrating.

―――――――――――

Fairly good day for Rea overall and a very good day for me since I managed not to cry even once. I did get a bit misty eyed at one point.

I'm still of the opinion that finally accepting what is going on has helped. This should also make it easier for me to give Rea the best possible experience in her remaining time.

9 May 2020

Day two of not being soul-crushingly depressed every time I think about our situation. I could get used to this.

Rea is probably 85% herself right now and in some situations you can't even tell she's sick. What was going on with me emotionally before yesterday was not sustainable. I still get a little teary eyed when I think too much about it, but it's manageable. All of which is making it a lot easier for me to be present for her while she's present for me.

We were working on our 2019 taxes most of the morning and still have a bit of work to do. The pandemic has given everyone an extension, but we need to get that taken care of before our big trip.

Rea and I both love music. She loves listening and dancing to it. I like that as well but am more interested in the writing side of things.

Her first musical love was The Grateful Dead. I went to a handful of shows with her when we first got together. Jerry Garcia died in 1995 and that put an end to that. Mostly we went to smaller shows and venues for the next 20 years.

Then in 2015 Rea saw Trey Anastasio, the lead guitarist and primary vocalist for Phish playing with the surviving members of the Grateful Dead during their 50th anniversary shows. This is where she discovered Phish, her second great musical love.

She's been to 50 shows since. I made it to most of those. We were scheduled to attend several of their summer tour shows this year, but those shows got postponed because of the pandemic. At this point it seems unlikely that she'll get to go to any more.

Our last shows were the 2020 NYE run at the Garden in New York City. I'm fairly sure I've talked a bit about that trip already. It was epic in a lot of ways. It was the second-to-last trip we did before the CJD crept up to the point where it couldn't be ignored.

10 May 2020

I've talked a bit about our New Year's trip to New York, but I haven't mentioned the hotel we stayed at. Here's a picture of the key card.

The New Yorker has been around since 1930 and has a very colorful history. For instance, it was where Nikola Tesla spent the final years of his life.

We landed on December 26 and came back on January 7. The signs of trouble were very subtle at this point, and it would turn out to be our last problem-free trip.

We were on the 24th floor and had a pretty good view of the Empire State Building.

For the first few days Rea had a bit of trouble navigating from the elevator to our room. The halls are a bit odd in the New Yorker but it wasn't that difficult. I didn't think much of it at the time. She was doing a number of other things that were fairly complex at the time without issue.

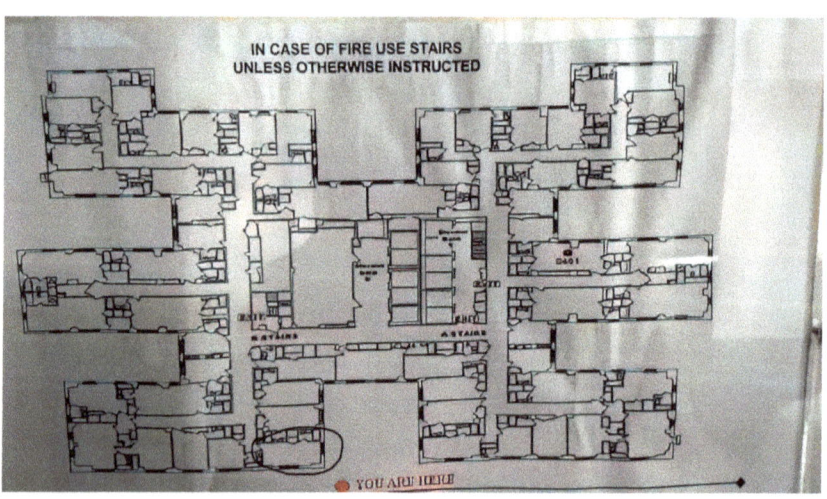

IN CASE OF FIRE USE STAIRS
UNLESS OTHERWISE INSTRUCTED

YOU ARE HERE

She's writing in her journal. That hasn't happened in a while. Something about a setlist? I decided not to clarify as I think I know what she means and I don't want to derail her.

God this would be easier if not for the pandemic. No place to go, can't easily see people, everyone is stressed. Fun times? No.

It's Mother's Day. Guilty admission, I haven't talked to my mother in a month or so. We can't get inside the care facility she is at, but with a bit of work I could talk to her on the phone. I did send her some gifts and a card.

I keep expecting to get a call saying she's passed away. She's so frail and yet tough at the same time. Although she's my mom, she will always be an enigma to me.

I've been kind of been responsible for her since her medical emergency. When we announced Rea's illness I asked my brother if he would be willing to deal with the arrangements if our mom passed away. He agreed immediately.

I'm a bit better at dealing with the situation now, but the thought of having to deal with my mom as well was pushing me even further toward the edge.

Rea's mood isn't that good today. I think she's noticing her confusion is a bit more present than it has been. Hoping this is just a bad day.

Her mood improved but overall this was by far the worst day she's had. She was mildly confused constantly. For instance, we were doing some laundry and she couldn't keep track of which was the washer and which was the dryer.

I had to explain the difference between "statement balance" and "current balance" for a credit card payment a couple of times as well. :-(

Basically I'd say she was in a mild daze the whole time today.

11 May 2019

She's asleep right now. Will she be better than yesterday? God I hope so.

Yesterday I decided we should wash our bedding. After we stripped it and got the first load started, I kind of forgot about it. Previously Rea would have taken care of that. Given how bad she was yesterday that didn't happen and it was evening when "we" remembered and was nearly bedtime by the time everything was washed and dry.

I got a little testy while we were making the bed. The downside of being less depressed is it's a bit harder to control my anxiety. I'm not making excuses here; I was a bit of an ass when she didn't seem to understand what I was asking her about which side of the sheet went up. I'm 53 fricken years old, I should know this already and getting pissy about it with somebody who has CJD is kind of the height of stupid and not cool.

We were both exhausted at the time. Not much of an excuse, though.

She seems to be having a good morning. Counting points during Cribbage went about as well as it has since her illness became noticeable. She also put away most of the dishes and washed the ones from breakfast.

I'm hoping this will be a good day. We need a lot of those to make our road trip work.

Still looking good after lunch. Point counting was good again when we played cribbage and she hasn't been as out of it as she was yesterday.

Just got word back from UCSF on her next round of testing. It will be the 19th and the 20th.

It's evening, and Rea is over at her friend Buck's house.

It's been raining on and off since about dinner time. The days are getting longer, particularly this far north. The view is gorgeous right now …

I'm kinda missing her. Today was a good day and yesterday was the latest reminder of where this whole thing is heading.

12 May 2020

We're nearly done with our taxes. The final form we needed arrived in email late yesterday. No refund for us, but that is okay. Not gonna lie, having no state income tax on Rea's pension is a big plus.

It is officially not a good day for me. Still on the shallow end of the pool compared to a week or so back though. I'm thinking it is probably a Xanax night tonight.

Rea is answering emails in the "special" mailbox we set up before doing the big announcement. Nothing new has come in there the past few days and I worry she might be answering messages she has already responded to, but if so, this is a subtle way of letting people know where she is.

I'm back to being worried about our road trip. I kind of wish we had left already but that would have made things tough in other ways.

Rea's plan is to stop along the way to New York and visit friends. My preferred plan would be that we drive to New York and see her family first so she is at her best.

Our current schedule gives us enough time for another UCSF visit and a few days to visit with friends in Livermore.

Rea has pretty much stopped using her iPad. I think it's because she gets confused going back and forth between it and her Windows 10 laptop. She mentioned that was starting to be the case a month or so back.

When we go to UCSF we'll be staying at a nearby hotel. It's about a mile away. We'll also be taking BART to get to the hotel. We'll have to reverse that route on the way back, though I may just have us take Lyft. We're doing this because Rea is concerned that the motion sickness medicine she needs to take when I drive would cause her to do worse than otherwise on the testing portion of the visit.

She's always been highly competitive academically but not in an obnoxious way. I think it's one of the things people like about her. She's a high achiever but in no way arrogant about it or dismissive of others.

She's been going over to see her friend Buck fairly regularly in the evening. Buck is in her late 80s and very much with it mentally. They watch *Jeopardy*, *Wheel of Fortune*, and whatever else is on at the time.

I kind of suspect this is Rea's last time here in Washington. It will really depend what sort of shape she's in when we get back from our big trip.

Even though I've pretty much accepted the reality of our situation I still pray for a miracle. Somebody has to be the first, right?

13 May 2020

Last night was a Xanax night. I think I feel a bit better this morning. Rea is still asleep.

Rea is in a good mood today and seems to be doing well so far. Counting points at Cribbage was as good as it's been recently. It's obvious, though, that math is where a lot of the damage to date has occurred. At one point she struggled adding eight to 16.

We worked on the "Up" puzzle a bit in the afternoon before Rea finally suggested switching to something easier.

The sorting of the new puzzle was a struggle with her becoming confused about which bins pieces went into and leaving pieces out initially.

Survivor finale night. Rea loves *Survivor*. I do not. To be fair, it didn't evolve into the debacle I thought it would many years ago when it first debuted but the world still kind of went steeply downhill since then so maybe I wasn't totally wrong.

The interesting thing is that this season probably started around the time she began to exhibit symptoms and as far as I can tell, she hasn't had any significant problems following it.

The bulk of her issues are really in math-related stuff with a bit of fuzz around short-term memory, at least on normal-to-good days. On her worst days those things are magnified.

Her social skills and love of music are still pretty close to normal. That is a huge blessing, as it prolongs her enjoyment and quality of life. She's retired; she doesn't need math.

14 May 2020

Her sense of time is pretty heavily impacted as well. I suspect this is related to the math issues. Last night just before we went to sleep we were discussing our trip back south. She was having a lot of difficulty with keeping track of which events happened in what order.

Putting together a pill schedule was a challenge this morning as well. We recently got some weekly pill containers to make it easier to keep track of her medications and supplements. The one we are using has two small containers for each day of the week. She was easily confused about which of the two containers to put the pills in that she only took once a day.

On the flip side we ran into our neighbor Dan when we went for a walk around lunchtime and she participated in a 15-minute or so conversation and I doubt he even suspected she's having problems.

Around dinner time we had a heart-to-heart about the trip, Rea's condition, and the future. This is the kind of scenario where it is hard to detect her decline.

The talk was tough on both of us, but we came away from it with a better understanding about where we both are right now and how set Rea is on making our big cross-country trip.

I think the stress of the packing is causing her to have second thoughts. The staff at UCSF seem a bit concerned about the trip as well. I'd been exchanging emails with them for the past few days and that came up as a topic.

Some of the decision we make will hinge on how she does during next week's testing. Ultimately it's our decision but we'd be idiots not to listen to the concerns of the medical staff. Particularly since they are experts in this disease.

15 May 2020

I slept kinda lousy again last night.

On the plus side we did talk some more about the big trip and have decided to scale things way back. I'll need to talk to Rea when she's up to be sure we're still on the same page. Her memory for this kind of stuff is still good, so I'm not worried about it from that perspective.

I still have a lot of stuff to pack and need to shower as well. I don't think we are going to manage an early start. Time will tell.

No, we are not getting an early start. I think she got a decent amount of sleep, though, which is good. I may have to stop at a rest stop and nap a bit somewhere along the way.

16 May 2020

Yesterday was brutal. I did a lousy job of helping Rea get organized and we didn't end up leaving until nearly noon. Sixteen hours later, we finally arrived at our apartment in Livermore. It didn't help that I'd managed to sleep just under five hours.

Normally this would be about a 12-hour trip with brief stops, but I ended up needing to nap a couple of times to make it and we stopped a bit more than normal.

Rea has never had a great sense of time and CJD has made it worse.

———————

On the drive we discussed the concept of a charitable nonprofit organization. I mentioned CJD/dementia, anxiety, and animals as possible focuses and Rea added in suicide. And thus "Rea's Song" is one step closer to reality.

———————

Today is mostly going to be a recovery day. Rea seems to be doing okay but the drive had to be tough on her. I feel bad about that but there isn't anything I can do about it right now.

———————

She did well today, although it's easier to see and acknowledge the decline when she is tired. I'm tired too, but at least I can attribute that to lack of sleep.

17 May 2020

It's Sunday today. We both slept really well which should help. Rea is going to visit her friend Andrea and I have some things to do in preparation for our trip to San Francisco for the UCSF testing over the next couple of days.

———————

I'm starting to explore the possibility of having us move into an assisted living apartment. There is a place nearby that gets really good reviews and they have everything from normal apartments through to memory care. Rea wants to spend her final days at "home", but we've already acknowledged that this will be in an apartment or rental home. I'm going to discuss this with her.

———————

Rea spent a couple of hours with Andrea at a nearby park. We need to finish getting ready to head to San Francisco. I just got a text from her that she is on her way home. It's getting to the point where I'm a little nervous about that. She made it home fine, though.

Rea did okay on the BART trip into the city. She got confused when we were walking from the station to the hotel. She thought at one point that we might have gotten turned around. I was following Google Maps, though, so we were fine.

We talked to her younger brother for half an hour or so and she was mostly normal. There was a point where she got a bit confused. I'm going to blame our schedule over the past few days for some of that.

San Francisco is a ghost town. Barely anyone was out, and it was mostly homeless people.

We saw a woman on BART and a man down the street from our hotel having meltdowns. Strange and sad days indeed.

Here is our schedule for the next two days…

Day 1 (5/18)
10:30am–12pm: Cognitive testing

12–12:45pm: Lunch break
12:45–1pm: Blood draw
1–3pm: History and neurological exam
3–4pm: MRI

Day 2 (5/19)
11:30–12:30pm: Motor testing
12:30–1:30pm: Lunch break
1:30–2:30pm: Conference with doctor
2:30–4pm: Lumbar puncture

18 May 2020

Hard to believe but it's been 40 years since the big blast of Mt St Helen's. Here's something I wrote on Facebook to commemorate the event.

Spring of 1980
We set off on a course
Stop at Mt St Helen's
Before it blew full force

I was 13 years old at the time and my family were in the process of moving from southern California to Oregon.

Ten years in California had brought no sustained success and a lot of disappointments. My dad had happy memories of the time he spent in Madras, Oregon in his mid-to-late teen years and so we headed north.

The four lines at the start of this section are from a song of mine called "Campground Stories" which is mostly about my family moving from southern California to Oregon in the spring of 1980. Along the way we did in fact stop in Battleground near Mt St Helen's.

The husband/SO of one of Rea's mouse collector friends died recently. I recall meeting both of them at some point along the way, but I seldom went to the various mouse collector events. I remember them being really nice people.

Not surprisingly this made Rea cry. It made me a bit teary eyed as well, mostly because it's a reminder of where this whole thing is heading.

Had a good chat with one of the UCSF doctors about our possible trip. It sounds like the concerns aren't outside of what Rea and I have considered. I'm going to tentatively push for us to go, though we still have more discussion on this topic with the medical staff.

We haven't heard official results yet, but she felt good about how she did on the cognitive testing this morning. That's the important thing, at least in the short term. If she did close to as well as last time, then we're as golden as we can be.

Her decline has seemed fairly obvious the past week or so to me. I try to be honest with her but not to the point of being cruel. I'm hoping the stress of the travel has been aggravating her symptoms. The MRI and the cognitive testing will tell the real story.

I keep going back in my mind to the fact that this is a one-in-a-million thing. It's mind boggling, particularly if it doesn't end up being genetic.

19 May 2020

Second day of our second two-day visit to UCSF. Rea had to wake me up a bit before midnight because I was having one of my REM sleep malfunctions and thrashing around.

It's been a few days since she had what I would describe as a good day. I'm thinking this is the new normal. She's a bit forgetful and seems to be walking around in a haze most of the time. Today is no different so far. It's depressing.

I'm not going to give up on there being one or two good days ahead, though. At the least I'm hoping she can stay at this level for a month or more. We have a lot of people to visit.

I know I whine a lot, but I'm really really tired.

———————————

Still tired but the news was mostly as good as could be expected given the circumstances. Minimal if any change between last month's MRI and this month, cognitive tests showed a bit of decline in one area and some improvement in another, so we'll call that a wash and the physical side seemed pretty steady as well.

Given my observations over the past week I'm a bit leery of these results, but some of the issues might be due to all our travel and travel prep during that time.

Three of the four tests on her spinal fluid came back positive for CJD and one was right on the border between positive and negative, so short of an autopsy the diagnosis is pretty much a lock unfortunately.

Right now I'm waiting for her second spinal fluid sample to be taken. Then we have an hour walk to the BART station followed by an hour train ride to our car. That will not be fun.

Yes, I just whined again.

20 May 2020

The trip home wasn't as bad as I thought it would be. The walk was around an hour and when we got to the Powell Street Station half of the entrances were closed but we eventually got in.

Once we did, we got to see just how different things are right now.

This was around 6:30pm when the station would normally be wall-to-wall people.

The picture above shows the train we took back to the Dublin/Pleasanton Station arriving.

There was confusion over where a lunchtime get-together was happening. This was organized by a good work friend of hers for people who she used to work for. Proper social distancing and masks were in place when we figured out the correct location. She basically confused two different parks in Livermore. Both are a bit obscure, and this hits right in the center of her time and place difficulties. I should have done a better job of vetting where we needed to be.

I could have stayed but politely declined. My social anxiety is at an all-time high right now and I really want Rea to be the center of attention for as long as that is feasible. I think I'm going to say that on Facebook in our private group. More or less, anyway. I might fudge a little on the anxiety thing.

Rea had a good time at the lunch get together. When I came to pick her up there was still a handful of people around, and we stayed and chatted for a bit. I've always done better with smaller numbers of people.

Overall it was a good day for her. More visiting planned tomorrow.

21 May 2020

We had left over iced tea in the frig from when we went to Panera Bread for breakfast takeout yesterday. Rea drank a bunch of it just before bed and slept poorly. Hopefully this won't have too much of an impact on her today but under five hours of sleep isn't a good thing. I didn't realize she had consumed the tea until after the fact.

———————

So far she seems to be doing okay today despite the lack of sleep.

She had a good time hanging out with more of her former coworkers at lunch. Tomorrow we have a couple more visits scheduled, one for her solo and one for the two of us. It's good that people are getting to see her and that she's still doing well enough that it is often not obvious that she is having issues.

———————

Rea asked about assisted suicide toward the end of her UCSF appointment on Tuesday. I'm not going to lie, that makes me both sad and anxious. I woke up at one-point last night while she was still awake and clearly depressed. I think we talked a little and I tried to comfort her but it's all a bit hazy. Sleep is my escape and it can be hard to avoid its grasp.

———————

I really need to talk to her about the whole assisted suicide thing. We've been busy and I've been putting it off.

I took this picture on the 19th while we were eating lunch outside during our visit to UCSF.

I posted it to her Facebook group earlier today after getting the okay from Rea. I think it's a good picture of her. We'd decided in advance that it was "Phish" day so she had a Phish shirt and jacket on while I had a black T-Shirt with Phish guitarist Trey Anastasio on the front.

More socializing tomorrow. I'm finding I'm okay in small groups of people I know. Rea is going to spend a chunk of the morning with her friend Julie and then we're both going to spend the afternoon together with Sue and Cheryl, a couple of work friends.

I can't wait to get on the road. I'll probably change my tune quickly, though. I'm pretty much a "glass is half empty" kind of guy.

22 May 2020

Friday, we have a full schedule today. One thing I need to do is call the motor home rental place and verify the pick-up time tomorrow.

I'm not great on the phone for reasons that aren't entirely clear to me. I think part of it is that I base a lot of how I respond to people on visual cues. The phone doesn't have that.

Okay, so there is video calling these days but paradoxically I don't like that either. This whole being human thing can be a challenge.

Rea seems to be doing okay this morning. Typically forgetful about small details but nothing out of the ordinary.

Pick-up of the motor home is 2pm tomorrow. Let the joy and the terror begin.

I just realized I forgot one little detail. Some friends are allowing us to store the motor home at their place while I do the loading. It's a mile or two away. I'm not clear on how I get back here. It's not a bad walk, or they might give me a ride. Likely will, but the whole C-19 thing sucks yet again.

It's only a mile and a half. I'll just walk.

We spent a chunk of the afternoon with our friends Sue and Cheryl. We also got to hang out with their three small dogs and Yogi who is a huge Bernedoodle. Rea did well in conversation and really enjoyed visiting with the dogs. Sue has been lobbying us to take on Yogi who was a surrender from a family and a dog she's spent a lot of time training. He's an awesome guy but at around 110 pounds is much too big for us. As Rea grows more unsteady, he would be a constant hazard to knock her over.

23 May 2020

Today is the day I pick up the motor home for our trip. Really hoping that goes well. It's bound to be more complicated than I'd prefer. Or maybe that is just the pessimistic side of me talking.

It's become clear to me that Rea, and by extension me, have a lot of very good friends. They have circled around us in a way, and to an extent that would be impressive even in normal times. These are not normal times, though.

The offers of help and the near-constant socializing for Rea have elevated her mood and given me an opportunity to prepare for our trip and get a little time away.

———————

She had some confusion between her phone and the key for the front door as she was preparing to head outside to be picked up by her friend Pam. I was a tiny bit sharp with her which she did not appreciate. She tends to fret leading up to these social encounters, and with everything else going on I was feeling stressed and didn't answer her in the kind way I should have. Really, I just said something like "That is your phone".

After she left, I nearly had the second panic attack of my life but I realized what was happening and managed to head it off.

This kind of thing is going to become more common, so I need to get used to it. Really, it's not that different from the general low level of confusion she has been having for a while now.

Motor home pick-up time is about one point five hours away. I'll be getting a ride over from our friend Jean.

C-19 means constant second guessing. Seeing our friends means risking that we infect them or they infect us. Asking for help is the same general deal. We (mostly Rea) have awesome friends and it would hurt hugely if any of them ended up getting seriously ill because of one of us.

24 May 2020

More preparation for our big road trip. Have I mentioned that we (mostly Rea) have awesome friends? Well, we do. The response we've gotten has been nothing short of amazing.

I'm hoping we'll be totally packed today. I'm working on being more proactive with helping Rea. Fingers crossed.

Rea is going to visit with her friend Andrea this morning while I get some fruit and do other things related to our road trip.

Life is so different now.

It's awesome seeing her friends wanting to spend time with her despite the virus.

She's still visiting with Andrea and I've managed to take care of the morning chores. I'm not going to lie, it's way faster doing this stuff by myself, especially now. Rea is very organized and methodical. I'm more a "just in time" kind of person. I'm constantly looking at what needs to be done and making new lists in my head of things to do along with scheduling. Sometimes stuff falls through the cracks which is the downside of my approach.

I'm not sure how much of the way I approach things is the result of my anxiety. I do know that if I think I'm going to do something and then I get derailed for some reason, it is a big-time de-motivator. I think a lot of that is the stress of not finishing something I've started. That probably is related to my anxiety.

———————

Had a really nice get together with a number of people who have gone to the regular Friday night get togethers over the years. Our friends Curtis and Ellen are letting us park the motor home at their home as we do the loading and final prep. They also organized today's get-together in their beautiful and large backyard. Masks and proper social distancing etiquette were followed.

Multiple people came up and told me that if anything went wrong, they would be happy to fly out and help if needed. CJD is a curse but we are blessed as well.

25 May 2020

Final packing and the first leg of our trip. We made it to just north of Shasta Lake in northern California. The weather was on the hot side so we stopped at a campground rather than roughing it at a rest stop. Shore power means air conditioning and that made a big difference in terms of our evening and sleeping.

26 May 2020

We have about another six hours to drive before we get back to White Salmon. We'll likely make it there in the late afternoon or early evening.

I'm contemplating hooking up the drains on the gray and black water tanks. We didn't end up putting much water/material in them, but it's something I need to "learn" to do.

Rea just decided to use the camp bathrooms. Her thinking is sound in that we don't want to use up our limited carrying capacity when we don't have to. Still, I'm worried she'll end up getting lost. I made sure she had her phone so I should be able to call or track her down if she isn't back soon.

27 May 2020

Rea made it back fine, though she didn't find the bathrooms. They weren't that far away but when she and I walked over to them we discovered they were locked with a key code that we didn't have. Not a big deal.

She was mildly confused several times yesterday. At one point we stopped for lunch and gas. She got a sandwich from Subway. I'd parked the motor home after filling the tank and was waiting for her. She got in the driver's side. For some reason she didn't seem to want to eat at the table. Eventually I talked her around to moving into the passenger side seat.

We got to our house in Washington a bit before 8pm.

I woke up around 5:30 this morning with "Box of Rain" playing in my dreams. It's a Grateful Dead song but unusual in that it was co-written and sung by their bassist Phil Leash. It's a song he collaborated on with long time Grateful Dead lyricist Robert Hunter. Legend has it the song was written as something that Leash could sing to his dying father.

Rea is the Deadhead, but I've been exposed to a lot of their music through her. Given the context of the song's creation it's interesting to me that I was dreaming about it. The last part of the song is especially poignant....

Such a long long time to be gone
And a short time to be there

On Facebook I described the motor home as one part sail, one part brick. It's about as apt a description as I could possibly come up with. It's pretty much a low-level wrestling match even when the wind isn't blowing. Add in a strong breeze and it's a workout for sure.

The progression of the disease is subtle but obvious despite the good results last week at UCSF. There is seldom a time when she's not mildly confused or seems fully herself, at least to my eyes and ears.

I still need to talk to her about the assisted suicide question. Between all her/our social commitments and prep for the trip, it's been easy to put it off.

I hate playing the "Is she worse today?" game with myself. Today the biggest deficit dealt with preparing for a shower. She wears special plastic shoes in the shower in part to lessen the chance of falling. First, we had to go out and retrieve them from the motor home. Next, she managed to put them between the two parts of the shower curtain and forgot. I eventually found them, showed her where they were, and wandered off. Then a few minutes later she had forgotten again and had to be reminded.

A while back this would have killed me. Now it just makes me a little bit more tired.

28 May 2020

I locked myself in the bathroom downstairs last night in part because I didn't want to visit our neighbors with Rea. I think it was a mild panic attack. The kind I've had on and off my entire life, but mostly when I was younger. Or maybe it was just anxiety.

I've mentioned before that dealing with people is stressful to me. Dealing with Rea's illness is, too.

I like communicating on Facebook. It allows me to say what I mean but at a distance. I've mentioned before that I like people, I want to help people, but I don't often feel comfortable, especially in crowds. I'm okay with people I know well, but even then I'd rather find a quiet corner to read or relax when the number of people edges toward double digits.

A couple of minor emotional meltdowns today for Rea. Preparing for trips has always been stressful for her and CJD has magnified that. I likely wasn't as helpful as I should have been at times. Basically, it was our normal level of mild dysfunction in these situations but magnified a bit.

29 May 2020

Did the final packing and set out on our cross-country trip. We'll hopefully make it a bit beyond Boise today.

At one point Rea said she didn't want to go. She always stresses during the packing, but once the travel starts she's fine, and so far that has been true this time as well. I reassured her when she got upset and we continued our prep.

I managed to forget to stow the foaming hand soap dispenser that was by the bathroom sink which caused a big mess back near the door to the shower/toilet. Luckily we had some towels that we rented with the motor home that seem to have done a good job of sopping up the mess.

We ended up at a rest stop an hour or two east of Boise. I tried to find a campground near Boise but the two I checked were either full or not answering their phone.

It's fairly warm since we have no shore power and getting to sleep isn't happening quickly. This probably won't be good for Rea.

She's definitely getting to be more out of it as time goes on. I hope we can make some good memories on this trip. Those memories will mostly be for other people unfortunately.

Me, sometimes I feel like I'm drowning. I'm human and frankly I'm fucked up and dealing with Rea's decline is challenging me in ways I never could have imagined. I pray regularly that I'll have the strength to make it through this.

30 May 2020

The overnight at a rest stop wasn't my best plan. It was hot and loud, plus we were not really prepared since I'd assumed we would stop some place earlier and have time to figure things out.

I booked two nights at a KOA near the west gate of Yellowstone before I went to sleep and that is where we are now. Rea is unsure where her Kindle E-Reader is or her wallet, although I'm fairly sure they are here somewhere.

―――――――――――――

Stuff found and Rea is napping. It's about 5:50pm.

Speaking of the campground it's nearly deserted. I kind of doubt that is typical for this time of year. The virus strikes again.

Tomorrow we're planning on heading into Yellowstone via the west entrance which was closed through today.

―――――――――――――

Being Saturday evening, it was time to refill Rea's pill box. It has slots for morning and evening where we keep her various prescriptions and supplements for the week. This was the first time we needed to refill it on this trip, and we initially thought we had left the prescription medications back in Washington. After a lot of panic and angst we managed to find everything.

Rea insists on being involved in the process even though it's not something she's very good at dealing with at this point. Which reminds me very much of her mother.

When Jean first came to live with us, she and I were dropped at home by Rea with several bottles of prescriptions and a pill box similar to the one Rea now has. Rea's mother was a force of nature. In an era when women were allowed very few opportunities, she managed to become a school principal and assistant district superintendent before retiring in the early 1980s. To say she could be intimidating is an understatement.

At that point Jean was still in the early middle stage of her Alzheimer's progression but when she decided to do the pill sorting while Rea was away, I was a bit worried as she was clearly not as coherent as she needed to be. Somehow I managed to subtly influence her to do things correctly, but it was like walking across a bunch of floating barrels while holding nitroglycerin.

31 May 2020

Today we'll be spending time in Yellowstone, then returning to our camp spot for the night before heading onto Tetons tomorrow.

———————

It turns out I was a day off in terms of when the west entrance to Yellowstone opens. Tomorrow would have been the right answer. We did spend some time in the town of West Yellowstone and got to see a bear, several raptors, and a couple different kinds of wolves at the Grizzly & Wolf Discovery Center.

We also ate lunch at a sit-down restaurant. They were seating people at least six feet apart when we went in and most of the staff were wearing masks. Rea seemed like she wanted to eat there so I went along with it.

The food was okay but it was mostly notable as the first time we've eaten in a sit-down restaurant since sometime in February.

———————

For the moment Rea has somehow managed to misplace her weekly pill box. She was looking for something else earlier and now I have no idea what she has done with it. I normally have trouble keeping track of my own stuff. I don't think there is any way to win here.

The motor home isn't that large so I'm sure I'll find it eventually?

———————

Never mind, she just found the pill box.

———————

I still haven't talked to her about the assisted suicide thing. Mostly it's because the moment hasn't been right but there has been a bit of putting it off as well.

———————

When all this is done I think I'm going to buy an RV and hit the road. I feel like I need to spend some time traveling and getting a better idea of who I am and what I want to do with the rest of my life. Yeah, I sound like I'm 19 years old rather than 53.

It's peaceful and relaxed here at the campground. Which is so much different from what is going on elsewhere.

I took one of my Xanax last night. I'm never sure how much or if it helps.

Chapter 4

(June 2020)

1 June 2020

Heading to the park today. It was very cold in the motor home overnight as it got down to the upper 30s outside. I finally figured out the heat once we got up. Should have done that last night.

I woke up at 4:30 and couldn't get back to sleep. It's gonna be a long day.

———————

Good day overall, though I was tired. We saw Old Faithful and a number of other sites in the south-western part of the park. Old Faithful was a bit of a disappointment. The eruption we saw was short and we waited a long time for it which probably colored my perception.

Yellowstone is amazing. It's beautiful and a place of extremes.

Offsetting the beauty is the fact that its numerous geysers, hot springs, and other volcanic features are evidence of an active geology. One that if things got out of hand could lead to an extinction-level event. Not the kind of thing we really want to think about right now, though, so let's not go any further down that path.

Last night the temperature dropped below 40 degrees. We hadn't figured out yet how the heater worked and that meant it was icy cold in the morning when we woke up. Borderline frostbite was a great motivator and I soon figured out how the heater worked and adjusted the temperature to a point where Rea was willing to get out from under the warm blankets.

We got to the park just a few minutes shy of 8:30am with no real idea of when it was supposed to open. There were a handful of lines, each with around a half-dozen vehicles when we pulled up.

This was the first time this year that the west entrance was open. Right at 8:30, the gates opened and vehicles started feeding through at a steady pace. We later found out that the normal time would have been 10am, so it was kind of like being at Disneyland with a ticket that allowed you the extra "magic hour".

Yellowstone is big and it wouldn't be hard to spend a week or two exploring the areas viewable by the public.

Early in the day the park wasn't crowded and we never had any issue finding parking for the motor home. It did get a bit busy by mid-afternoon, but even then it wasn't bad.

We had a good time and saw a number of Bison in the morning including several of various ages on the road as well as a couple of huge males, one of whom got onto one of the boardwalks and broke a board.

2 June 2020

It wasn't as cold overnight, and I slept much better. Today we plan on spending some time in Yellowstone before heading over to Tetons.

———————

We had a good day, first at Yellowstone and then driving to Jackson Hole Wyoming. Well there was an exception. Some dude didn't want to go "every other" at a construction lane merge. He was dropping the F bomb and flipping me off. I get really stubborn in those situations. As far as I was concerned he wasn't coming over and he didn't. I might have flipped him off and muttered a few F bombs myself. I've occasionally thought that Testosterone should be a controlled substance. That comment cuts both ways in this case.

We're at the KOA outside of Jackson Hole. It's a lot further from Tetons national park than I'd thought it would be. I've got a lot of work to do on my planning skills.

3 June 2020

Driving around Grand Tetons national park today. A lot isn't open yet including most of the camping and some/all of the visitor centers. Mother nature on the other hand is certainly open for business. It's in the mid-seventies and gorgeous. We're going to do the scenic drive and then take it from there.

I'd been hoping for a hotel room tonight but I'm thinking that may not be feasible.

———————

We're at a campground near Jackson Hole. Power but no sewer or water. Early tomorrow we'll head to Casper Wyoming for a night at a hotel. Looking forward to that.

Tetons was neat. We stopped at Jenny Lake visitors center and walked around a bit. There were hardly any people there.

At one point it rained a bit and I started singing "Raindrops keep falling on my head". I don't generally do that kind of thing in public but we were alone. The chorus is awesome

There's one thing I know
The blues they sent to meet me
Won't defeat me
And it won't be long
Till happiness sets out to greet me

Kinda hard to explain why that whole thing felt so right. I think perhaps it's because I believe there is something after this life and while I'm dying a bit inside watching Rea's decline that gives me hope.

———————

Listening to a 1970s station. Let it be noted that "Seasons in the sun" is a crap song

---

Rea is sitting here working through Algebra I problems. I know she understands the nature of her disease but she's going to fight it as best she can, that much is clear.

Rain, thunder and lightning this evening in Jackson Hole. It's nice not to be in a tent.

4 June 2020

Some seepage of water at the windows so not being in a tent isn't a guarantee of moisture remaining outside apparently.

Same level of general confusion for Rea when she woke up as has been normal recently. Recalled we are seeing a one-man Teddy Roosevelt play in Medora ND, but thought it might be tonight. It is two nights from tonight on Saturday.

Today we drive to a hotel just east of Casper Wyoming where we will stay the night.

It was nice to have a short day yesterday. I got caught up on some things and got to relax a bit. Even so, I'm feeling a bit more tired than normal today. I suspect the clouds and rain aren't helping.

The drive is about five hours which shouldn't be an issue.

About two hours in and so far so good. It's beautiful country but oh so stark at times. We're driving Highway 26 for the first part. Not sure what is next. Right now we're stopped at a rest stop taking a break and eating lunch.

Made it to our hotel without incident. I'm in a bit of a funk. My mood varies a bit outside of what is going on in my life. I'm fairly good at ignoring it at this point but I still notice it at times.

Showering on the road is a challenge. Showering in a hotel room is a wonderful experience. The bed doesn't make much of a difference but it seems fine.

Here's my favorite picture of the past few days. I love taking pictures of flying bees around flowers for some reason.

Modern digital camera's take fairly good pictures at ISO settings between 400-800 and there is software available that largely eliminates the "noise" seen at those settings. This makes it possible to take pictures at a much faster shutter speed which in turn makes capturing images like this one where the bees wings are nearly stationary.

I think the shutter speed was 1/2000th of a second.

5 June 2020

Motion sickness medicine makes Rea sleep more than normal. Over nighting in a hotel is going to have to be at least a weekly thing.

I appear to have misplaced not one, but two USB-C cables as well as the power brick for my Mac Book Pro and the fiber case I bought for it. Most likely I left them at the hotel we stayed at last night.

We made it to Medora, though the wind was bad at times and the roads in South Dakota sucked.

The North Dakota suck comes from their apparent inability to comprehend that we are still in the midst of a global pandemic. I'm not happy about being in this state but Rea has things she wants to do and hopefully neither of us gets ill.

6 June 2020

Rea was really confused just before bed last night. I suspect the decline in her executive function is starting to impact how she interacts with the world in real time. It's also the case that the motion sickness medicine she takes while I'm driving isn't helping. Hopefully that was just a preview rather than the new normal. She a bit better this morning.

———————

Rea forgot the word for toothpaste today. She remembered when I reminded her. In spite of that she's having a fairly good day.

Things aren't going so well on the weather front. Rain, wind and the twin threats of thunder and lightning are both here and forecast. I'll need to drive us downtown and back in the motor home which means taking everything apart and stowing things for a trip that will be two miles total.

7 June 2020

I'm having yet another not so good day. I took a Xanax about a week ago so maybe it's time again.

Rea is doing OK. I think her shaking is getting a little worse. She has been taking her walking stick along more when we go out to do things.

We went to see the one-man Teddy Roosevelt show last night. It was good. Rea had seen it last September when we were here for the first time but I'd skipped. I'd been feeling a little overwhelmed by all the travel at the time and needed a break. That is one of the reasons we're here, as Rea really wanted me to see the show.

At the end they gave away a "Teddy Bear". Rea got it. The actor who plays Teddy has a good arm and Rea managed to catch it when he threw it to her. We were about halfway back in the theater. Call it ten rows or so plus a bit of the stage.

Every other row was closed and groups were asked to leave two spaces between themselves and others. The theater was maybe 1/3rd full overall but a bit over half given the restrictions.

We were going to try to make it to the zoo in Fargo today but the time zone switch made that infeasible. Instead we'll do the zoo tomorrow (weather permitting) and then drive to Sioux Falls.

The wind was blowing hard on our drive from Madera to Fargo and it started to rain a bit as we were moving stuff into our hotel room. I wanted to camp tonight but couldn't find any good places near Fargo so we're at a hotel.

Price wise it tends to be close to a wash when comparing a hotel room with a camping spot.

I'm still in a bit of a down mood. I thought about taking a Xanax tonight but will pass for now. Gotta make them last and I don't want to get addicted.

8 June 2020

Travel day from the Fargo area to Sioux Falls. More traffic around Sioux Falls than I would have expected. It's arguably the most developed area we've been in recently.

I'm still in a down phase but dealing with it OK. Rea had a good day which helped. She reminded me that I'd shoved a wad of paper towel into the air conditioner vent on one side to keep it closed as it's defective and won't stay closed like it should.

The campground here is right by the freeway but that doesn't mean the same thing it does in more populated areas. It's still a little loud but not bad.

9 June 2020

Another travel day. It's hard to write much when I'm driving so much.

4115 Barbican Avenue, Weston, WI is our destination tonight. Nothing in particular there, just a stop along the way to Adams.

I'm hoping my mood makes an upswing soon. Really need to think about taking a Xanax tonight if this keeps up. Mornings are the worst. Or maybe it's evenings. In fact, maybe there isn't a good time of day. Except when we're doing a fun activity and I can pretend none of the bad stuff is happening.

Gotta hold onto that I guess.

––––––––––

Ugh, didn't get to the hotel until about nine PM thanks to various bridges being out and other construction closures not being known by our GPS software. It didn't help that it was raining hard by then and the wind and lousy road conditions only added to the "fun".

We're going to take tomorrow as a rest day. I was leaning in that direction even before things went bad drive wise. The late arrival cinched it and we were able to snag our room for a second night.

The complimentary breakfast is being served here. I'm not sure how I feel about that. I'll likely make a quick trip out in the morning and scrounge some stuff for the two of us. I brought some food related things in from the motor home so we shouldn't starve even if we lounge about in the room all day tomorrow.

10 June 2020

No Xanax and I don't think I'll need it tomorrow. Having a day off was a big help. This is a good thing since I left it out in the RV.

11 June 2020

Nothing new to say recently.

Today is a travel day. We're getting closer to Adams which is good. We're also going to need to extend the motor home rental at least a week I suspect.

We cuddled a bit last night before going to sleep. It was good.

––––––––––

I posted this to Facebook earlier today…

One of the hardest things to do in life is to experience it with comprehension as our main focus rather than confirmation of our previously established biases and beliefs.

I think it's accurate and encapsulates a lot of the human experience and condition.

———————

The drive went well. It got windy at times but nothing I haven't experienced several times so far on this trip.

It feels like Rea's memory is less of a problem then her cognitive abilities right now. I'm hoping the motion sickness medication is causing some of this. I'll have a better idea when we have been in Adams for a day or two as she will hopefully have to take less/none while there.

12 June 2020

We should end up in Ohio today and then in the Adams NY area the day after if things go as planned. Rea grew up in Adams and we'll be staying with her younger brother's family.

There are a lot of things I need to take care of in Adams including getting an oil change for the motor home. This will give me some time to myself which I need right now.

I know this is just a variation of things I've said many times before but watching someone you love erode away in the blink of an eye is the most horrible experience I can imagine.

Rea and I witnessed it in extreme slow motion with her mother and that was a different kind of agony. Much more so for her then me as her mother and I weren't very close.

At this point it looks like we'll be extending the trip a week or two. There is no way we'll be able to complete the things she wants to do by July 2nd and I don't want to rush her. Hopefully that won't be an issue in terms of the RV rental. I'll be calling the rental company once we reach Adams. I had a brief informal conversation with one of their guys when I picked up the motor home and he said it wouldn't be an issue but I don't have a lot of confidence in them at this point.

13 June 2020

Today we drove from Ohio to Rea's brothers' home near Adams NY.

Nothing particularly exciting happened outside of the typical stupid tricks people get up to on the roads. I'm starting to wonder how long-haul truckers keep their sanity.

Tomorrow is Sunday and our plan is to just hang out, visit and relax. Very much looking forward to it.

14 June 2020

Rea worries both about her own wants and desires, as well as mine. Especially when she thinks they are in conflict.

She told me today that she wasn't sure if she is getting worse.

I believe she is. It's inevitable given the disease but it's hard to be sure given all the motion sickness medicine she's been taking. We'll be staying still the next few days so that will help me assess her situation.

———————

Rea is having a good visit with her brother and sister-in-law. After a few hours I decided to take a break. She's doing a fairly good job of communicating with them and seems mostly normal. Perhaps her decline is not as bad as I'd thought. The motor home is so loud that it is difficult to talk and I'm so exhausted at the end of the day that I just want to relax a bit and sleep.

———————

Me and my stupid optimism. We showered in the guest bathroom this afternoon, and I accidentally caused Rea a lot of confusion when I talked to her after she had gotten out of the shower but wasn't completely done. I was going second. Between dealing with her confusion and the dogs it was not a pleasant time. She became upset at one point.

15 June 2020

I took a Xanax last night. I think it helped me sleep a bit and I don't think I'm in a down phase right now, but Rea's situation is hitting me fairly hard at the moment.

I think there are two reasons for this. First, being stationary and avoiding motion sickness medicine hasn't seemed to make much of a difference.

Second, and paradoxically, multiple people have expressed their sympathies to me. Somehow that makes the situation more real. Though I think it's also the case that it will help in the long term.

On some level I'm never going to stop mourning but bottling things up too much right now isn't good either. I need to vent a little in private when I can to keep the pressure at a manageable level.

It's becoming clear that the motion sickness medicine wasn't having as large an impact as I'd hoped. She's had a noticeable decline in the past couple of weeks.

I say with complete sincerity that I would trade places with her in a heartbeat if I could. I'm upset and I'm going to miss her big time but what is killing me more than anything else is how unfair this is to her. She is such an awesome person and this is the shitty ending she gets?

I don't blame God. This is just the way the world works. Maybe I've said this already, but this place is neither heaven nor hell, but it can be a healthy helping of either depending on our actions and the actions of those around us, and in this case random chance.

16 June 2020

It's clear that our toilet in the RV is broken. Likely both clogged and with a mechanical failure that may or may not be related. I called the company and am waiting for a call back on where to take it.

Rea and I had another tough conversation last night around bedtime. She was mostly herself but there were a lot of tears. Her big stress was not being sure about what I wanted.

What I want doesn't matter. Because what I want is for her to somehow recover. I couldn't just say that so I went with my distant second want, which is to make her as happy as I can in whatever time she has left. In my weaker moments I also want it to all be over.

It is so so hard to be in this situation. I know I whine a lot but it's true. The worst times are when I can't manage to lie to myself a bit about how she is and what is happening. It's exhausting, heart rending and horrible in equal measure and all of that comes on top of my own issues.

When 2020 started I was actually optimistic. This was going to be the big year. I'd fully retire, we'd have time to start dealing with various fixes and enhancements at our house in Washington, we'd travel around the US and I'd get to work on my own hobbies as well. Here we are six months in and it is the worst shit show of my life both on a personal and global level.

17 June 2020

Rea was confused just before bed last night. She thought the Phish "Dinner and a Movie" was on TV until I reminded her it was on YouTube.

She seems good today. We put a deposit down on a puppy. It'll be ready in three weeks. Rea and I both love dogs. I'm not sure a puppy is the right choice –in fact I'm pretty certain it isn't –but it's what she wants so here we are.

Shower day. It was an adventure. That is about as much as I will say about that other than she got frustrated because she was confused about how to get from point A to point B even though the path was relatively simple.

She enjoyed the latest "Dinner and a Movie" from Phish. We actually stopped a bit before the encore since the network kind of went away. I might queue it up later but halfway thinking I won't.

She might remember or she might not and it would be a bit of a production.

I am so tired.

18 June 2020

I'm not sure how much longer I'm going to be able to make regular updates to this journal. The disease is progressing and I'm depressed and sometimes a little angry when I'm not in some form of denial. There are only so many ways I can say that.

Starting tomorrow we'll be traveling again. That will probably give me some opportunities to say something new. We'll see.

I have tried making deals with God, but not surprisingly that hasn't worked. The world is mundane except at the spiritual and quantum level.

My sister-in-law just said Rea told her she might live another five to 10 years. That is outright denial in action but nobody is going to tell her she is wrong.

18 June 2020

New plan: we may be moving to the Adams NY Area for the duration. Rea had turned this down initially but now seems interested in the idea. She doesn't recall saying no though.

We have a good network in California but Rea has a good one here as well. I'm not a fan of the weather in this part of the country but it is what she wants, so it is what she will get.

Tomorrow we head to Watkins Glen then on to Vermont and Maine. In theory we are supposed to have the rental RV back on July 2 and there is a $25 an hour late charge. I called the place we rented it from. At the time they said an extension would not be a problem. Their story has changed now. These are the same bozos that haven't returned my call about our slightly broken toilet even though I've been assured multiple times that they will.

There is a decent chance I'll be eating a one-way charge and returning it on this side of the country.

21 June 2020

We've been visiting some friends in the Corning area the last day or so. Rea has been doing very well. Arguably her best day or two in a while. When her deficits are exposed, though, it's easy to see how much she's declined since the start.

22 June 2020

The RV company we rented from is driving me nuts and upsetting Rea. We want to return the RV here in NY. I'm willing to pay the full term of the rental and the one-way fee but I can't get them to answer me on whether they will allow this. When I picked up the unit I asked if it would be a problem to extend the rental and the guy said, "No problem". When I called back a couple of days ago the same guy essentially said, "Hell no". Rea probably has a month or two more of decent quality of life. I sure as expletive don't want to spend 25–50% of it returning the rental unit and getting back over here to do the remaining things on our list. In retrospect I should have just rented it for an extra week or two at the start, but we weren't sure how it would go. Assuming we'd have the option to extend was a mistake.

24 June 2020

We don't have the final bill yet for the rental RV, but it has been dropped off in Syracuse. Turns out there is an emergency drop-off, either due to mechanical or personal reasons. I wish the first three or four people I'd talked to had mentioned this. Thankfully I finally got a guy on the phone who knew this and was willing to tell me.

Tomorrow we're going to Syracuse to look at a new RV. Hopefully that will work out. It would be a significant upgrade over the rental. Fingers crossed, knock on wood and all that.

25 June 2020

The C-19 thing continues to be a slow-moving train wreck here in the US.

26 June 2020

We did some planning for the trip to Maine this week first thing this morning and then got our food all sorted out. I did all of the packing and loading of the rental RV and it was total chaos. In part because that is who I am, and in part because of the situation and my panic over how fast the disease would progress. Throw in the fact that it happened in both California and Washington.

Rea is dizzy today. Not sure how much of that is directly attributable to the disease. She's struggling a bit with words at times but in casual conversation does fine most of the time. Her general confusion level is increasing, though.

We've been confirmed for financing and set the date/time of pickup as 1:30pm on July 3. We'll spend a day or two in Rodman getting loaded and organized, and then head back west. We're going to be getting in touch with the puppy people to hopefully get a confirmed pick-up date. Fresno is a long way from here.

Rea's progression looks a lot like her mom's at this point, only accelerated about a hundred times. She's increasingly confused and forgetful. We had to call to get the account number for her personal checking so we could reset the password and I had to repeatedly tell her what we were doing.

Hopefully we'll be looking at a place near here in the morning and then heading to Maine.

27 June 2020

For the record I still cry sometimes, but almost never when I'm near Rea.

———————

Today was a bit of a debacle. Turns out Vermont won't let out-of-state people stay at their hotels. Traveling without an RV is not nearly as fun. Five hours of driving without a bathroom and then denied when we got to the hotel. Luckily we found a gas station with an open bathroom before we headed back to NY.

Tomorrow we are driving to Maine. Research indicates there shouldn't be an issue with the hotel, but I should probably call in the morning to be sure.

We have a real estate agent now. She went to school with Rea. She sent over a really nice listing that will probably be gone before we can move on it.

29 June 2020

No issues on the drive yesterday. I called the hotel first thing to be sure we wouldn't have an issue when we got there. Today we're heading to Lincolnville to see the general store that is owned and operated by the wife of Phish drummer John Fishman. It's been on Rea's bucket list for a while.

We're not sure how accessible it will be, although we think it is open. Worst case we'll take some pictures outside.

Lincolnville is an hour or so from where we are staying, which is Augusta Maine. There weren't any hotels closer that are part of the conglomerate that we normally get rooms through and Augusta is in the correct direction to get us back to New York. We'll be staying in Augusta again tonight.

The virus continues to be in the news with both cases and deaths trending upward in the US and a few other places that didn't take it seriously enough.

We're tentatively scheduled to see a house in the Adams area Thursday afternoon.

30 June 2020

Today we drive to Burlington to see the sites, then on to Plattsburgh since we can't currently stay in Vermont hotels.

Rea is depressed about her situation which is making me extra sad as well every time I make a mistake, like forgetting to remind her to take her medicine or when I'm less than 100% caring and understanding which thankfully doesn't happen very much but does happen sometimes. I'm constantly exhausted and distracted. Plus, I'm human. Crying in the shower helps.

Okay, let's try for some optimism? Not much to work with, but I need to do what I can to make her final days better.

Chapter 5

(July 2020)

1 July 2020

The RV is delayed, possibly for a week, as Mercedes needs to do some recall related work on it and likely won't be done until next Wednesday. This in combination with some other things has Rea kinda upset. I think I need to stop telling her stuff that will make her worry.

2 July 2020

You haven't lived until you've had to show your wife what you mean when you say "underwear". Rea was getting ready to shower and had socks, but no underwear. Once I showed her, she was fine.

The RV rental company is trying to charge us nearly $5K for the drop-off. I'm contemplating how much energy I have to devote to that. Very little is the answer but I might stick our credit card company on them.

Today we are going to look at houses. We are also going to pay cash. It just seems easier than dealing with a second mortgage and it isn't like we'd be able to write off the interest anyway. At least not most of it.

The virus continues to explode in the US while most of the rest of the world is pretty much in containment mode. Yay?

We looked at two houses. One was well placed but meh, and the other was gorgeous but too small and too far from anything.

3 July 2020

Two more houses on the agenda today. Hoping for a winner. Also have tentative plans to fly back to the west coast on Tuesday the 7th.

The first one we looked at was a winner. We're planning on putting in an offer. It's the 4th of July tomorrow, though, and our agent has a family reunion so Monday at the earliest I suspect.

Texas is in trouble with the virus. Hospitals are filling up and their governor is finally calling for people to wear masks.

4 July 2020

The 244th anniversary of the founding of the US is today. It's hard to care as much as I should, all things considered.

You can roughly break the US into thirds right now. Two of the thirds hate each other and the other third is some combination of apathetic, despondent, and clueless. As I've probably said before, it's not hard to see where things are likely heading at this point, though I hope I'm wrong.

I was just talking to my sister-in-law and she told me Rea didn't recognize her brother a couple of days ago when we got home from our Vermont/Maine trip. She's been better since and had a good day today. This might explain in part why Rea started to cry when she came to bed that evening. The two events were very close in time.

On another note, I'm fairly sure the puppy is a scam. Too soon to be 100% sure but now that I look into it there are plenty of signs that point in that direction. I blame myself 100% if this turns out to be true. I barely checked into it. I have some backup plans if I'm right about it not being legit.

5 July 2020

I sometimes think about what my life will be like after Rea is gone. I'm one part depressed and one part hopeful when I do. This is much better than thinking about what Rea is going through and how unfair it is. I've talked about how that makes me feel already. I'm sure I'll talk about it some more.

Having hope of some sort of a future where I can heal and create a life for myself helps me keep going. That, and lots of denial. Never underestimate the effectiveness of denial.

6 July 2020

Sleep has always been an escape for me. I love to dream and remove myself from the world. It's probably not too much of an exaggeration to say that sleep is my drug of choice. I'm not very good at it, though, which may explain why I'm anxious to embrace it when I can.

Rea woke me up a few times last night saying she was warm. Which was weird. It wasn't really all that warm. I think the real truth is she gets confused and lonely sometimes at night, so she clings to me. I need to be better at how I react to that. Reassuring her and going back to sleep isn't really the best answer but sleep can be elusive; it's hard not to grab back onto that wave when it is available.

We have three or four places to look at this afternoon. None of them look like slam dunk winners. We lost out on the house we thought we had when the sellers took it off the market after panicking about what is going on in Florida C-19 wise. Smart choice on their part, but major pain for us. It looked like a perfect situation.

7 July 2020

One more house to look at today. Though I already know which one we should buy. It has two steps in and out, and everything Rea would need is on the main floor.

I need to finish our packing today. Hopefully we can make it to the hotel in Syracuse at a reasonable time. Fingers crossed on that one. I'm also hoping tomorrow won't be too much of an adventure, but I'll likely not get my wish. Flying right now is a bit of an unknown to me and I don't have the energy to research it.

8 July 2020

Packing was a chore but we got through it and made it to the hotel near the airport around 7:30pm. We also electronically signed the offer letter for our new home. We should hear back today. Obviously acceptance or a counter offer would be great.

Rea is still having trouble sleeping, though she is almost always out when I wake up. This is problematic today but I'm going to let her sleep as much as I can.

The C-19 deaths are starting to spike again. Not a surprise given the upward trend in confirmed infections. The next few weeks will almost certainly see those numbers continue to trend upward. I'm hoping we can make it back to the Watertown NY area before everything goes massively south, because I'm fairly sure we're heading back to something close to what we had a couple of months back and it could end up much worse.

I'm still a bit unsure on the whole puppy thing. They are offering to refund our money after I refused to send any more until we came to pick up the puppy. We'll see. The whole thing feels way too shady for me at this point.

9 July 2020

Looks like Facebook pulled the plug on the puppy scam. Yay?

On the plus side we got a lot done today. The check for the down payment on the RV is on its way as is the check to open the escrow account on the house. We also returned some stuff and went grocery shopping. Oh, also we got notice from the mortgage broker that refinancing our Washington house could save us a lot of money.

Rea had a good day; particularly given how poorly she's been doing recently. Hoping and praying this will last for a while.

11 July 2020

I think this is only the second time I've missed a day updating this journal.

Yesterday was Friday and it was uneventful. We did run some errands and got together with friends in the evening for a socially responsible and distanced gathering. Depending on how things play out that may be the last time Rea gets to attend this particular gathering. The core group all went to graduate school together back in the early-to-mid-1980s.

Rea's continuing to do well relative to her recent range.

No word back yet on our Washington refi. Not sure what is happening there. I'll contact our broker in the next day or two.

I'm doing okay. At this point I'm tired but I'm managing to mostly keep all the balls in the air. We have a schedule for the next couple of weeks and I've taken care of most of the immediate "To Do" items.

Right now I need to put my shoes on, gather Rea up, and get going on some errands.

———

Rea is getting frustrated with not being able to drive. In a sense that is good because it means she's aware enough of her surroundings to feel that way. It's also bad, though, because her mental processes are clearly a bit broken, and given where this disease progresses I suspect she'll be less understanding at some point, even though her ability to interact with the world is already noticeably impacted.

11 July 2020

Today is not shaping up to be a good day in terms of Rea's overall mood and cognition. She was confusing socks and shoes and even different kinds of shoes when trying to get ready for the day.

She's supposed to visit a friend and at the last minute decided she needed to shower which I hadn't accounted for. She also asked about her cane which we left in New York since she said she didn't need it. Yes, I'm an idiot. I listened to a woman who is in serious cognitive decline and didn't even give it a second thought.

I'll buy her another one once I drop her off, assuming the visit happens. It's very hot right now and most visits happen outside. Not being on time means either rescheduling or shortening the visit.

The visit happened and was apparently fine. Rea had no complaints, but I didn't ask her friend what she thought of Rea's ability to interact. They last talked about six weeks ago when Rea was still in the mildly impacted range. I'm fairly sure she would be considered moderately impacted at this point, though on her really good days she might still be on the border between mild and moderate.

12 July 2020

I haven't written a song since this whole thing began. I've been fiddling with my guitar occasionally and have some musical ideas, but most of the lyrics I've written recently have sucked.

Here's a snippet I came up with just now. I think I like it, though it might not age well.

Come walk with me, darling
We'll feel no despair
Unchained from that emotion
It only seems fair

You are my religion
The one I love most
Though we will be parted
You'll still be my ghost

Or maybe it's horrible. It's always hard to tell for me.

I just heard that New York is buckling down on people entering the state. We'll be asked to self-quarantine for 14 days when we exit the airport in Syracuse. This is a pain, but I get it. I'm in the process of figuring out what makes the most sense in terms of how we deal with this.

13 July 2020

Well, we own a puppy. At least we're on that path. Rea has been looking at puppy sites for a few days. I've never been good at saying no, and with the whole terminally ill thing I'm pretty much horrible right now, but if it is something that will endanger her then no is still going to be the answer.

The puppy is only four weeks old, so it will be another month before we get it.

We have no idea where the puppy is, as the site we got it from acts as a go-between. They seem much more legit than the scammers we dealt with before. I'm supposed to talk to somebody on the phone this morning.

On a different topic, we've been getting calendar notifications for the Phish summer tour the past several days. The tour was cancelled months ago of course, but with everything else going on we never got around to removing the calendar entries. It's a reminder of a much nicer world that I'd give almost anything to be living in.

———————

Rea has a lunch get together with some of her former coworkers today. Socially distanced, of course. I have a ton of things to do including stuff related to the puppy, getting her lunch, dropping her off and picking her up, working on the refi of our Washington home, and talking to a lawyer about the place we are purchasing in New York. It's starting to feel like a Xanax day.

———————

Just because, here is a picture of the house in New York.

And yes, it was a Xanax day.

15 July 2020

I think I'm in one of my periodic down phases. Maybe it sounds weird that I'm not sure, but all I can say is that I learned to live with my mildly bipolar self a long time ago and one of my coping mechanisms is to keep a wall between myself and my mood.

Speaking metaphorically, it is not a tall or thick wall but it does provide a bit of a buffer. I've been doing it for so long that a lot of the time I don't even notice when I'm at one end of my relatively modest extreme or the other.

Today is the last semi calm day until next Monday. I have to prep for the CR-V getting picked up on Saturday, finish the paperwork for our refi on the Washington home, talk to the lawyer doing the paperwork on our New York house purchase … I'm probably forgetting something.

Rea has had a couple of moderately bad days in a row after three really good ones. That doesn't help my mood. She's still asleep so I don't know what today holds.

Above I said that I have a lot to do over the next several days. Rea is essentially no help at this point and requires a lot of my time and effort. She is becoming more childlike in the way she deals with the world. Thankfully she seldom gets angry though she does get sad, which isn't easy to deal with.

I think today was a sad day for both of us even though I got a lot done.

At some point Rea will pass over the "event horizon" where she will no longer be aware of how sick she is. That will be a very sad and a little happy day.

15 July 2020

Phish has a song called "Death don't hurt very long". Despite the title it's meant to be whimsical and is one of a suite of songs they wrote for the music-al gag portion of their 2018 Halloween show. The concept was that they were covering an extremely obscure (and it turns out fictitious) Scandinavian band from the early 1980s named "Kasvot Växt".

We were seated behind the stage toward the right side at that show.

Many of the songs from that set are already fan favorites and "Death don't hurt very long" tends to get played often.

It's been stuck in my head for a day or two now and I'm not enjoying it because I can tell you from the observer's side that at least in this case death does in fact hurt for a long time.

This is not meant to be a slam on the band. That set was genius, and there are a lot of excellent songs and some very good memories associated with it. That song in particular, though, is no friend of mine right now

---

Getting back to New York is turning out to be more difficult than I had hoped. At this point we'll be on the west coast (most likely in Washington) until we either close on the house or the RV is delivered.

Meanwhile Rea's level of confusion continues to increase. Actually, that isn't entirely accurate. I should say she's confused more often and in more obvious ways. Changing the toilet paper for instance. She just wandered in wondering where to put the new roll, which she had on the barrel thingy already. The real issue was that the roll she had was too big for the holder. Generally we just sit the roll on the sink until it is a bit smaller and then put it in the holder.

16 July 2020

Tomorrow is UCSF. I know the news isn't going to be good, but hopefully they'll get some useful data. The doctor won't be able to meet with us in person. That will likely happen via teleconference next week sometime.

I'm more exhausted today than normal. I had to return our first rental car today to SFO. For some reason I scheduled the pick-up of our second rental in Livermore. It's a different company so it's not as absurd as it sounds.

No, it is as absurd as it sounds. It just never occurred to me. Oh well, two hours on BART gave me some alone time and allowed me to get a bit of reading done.

17 July 2020

Traffic into San Francisco was still very light at 10am or so when I started my drive so I'm not too worried about getting to UCSF tomorrow morning.

Reading more on the NY State quarantine, it looks like Rea and I would be fine if we stay in Washington for two weeks as Washington isn't one of the "bad" states on the NY list. At least it isn't at the moment. Who knows what will change in the next few weeks. Still it seems viable to plan on staying in Washington for two weeks before heading east. There is a decent chance either the house or the RV would be ready at that point.

UCSF has been mostly Rea getting tested. It's been relaxing in a sense. She seems to be at the high end of her current range and is in a good mood which has made the whole experience better than it might have been otherwise.

She thought she did a bit worse at the more difficult parts of the cognitive testing but that didn't seem to faze her much when we talked while eating lunch outside. Eating inside is not allowed right now.

18 July 2020

UCSF went well. Rea was having a good day, but the MRI and other testing will give a better indication of her overall condition. She had some pronounced physical shaking in one of the tests I wasn't present for and yesterday evening she was having mild spasms initially after she went to sleep. I'm fairly sure that is new.

Her physical symptoms were some of the first to emerge, but until now they've lagged behind other areas of decline.

Our CR-V is supposed to be picked up today and I still don't have a time.

Rea wants to see the agility dog training some friends do at 9am. I have this horrible feeling I'll get a call at 7:30 saying they are ready to get the CR-V, which would prevent us from seeing the dogs.

The pick-up window on the CR-V is 9am–9pm, but they'll call me two or three hours prior. It's lunch time already so at this point it looks like late afternoon or evening is most likely. This in turn means tomorrow for our trip north.

I'd like to leave early but that will be a chore with Rea. She's going to want to help and that is going to take four times as long. Frankly I don't have the patience for it. I think I may be coming out of my down phase which will help.

19 July 2020

We're heading north today and some friends are going to handle coordination of the pick-up. I don't know what I'd do without all the support and prayers we've received. Time to get up and get going.

I cried a bit while splitting Rea's English muffin this morning. She has a way of doing it that I'm normally too lazy to do. It's just inserting a fork all the way around and twisting slightly. She was still in bed so it was "safe" to do that.

Thankfully the shipper who is going to pick up the CR-V called a bit ago. He should be here soon. That will be one more thing I don't have to worry about for a bit.

20 July 2020

We made it to Washington just before midnight. The CR-V went onto the top of the trailer and is currently on its way to New York.

The best part of the drive was the two of us trying to come up with puppy names. The worst part was Rea's balance being so bad that we used a companion restroom at one point, and I had to help her to and from her bathroom the other times. She was upset with her balance issues once we got to our house and got into bed.

We failed to bring any of the pillows from the apartment because I was too stupid to figure out that most of the ones we took on the trip in the rental RV came from Washington. I was able to improvise something but will need to buy pillows today along with completing several other tasks.

Favorite puppy name was Abby. Too early to know if that will be the winner. Piper and Fluffhead have also been in the running.

———————————

I left Rea at home and drove over to the Oregon side to get the mail and pick up some things that we needed (including pillows). In the original plan we were going to drive the rental RV back through here and drop stuff off. Since the rental RV got dropped off in NY instead, we are short pillows and had no frying pan. There are probably other things missing, but those are the ones we've run into so far. Oh wait, I just realized I talked a bit about that above.

———————————

New puppy name suggestion. Cassidy. This is Rea's. Yes, it's a Grateful Dead reference.

The whole dizziness thing has Rea really bummed. Heck, it has me really bummed as well.

21 July 2020

It's been really hot recently. I was sweating like crazy yesterday while we were outside in the shade talking to our neighbor Ken who is helping us with some repairs that need to be made to the house. I don't normally have that issue.

I've been freaking out for the last day or so about having to be Rea's primary care. First of all, it's depressing as heck seeing her go through this and then there is the thought of trying to deal with it mostly by myself.

We have long-term care insurance but it has a 90-day deductible which I've only just realized. We can afford to pay that first 90 days but we need to somehow get the clock ticking sooner rather than later as CJD takes no prisoners even when the progression is relatively slow.

Video conference with the team at UCSF went well today. This was a follow-up to the appointments last Friday.

The MRI showed some progression, things I've observed a fair amount over the past six weeks or so since our last visit. Overall, though, she's doing very well. They did recommend Aricept, a drug used to treat mild-to-moderate Alzheimer's. The primary doctor wasn't confident that it would help, but given Rea's relatively slow progression he seemed to think there was a better-than-normal chance.

22 July 2020

The inspection of the house in NY came in and there were no major red flags. I suspect we'll attempt to move forward ASAP, but we're waiting to hear back from our realtor to see what she thinks.

We have some friends coming to visit from the Seattle area this afternoon. Rea should enjoy that. Mostly people seem to avoid talking about the whole death thing which is good. We all know it is there, but just being as close to normal as we can manage is therapeutic.

The inability to do anything is really getting to Rea. She's aware enough to know that she is seriously impacted but her instincts to be doing something are still present. Luckily, our friends should be here in an hour or two and that will provide a distraction. Tomorrow I'll take her out some place.

Apparently Washington has been added to the quarantine list for New York. It doesn't make a lot of sense based on the data I have access to, but what can you do? This means we'll need to self-quarantine for two weeks when we get back there.

23 July 2020

Progress has been made on the house purchase as well, though we're still a ways out from that resolving. Likely a couple of weeks. We might be able to work it so we can take possession early though. We'll see.

———————————

The past two or three days have been really good ones for Rea despite the ongoing dizziness issues. Her mood hasn't always been good, but her level of confusion has been relatively low and that hasn't been true for a while.

Today was a Xanax day.

24 July 2020

Friday and payday for me. Coming up on payday for Rea. I know I've said it before, but we are so blessed to be in a position where neither of us has to work for now and we still have a good income.

We worked a lot of years for that and saved like crazy for a decade-plus to get into this position, but there are plenty of people out there who can say the same and didn't get as lucky.

———————————

The probable plan for the next couple of weeks came together today. Flight to Syracuse is on the August 2 since we should be able to occupy the home as of the 31st if things go as it appears they will. Closing would be a bit beyond that time. The lawyers are still negotiating the details.

The RV is moving forward as well but likely will be a bit slower. At this point I don't care since we should have the house before we plan on flying back.

On the one hand Rea has had several very good days in a row mentally, while on the other her mood has not been very good. I think in part because she realizes how impacted she is. I need to figure out ways to improve her mood and distract her. I suspect a dog or dogs would help.

25 July 2020

We're two weeks out from the scheduled puppy delivery and a little over a week out from when we are scheduled to fly to Syracuse. Other than finalizing various paperwork there is not a lot for us to do between now and then.

Keeping Rea engaged and positive is really my main job. The first battle of course is doing the same for myself.

Being in this position is more brutal than I think most people could imagine. Sometimes I'm terrified. Other times I'm exhausted. Occasionally I'm joyous when Rea and I have a good experience together. I am so grateful that still happens on occasion. If not for the virus, I'm sure we'd be having a lot more.

Right now I'm a little numb. I know it's a self-defense mechanism, but intellectually I don't like it that much. I suppose it is better than being pushed further into depression or heavily self-medicating, though, so I guess I should just accept it.

Both of us have been feeling a little sick the past couple of days. I'm thinking it might be a good plan for us to minimize our outside contacts even more just in case. This is not going to help Rea's mood.

———

Memory is weird. Rea recalled that I said I'd prefer to walk first thing in the morning today. Later, more of our neighbors are out and while they are awesome people, the walk becomes a meet-and-greet and that tends to make my anxiety worse, as on the one hand meeting people always makes me a bit uncomfortable while on the other I'm mentally geared up to be getting some exercise and that isn't happening while we're talking. It's a double whammy.

My brain is annoying.

26 July 2020

I feel like I spend a lot of time whining in this journal. Probably because I do :(

Rea has become more clingy recently. It's another situation where I feel guilty because sometimes I just want a few minutes of alone time to focus and center myself and boom, she's there.

Today will be the first day she takes Donepezil. Have I mentioned this before? It has another name as well. Most drugs do it seems, and doctors and pharmacists tend to use the one normal people have never heard of.

Donepezil is used to mitigate memory issues in people with Alzheimer's disease. It might help Rea and it is unlikely to hurt her.

———————

When Rea is clingy, I can feel like I'm suffocating. On those rare occasions when I'm away from her, I start to feel a bit like I'm drowning.

I've been so lucky in my life up to this point in that I've had very little experience with losing those close to me. A college friend when I was around 30, my dad when I was 22. The past few years, though, have been kinda brutal. I guess that is inevitable when you pass the half century mark.

Her good and bad days tend to cluster. We're in a bad phase again. Yesterday and today have featured periods of significant confusion. The three or so days prior to that were really good ones for her. I wish I had a clue as to why some days are better than others.

One week until we head back to New York and about two weeks until the puppy arrives.

———————

I'm doing a bit of research on enhancing executive function since that is Rea's biggest deficit currently. Her memory is spotty, but her ability to reason and interact with the world is more impacted. Last night I was looking for her cane and she equated the cane with a couple of different books when she pointed out that the books were not the cane. Which was true, but it felt like she really thought they were similar.

Tasks like this help me maintain my sanity (I hope).

27 July 2020

It's supposed to get to 100 degrees here today. As a planet we've been dumping a lot less C02 into the atmosphere over the past six months thanks to the virus but that is a drop in the bucket comparatively, I guess.

Speaking of the virus, the numbers are trending grim again. I'm a bit worried about our flight on Sunday. I'll just have to keep my fingers crossed and hope for the best. The best has been in short supply for a while now, though, so it's not as easy as I would like to stay positive.

Rea has been in a down phase the past few days, so I'm hoping she'll be a bit better today. She's still sleeping so it'll be a while before I know what today will be like.

28 July 2020

Mostly I think I've been a numb the past several days. I think I'm burned out. It's not that I don't care. I still do, very much, but everything is blunted and fuzzy. I don't think I'm in one of my down phases. Maybe I'm on the other end of the cycle?

I don't know that I'm bipolar and if I am it's fairly mild but being near the top of my arc might explain this.

We're still far enough away from our flight that I'm not panicking. That will come in a day or two. Especially if either the house or the RV aren't going to be available when we get there. Speaking of which, I need to bug some people again.

———————

The paperwork for the RV came today. I filled it out and sent it back. In theory it might arrive tomorrow, but it should be there by Thursday at the latest. Which might mean we can take possession of the RV as early as Friday. Well, I use possession in a very loose sense since we are 3000 or so miles away from where it is.

Rea is having a pretty good day. One way I can tell is by looking at the curtain in the window of our main floor bathroom …

It's not a very neat job, but she rolled the curtain up and tied it on both sides.

Before she got sick, she'd do this every day in the morning when we were here. Now she only does it occasionally, generally on days that she seems to be a bit more with it.

29 July 2020

We had friends over this afternoon. It was good to visit. Fingers crossed nobody had the virus or spread it. We were all fairly cautious.

I think I got the RV completely squared away. I should know for sure tomorrow.

The house is still in limbo and things have to happen tomorrow or I don't think we can get the money in place. I'll be pinging our agent first thing.

We're going to fly on Sunday even if we don't have the RV or the house in place. Worst case we'll spend a few days in a hotel. Living in the COVID age is constant fun.

———————————

Rea asked for floss tonight. That is the first time in a while that she's done so. Today was the first day of her taking Phenylpiracetam(a supplement), and about the fourth day or so taking Aricept. One or both may be helping, or maybe it's just a coincidence.

30 July 2020

The RV is a done deal. The problem now is figuring out how to get it someplace useful. The house on the other hand is still in limbo. Today is Thursday so if I don't hear something good in the first few hours of the day tomorrow I'm thinking we're not going to be moving in for a while.

My latest theory is I'm numbing emotionally, mostly out of self-defense. I can't afford to lose it. This is especially true in the days of COVID.

———————————

It's 1:30pm pacific and the early move in of the house is nearly a done deal. We're close to having all the pieces in place and it feels good. Tons of hard work ahead, but we'll have a base of operations and a plan once we get there.

———————————

It's bedtime and my last task is to make sure the keys to the Watertown house get to our friends/Rea's relatives in New York so they can drop off all of our stuff.

So looking forward to having this part dealt with. Not looking forward to having to manage Rea during the packing. Flight is Sunday.

Chapter 6
(August 2020)

1 August 2020

The thing that is going to drive me nuts is shower days. We just spent an hour going back and forth trying to get a combination of clothing that Rea approved of. She kept changing the shirt when she should be looking for pants. Then we went through numerous sock permutations as she wears between two and three pairs on each foot. This last bit is largely due to a physical disability.

Between her confusion and her pickiness, I was about at the end of my rope at the end.

I'd never understood how important the ritual of dressing is to her. I think in some ways her inability to navigate that is one of the hardest things she's having to deal with, so it isn't only me that is suffering.

———

We made the rounds today of the people we've grown closest to in the neighborhood here in Washington. Tomorrow we fly to Syracuse. It was a bit hard as they all knew this was likely their final time seeing Rea. Even without C-19, it is unlikely we'll make it back. Travelling is just getting to be too hard for both of us. With the virus we have two-week quarantines being put in place and many other complications that make things worse.

Today ended up being a Xanax day.

2 August 2020

Today we fly to Syracuse and from there drive to our "nearly ours" new home in Watertown, New York. Fingers crossed everything will go as planned.

Rea is still asleep. I'm going to wake her up at 6am.

3 August 2020

The trip to Watertown went reasonably well.

Two hiccups were that the airline luggage check didn't open until about an hour and a half before our midday flight, and once we got to Syracuse, luggage carts were impossible to rent. We staggered into our new house a bit after midnight and then it took an hour or so of cajoling before I managed to get Rea to go to sleep. Her ability to deal with new and unusual situations is significantly reduced.

I'd never realized before how much of her life circles around ritual. She has/had a way of picking her clothes for the day. A list of things she did in the morning after getting up, the same for the end of the day. Her inability to navigate those rituals is causing both of us a lot of stress.

In general I'd say her mood is fairly low today. Neither of us slept that well and jet lag is probably playing a part as well. At least we have a mattress and a decent supply of groceries after a couple of deliveries.

4 August 2020

Rea isn't sleeping well. This of course magnifies her confusion, which has been fairly bad at times. The new house isn't helping, as she's having to learn where things are. I knew that would be an issue which was one of the reasons I wanted to get moved in as quickly as possible.

I hope the puppy is a sweetheart. I'm already stressed dealing with Rea, particularly given our current quarantine. Rea seems to need me constantly and that is not making this any easier since we can't have anyone over who could distract her.

Rea stopped being the woman I've spent the past 25-plus years with a while back; it's probably been more than a year. But even now she's still there. The essence of who she is remains, and if anything I've grown to have a greater understanding of who she really has been all these years.

It's ironic that this horrible disease has given me a greater insight and appreciation of her.

5 August 2020

We have water in the basement. It's been raining a lot and was pouring early this morning, so I'm not totally surprised. There isn't a lot and we haven't completed the closing so we'll see what happens.

Short of a biblical-level flood there is no way we're aborting at this point. We like the house and it wouldn't make sense given Rea's situation.

I have no clue how I get from where I am now to Rea's passing. Absolutely no clue. I don't mean the logistical side – that is fairly obvious.

I've felt constantly overwhelmed for months now. I've built a bit of a wall between me and the sadness but even that is brittle.

It's getting harder to update this journal as she's nearly constantly wanting to be by my side. I'm being a bit short with her at times. I suck :-(

6 August 2020

I've been thinking about it a bit, and I think it's not really true that I can't imagine the non-procedural parts of the time between now and the end for Rea. I think I just don't want to. It's just too painful.

Virus deaths are leveling off again. At this point it amazes me how many people still don't get it. Wear masks and follow safety guidelines and the virus stays at a dull roar. Don't do that and it starts to explode. It's a simple enough equation.

There is talk of a vaccine being available later this year. I'm not that optimistic. This whole thing looks way too much like the opening chapter of a zombie apocalypse story to me.

7 August 2020

Yesterday's virus data showed a slight downward trend. I can hear the virus deniers already saying, "See, we told you it wasn't so bad". Which ignores the fact that when the trend started to be up again four weeks ago states started rolling back the relaxation of the rules. In other words, this downturn is 100% expected and happening pretty much exactly when we'd expect it to.

The new supplement I'd been trying to get for weeks finally arrived. No immediate impact but we'll see if she's a bit more with it cognitively tomorrow. I tried describing to her where the light switch was for one of the fixtures in the bathroom. I patiently explained it was on the wall between the sink and the mirror and to the left.

Suffice to say a five-year-old would have easily understood but she couldn't. This would have killed me a few months ago but at this point it's just one of dozens of similar incidents every day.

8 August 2020

Puppy arrival day, assuming the delivery people know what they are doing which I'm a bit doubtful of. Time will tell.

———————————

Just got a call from the puppy dispatcher. Marley (we decided on this name yesterday. Rea chose the name from the list we had compiled over the past month or so) is scheduled to be here between 1:30 and 4:30 this afternoon.

Rea is doing a bit better this morning than she has in a while. It might be the new supplement or I might be imagining it, but she got dressed without prompting and put on some earrings for the first time in I don't know how long.

The final part of CJD progression is bad and I know neither of us has any desire to prolong it when it gets to that point, but increasing the duration and quality of her time before then is something I've been working hard to achieve since the start.

Latest ETA is around 2:30 in the afternoon for Marley.

Marley arrived on time. She was great out of the gate, but the evening isn't going so well. It's a challenge as her crying is pretty darned heart-rending but we can't afford to encourage this level of separation anxiety. She's all of 15 feet away and can hear us so she knows we are nearby. We'll relent a bit in an hour or two if we have to, but she will get used to being on her own, or she won't be with us/me long term.

She should be exhausted at this point, but she is a bit like the energizer bunny. Even though she's been awake almost all of the past nine hours, she still keeps on going. Puppies her age supposedly sleep 18 to 22 hours a day. Once she's out she's hopefully going to sleep most of the night. I can dream, can't I?

9 August 2020

After much initial drama Marley has been an angel. I got up at about 2:30am to take her outside and she cried a little after being put back in her crate but that was it.

Her kennel should be here today. We may try her in there tonight.

Marley has been much more mellow today. I think she's still exhausted from the travel and excitement yesterday. I'm a little frustrated by how much she prefers eating the bark out in the planter by the back door to her food, though.

Here she is with Rea. This was taken yesterday, one more week of quarantine.

10 August 2020

Last night was not fun. Marley started barking at midnight. I took her out and after I brought her back in she made a near-continuous din for the rest of the night. Eventually I was able to mostly sleep through it. Rea, not so much.

I took Marley out to go to the bathroom at 3am as well and that had no impact on her noise level. A bit before six I decided it was time to get up and after waiting for her to be silent for a bit I took her out to our sun room which is where she's spending her non-sleeping/noise-making time for now.

Rea is hopefully sleeping at the moment. I'll have to check her watch to see how she is doing, at least as far as Fitbit is concerned.

———

Rea is up and has had breakfast. I'm exhausted, but not for the typical reasons. I'm not sure how I'm going to make it through the next six days but somehow I will.

This afternoon we have somebody coming to do an estimate on a walk-in tub/shower upgrade. I'm hoping that won't be too terrifying cost wise but it's not something I have a lot of experience with so I'm just not sure.

11 August 2020

I think the supplements are helping, but in a sense they may be hurting as well. Yesterday Rea told me she was scared. She's said this a few times along the way, but this was the first time recently. I never know what to say so I just hold her and mumble something. We're more than halfway through the quarantine and being able to go out should help her mood.

I'm confident that there is something after for us and I'm also confident that she and I will meet again someday after she is gone but I don't think she has that kind of faith.

I've been able to maintain my faith through this whole ordeal, but I wonder if I'll be able to do so when my time nears? I think I will but we can never be sure of how we'll react in a particular situation until we're in that place.

God, I hate CJD and I hate being in this situation. I do my best but I'm just not a very strong person and at times it is nearly overwhelming. I just have to keep on keeping on, though.

I've said I'd switch places with Rea in a heartbeat and sometimes that is true. Other times it isn't and that makes me feel small and selfish. Really there is no winning place to be mentally in this situation. Minimizing and sometimes burying the hurt for a short time is the best I can do.

I think I may be in a down phase. I've said before that it is hard for me to be sure. Which probably makes it seem like there is no chance I'm a bit bipolar. Maybe I'm not; maybe I am. I live my life with a metaphorical layer of fuzz between me and the real world. It's almost (though not really) like I have a second personality that I keep a bit apart from myself. That other me is how I interact with the world. It's just a bit removed from the real me, a tiny bit shielded and shielding. Often I think of that surface personality as the real me which can make it difficult to know how I'm really feeling.

Maybe everyone is this way – it's impossible to know. I'm stuck in my own head with only the most superficial understanding of others. We don't understand ourselves, so how can we expect others to "get" us?

Marley had a very good night. Being in our room made a big difference to her for reasons that aren't entirely clear to me. Before she was all of 10 feet further away with both doors between us wide open. If she's happy, then we're happy.

I'm still exhausted, though, even after a good night's sleep. This is probably due in part to me being in a down phase.

I haven't had a chance to write this much in a while. The puppy is being very mellow and Rea slept in this morning. I got her breakfast mostly ready in advance, so when she woke up I was able to get it to her quickly. She'll be out in a bit and we'll have a lot to do at that point. It's a never-ending list of real and not-so-real needs for Rea, the puppy, and even me once in a while.

As if this year couldn't get worse, I managed to accidentally poison Marley. It turns out grapes and raisins are toxic to many dogs. Really toxic. As in kill their kidneys. I found this out by making a posting on Facebook about how she liked grapes and carrots. She only had three or four grapes but for a tiny puppy that could be deadly. Or totally harmless. I had to take her to the emergency vet in Syracuse which is an hour away since none of the vets here in Watertown are taking new patients. They pumped her stomach and got maybe one grape so she's spending three days there getting her kidneys checked frequently and constantly monitored regularly.

Chocolate I knew about. Artificial sweeteners I knew about. I had no clue about grapes.

She seemed okay when I dropped her off, so fingers crossed she will be fine. I was balling my eyes out at one time on the drive back from Syracuse. Frankly I almost completely lost it but I just don't have the time for that now. Besides, doing 70 miles an hour is not the time to have a nervous breakdown.

While I was waiting out in the parking lot for word on Marley, Rea asked me to call her because her phone battery was getting low. It took me 15 minutes to talk her through plugging the right cable into her phone and an external battery pack. She was never all that into the hardware side of things but before CJD this would have been a trivial task for her. The decay in her executive functioning is likely the primary culprit. She's still doing well with language, and if you didn't know her well you could be fooled depending on the topic. Heck, in some ways her memory is surprisingly good still. She remembered details of our trip through Vermont and Maine that I was hazy on, for instance, and that happened during the last few days of June when she was nearly three months beyond diagnosis. Plus, we're talking about something that happened six weeks ago.

A lot of the knowledge and problem-solving part of who she is has eroded, but her personality is still mostly there. Thinking about it makes me both grateful and extremely sad.

I feel like I'm constantly being pulled in seemingly diametrically opposed directions emotionally.

12 August 2020

Last night Rea started writing a letter to Phish. It's something she's mentioned before, but I've never been clear on what she wants to accomplish and other things have always distracted me from helping her. I've wanted to write a letter to them as well, so maybe I'll combine the two. She's at the point where she needs a lot of help to get things done, but as I mentioned yesterday, her memory is still surprisingly good for some things.

I was reading that blueberries might promote new brain cell growth. Rea loves blueberries and I frequently include them in her meal. We haven't been able to get very good ones here in New York, but I've been the only one complaining about that. I decided to order a blueberry extract pill to add to her daily supplement regime. I'm sure other loved ones have tried similar paths to slow CJD, and as I've said before, I have no clue whether it helps but I have to try.

She's been sleeping better recently, with the exception of puppy Marley meltdown night.

Marley is doing very well at the 24-hour mark. If she's still fine at 48 hours I'll be able to pick her up tomorrow. As an added bonus, the emergency vet was able to recommend a place that is taking new patients. It'll be a 50-minute drive each way from Watertown to get to them, but they were very friendly on the phone and best of all they were willing to see us.

I've spent most of the afternoon trying to cajole Rea into the shower. She's getting a lot like a kid in some ways.

Our walk-in tub was initially promised for the 24th of this month but apparently they are just starting to hit shortages and we've been pushed back to September 15. Not enthused about that but even stuff that is made in America is going to be impacted by C-19 restrictions. The company manufactures in Texas near Dallas so that is an added challenge given how the virus has been spreading there.

Rea has been complaining about her left ear feeling plugged for a while now. It didn't seem all that serious and with our quarantine status I decided not to worry about it. It turns out she had a partial earplug stuck in her ear. This was likely left over from our flight back on Aug 2 :(

I was able to carefully remove it with some tweezers. Not a huge deal given the outcome but it's frustrating I didn't think to look in her ear sooner. In fact, I didn't think to do it at all. She figured it out herself. Ugh.

13 August 2020

Hopefully we'll be able to bring Marley back home today.

I'm a bit of an introverted hermit but even I'm ready to escape from this place. Quarantines are not fun, even if they are necessary. The infections and fatalities are trending back downward, though, which will probably rile up the idiots again. What can you do though? It's exhausting to argue with them.

Marley's third round of test results were fine, so I got to go pick her up today. Rea was feeling dizzy so I went solo again. I got home about 4:30 in the afternoon.

Marley was a complete brat for the first couple of hours and then she had a couple of hours of being good followed by a bit of back and forth. She is a smart dog and very even-tempered. She's only about 10 weeks old, though, and she has a lot of mischief in her.

The finance stuff on the house is pretty much done. We will probably sign the final paperwork on Monday. It will be good to be done with that finally.

14 August 2020

The riding lawnmower is scheduled to arrive sometime in the late morning to midafternoon today. We'll need to get a snowblower as well in a couple of months.

The money transfers are all done on the house purchase. At this point we just have to do the paperwork. That will wait until Monday most likely. I'm also working on getting power of attorney for Rea set up at that time. Her command of language is still good, but her confusion can be pretty severe. She wasn't sure where the bathroom was this morning. Yesterday she was confusing her shower seat with the toilet :(

The riding lawn mower has arrived. Without gas. Which makes sense in retrospect, but I'll have to figure out how to fix that with two more days of quarantine left.

Almost every day I wonder how I'm going to make it to the finish line. Then another day passes and I'm one day closer.

15 August 2020

To be clear, I'm in no hurry to see Rea gone, though to a degree she already is. Anyone who has watched a loved one fade, particularly due to some form of dementia, will have a good idea of what I'm going through. Being done with the quarantine will help, I think.

16 August 2020

Rea is still mentioning that she's scared. I suppose that is in a sense a good sign, as it shows she still has that level of cognition. I don't have any good answers for her, though, as I'm scared as well. My faith provides me some level of comfort, but she doesn't share it, at least not on a conscious level. I firmly believe she is going to be fine if there is any sort of afterlife.

Rea's balance has been getting worse recently. She's complaining a lot about being dizzy. I don't know if that is the cause, or an effect of her unsteadiness. I thought putting her shoes on early in the day would help but so far there is no evidence to support that theory.

Marley is making progress. She's smart which helps. She's also learned the word no and mostly listens when it is used. I get the impression that it's verboten these days to say no to dogs, but frankly I only have so much patience and while I am willing and enthusiastic to give her a lot of love and positive reinforcement, she is getting the occasional correction. Which is mostly me talking in a stern voice or occasionally grabbing her and giving her the stink eye. When she started chewing on an electric cable, she did get a bop on the nose. Doing that could freaking kill her.

17 August 2020

Last night Rea insisted she had a Vote Biden hat. I'm nearly sure she doesn't. She wanted to get one a week or two back and I argued against it. I'm not a fan of political stickers or apparel. Add in the fact that in this part of the country things tilt strongly to team red and we just don't need the aggravation. Selfish of me? Yes, but frankly I have to be selfish at times. I'm no paragon.

Bottom line, she does not have a Biden hat. She might have figured out how to order one and it could be on the way but at this point that would be a major challenge for her.

Why do I bring this up? Because to the best of my knowledge it's the first time she confabulated something out of nothing. This is yet another step along the path of the progression of the disease.

Marley was being a brat this morning. I moved the throw rug that had been by the front door (which we don't really use) to the back door in the sun room and she immediately tried to rip it apart.

18 August 2020

Marley eventually figured out that I didn't want her messing with the rug. I had to go Godzilla on her a few times first, though. This basically consisted of me making myself large and demonstrating in a non-physical way that I was very unhappy with her doing that. If anyone else ever reads this, I'm sure somebody will be thinking "oh the horrible abuse". Put a sock in it if you are. Teaching a dog or animal the meaning of the word no and discipline is not automatically abuse, though it can be.

As much as I would like the world to be full of rainbows and unicorns, it is not. To the best of my ability, I live in reality and reality is I do not have the time to distract and subtly cajole Marley into correct behavior. I do have the time to give her a lot of love and positive reinforcement if I can also teach the meaning of the word no in parallel. That is the math I live with.

––––––––––––––

Rea's mood today is poor. She essentially said she wishes she were dead. It doesn't get much worse than that :-(

I had a plan for California. New York not so much. Looking back, I think my biggest mistake was not questioning her more when she said she wanted to come here. The house is gorgeous and I'm confident things will work out but in the short term the stress is a lot greater than it would have been if we had stuck with California.

What is done is done, though. We're going to take Marley for a walk. That will hopefully help.

19 August 2020

The walk was short and 90% of it consisted of Marley sniffing everything and trying to trip us. Probably typical for puppy's first walk.

In the early evening I spent 45 minutes outside with Marley waiting for her to do number one and/or number two. Nothing. She'd been back sliding on the potty training, so I was hoping to give her some positive reinforcement. Five minutes after we came back in, she pooped and peed in the house. Godzilla was back and he was feeling vengeful. She ended up outside while I cleaned up the mess and we spent the time up until bedtime outside. She didn't do a number two but probably did a number one once or twice. I wasn't paying that much attention. Marley also spent a lot of time trying to get me into a better mood. Mostly it didn't work, though I did play with her a bit and give her treats and positive encouragement when she was good.

We now have an appointment with the recommended neurologist. It's for a week from this Friday. Rea's mood seems a bit better today. Mentally she's doing as well as she has in a while.

Marley on the other hand was a big brat this morning. I've emailed our friends who are dog trainers for advice.

I got some good pointers on how to deal with Marley's issues. I feel a better having a path forward but she's skating on thin ice. I'm not sure it's fair to her or us if we can't start to make some progress soon.

And then Marley broke through the ice with a vengeance. :-(

We bought a cheap 50-inch TV. This should make watching stuff more exciting. Maybe it will distract both of us. When Marley isn't making me want to tear my excessively long hair out.

20 August 2020

Marley had a much better day today. It was a huge relief to be able to give her positive reinforcement for doing things correctly.

I've been told by Rea's new neurologist that her recent balance issues are likely caused by CJD. Not what I wanted to hear of course. Mentally she's doing as well as she has for the past couple of months. It really is a bit of a miracle. I'd like to think it is also related the supplements I've been giving her.

I won't lie, there are times I think about loading up the RV and driving back to the west coast with Rea. Everything is so much more difficult here since we don't have all the doctors and such in place. I often feel like I'm flying solo in terms of her care which is not a good place for me to be.

———————

Okay, so Rea does have a Biden hat. I had no clue. I can't complain about that. It's a positive thing for sure.

She's watching the Democratic convention broadcast right now. I'm not interested. I will say that I want the president gone in a big way and for a lot of reasons and I'll vote for Biden because of that, but I'm a political independent and there are things in the Democratic Party platform I'm not very happy with.

21 August 2020

We discussed heading back to the west coast. No firm plans on that yet, but it's a real possibility. We talked about it a bit with the wife of Rea's older brother yesterday when she stopped by. That information may be circulating.

There are really three primary issues. First, my social anxiety hampers my ability to interact with people, even on the phone. Second, C-19 makes getting anything done much more difficult. Everything is in short supply even if things aren't as bad as they were a few months ago. Finally, people here have busy lives of their own and our ties aren't that tight at this point.

I took a Xanax for the first time in a while today. I still have a decent number of them since I use them so infrequently. They make a noticeable difference when I take one in the morning, which is what I did this time.

Tracking down the legal paperwork we put together a few years back related to our own mortality is a pain. My brother doesn't appear to have a complete set and I was sure that he did. I can't seem to figure out which lawyer we used either. :(

———————

Figured out who the lawyer was and pinged them via their contact page this morning No word back. It's a Friday so I'll have to wait until Monday to call.

One of Rea's high school classmates dropped by. It was a good visit for Rea. Three more friends are coming by tomorrow afternoon and taking her out. Which should be good for both of us. I could really use a bit of alone time. Well, mostly alone. Marley will need to be kept company but that is fine.

22 August 2020

No word back from the lawyer by the end of the day. I guess I'll have to call them on Monday.

Rea had some friends from her high school graduating class over today. She had a good visit, and I had a chance to go out and complete a couple of errands while she was busy.

Marley has been mostly good. It's really key for us to keep to the routine she is used to.

Sometimes I wonder if I'm getting better at coping or if I'm just losing my mind.

C-19 cases and fatalities are trending down again. This is a good thing, but winter is in theory the worst time for viruses. We're heading into the later part of summer.

I'm going back and forth on the whole return to the west coast thing. There have been some positive signs the past day or so, but it's not feeling like a sure thing to me.

Of course, going back to the west coast isn't a guarantee either.

23 August 2020

I'm arguing on Facebook. Which isn't particularly effective but cathartic – at least in the short term.

I feel like I'm going to have to start being more honest with people about our situation. Mostly my own. In particular my anxiety. In a way that feels a bit narcissistic and maybe it is, but I don't feel right sharing where Rea is in her progression.

There are times when it is clear that Rea is either forgetting or ignoring that she is terminally ill. I don't want to remind her of that given her frequently down mood. This also makes it difficult to share my own challenges as that doesn't help her mood any either.

24 August 2020

Another Monday. We're both still homesick. Lots of errands to run today. Having something to do helps.

In other news, Marley is still adorable …

Rea's dizziness continues to be an issue and is going to get worse.

She hasn't slept well the past two nights. I almost always sleep like a rock. I realized recently that I haven't had one of my REM sleep disorder episodes in a couple of months. That wasn't an unusual lapse in the past, but I was having frequent occurrences initially after Rea's diagnosis.

We've introduced Marley to the wonders of the Kong. Right now she is trying to get the treats out. The Kong in question is small, maybe three inches or so, and I have a flat treat blocking the big end.

Oooh, she just managed to get a few pieces of treat out of it. Progress :-)

Finding the time and energy to play with her can be difficult, so it's nice that this appears to be a winning thing. And it's therapeutic watching her try to get the stuff out of the Kong.

———————

Earlier today we were running around doing errands when we passed an ice cream shop. Rea mentioned that it wasn't the one we stopped at in Watertown a couple of months back and recalled that we chatted with a fellow about how we liked our rental car at that time.

26 August 2020

Marley is resisting all efforts to potty train her. She's so smart and quick to pick things up that it's very frustrating. She'll figure it out eventually.

My great-uncle passed away on the 17th. He was 89 years old. I don't really recall him, though I remember his mother. She would babysit me occasionally when we were still in Illinois. We left when I was about four years old, so those are some of my earliest memories. They lived on and owned a farm near Seneca Illinois.

———————

Have I mentioned that the DNA results are back? This is the test to see if Rea's CJD is genetic. We don't care, but she has relatives who are understandably concerned about the possibility of Rea's situation having a genetic cause.

27 August 2020

Xanax day.

Rea's brother, sister-in-law, and nephew visited. We had a good time chatting over dinner.

28 August 2020

Turns out Rea's appointment in Syracuse is actually a month from today. Who schedules a CJD patient nearly six weeks out?

I'm starting to hate the roads around Syracuse. Crap on-ramps and lots of twisty little side streets that don't make sense. We didn't find out about the mix up on the appointment until after we got there. Not a good time.

29 August 2020

Another weekend is here. Marley was good on Thursday and not so good yesterday. Hoping for better today but it's raining which is going to make it tough to keep to our normal routine.

I need to mow the lawn. Hopefully tomorrow.

The first few times it has rained a lot we ended up with a bit of leaking in the basement. On Thursday we had a mini flood. There is a sink and cabinet around the sump pump and I had to drill a couple of holes in the base of the cabinet to allow the water to pass to the drain more quickly. In theory this shouldn't be needed as there is a system in place that is supposed to prevent this from happening. Apparently that system has been slowly failing over the past half-dozen years and Thursday may have been the final nail.

31 August 2020

Last day of August, another month nearly in the books. Rea is doing amazingly well and in certain contexts still seems normal. In other contexts (Me: "Rea, the table in front of you." Rea: "What table?") she is profoundly impacted.

Marley is making progress. She's awesome and a little bit frustrating. Speaking of Marley, I need to go spend time with her before we head out to run errands.

———

Today has been a really bad day balance-wise for Rea. Some of it might have been related to low blood sugar but it seems clear that this is the next area that CJD is attacking.

———

This may be both the happiest and saddest picture I'll ever take.

Looking at it makes me smile and cry at the same time. I guess maybe that makes it a perfect moment?

Chapter 7

(September 2020)

1 September 2020

Rea is getting taken to have her hair cut today. This is the first break I've had in weeks, if not months. How am I using it? Catching up on some chores, relaxing a little and crying. I hate CJD so freaking much.

My typical winter depression is going to be brutal this year.

Having said that, the crying is probably good for me. I'm keeping a lot of stuff bottled up right now and that isn't healthy.

I need to take Marley outside and spend some time with her.

2 September 2020

We went to the Watertown Farmers Market today. It runs through the first week of October. There was a good selection of fruits and vegetables. My right arm nearly fell off, though, as I had to help Rea balance with my left and carry everything with my right.

Marley peed in her big kennel. This is the second time that has happened.

Rea seems to be having a good day mentally.

I really need to do the bills. I have a couple of days left but the sooner the better. Rea used to do all this and it's another reminder of our situation.

3 September 2020

I managed to get things set up for a couple of conference calls on Rea's DNA results. It's looking like next Tuesday will be the day.

4 September 2020

Friday again. The days seem to blur together.

Lots of progress on various things, plus Rea had a visit from her friend Gwen this morning which was nice. We'll likely run some errands this afternoon.

5 September 2020

Today was a decent day. Bad at the start and at times late in the afternoon, but good otherwise both mentally and emotionally. Neither one of us slept well last night which contributed to some unevenness.

After three good days Marley had a setback today. There was a suspicious wet spot on the carpet in the sunroom. Still, she's making progress.

I rescheduled the contractor visit to quote the gutter install. I'd double booked us accidentally and Rea really wanted to do the stuff that didn't involve getting a quote on gutters. The gutters will redirect water away from the house, which should prevent the basement from flooding.

A good day mentally for Rea. We had a nice dinner with Rea's older brother, wife, kids, and grandkids.

6 September 2020

Rea had a really good day mentally and a pretty good day mood-wise.

I moved one of our chargers for USB devices to the headboard area of our bed and she actually plugged her phone in without help or prompting. This may not sound like a big thing but a few weeks or so ago when I had to take Marley to the emergency vet in Syracuse after the unfortunate grape feeding incident, I had to explain to her in excruciating detail how to plug her phone in while waiting for word back on Marley's condition.

Marley is still a challenge. She's improving but today she peed right in front of me. I was not amused and after a visit from Godzilla she got to spend a lot of the time she would have had free rein in the Sun Room in her big kennel instead.

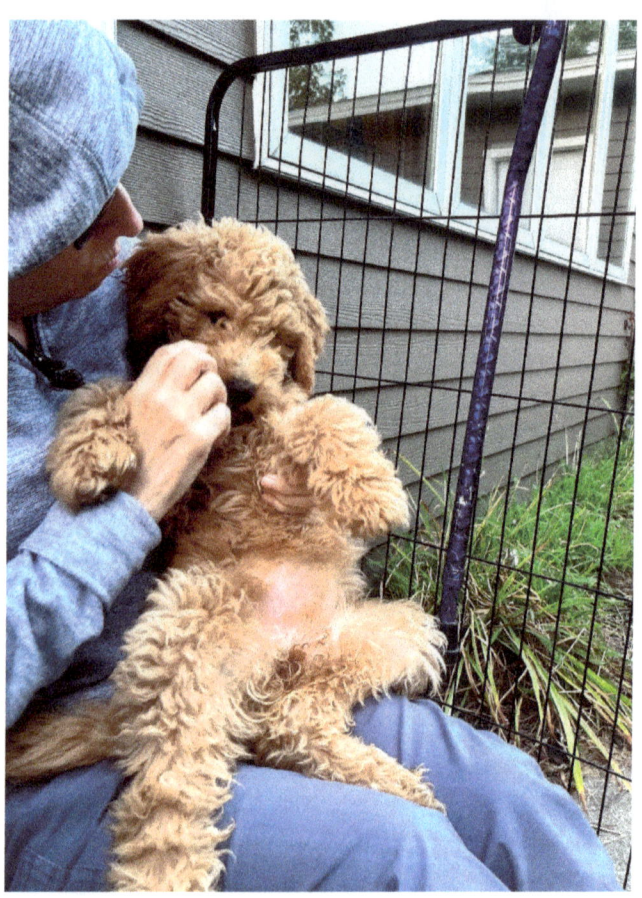

9 September 2020

We went to SUNY in Syracuse yesterday. It was a good visit. This was a rescheduling of the appointment that I'd thought was a couple of weeks ago but was in actuality later this month.

The results of the genetic test came back normal, meaning that Rea does not have a genetic predisposition for CJD. This was an immense relief to her family but bittersweet.

10 September 2020

Marley has a vet appointment today. It was scheduled a few weeks ago and is for inoculations. She's had issues though with diarrhea pretty much since day one and it has gotten worse over the past couple of days. She seems fine otherwise, but I'll be mentioning it to the vet.

Yesterday Marley pooped on the couch in the sunroom. Actually it was more like a thick soup. I was not amused. She'd been outside a few minutes earlier, and while she barked, it was brief and she didn't wait. We still don't have a washing machine and likely won't for a few more weeks. The PITA factor is high given that.

I rinsed the cover off outside. It's still filthy.

When I get upset with Marley, Rea gets upset. I hate that, but not enough to stop doing it apparently. I'm hoping for a better day today. I seriously need a break.

Rea looked after her mom for years. I wonder if she has ever thought about what I'm going through? I think some of the things she said early on point in that direction. She's far enough gone now that I'm not sure she could now.

The fact that her CJD is not genetic really is a bit of a two-edged sword. I'm really happy for her family, but I'd be lying if I didn't admit it makes me sad as well. So far as we know now this was just random chance. I've said before that I don't blame God. The way the world works seems self-evident to me and believing that God is highly involved in day-to-day events requires mental gymnastics that I am not capable of.

Marley vet appointment went okay. She got her latest round of immunizations. I got some probiotics and special food for her which will hopefully help with the diarrhea.

She got carsick on the way back. First time for that. I suspect it was all the shots.

11 September 2020

Friday again. The house is a bit of a mess. I need to work on getting things tidied up as we may have guests tomorrow afternoon.

13 September 2020

Saturday was a fairly good day in spite of it appearing that Rea's confusion level has increased. A childhood friend and his wife stopped by and took us out to lunch, and we got to chat for a few hours which Rea really enjoyed.

I ordered a digital piano on Friday. I can hardly play but I love the sound of the piano and retail therapy is a thing.

Friday night we had dinner with Rea's younger brother and his family at our place. That was nice as well.

Rea has been sleeping poorly for the past couple of weeks. That is probably contributing to her confusion. I'm not sure what to do in order to help that. I should probably talk to her doctor.

Rea bought a $550 Phish-related poster today. I'd spent more than that on a good beginner's digital keyboard the day before so it was hard to argue. As much money as we've spent, we're still okay financially and with a bit of discipline I should be fine when this whole thing has run its course. Still, we need to get the spending under control a bit.

The walk-in tub is supposed to be installed on Tuesday. Hopefully we'll hear something positive from them tomorrow.

14 September 2020

Texted early evening by the walk-in tub people. They will be here as scheduled.

15 September 2020

Walk-in tub day. The work is scheduled for one day with the possibility of two. Hoping for a good result. This should make bathing a lot easier for Rea.

16 September 2020

The walk-in tub is still in process. They got a late start yesterday and it's a complicated operation.

The local hospice people called yesterday. They are going to stop by today and talk to Rea and me. At least that is the plan. The tub delay may push that out.

This morning while I was out back with Marley, I had the thought that I am a lobster in a pot of water that is very slowly coming to a boil. Not a good thought.

Farmers market today. I don't think we'll make it there.

17 September 2020

The walk-in tub is mostly a win. The final cleanup could have been better. We'll likely be working out how best to use it for a while.

18 September 2020

Rea had been having trouble sleeping but did well last night. I've been having trouble as well, so I took a Xanax last night. First one in a while. Thirty minutes later I was sound asleep. Let's hear it for modern pharmaceuticals.

Rea has some high school friends coming over today. It will be a mini reunion. There will be four of them including Rea so it should hopefully be safe even with C-19.

Speaking of C-19, early signs that it is trending back up again and now the news is reporting that a widespread vaccine likely won't be seen until mid-next year at the earliest.

20 September 2020

Marley is showing signs that she might have figured out the whole potty-training thing. I'm slowly allowing her more freedom again and so far she hasn't blown it.

I've been accumulating additional cooking tools. The latest are an air fryer and a waffle maker. This is leading to better meals with more variety. I guess that's kinda trivial, but anything positive is worth mentioning.

21 September 2020

My life is mostly sad. There is Rea, the virus, and the state of my country. The death of Ruth Bader Ginsburg is just another nail in the coffin of this country I suspect and it's hard to watch.

The hospice people have a set of three drugs they prescribe to all their patients. One is for anxiety, another is morphine, and the final one is for "death rattle". The morphine is unlikely to be needed by Rea, but I suspect most of their patients have cancer and it makes lot of sense in those cases.

The whole "death rattle" thing has me rattled. In the back of my mind, I knew it was coming someday but that medication makes it a lot more real.

Marley has been doing well recently. She's either been contained or supervised the whole time which has limited her ability to do the wrong thing. This means she's gotten a lot of reinforcement in doing things the way we want. No guarantees of course, but it's been a step in the right direction which is nice.

In theory our washer and dryer should be in stock in a few days. I'm hoping that is true. If it isn't then I'll have to come up with a plan B.

22 September 2020

Rea's younger brother dropped off a table and chairs. Having this has allowed us to move the smaller table we already have into the sunroom where we can work on puzzles.

We'd be working on a puzzle today if we weren't both exhausted. Rea woke me up around 1am because she couldn't sleep. I got her some yogurt and then couldn't get back to sleep. This has rarely been a problem since this whole ordeal began. I think I got maybe four hours of sleep total. Tonight I'll be taking a Xanax for sure.

Grocery shopping done, Marley only mildly neglected and it's already four o'clock. Five more hours or so and I can take a Xanax and call it a day.

24 September 2020

We're giving some thought to returning briefly to the west coast. We have friends who train dogs who would be willing to take Marley on, and this would give us a chance to see people and possibly clean out the apartment as well.

———

Rea saw a plate glass window on FB marketplace for $30 that was nearby. She wanted to get it and I freaked out as it would be one more thing I'd have to deal with and I'm at my limit. Also, we were supposed to hear back about our washer and dryer today. That didn't happen and my mood was not enhanced.

Still, I wish I were less of an asshole.

Rea got to socialize a lot today, both in person and via video chat.

25 September 2020

Our washer and dryer are now due on October 1. COVID is the excuse of the day. It pretty much works for everything.

———

We bought a small plate glass window today from an estate sale. I should say that Rea offered to buy it last night on FB. I was a little perturbed and made an ass of myself which upset her :-(

My social anxiety makes dealing with people I don't know very uncomfortable. Not an excuse, at least not a good one.

26 September 2020

It occurred to me this morning that Rea is solidly in her twilight time. I'm not very good with metaphors. I understand the general concept but something in my brain just doesn't quite click most of the time when it comes to feeling them on an emotional level.

The sunset and our current situation are exceptions. Rea can still speak and with a bit of help she can get around, but she's unsteady on her feet and her level of confusion continues to increase. The times and situations where she seems more or less normal are also becoming rare.

I can no longer tell her I'm going to be in the bathroom or outside with Marley and have any expectation she'll remember. Last night I came in after having been outside with Marley for a while and she was sitting on the couch in the living room upset because she hadn't been able to find me. I'm frequently outside with Marley so it shouldn't have been difficult to figure out where I was, but her mental state just isn't up to that most of the time now.

Politics here in the US continues to be horribly depressing. The death of Ruth Bader Ginsburg is yet another flash point that we didn't need.

27 September 2020

It occurred to me recently that the downside of Rea wanting to spend her final time at home is the reduction in opportunity for social interaction, particularly in the time of COVID. A home would have other people around including staff. Seeing her would be much more difficult though so even that would be a tradeoff. I hate this virus nearly as much as I hate CJD. Without the virus Rea's final days would have been so much richer. She deserved better.

But here we are, and so I have to work at making things as nice as I can, while also knowing I'm failing miserably at least in part, because I'm not all together myself.

28 September 2020

Another month nearly in the books.

29 September 2020

Rea had a slightly better day today than the past few. Her mood wasn't great, but she was more engaged and not quite as down as she had been. Which is surprising since it's rainy and gray outside.

Today is the first presidential debate. It's amazing to me that there is any question at all as to who will win this election. I'm a political independent so it isn't like I'm strongly biased either way. I've voted for members of both parties in the past and haven't voted for any of the Democratic presidential candidates in decades. To be completely honest I haven't cast a vote for president in around 20 years. I almost voted for both McCain and Romney but then they picked VPs whom I couldn't stomach.

It's funny in a dark kinda way that the Republicans are trying to pretend that Biden is a socialist. I'll ignore for the moment the fact that we use that word in this country for two or three different largely unrelated things and point out that Biden is neither a socialist of any stripe nor a progressive. The progressive wing of the Democratic Party is holding their noses and supporting him because anything is better from their perspective than our current president.

30 September 2020

The installation of rain gutters is happening today.

The hospice nurse will be coming over this afternoon to do the biweekly examination of Rea and discuss a few issues including dizziness.

———————

Rain gutter installed; nurse appointment delayed until tomorrow because Rea's hospice nurse had something else come up.

Lots of rain over the past 24 hours but as of a few hours ago zero sign of moisture in the basement even before the rain gutter was installed.

Chapter 8
(October 2020)

1 October 2020

It's a brand-new month. Rea's level of confusion is certainly increasing. It had held steady for a long time but that no longer seems to be true. I can't help but wonder if it is going to continue to accelerate. We're getting closer to the point where her quality of life is constantly negative. I try to live in the moment and not think too much about the past or the future.

I've probably said something similar to that a dozen times or more in this journal. It's my truth, though, and it helps keep me going.

Tomorrow we are heading south to visit some of Rea's friends. Given her recent trend this may be our last road trip. I was thinking we might try to drive out west and back one last time but between her decline, COVID, and the upcoming election, that is starting to seem like a bad idea. We'd need at least a week to drive each way and a couple of weeks out there, so it's inevitable that we would not be home during the election since getting ready would take about a week.

The hospice nurse visited today. It was a substitute for our regular one. He seemed like a good guy and got back to us promptly with some recommendations.

2 October 2020

I've found that a bit of crying on the way to or from the vet is pretty much standard. Actually I'm fairly sure I've been crying more recently than I ever have. Rea's most recent decline is making that pretty hard to avoid.

I'm hoping she has a good few days on this trip. Her friends deserve to have positive memories of her final days.

I don't lie to people about her condition, but I have left out information. She still kind of knows what is going on around her and can read. I don't want to make her sadder than she already is.

I woke up at 4am, and then Marley started crying around 4:45 so I took her out and gave her breakfast. At that point I wasn't going to get any more sleep. I'm hoping for a good day.

———————

We didn't make it to Corning today. We were supposed to leave mid-morning but Rea was very dizzy and didn't want to go. We'll see how she feels in the morning.

3 October 2020

No trip to Corning. Rea was still feeling dizzy; in retrospect I don't think she fully understood that we weren't going as she later talked about going to the Corning Museum shops.

4 October 2020

I could be wrong but it feels like her decline is accelerating.

At first, I was hoping she was just having a couple of really bad days in a row. At this point it's been four. I don't know if I can leave her alone even briefly now. Certainly not for very long.

We did manage to go on a short walk yesterday near the house. She was very unstable on her feet. We made it maybe two blocks each way.

Rea's sister-in-law and brother came over to visit. She had offered to do a bit of house cleaning which is something I've been falling behind on. Rea wanted me to pay her $40. I was kind of appalled and told Rea no. It was being offered out of love for her and us. I don't think Rea in her right mind would have ever suggested such a thing.

Rea is increasingly childlike.

I feel like I'm getting close to some kind of breakdown. Not anything serious or dangerous, I hope; just a long hard cry. I've done that in bits and pieces for months now but haven't really had much time to fully let go. Her rapid decline recently has been ratcheting things up and the metaphorical water is getting closer and closer to a boil.

5 October 2020

We had lunch out today. Rea was confused both before and during about where Marley was going to be while we were out. I'm going to go out on a limb here and say she's got a month or two before she'll be confined to bed. At that point three to six months seems the most likely timeline.

We stopped at our favorite pet store and scheduled a grooming for Marley. She'll get sheared for the first-time next Wednesday. She really needs a haircut as she can barely see at this point. A downside of being mostly poodle.

7 October 2020

I've probably said this dozens of times already, but I am tired. So very tired.

We had a good visit last night with Rea's younger brother and wife. Marley got to play with their dogs for a couple of hours which was good as well. Unfortunately she also pooped and peed in their home but that was mostly my fault since I didn't take her out when I should have.

The b key on the keyboard I'm typing this on is broken. I'm having to bring up the soft keyboard almost every time I need to type one. Word completion/correction is saving me some of the time thankfully.

Rea is watching the VP debate right now. As far gone as she is, she still has a passion for politics. I can't stomach it myself. Especially not given her situation.

9 October 2020

Another Friday. It's clear I'm on a bit of a downward spiral and need to do something. I'm working on that.

Rea's birthday is 10 days away. My mom's is four days away. I've been meaning to order something for my mother. Time to do that.

10 October 2020

Mission accomplished; I ordered something for Mom. A failure, though, in that it isn't scheduled to arrive until the day after her birthday.

I'm confident that Rea's fade is accelerating.

12 October 2020

Rea is spending the day over at her younger brother's house. Our sister-in-law, offered. I haven't been as productive as I could have been thanks to a combination of things not going well and me being lazy. I'm about to get my first hair cut in six or seven months, so that is something.

13 October 2020

The haircut ended up being shorter than I would have liked but I gave lousy feedback and it turned out fine otherwise. It's hard to know what you want when the same person has been cutting your hair for 25 years or more.

Rea had a good day today by her recent standards. We got to talk to some of her work friends in the afternoon via video conference which helped.

Marley gets her first haircut tomorrow. I'm looking forward to seeing how that turns out.

14 October 2020

Marley's haircut turned out great. She looks a bit more like a poodle now. She also got an expanded fenced area out back after the modular fencing expansions arrived today.

Rea was tired and confused. I also realized she put the toilet paper on backwards to what she normally would. To qualify that, when we first met she put it on with the paper inside. I convinced her to do it the opposite way by pointing out it was easier to manipulate that way. So this might have been her reverting to the way she did it when she was young.

15 October 2020

The hospice nurse visited today. I think I've mentioned that they come every couple of weeks? It's amazing how quickly time passes.

Rea is having a hard time completing her thoughts. Even simple ones stump her. She's frustrated and depressed about that.

I know I've said it before, and I've gone back and forth on this but as of this moment I would trade with her if I could. I am so terrified about what is coming and frankly I doubt I'm strong enough to deal with it.

Though if you had asked me six months ago if I would have made it this far, I would have had my doubts then as well. I need to hold onto that thought.

At dinner she sat in the chair I normally sit in. She's done that a time or two before and I've always gently corrected her. Tonight I just let it slide. I suspect at some point in her past there was a similar setup and she sat where I normally sit. She's regressing more and more.

The virus is resurging. No surprise there when a third of the people in this country are living in their own fantasy world where it is no big deal, and the rest of us are fatigued to one degree or another.

The election is only a few weeks away. I'm terrified about what is going to happen. People are voting in record numbers and I suspect that will bode well for Biden, but we'll see.

Keeping up with this journal is tough. Rea wants to be by my side most of the time. Writing here also forces me to think more about our situation which isn't easy.

Way back at the start of this I remember saying something along the lines of "I now understand why people drink themselves into oblivion." For a long time I had found a place where I didn't feel quite that bad. I'm almost totally back there now.

The funny thing is, I think I'm actually in the up part of my cycle. Thank God I'm only mildly bipolar if I am bipolar at all.

17 October 2020

It was rainy yesterday and I didn't manage to get Rea to spend much time out of bed or get dressed. I didn't push things though given the weather and my own low energy level. I'm working a bit harder to get her going today as the weather is looking nicer.

A trip to Target to pick up a prescription and a surprise visit from one of Rea's high school friends made it a good day for her mood wise.

Her ability to think and carry a thought through to completion is mostly gone now. She can seldom complete even simple thoughts. It's like she knows where she wants to go but she just can't get there.

I try to ask clarifying questions but that doesn't help.

Her vocabulary is still good and her long-term memory is not as impacted, but it's only a matter of time.

We're going to celebrate her birthday tomorrow with her younger brother's family.

18 October 2020

I should mow the lawn and mulch the leaves today. And vacuum. I'm not sure I will.

I did neither. I may have time but at this point I don't think I'll bother.

On the plus side I did manage to feed all of us and pay the fine from the NY state DMV for letting the insurance on the RV lapse. That happened because our idiot insurance company never told me I had to send them a proof of residency and then forgot to tell me they would be cancelling the insurance when I didn't respond to the request they didn't make. I found out when the state sent me a nasty letter. Very frustrating.

The fine wasn't huge, but most people in this situation probably got there because they didn't have the money to pay for insurance. I question the wisdom of levying a fine on people in that situation if they fix the problem promptly.

One of Rea's work friends has a charity dedicated to helping teens and others dealing with anxiety. The charity was started after his 15-year-old son committed suicide a day or so before his 16th birthday. There was a fundraising ad on Facebook today for the charity and Rea leaned over onto me and said "Sad". I asked her if it was because of Zachary (the son), and she said yes. This shows who Rea was and still is. The disease will someday erode the last of her away, but it hasn't gotten there yet.

She still talks in full sentences at times but in this case, few words were needed.

The mini birthday celebration was good. The veggie lasagna and ice cream cake were major hits with Rea and the rest of us as well.

Rea went to the bathroom just before leaving but still managed to pee her pants a bit on the 25-minute drive home. It would have normally been 15 or so but she wanted to drive through downtown, and I'd taken some slight detours along the way to avoid the deer and dark curvy roads. This is the first incident of incontinence. I cried while sitting out back on the step waiting for Marley to do her business. It was dark and with the wind I'm sure nobody saw or heard me.

Just before falling asleep, she said she might need my help in the middle of the night if she had to get up to pee. I thought it might have been because of her worsening issues with balance but she said something about the bathroom having moved. I pointed out that it was right across from our bedroom.

I hate this disease.

19 October 2020

Happy 62nd birthday to Rea. So far she seems to be having a good day. Hoping that continues. She had two homemade blueberry waffles for breakfast which is what she wanted.

It's rainy and dreary outside unfortunately.

I didn't get to sleep until nearly two last night and it took a Xanax at that. Tonight should be better I hope.

Or maybe not.

20 October 2020

I got to sleep at a semi reasonable time but then woke up about 6am. Rea woke up a half hour later and ended up falling on the way to the bathroom. This is her first fall at home, though she did fall in a restaurant bathroom a month ago.

She's increasingly unsteady on her feet which is not unexpected. She often gets up in the middle of the night to go to the bathroom. I seldom wake up for this. So now I have another nightmare scenario to deal with. I cuddled with her a bit before sleep, as well as after it became clear we were awake for the day. I need to do that more.

On the positive news side of things our washer and dryer finally came. I'm currently running the first load through. This is not a skill I've developed much, as Rea would never let me do the laundry; she could be very picky and I'm a bit too loosey goosey. I'm washing the furniture covers that Marley managed to get poop on a month or so ago. They've been out in the garage. I didn't feel right asking to use anyone else's washer and dryer for that.

Rea complains a lot about feeling tired. She may be a bit tired, but it's mostly the disease I suspect. Someday soon she'll cross over into the twilight and no longer suffer.

I'm continuing to cry a lot more than I have in a long time. More than I've cried in my entire life.

21 October 2020

I'm now having to help Rea walk everywhere in the house.

She had a decent day otherwise. We watched some good animal-related shows on TV. She's always loved animals. When she first went to college, she wanted to be a biologist but she once told me that having to dissect dead animals changed her mind. That, and organic chemistry.

Having the washer and dryer has buoyed my mood a bit. I'll take what I can get.

Marley has a vet appointment tomorrow and Rea has a friend coming over to keep an eye on her and visit.

23 October 2020

Yesterday I took Marley to the vet for her final round of vaccinations. It turns out she has six adult teeth and I never realized. She had been a bit off on her eating the past couple of days and that is probably why. It's also about time to consider getting her fixed. Which freaks me out a bit if she's scheduled for a couple of weeks out as of now.

A friend of Rea's came over while I was gone with Marley and hung out/watched her for the three or so hours I was away.

A grow light arrived yesterday. The only problem being I'd forgotten I ordered it. I actually ordered a different one the day before, the idea being to hopefully minimize seasonal depression in both myself and Rea. It is really bugging me that I ordered two without realizing it. That is not an encouraging sign.

It's Friday today. Nothing big planned, though one of Rea's friends is coming over this afternoon so that will be nice.

24 October 2020

It's getting increasingly difficult to get Rea out of bed and dressed. I did manage it yesterday since she knew her friend Gwen was coming over in the late afternoon. They went out for a drive that lasted a few hours. It was good for me to get some time alone. I got the garage cleaned up enough that I could get the car into it and did a couple of other chores. I also relaxed a bit.

Marley is teething and it is causing her to eat a lot less. Speaking of Marley, she's telling me she needs to go out.

Marley just wanted to eat maple leaves. Of which there are a lot.

I managed to get Rea out of bed and into the kitchen, but I think she'll be heading back to bed soon. It's likely only weeks until she spends almost all of her time in bed. Maybe that's for the best?

My wife and best friend is mostly gone at this point. I still get to see glimpses of her at times but those are further and further apart. I don't believe God is punishing me for an instant, but I have to say that it sometimes feels like I drew the short end of the straw somewhere along the way.

When that happens I try to think of all the people who have clearly had worse hands dealt to them then me and I remember that it's a big, complex, and often cruel world, and my life isn't that bad in comparison to many others. Rea's for one.

The virus is starting to spiral out of control again and the presidential election is just around the corner. Both of our ballots are in the mail now, though odds are the results won't be impacted at all since Washington is a blue state. Still, it was Rea's final chance to vote and I'm glad she got to express her will one more time.

I ordered a bunch of survival stuff today. Hopefully it will make it before the election. The bulk of it should, but the big rechargeable battery I ordered may not. I should have thought of it sooner, I guess.

We are near Fort Drum; I don't know whether that is going to be a good or a bad thing. Hopefully it's going to be a null op but given the way this year has gone so far, it's hard not to be paranoid about what is yet to come.

25 October 2020

The election is getting close. God help us all.

26 October 2020

The virus continues to escalate. The big difference being now it is more widespread in terms of where the outbreaks are happening. This is as close to a zombie apocalypse as we are ever likely to get, or so I hope.

27 October 2020

We both kinda cried ourselves to sleep last night. I thought Rea was beyond that but no.

She didn't say why she was crying but it's pretty obvious. A bit earlier she asked about appointments for a breast exam and the dentist and I said neither was scheduled. She asked why not and I couldn't say anything. I think this reminded her of her situation. I suck.

Today she's been very confused at times.

She got a new walker yesterday that is giving her more mobility in the house. For the past week I had to help her go everywhere but now she's able to do that herself, assuming she can recall where she is going.

28 October 2020

Rea's younger brother and family came over for dinner. At one point Rea got confused/upset that the two of us weren't going out to do some sort of shopping that she couldn't explain.

It's difficult most of the time to be sure whether the problem she is having is related to an inability to find the right words or if she is just confused. It is likely a bit of both.

She was more coherent later in the evening.

29 October 2020

I just noticed that she no longer flosses her teeth. When did that happen? Sometime in the last month, I think.

The leaves are mostly off the trees and the temperatures have been down near freezing the past couple of days. This weekend clocks get pushed back an hour so it's going to be dark extra early.

Chapter 9

(November 2020)

1 November 2020

It's a new month and we have a winter weather advisory here in Watertown with the possibility of six or more inches of snow. We're well stocked so things should be good on that front.

I have a big battery/UPS on its way that I'd prefer to have on hand. It might come tomorrow if things don't get too bad weather-wise.

The election stuff continues to cause me angst, as does the virus. What doesn't, though?

There was some crying by both of us at lunch time. I was a bit short with Rea when she didn't want to get out of bed for lunch. We have a rule that she only gets one meal a day in bed. That is almost always breakfast. She's often reluctant to get dressed and get out of bed, and so long as she can, I want her to. The day isn't far off when physically and/or mentally she won't be able to. That day will remain a little further off if I can get her out of bed every day, even if it's only to go out to the kitchen and then the living room. She was visibly upset at my arm-twisting, and I said I was sorry and we both ended up crying. I think she realized that I was saying I was sorry for being a bit of a jerk as well as for the situation.

Despite that, it's been one of her better recent days.

2 November 2020

We're having our first snow of the season. It started about 5pm. I think this is going to accumulate.

Rea is not having as good a day as yesterday. She said something about Trump and socks this morning that made no sense and she's been confused most of the day.

The election is tomorrow. God help us all.

3 November 2020

I've felt like I'm on the edge of a panic attack a couple of times already today. It is just after lunch. Even in her current state Rea is passionate about politics. I am as well, but I can't look too closely at the current train wreck in progress. Rea is different. She needs to know what is going on. So she's out in the living room watching while I'm hiding in our bedroom.

The polls all show Biden well ahead but we know how that ended in 2016.

As I think I've said before, it's not that I'm a Biden fan. I'm just not a fan of what the president has done to the heart and soul of this country. Four more years would either kill or cure us, I suppose. I'm thinking kill is more likely.

4 November 2020

Well we're still waiting for a final result midday and it's too close to call. This is a damning indictment of the Democratic Party and their inability to bridge the gap. If Biden manages to pull this out, though, there might be a silver lining which is that there is no way the Democrats can claim any kind of mandate.

The fly in this ointment being Mitch McConnell. With him in place no compromise or progress is likely.

I had to take a Xanax last night. I'm down to a handful of those. It didn't help that much but at least I got five hours or so of sleep.

Rea is having a really good day relatively speaking on both the mental and the mood side.

The weather today is beautiful. Sunny and hovering in the mid-60s. Hard to believe we had snow just a few days back.

Her evening was not good. She was very confused when it was time for bed. I think she thought it was still day, perhaps? I couldn't get her to choose between brushing her teeth first or getting into her jammies. It was frustrating for both of us.

5 November 2020

Today is a not-so-good day for Rea. It's a not so good day for our country as well with the election stuff dragging on, though it looks like Biden is going to win, which I view as a good thing even if I'm not a Democrat.

I had a thought earlier about good days versus bad days. At some point there is going to be a last good day. Maybe yesterday was it. Then I thought about how six months ago yesterday would have been a very bad day. It's all relative, I guess.

I've mentioned many times that I'm tired. Funny thing, I keep reaching new levels of fatigued. What is the opposite of a plateau? I've reached a new one, whatever it might be.

6 November 2020

A Biden win is looking likely. Hopefully things will stay calm if that is confirmed.

The virus is continuing to explode. I feel like I'm getting close to being able to make the claim that I've lived through times similar to those experienced during the Great Depression of the 1930s. I hope we avoid the worldwide war that came after that, or any war for that matter.

8 November 2020

Biden was unofficially declared the winner yesterday. Nice speeches by him and his VP elect Kamala Harris.

So far things aren't getting too crazy though there are still elements in the media and politics trying to muck things up.

We had visitors yesterday. Rea's childhood friend Steve and his wife, Lora. It was a good visit though Rea wasn't having a very good day. She's been doing a little better today.

The weather has been incredible the past few days. We made a trip to Target today to pick up some things we needed and then went on a drive around the countryside.

Most of the leaves have fallen off but it was still a scenic drive and a nice break from being stuck in the house.

10 November 2020

I dropped Marley off at the vet this morning to be fixed. I'm feeling guilty about that since today is her five-month birthday. I hope everything goes well.

We're watching *Finding Dory*. Given Rea's condition this is a bit too much on the nose but I didn't think about that until the movie had started. We hadn't seen it before and it seemed like a good choice to kill a couple of hours.

11 November 2020

Rea's younger brother and his wife came over this afternoon and gave me a few hours off. The weather has cold a bit and it rained earlier but the temperature is still in the 60s so I just went out to the garage, got into our car, and relaxed. I haven't been sleeping well recently and I was able to nap for an hour or so which was great.

It took me a bit of time to work up the courage to come back in. I'm not proud of that, but that is my reality.

12 November 2020

Had a good video chat with several former coworkers of Rea's and mine this afternoon. Rea also got her haircut earlier today.

Marley is more or less back to herself, though she has to keep the cone on for another week.

13 November 2020

Today was a Xanax day. I won't go into why here on the off chance this someday gets shared with anyone else.

Rea actually calculated on her phone the distance to the SF Bay area. This is really impressive, given how she currently is. She's asked a few times when we are going home.

I have to say I'm sorry we ended up here. Lots of good people nearby, including close family of Rea's, but I know next to nobody and our network is a tenth the size it would be in California.

Marley is doing well. I wish I could say the same for me. I'm not doing horribly but I could be better.

The virus continues to escalate, particularly in states where people failed to heed the warnings. The election is also causing a lot of angst even though Georgia and Arizona have now been called for Biden and he's way above where he needs to be to win the electoral college.

We've been watching recorded and semi live music on the computer. We were watching a Tim O'Brien concert recorded a few years ago and he mentioned there would be CDs downstairs. Rea asked if we should go downstairs and buy some CDs :-(

Despite that, this has been one of her better recent days.

15 November 2020

Yesterday I finally had my breakdown. It had been coming for a long while. I'd been feeling kind of left out in the cold in terms of support and I threatened to take Rea back to California or possibly to just leave myself after warning her family with it being uncertain whether I'd be seeking help or just ending things.

Yeah, I was thinking about that. I've been thinking about it for a while. Depression has always been part of my life and while I've gotten much better at handling it over the years, the current circumstances both personal and global would be enough to stress just about anyone, I think.

I had a really good chat with Rea's younger brother and wife, and I feel much better now. Which isn't to say I'm totally out of the woods.

It would not be an exaggeration to say I had a hard time looking after myself before Rea and I met. Here I am the better part of 30 years later and I'm having to take care of her and me while dealing with the stress of a pandemic and a totally broken political system. Add in the fact that I haven't seen my now 88-year-old mother in months.

I think we're on a more sustainable path. Time will tell.

17 November 2020

The care facility my mom is at called last night and said she's in decline. The hits just keep on coming. We nearly lost her about six years back and she's been bedridden for a few years so it's not really a surprise. I've been expecting it for a couple of years. At this point I'm not planning on heading back out there. We'll see, I guess.

I have an appointment with a local in-home care company on Friday. We're hopefully going to get some help in here soon which will be great for me and for Rea as well.

Rea has been in a down phase the past two or three days. It's hard to be sure at this point if this is another decline or just normal variation.

I was just chatting with my sister-in-law on Facebook about Rea. I had an epiphany when I texted the following …

I think this is the hardest time in this whole ordeal. It's like she's just barely visible and about to pass out of sight.

I had to suspend the conversation just after that and I'm having trouble not breaking down again.

My mother is dying, the virus is raging across the country, a third of the country including our president is hellbent on destroying everything so many worked for over the years, and Rea's mental acuity is declining every day. She's down to maybe 20% of what she once was.

This disease ends with a long period of near coma. I'm sure that's going to be hard in its own way, but at that point she will for all intents and purposes be gone. This twilight state is more horrifying than I can possibly describe.

So yeah, I was borderline suicidal a few days back. Now I'm just deeply depressed. Yay for progress.

If I make it to the other side of this insanity, I hope I never forget to be thankful for any time that isn't a living hell.

18 November 2020

Rea just talked about a wedding tomorrow. There is no wedding tomorrow. I didn't ask her what wedding she was talking about. I doubt she could have told me. She also seemed to think that her younger brother was a football player.

She keeps wanting to go to sleep around four o'clock and then can't sleep at night. It's frustrating for both of us.

19 November 2020

Today she wanted to go to bed at 3pm. She didn't want to nap either. She didn't actually manage to get to sleep until around 9pm. I think in large part that she's attributing her confusion and inability to think to being tired.

I'm escaping a bit by concentrating on technical work. Just hobby stuff at this point but it feels good to get something done and to be distracted.

Tomorrow the in-home care company owner will stop by. I'm hoping that works out.

20 November 2020

Phish has a song that contains the lyric *"God never listens to what I say"*. Phish lead singer Trey Anastasio is doing a series of online concerts on Twitch which is normally an esports thing. He's playing that song currently and Rea has been singing along quietly. She never used to do that but as the disease has progressed it's become more common.

It looks like we'll be getting help starting next week. I'm still working out the final details. This will be a big change and likely a challenge for Rea who is incredibly dependent on me at this point.

21 November 2020

Rea just commented that she wondered how her mother is. Her mother passed five years ago. I did not remind her that this was the case.

24 November 2020

I could have sworn that I made at least one entry after November 21 but apparently not.

Today was the first day of having somebody here doing in-home care. It's going to take a bit of adjustment but it was so good getting some time to myself. Rather than leave, I hid in the basement so I'd be nearby but out of sight.

We'll likely move to eight hours, seven days a week soon, but for this week we're doing six hours a day. We can afford either for now. Things get trickier when we have to ramp up to 24/7, but I'll cross that bridge when I get to it. In the meantime I'm going to try to build up a cash buffer. We have a decent amount of money in our retirement accounts but the tax burden on pulling much more out would be brutal.

27 November 2020

Thanksgiving was yesterday. We spent it hanging out alone during the day and had dinner with Rea's younger brother and family. It was a low-key day.

Today I'm having my second real break in three days. The head lady from the in-home care company is here. I'm hiding in the basement working on personal projects.

Next week we'll be doing six hours a day again. We'll see how that goes.

30 November 2020

Last day of the month. Rea is more and more in a fog, though she's been a bit more talkative the past few days. I increased one of her supplements about that time. I'm not sure if that is a coincidence.

Getting regular breaks is making it easier for me, at least for now to deal with the situation.

The virus numbers have been down the past few days, but that is likely due to reporting delays related to Thanksgiving. We'll start to see the true story today and tomorrow and the fallout from all the family gatherings over the next several weeks.

Chapter 10

(Dec 2020)

1 December 2020

It's funny the things Rea has held onto. Hand sanitizer is something she still wants to use before she touches anything. On the other hand, she will put her shoes down on the bed while the covers are off without a second thought.

3 December 2020

My mom passed away earlier today. It wasn't a surprise but it was still a kick in the gut.

Every time my phone rang recently and it was a 541 area code I half-expected to get this news. This call was like the previous couple. Initially it sounded like she was struggling but still present and then boom, I'm told she's gone.

I have some regrets of course. My life is 2/3rds regrets right now and 1/3rd promises to myself and God to do better in the future.

I told Rea my Mom had died and she hugged me and said she was sorry. She will most likely have forgotten in a few hours, but it was nice to share that moment with her.

If 2020 isn't the worst year of my life, then I fear for the future.

4 December 2020

It's 6am and I've been awake for a couple of hours. I had a bit of a breakdown a few minutes ago. It will not be the last.

I've started working on my mom's obituary. It's going to be posted to Facebook today if things go as planned.

Nearly lunch time. Rea now thinks her friend Tutti is alive. Tutti was her mom's best friend and a second mother/aunt to Rea growing up. She passed away 10 or more years ago.

I suppose a deeply spiritual person might say that as Rea gets closer to death, she can hear those on the other side and that her mother and Tutti are talking to her now. I'm not that person but in a way it's a comforting thought.

I think I've mentioned keeping a bit of distance from the reality of Rea's situation as a method of coping. That's still the case and my mom's passing yesterday isn't likely to change it anytime soon.

I think we've all seen situations depicted in fiction where somebody in a very stressful situation loses track of reality and starts believing things that aren't true. It never used to make sense to me. It does now. I'm not the kind of person who can completely disengage from reality though. Or so I hope.

So I'm hiding in the bedroom with the door closed to get some grieving time and to try to distract myself with a programming project I'm working on and I hear Rea come down the hall. It turns out she's looking for her mom. Luckily the nice care lady distracted her, but this is a good illustration of why I need to go down to the basement when I'm trying to decompress. I still hear the wheels of her walker across the floor when I'm down there, but I don't have any idea what she is saying or doing.

5 December 2020

At 4am I woke up to Rea saying "Mom" loudly.

At 5am I was sleeping lightly when she made a sound nearly like a scream. She seemed okay when she said my name just after that.

7 December 2020

Just over a week until my birthday. My 53rd year was not a winner. Number 54 is likely going to have a lot of suck as well. Okay, enough on that.

Rea is having a better-than-average day. Her speech is a bit clearer and she's been more capable of figuring out what she needs to do. It's still nothing compared to what she was like even six weeks ago, but as I often say, I'll take what I can get.

I mentioned that she sings along to songs. The interesting thing is that she often gets the words right. She will mumble when she doesn't know a song.

The thing that makes this odd is that I often have to instruct her on how to take her pills. She'll forget she needs to take a drink with each one to assist in swallowing. Yet she remembers song lyrics.

I got about four and a half hours of sleep last night. I remember early on I was so exhausted at the end of each day that I fell asleep instantly. These days, between Rea sometimes waking me up and my own ongoing anxieties, I'm getting a lot less sleep than I need.

11 December 2020

It's a beautiful day outside. If I'd had a bit of foresight, I'd have scheduled Rea and my Tuesday lunch for today. There was lots of snow that day so my bad. Rumor is that restaurants will be closing again on Monday. COVID is going crazy and we still have people with no clue. It's not a particularly good sign for the human species.

12 December 2020

I took the time to just cuddle a bit with Rea first thing today. I've been bad about that. I'm trying to balance maintaining my own wellbeing with being there for her and if I'm going to be honest, I've been neglecting her a bit. The irony being that if I don't get my shit together it's going to impact my wellbeing in the longer term because I'm occasionally self-aware enough to call myself on my own bullshit.

I've read a lot about how resilient human beings are. I'm confident now that a lot of that resilience is built on denial and self-deception. We're much more fragile than we care to admit. Or I am at least.

———————————

Rea just asked if my mom had called. I told her no. It's oh so tempting to try to correct her but there is no reason to.

14 December 2020

Tomorrow is my 54th birthday.

Year 54 mostly sucked with a few bright spots at the very start. New Year's in New York seeing Phish was good. Then things went rapidly downhill.

Year 55 will likely feature Rea's final decline and passing.

I'm already looking forward to year 56.

15 December 2020

I think Rea is having another rapid Decline. Both her balance and her mental state seem to be getting worse after several weeks of relative stability. This has been the pattern all along unfortunately. I think we'll be looking at an increase in-care hours come the new year. Thankfully we can afford it.

Rea has always been a workaholic. Even now it bugs her to do nothing, though at this point she isn't capable of anything beyond listening to music. I can't even ask her simple yes or no questions and have much hope of a coherent response.

About a year ago I was at a songwriting workshop in Nashville. It was a dream come true.

Rea had been having very early symptoms for a year or more at that point but was still completely normal, at least superficially. Two months later her Decline would become obvious.

17 December 2020

The feared rapid Decline may have been overstated. She's had two better days. She's still a bit worse than she was a month ago, but nowhere near as bad as she was a couple of days ago.

Guilty admission: if I could feasibly put Rea into a high-quality around-the-clock care facility then I'd seriously consider it, especially as she gets nearer to the end. This place has been our home for all of four months and she lived nearly two thirds of her life very far away from where we currently are.

Does that make me a terrible person? In some sense, yes. I'm currently dealing with my mom's passing, Rea's rapid Decline, with COVID, and the ongoing political insanity. Plus, there are my own shortcomings.

Another guilty admission: I've failed to open most of the cards and letters people have sent. I know having to read them would make the reality of our situation even more real than it already is, and as I've said before, I'm partially hanging on by not entirely acknowledging the reality of what is happening with Rea.

I continue to be paid through the generosity of others. There is a program where I work that allows people to donate unused vacation time to those in situations similar to mine. I never imagined I'd need to take advantage of this, but I am so grateful that it was available and that so many people were willing to help. I think it's in large part a reflection of how people feel about Rea.

20 December 2022

Five days until Christmas and I'm shading back to thinking she's had another big downturn. Her balance has been much worse recently.

Mentally she's about on par with where she has been the past month or so.

She's been waking me up a lot for a snack or to go to the bathroom. The weird thing is she sounds more like her pre CJD self in the middle of the night. I don't know if this is just coincidence or because she's as well rested at that point as she ever is.

Five days until Christmas; today is Sunday.

The hospice nurse should be stopping by in the next day or two. It's time to discuss next steps, I think. I'm not sure how much longer Rea is going to be able to get around even with assistance.

It's been a while since I put a picture in here. This one is recent. She does enjoy hanging out with Marley – when Marley isn't being a total spaz. She's also enjoying watching game shows and music still. She can talk to a limited degree, but real communication is really hard.

Recently she's also lost the ability to tie her shoelaces, something she's done herself up until the past week or so. Brushing her teeth is becoming more of a challenge as well. It's an electric toothbrush and she forgets to turn it on. She frequently brushes for 30 seconds or less which is not like her at all.

Merry Christmas?

22 December 2020

Rea's younger brother, myself, and our hospice nurse met today to discuss possible changes in Rea's medication as well as coming up with a tentative plan for how to deal with her Decline. It was a sobering chat, but I got through it, albeit with a couple of semi close calls on the emotional front.

My "me" time has been limited the past two days which has pushed me closer to the edge. Yesterday it took a while to get a prescription filled and today was largely taken up by the meeting.

24 December 2020

Rea said thank you to me first thing this morning soon after waking up. At least I think that is what she said. She is hard to understand. I'd had my nose in my laptop and she had been half awake. We cuddled a bit after that.

Of course I'm left wondering if I misheard, but it isn't like I can ask now or could request that she clarify at the time.

That self-doubt is intrinsic to who I am, I guess.

I've been having mini crying episodes throughout this whole thing. I think I need an extended cry. Maybe this afternoon when I have my alone time.

Well, the thank you was nice and timely. Twice today I've had to pry wet poopy toilet paper out of Marley's mouth. Once was my fault as I forgot to flush the toilet after Rea was done and left the bathroom door open. The second time was arguably my fault as well. I had a bathroom crisis of my own while Rea was in the middle of going and went to our half bath which is all of 10 feet away. I tried to get Rea to sit still but she got up and headed out of the bathroom by herself, though luckily with the walker. Marley snuck in again and did a toilet paper grab.

So yeah, not a red-letter day in some ways.

We'll have no care tomorrow, so I'll have a full 48 hours with Rea. Given her level of need that will be a challenge, but I won't ask the caregivers to work on Christmas.

This time last year we were getting ready to head out to New York City to see Phishes four-show new year's run. At the time COVID was just a vague rumor, Rea's symptoms were easily missed, and we had no idea that those would be the last Phish shows we attended together.

The final show of that run featured Trey being trapped 30 or 40 feet in the air on the platform that was part of their traditional New Year's Eve musical extravaganza. Trey being trapped above the stage turned out to be a harbinger of things to come. Thankfully He was unharmed in the end. There will be no happy ending for Rea unfortunately.

We had dinner with Rea's younger brother and family. It was good. They hung around watching TV with us afterwards. Eventually they had to leave and Rea grabbed onto her brother's hand. He was sitting on one side of her and I was sitting on the other. They ended up staying another ten minutes or so.

Eventually Rea let go. I suspect he'll remember that moment for a long time. I know I will.

Tomorrow is Christmas. No in-home care. We'll make the best of it. I got a bunch of groceries in today, so we are well stocked if the weather turns out to be as bad as it is supposed to be over the next few days.

26 December 2020

Yesterday was a mix. It started well and then Marley pretty much destroyed my $500 night guard which protects my teeth from my nightly grinding. Everything after that was back and forth, in part because I was in a foul mood for a while. The fault was mine for not having put it away when I woke up and then leaving the bedroom door open. She'd been caught with it once before, so it wasn't like I was unaware of the risk.

We didn't get a white Christmas, but we are getting a white Boxing Day. At least I think this is Boxing Day. It's a British thing, so in theory I should know.

———————————

Rea's tried to call her mom and called for her as well today. This isn't new, but it's painful to hear. I told her that her mother wasn't here. When she asked where she was, I said, "I don't know". Which is truthful in a meta-physical sense. I do know where her ashes were spread, and it wasn't that far from here.

Sometimes the right answer is the less obvious one.

28 December 2020

Tutu, childhood nickname for Tutti? Rea was thrashing around a bit and woke me up around 2am. I heard her cry out something that sounded like "Tutu" which immediately made me think of Tutti, her mother's best friend and Rea's second mom/aunt, if not by blood.

I don't know if this is a sign of her regressing or not. She almost immediately went back to sleep, and I don't think she could have answered even if I had asked.

29 December 2020

I'm not in a great place. Nothing new there.

I finally figured out how much I've short-changed Rea along the way because of my inability to fully deal with her situation. This is not a good thing. It's too late now to do anything about most of it.

One of the crazy hard things for me is that I'm always trying to minimize the impact of Rea's situation on others. Actually, that's partially a lie. What I've realized is that in part I'm minimizing the impact on me by not having to talk about what is going on with her. I hint to others, much like I hint to myself. So in the end, I'm really just being selfish.

When I think back to the original plan Rea and I had, to stay in California and ride things out there, I can't help but feel that would have been the right approach. But with the best of intentions and blind optimism, I allowed the plan to change radically halfway through and I've never quite managed to recover. That is 100% on me, as is my continued inability to completely resolve the issues.

A lot of people are hurting over this and people in pain don't always make the best decisions. I know I'm guilty of that.

It doesn't help that I don't communicate well. I mean, I try; I really do. It just doesn't come naturally to me. I try to be honest and straightforward, but it seldom seems to work out the way I would prefer.

I'll just do my best to keep slogging on and do better going forward.

31 December 2020

New Year's Eve.

2021 can't come fast enough, though I know it is going to have a lot of suck, barring a very major miracle.

My anxiety is spiking for reasons I won't go into here. On the plus side, I finally managed to let everyone know on Facebook what is going on with Rea in terms of her condition. That is a big relief, though I should have done it a lot sooner. With Rea no longer capable of perusing FB, I no longer had an excuse.

I'm down to one Xanax.

I doubt either of us will be awake when New Year's comes. Rea zonks out around 7pm recently and I think I've been awake since around 3am. It was another one of those nights where she woke me up multiple times just when I was getting to sleep.

She often thinks she needs to go to the bathroom when she doesn't. It's frustrating, but it's not her fault and I try to keep that in mind.

Rea once again mentioned she was scared earlier this evening. I asked her of what but she didn't elaborate. I suspect it was a rare moment of lucidity.

She also asked me if I was coming with her to the next game at one point. I don't know what to think of that. She's been talking a lot about games recently when she talks at all. I think she means football, but there is no way to be sure.

I'm pretty sure I said yes.

Chapter 11
(January 2021)

1 January 2021

Rea and I greeted 2020 at Madison Square Gardens in New York City. This year we slept through the year's demise. It deserved no better.

———————

I don't know if I'll keep this journal up after Rea is gone, but in a way I hope so. I also hope I'll be able to write about things that aren't so depressing.

Rea slept well last night which was a relief after the night before. Both she and I were exhausted yesterday which is never good, though I survived it somehow.

C-19 vaccinations are rolling out, but they aren't a quick fix and as has typically been the case recently we have a bunch of people who are freaking out over the whole thing. It's not nice, but I'm really tired of a decent percentage of my fellow human beings.

Rea will not be here this time next year barring an epic miracle. I'm resigned to that and we're getting closer and closer to the point where it would be a mercy to her and those who love her.

Near the start of this whole ordeal, she and I discussed assisted suicide and she decided against it. The thinking at the time was that by the time she was incapacitated enough to want to go that route she wouldn't be able to make that decision. It's certainly not one I would make, even if I could. I don't have any religious objections against it. I know it's supposed to be a sin, but frankly nearly everything is, and if you're forgiven, then why does it matter? I'm sure a theologian could rip me apart on that one if so inclined. Thankfully I won't be judged by a theologian.

3 January 2021

It's hard to believe it's been a month since my mom's passing. I'm going to try to put together a video to go along with a rough demo I have of "Part of a Chain" which is a song I wrote four or five years ago about my, at that time, incomplete family tree. It features both her and my biological father Dennis, along with my dad.

Rea often mumbles or says things that she doesn't complete or that don't make sense. Sometimes she'll express her desires by implying that somebody else, often a person not present or no longer alive, wants something. For instance, to go to the bathroom. I think she's also having trouble recognizing people, including me. Yesterday she said something along the lines of "Mike is a very good writer" to me. Which was both incredibly flattering and really really sad, since I was sitting right beside her and she said it to me.

On the off chance that somebody else reads this, particularly somebody "guilty" of the following, please don't feel bad.

People expressing their sympathy for the situation Rea and I find ourselves in is understandable and good. There is a variation, though, that I don't really enjoy. It's when they say things like "You must be feeling awful". Why yes, yes, I am feeling awful. Thank you for reminding me.

While I'm venting, no disrespect to people who believe in karma, but I don't buy it. Too many people do bad things and get away with it while others are for the most part good and suffer. Rea is my exhibit one of that second case.

4 January 2021

Rea's friend Debbie called today and they got to chat for a bit. Rea was having a good day but still struggled when asked anything but very simple questions from what I could tell. Still, it was good for her to have a chance to talk.

I'm far from the only one struggling with Rea's recent decline. She is truly loved by her family and many friends.

I suspect we're less than a week away from going close to full-time care for Rea. Financially I can swing this but it's going to take some work.

Money may not be able to buy happiness, but it can buy peace of mind, and that is more than enough sometimes.

It turns out that Tutu was the poodle they had when Rea was growing up. One mystery solved. Her younger brother had no idea who Karen might have been but that is another name Rea has called out.

5 January 2021

I have gathered enough money together for two months of full-time care for Rea. She seems to be fading very fast now. Current scheduled start is Monday the 11th but I'm not sure I can make it that far. Tonight will tell the tale.

8 January 2021

We got a hospital-style bed installed in the living room yesterday. Rea slept there and I slept on the couch. This is how we'll likely do things until we start 24-hour care on Monday.

9 January 2021

I'm trying as much as possible to enjoy these last couple of days before we go to around-the-clock care. I know it will be different then. Given how sore my back is getting, though, I also know this is needed.

I think one of the best things about the caregivers is that having them here full time means that Rea will almost never be alone. One of the things I've learned about her over the past couple of years is that even though she's always been a very independent woman, she hates to be alone. When I look back over all the time I've known her, this becomes more and more clear.

The past two years or so that was magnified, likely because of her illness. I think she knew well before she told me that something was seriously wrong.

10 January 2021

Marley is seven months old and this will be the final day I am 100% responsible for Rea for some part of the day. I'm happy to be getting full-time help starting tomorrow, but it's also bittersweet for a lot of reasons. Not the least of which is what it means in terms of her decline.

My back is unhappy, though, so from a physical perspective I just wasn't going to be able to keep this up much longer. Hopefully I can make it through tonight.

I'm an hour or so away from my final night with it being just Rea and me here. It's weird, at times I feel completely calm and in the moment, and then I'll think about her and how close we are to the end and I have to fight the urge to cry.

Rea seems to have taken a significant downturn since this morning.

While the caregivers are present, I've been spending noon to five or six down in the basement working on various things and trying to recharge. She was in the bed when I came up. She'd been agitated most of the day. I gave

192

her some leftover mac and cheese and put a paper towel down between the tray and her mouth to catch any spillage. When I came back she was trying to eat the napkin and ignoring the mac and cheese :-(

I hand fed her from there.

11 January 2021

Rea wet the bed this morning. She'd been having trouble going for the past 24 hours or so and I was a little slow getting going this morning, mostly due to lack of sleep.

Full time care started this morning at 9am.

About now I'm wishing I had more than one Xanax left. Slept poorly last night, can't seem to sleep today during the day.

I really wanted to get some sleep and then spend time with Rea. So far, no good :(

Despite the extra sleep, she seems to still be very out of it today.

I've given up on sleeping for now. Hopefully tonight will go well.

Have I mentioned last week's coup attempt? Hopefully it wasn't just a warm-up, but given how lightly some people are taking it I can't help but be even more worried.

Because I need more things to be stressed over apparently. It's not all about me, of course – not even a little bit. But sometimes it's hard to keep that thought front and center.

12 January 2021

Well, I screwed up yesterday. Which may explain the mystery of Rea being so out of it. She's had a prescription for an anti-anxiety medication for a while now and on the 10th we got permission to double the dose as needed. This means going from one pill every four hours to two. I gave her one first thing yesterday and she started to get agitated about an hour and a half later, so I gave her a second dose.

Big mistake. I'll blame sleep deprivation in part for that choice, but the prescription is for one or two pills every four hours, not one pill every couple of hours and apparently my ignorant and tired assumption that it wouldn't matter was very much wrong :(

This made me feel like shit when one of the caregivers rightfully questioned the decision and sought additional advice. This in turn made it difficult to get to sleep last night, but in the end I managed just under seven hours, with an hour and a half awake in the middle of the night.

Hopefully this will make me marginally less stupid.

I just realized we're just over a month away from our 21ˢᵗ wedding anniversary. I think there is a good chance she'll make it to then, but I doubt there will be enough of her left to realize what that means. I don't think there is now actually.

On the plus side she's having a much better day. It's amazing what can happen when some idiot doesn't screw up her medication.

13 January 2021

Communication is hard for me. Or maybe it's too easy?

I want to live in a world where I can be honest with people and not have them get upset. I'm not generally cruel and I seldom if ever have bad intentions, so I don't feel like that is totally unreasonable.

14 January 2021

Rea mentioned she'd missed me yesterday evening when I came up from the basement. I was amazed and moved that she is still capable of that. If I think too much about it though I'm going to have another mini breakdown. I already did that last night at bedtime.

We were watching various musical artists on YouTube this morning. Del McCoury, Tim O'Brien and John Prine. One of our favorite songs of Prine's is "Angel from Montgomery" which he played as part of the encore on the performance we were watching. This was his 2005 Austin city limits appearance if I'm remembering correctly. Rea was singing along and getting a fair number of the words correct. It is such a beautiful song. I decided right then that I'm going to include it in the soundtrack for her memorial.

15 January 2021

I was looking at Rea earlier today and it struck me that she looked old. I understand she's 62 years old, but she's never looked old to me before. Not even after she stopped coloring her hair.

The caregivers had to take Rea's wedding ring away from her earlier. She was trying to eat it. I ordered a chain that I can attach it to so I can wear it around my neck. I'd been planning to do that for a while now, but I didn't figure it would happen until after she was gone. It was yet another kick in the teeth.

16 January 2021

I haven't left the house in a couple of weeks. I'll have to on Monday to pick up a prescription for Rea. I need to make Marley a grooming appointment as well. Some of this is the weather, but some of it is my tendency to be a recluse.

I've been trying to figure out how to make this house more sellable without ruining it. Sometimes, though, I feel like it would just be easier to stay here. Then I remember that one of the reasons I don't go out much is I hardly know anyone and I don't feel comfortable here. A bit of it is the weather, but I don't think that is anything close to the main reason.

The virus continues to spread and now we have a more contagious version. The SOB was already far too easily spread. This is the residue of too many people not being smart enough to follow basic instructions. The virus will continue to mutate. It's what they do. The more cases there are, the greater the odds of a mutation that will be detrimental. We're lucky in that this one apparently didn't make it any more deadly.

The inauguration will be here soon. Given the security concerns, our soon-to-be ex-president will be able to brag that there were more people at his swearing-in than at Biden's. I suppose he can count that as a small victory, though it seems clear it is not the one he had hoped for.

Rea slept badly last night and is very lethargic this morning. She's having a lot of trouble speaking. A bad day, or another downward step?

Steve and Lora will be here around lunch time. Hopefully Rea will rally by then. It's 9:35am right now, so she has a bit of time.

––––––––––––

Well, the Steve and Laura visit was good but in a very sad way. Rea was out of it yesterday and even more out of it today. She seems to be having trouble holding her head up. Given the way things have been going for the past week I think the end might be less than a month away. That is a mercy at this point.

I've decided I won't be staying in Watertown once Rea is gone. There are lots of good people here, but I've never felt comfortable and I don't think that is going to change.

17 January 2021

It's 2:41am and I have been awake for a bit.

I don't understand people. I just don't. I don't think I want to either.

I get that I'm a "people" too and I'm probably not any different, but that doesn't make it easier for me to reconcile my confusion.

As I get older I'm increasingly confident that we will end up being a failure or at best a mixed success as a species. I suppose it's good that there is no judge visible to make that determination. Though perhaps that is the biggest tragedy of all.

I do believe that we are all judged eventually. Maybe that's where justice, humility, and honesty all come into play. I certainly hope so, though I'm not going to pretend that I have no fear of that day.

––––––––––––

Last night I told Rea I loved her and she managed to say "I love you too". It was a real struggle for her, but she said it. She kisses my hand as well at times.

––––––––––––

She had a good morning relatively speaking but then faded badly the rest of the day. The first thing she said to me this morning was "I feel better". This was the most complex sentence I've heard her initiate in weeks. It's hard not to think that it might be the last one given the past few days and this afternoon.

The recliner I ordered and paid for yesterday came today. Her younger brother and his sons picked it up, delivered it, and put it together.

I went out to pick up some stuff today and the battery in the CR-V was dead. It's only a little over two years old so that was a surprise. It hasn't been that cold the past few weeks.

I struggled to find the battery jumper thingy I bought a few months back. I looked all over before it occurred to me that it would probably be in the car. Sure enough, it was. It took a good 10 minutes of the charger being hooked up to the battery before I could get it to turn over.

I've alternated between extremely depressed and resigned throughout the day. I only got a bit over four hours of sleep last night which made everything feel a bit more distant. A bit of distance can be a good thing at times.

18 January 2021

I slept a bit better last night but I'd swear I lost an hour or two in the early morning. I woke up around five after getting to sleep a bit after midnight. I went to the bathroom, had some melatonin gummies, and got back into bed. I didn't think I slept, but the next thing I knew it was a quarter after seven.

I worry a bit that I'm losing it.

Now I'm lying on my mattress down in the basement trying to work up the energy to head upstairs. Marley really needs to go out, so I should get up. I'm really tired, though.

Rea and the caregivers were still mostly asleep when I took Marley up just now. I suspect it was a tough night since it was almost 8:30 at the time.

I truly could not have imagined both how horrible this experience was going to be and how I would somehow (albeit barely) be standing at this point.

I am torn between wanting to hold onto her with a death grip and wanting her to be at peace.

I think I see the hand of God in this. Not in a bad way. It is hard for me to see what purpose this intense grief and confusion could possibly serve in a purely mechanistic universe. Why would evolution have led us to this destination?

Which isn't to say that I don't believe in evolution. I do; I just think I am getting glimpses of the divine occasionally.

Rea passed at 2:55pm. I will never be the same.

I kind of had a feeling this morning that this would happen. It was so hard to get out of bed. She seemed more or less okay in the morning but things went rapidly downhill in the early afternoon.

I'd been out running errands when I got a text that she was having trouble breathing. I'd been thinking about making one more stop but headed back immediately. She was gone within minutes of my getting there.

Rea was one in a million. I was not ready for her to go. I was never going to be ready for her to go. Thankfully it turns out I have one more Xanax. I'd been saving it for some reason, and I guess I know why now.

To be clear, I'm one part devastated and one part relieved that she isn't going to suffer through days or weeks of being in a coma. I think she chose her time and she chose well given the circumstances. I'm glad her suffering is over. My grieving started months ago and will to a degree never end, but now I think I can start to heal a bit.

19 January 2021

This is the first day of Rea being gone. I was awake about half the night, and I have to meet with Rea's family in a couple of hours at the funeral home. It's supposed to snow a lot today. Yes, that matches my mood.

I'm alone in this house for the first time ever. With the caregivers there have been three and sometimes four other people including Rea at shift changes.

My sadness and regrets haunt me today. Yet in between crying I feel detached. Dissociation is the word I'm looking for.

In a post on Facebook a few days before Rea's passing I mentioned that I was suffering from survivor's guilt.

After Rea passed she was cleaned and laid out on the hospital bed that was installed in the living room a couple of weeks back. Various people took time to sit on the love seat beside her and pay their respects, including me. It seemed as if she were still breathing, though the paleness of her face distracted from that illusion.

I don't know if this is odd, but I don't feel wrong sitting in the recliner I bought for Rea the day before she passed. This is also the recliner she was sitting in when she died. I kind of feel closer to her when I do. Right now I'm in the living room, which is where she passed. With the lights on I feel fine, but I'm not sure I'd want to sit here in the dark.

I've been missing her terribly today. Mostly I've managed to keep it together, but there have been several crying fits. Sometimes they sneak up on me and sometimes I see them coming. Looking at a picture of her, especially when she is smiling, pretty much always does it. I miss her smile so so much.

I know I'm not unique – many people have lost spouses and loved ones. Along with the grief though there is the huge void that I now need to figure out how to fill. Rea has always been a big part of my life, but for the past year or so she's been my everything. Now she's gone, and other than a few details related to her passing I don't have anything to do.

The first thing I put on yesterday morning when I went out to sit with Rea was *December*, the duet album by Trey and Page of Phish.

I just started to cry and Marley came running. She is such a good dog.

She's probably pooping out in the sunroom now that I've said that.

20 January 2021

I've been averaging just over five hours of sleep a night the past few days. I don't know how long this can go on. I'm managing to distract myself at times during the day, but then reality comes back and punches me in the mouth and I'm sobbing again.

I don't think I'm suicidal. I am depressed, though.

It's hard not to feel guilty about all the mistakes I made along the way, both before and after Rea's diagnosis. I never cheated on her, but my anxiety sometimes made me a pain to deal with, I'm sure.

She wasn't perfect either, though she was in most ways perfect for me and much better than I could have hoped for.

COVID and the weather are adding a bit of stress. Thankfully I have a ton of food at hand so there is no need for me to go out for now. Marley is set as well.

I have a grooming appointment for her next week and will schedule a haircut for myself at the same time when it's a bit closer.

The new COVID variant is spreading rapidly here in the US. I'm being cautious but not paranoid. On the one hand, social isolation is the best way to avoid it, while on the other, I need to be around people occasionally even if I am a bit of a loner.

I'm hungry but nothing appeals to me. I'm lethargic but I have trouble sleeping and feel the need to be constantly doing something. My concentration, which is never great, is even worse.

I don't know if I'll keep journaling. I think it's a good thing, though, so I'm going to try.

I wrote a line a bit ago that I really like. I can only hope it's original. Which is selfish because I think it says something important.

I don't believe in perfect love
But I believe in love true

That feels like the bridge of a song to me, and I have a couple of verses and a chorus that I think it goes to.

Earlier I ate half a golden crisp apple that was in the fridge. The caregivers had fed the other half to Rea a few days before her passing. I didn't think about it initially but when I was halfway through, I realized that in a sense she and I were sharing that apple.

And then I cried because I realized it was the last time we'd ever share in that way. Maybe that doesn't make sense but it's how I feel.

Maybe this is part of the grieving process, but I've been talking to Rea out loud on and off today. I have a lot to apologize for and a lot I need to say. Some of it I should have said a long time ago. Neither of us was ever very good at communicating the mushy stuff. Some of the very positive things I've been told she said about me have me floored.

I could be a bit sarcastic and arrogant at times, and she was sometimes on the receiving end of that.

My inability to deal with her illness meant that some of her final wishes were not fulfilled before it was too late. I want so badly to have the power to change history. Obviously I'd make it so she never got sick, but if I couldn't do that I'd still be grateful to get a do-over on how I handled her illness.

It wasn't all bad. I did a lot of good things, but I wanted it to be perfect for her and I spent too much time doing things I thought were important rather than talking to her as much as I should have about it.

COVID made the whole thing worse. We would have flown back to the west coast to visit people there at least a couple of times if not for COVID. But that just magnifies my failures.

I don't want to lose my ability to say I'm sorry, but I do want to be better at not doing things to be sorry for.

Which brings me back to anxiety. I hate it. I spent so much of my life not understanding what was wrong with me.

Back near the start of this I think I wrote about how I finally understood why somebody would want to get drunk or otherwise self-medicate.

I think I've reached the next level of understanding. Thankfully the hospice nurse took the remainder of Rea's prescriptions, including the morphine.

I should probably avoid alcohol for now. Thankfully there is none in the house.

21 January 2021

Another day. I'm feeling a tiny bit better today. I just looked at some pictures of Rea and didn't cry, so that is something. I did cry a bit when I first went upstairs and looked over toward the corner of the living room where Rea took her last breaths. The look on her face when she passed will haunt me forever. Thankfully memories of her smile and laugh mostly distract me when that happens.

Given Rea's political leanings it was in some ways appropriate that she passed on MLK Jr Day.

My portion of the flowers is dealt with. I also decided to get an urn. I'm working on the music and pictures for the calling hours next Tuesday.

My mood trajectory has been mostly down today. I think having to look at so many pictures of Rea has something to do with it.

I also just realized that I don't want to listen to Phish. I was really starting to get into their music on a new level over the past few months, so I suspect this is an association thing. I will probably bawl my eyes out for a while whenever I hear them.

22 January 2021

I'm not making any decisions, but I am thinking about the future. When I'm not crying about the past and all the mistakes I made during Rea's decline. I try to balance that with the good things I did but it's hard.

It could have been better for her if I hadn't been partially in denial. I suppose in a way that shows how much I loved her since I couldn't completely embrace the thought of losing her. I don't know, maybe she realized that? She managed to tell me she loved me just a few days before she died. It was one of the last complete sentences she uttered.

I talked to Dave, the fellow who runs the funeral home today. He stopped by to show me a couple of different urns. Both were purple since that was Rea's favorite color. I chose the one with the more complex pattern. I don't know why, but it appealed to me.

I miss her so much. There are so many things I'd like to say to her if I could. Actually, I've been saying them to her anyway even though she's not here anymore. Or maybe she is. I know it's not logical, but as rational as I try to be, I don't believe we completely understand how things work.

23 January 2021

I need to get through the last of the pictures I've chosen for Rea's service. I think I'm about 80% of the way there and it isn't even lunch time.

I'm slowly getting better about not breaking down when I see a picture of her. Partially this is a result of the scars starting to form, I think, but it's also a bit of subtle denial on my part. Being in the moment and not thinking about the past, or the future. The first makes me sad and the second causes me a mixture of terror and a tiny bit of anticipation. I need to find a path forward and I have only a very slight idea of what it might be.

The truth is I was an emotional wreck before I met Rea and I barely functioned. I think I've grown a lot since then but I don't know if I've grown enough. If I take care of myself and get a bit lucky I could have another three or four decades left based on what I know about my ancestors longevity.

I'm terrified of love or commitment right now. I suspect a lot of people in my situation go through this.

Distracting myself is just something I have to do. I can deal with the pain in small doses. It's like a game of hide-and-seek.

I managed to sleep over six hours last night for the first time since Rea passed. I still wake up in the middle of the night. I then spend an hour or three trying to get back to sleep.

24 January 2021

I am really tired today, but I was productive. I bought a bunch of stuff for the service on Tuesday and if I'm productive again tomorrow I'll be in a good place preparation-wise.

When I was chatting with my sister-in-law yesterday on FB she sent me the following.

"When I visited her by myself on Sunday she said to me, 'There's a spirit.' I said, 'It's okay.' She just nodded. On Monday when we were with her while you were running errands, she didn't really say anything. … we sat with Rea. I just knew … I kissed her on the head and said, 'If you need to go *home* it's okay. We all love you. Don't be scared, if you need to go then it's okay.' She nodded yes. Buzzy went and opened the window by the dining room table so the angels could take her home. Her poor body had enough of that Godawful disease."

I responded …

"I don't think she said anything all morning either. She just kind of dozed. I sat on the floor beside the recliner holding her and crying."

One week tomorrow. I miss both the idea and the reality of her. Those two things are not the same but close enough that it probably doesn't matter.

26 January 2021

I spent most of yesterday getting ready for Rea's calling hours today. I have 80 or so pictures of her and others that I've mostly organized into groupings for a handful of poster boards. The weather report was a bit iffy for this afternoon/evening when I looked at it last night. Time to check again …

It's still looking iffy but a bit better, I think. There is nothing to do about it but hope for the best.

I slept okay last night but I'm very tired. Marley is at the groomers and should be ready in about an hour. I've made a lot of progress on the picture displays and I have the Trey song Rea wanted ready.

————————

Mostly I'm trying to listen to go with the flow and let Rea whisper to me what the right thing to do is. I don't literally hear her voice as much as I'd like to, but I feel like I'm being nudged in certain directions. Serendipity may also be playing a part.

————————

Attendance was good at Rea's calling hours. Everyone wore a mask and kept things reasonable. Hopefully no one was sick and if they were, fingers crossed the virus was not spread.

It snowed before I headed over, while the service was going on at times, and then all the way home. I'm not an expert at driving in the snow but I managed to get back without incident. The roads were not great either so apparently I'm not a complete novice.

Tomorrow I need to head back over to Adams to pick up Rea's ashes and a few other things I left behind. Dinner after with her family at the country club in Adams was good.

27 January 2021

I picked up Rea's ashes around lunch time. The roads were fine. I belted the urn into the passenger seat after letting it sit in the driver's seat while I retrieved the poster boards and pictures I'd also left behind last night.

I looked at my Fitbit app a bit ago and realized I slept under four hours last night. Ugh.

Between Rea's service and going out to dinner with her family afterwards I was out late but I hadn't realized I'd done that badly in the sleep department. It does explain why I'm exhausted at just short of 6pm though.

I'm going to try to stay on my schedule of heading downstairs and getting ready for bed at 8pm. I likely won't wait to get into bed until nine, though.

28 January 2021

I slept as well as I have since Rea's passing last night. My Fitbit recorded six hours and 51 minutes of sleep. That is pretty much my normal, or at least it used to be. Maybe a bit better than that really.

I drank two thirds of a 52-ounce bottle of unsweetened tea as part of breakfast. I was a bit surprised when I realized how much of the bottle I'd gone through. It's not bad manners to drink straight out of the bottle when you are the only one around, right?

I also had the last piece of pumpkin pie from a pie I'd bought Rea before she passed. She ate the first half and I finished off the second half over the past couple of days. It was a small pie and the pumpkin filling was starting to shrink. Much like the half an apple I ate a week or so back, this felt like I was sharing a meal with Rea.

The grief comes and goes, and sometimes hits me with little warning. I'm a long way from being okay.

Right now I'm sitting in the recliner that was delivered the day before she passed. It is where she was sitting when she died.

I know I'm working my way through this, but sometimes it seems like one step forward and two back.

I need to get out of the house some tomorrow. Maybe take Marley for a ride. I should take my camera as well and see if I can get some good pictures. It's not supposed to snow, and the roads should be clear. It will be cold, though.

Time is dragging something crazy. It's been 6:40-something pm for what feels like an hour. I really don't want to head downstairs until eight but I'm starting to think that's going to be tough to accomplish. Seven might be pushing it.

Generally I've been going downstairs around eight and going to sleep between nine and 10pm.

29 January 2021

Grief comes in waves. I'd heard that before but now I feel it. She is gone, and in this life I will never see her again. And that hurts so bad. Yesterday was bad and today isn't starting out great either.

It was two below zero when I took Marley out at about 7:45am. I said I was going out today, hopefully with Marley as well. We'll see.

For now I'm going to read something light and funny and try to get my shit together.

30 January 2021

Another night with six-plus hours of sleep. Though according to the Fitbit app last night was only of fair quality after two nights of good-to-excellent sleep. Oh well.

Mood wise I'm doing a bit better today I think. It's still hovering near zero degrees here in Watertown, though, which kind of discourages me from spending much time outside. Any excuse I guess?

Monday I start work again.

I have a bunch of tasks that Rea wanted done after her passing related to contacting people. In theory she was going to write them notes, but I think I've already talked about how I fucked that up.

I ordered an inexpensive queen bed frame today. I've been sleeping with the mattress on the floor downstairs. I don't see myself moving back upstairs any time soon and the bed frame in the master is built in so getting a replacement for it was my best option.

It's 4:06pm. I'm looking forward to it being four or so hours later so I can go to bed. I'm kinda just killing time currently.

31 January 2021

I'm still waiting for it to get easier. If anything, it's been getting worse the past few days. I hope/pray that getting back to work tomorrow will help.

I always knew I was kind of fragile but I didn't really think I was this fragile. Or maybe this really is just a totally horrible situation and I'm doing as well as can be expected.

Earlier I was reminded of the phrase "Death is a permanent solution to a temporary problem". While the problem that is ripping me apart is anything but temporary, I know intellectually that it will get better. Marley is trying to help which is good. I just need to make it through the next couple of months.

Politics and COVID continue to add to the poop sandwich that is life in the good old US of A at the start of the third decade of the 21st century.

I guess the less said about that the better.

Chapter 12

(February 2021)

1 February 2021

Two weeks today since Rea's passing. Though given her decline, especially towards the end, it was much longer than that. It's also a bit under two weeks until what would have been our 22nd anniversary. Maybe I should stop going down this path as it's making me upset again.

I woke up at 4:30am again after going to sleep around 10. It's become a regular thing the last several days.

First day back to work. I'm only doing 60% time, which is 24 hours a week. I plan on doing five hours a day Monday through Thursday and four hours on Friday. We'll see how that goes.

———————

Have I mentioned food? I haven't done a grocery order since a few days before Rea's passing. I'm not going hungry, though, as the house is still well stocked. But I did run out of milk yesterday.

One knife to the gut is all the food I'd bought for Rea. She preferred Colby Jack cheese, I prefer cheddar. She loved yogurt; I'm indifferent. She liked cheese pizza; I prefer it with olives and mushrooms. So I have a bunch of food that caters to Rea's preferences rather than mine. I don't want to let it go to waste, but eating it and seeing it just makes the whole situation more painful.

———

So here's the thing about depression. It is the great deceiver. Earlier I was thinking about my belief in the afterlife and that Rea is there waiting for me. Then suddenly I got to thinking "Why wait?"

Yeah, bad thought. Really bad thought. I'm past it, but ouch.

What a fucking horror show this is.

Work went okay. I didn't manage to get logged in beyond the lowest level access, as my credentials had expired. I did get a number of other things taken care of, including some training, and I should be in a good position to get stuff done tomorrow.

2 February 2021

Wow, I didn't wake up until about 10 after five this morning. I feel better than I have in weeks, if not months. It probably won't last, but it's good to have an up day.

Depression and guilt are soul crushing.

Maybe I shouldn't think about that right now.

———

It turned out to be an okay day. Well, other than the foot or two of snow that fell with more coming. Maybe I'm just in one of the up parts of my cycle. Hard to say. It could also be that the pain is starting to fade a little.

I still find myself wanting to cry when I think about Rea, especially when I think about all the ways I could have done better. Neither of us was perfect but I guess we both did our best in our own ways. Knowing what I know now, though, I could do a whole lot better given a second chance. Which is probably why there are so many stories about people getting second chances. Too bad they are all fiction.

3 February 2021

I woke up crazy early – 3:30am or so. Which means this was my worst night in a while. I'm feeling kinda meh today. I'm speaking relative to the past year for me. So probably fairly down in pre CJD terms. I feel as if my ability to judge my mood is all sorts broken currently.

Newsflash, I'm really not happy alone. Marley helps, but she isn't a person. I can't talk to her, plan and scheme with her or, beyond a fairly limited level, experience new things with her.

Given how bad I am with people it's hard for me to imagine finding somebody else. I guess I do have the fact that women tend to outlive men going for me.

Which isn't to say I'm anywhere close to being ready to look for somebody else. Hearing Rea say "I love you … too" in my head just days before she passed still makes me cry and probably always will. I can't believe she's gone. Actually, I don't want to believe she's gone, and I still can't 100% acknowledge it.

I got through about half of the training I needed to do immediately yesterday so I should finish that today. Work is a mixed bag. It's good to have the distraction but the west coast is so far off the east schedule-wise that they are having their virtual morning status meeting at noon my time which would be the end of the day for me if I got an early start since I'm only working five hours Monday through Thursday and four on Friday.

I need to invent or invest in legit time travel research. Who am I trying to fool, I'm sure as heck not going to invent it so that really only leaves one option.

Actually, that sounds like the introduction to somebody getting screwed out of all their money with that somebody being me.

Yep, grief makes you crazy.

4 February 2021

Today was a mixed day. It didn't snow and I bathed. Both good things. I also had a bit of a breakdown in the shower. Not good. It's supposed to snow four of the next five days. Actually, that is good exercise. Especially now that it's starting to get deep. I have to shovel out a channel around the inside of the Marley's fence out back. Otherwise she'd soon be able to walk right over it.

She could probably jump over it now but thankfully she either doesn't want to or hasn't thought of that yet.

6 February 2021

I'm wondering if I'll ever get to a point where I can think of Rea and not cry.

7 February 2021

For the record I've cried at least three times today. Any time I stop to think about Rea there is at least a 50/50 chance it will happen. I'm going to stop talking about that though because … Well, because I don't want to cry again.

We got more snow today which meant I got more exercise. The weather reports keep going back and forth so it's hard to be sure what the next several days hold.

I threw out some rice cakes I bought for Rea. She got through about half of them before her appetite declined. Which meant they were old in addition to being something I don't really care for.

Marley is doing well. She gets to spend a lot more time with me since Rea's passing. She's good about comforting me when I lose it too, which helps.

9 February 2021

Yesterday was not a very good day. Or maybe it was. I cried a bunch, and I did it a lot more freely than I generally had before. I think I'm getting better at processing things. It hurts so much though that I really have mixed feelings about that.

It feels like if I totally let go, I'd cry for hours. Maybe I'd never stop.

That is a scary thought.

––––––––––––––

I've cried more in the past year than I did in my entire life prior. I've probably cried as much in the past month as I did my entire life. Well, excluding when I was a baby.

I've been looking at some of the last pictures I took of her. The final ones are from the day before her passing. They aren't very good. This one is from the 14th, so four days before.

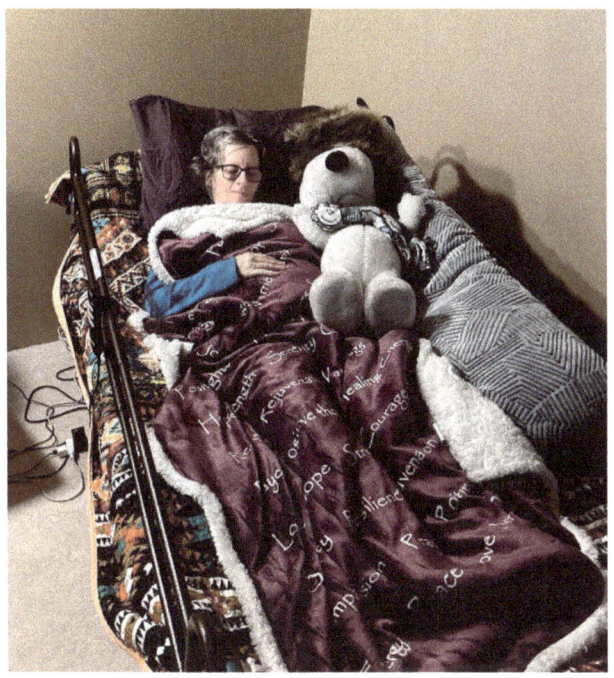

It's hard not to smile at that smile and cry as well.

———————————

I think in part that we build our world around people. As we age, these people often leave our lives, either through changing circumstances or through death's door. It feels as if my world is a lot smaller now with both Rea and my mom gone.

10 February 2021

I wrote my first thank you letter today in response to a condolence letter. Actually I started it a day or two back. This is extremely difficult for me, as is the case with anything associated with Rea. I need to get through it, though.

11 February 2021

I haven't left the house (other than to shovel snow) since Rea's service on the 26th of last month. It looks like Watertown has a really good guitar shop downtown that I plan on checking out this afternoon.

One of the guitars I bought recently came with a horrible set-up. Meaning the strings buzz like mad even when none of them are depressed. I tried messing with the truss rod but that didn't do me any good. This was a very cheap guitar bought through the mail, so the lousy set-up is not a surprise. I'd bought another more expensive guitar from the same dealer and it came with a decent set-up. I'm guessing that was because it came from the factory that way.

So in short, I need some work done on the cheap guitar and I want to check out the local guitar store. Plus having been a shut in for two plus weeks is more than enough I think.

12 February 2021

I dropped the guitar off yesterday. It might be done today. They are going to give me a call.

I've been going through all my old unpublished songs and fragments. There is a lot there it turns out. I've started seeing what I can salvage.

Tomorrow would have been our 22nd anniversary. I've probably said this before here. I've certainly said it on Facebook, but until mid-December I was certain she would be around long enough to see that day. It still seems unreal that she will have been gone almost a month instead.

13 February 2021

This would have been our 22nd wedding anniversary. Here is what I posted to Facebook today.

My grief over Rea comes in three distinct parts.
The first is the loss of her from my life.
The second is the sadness that her ending was so unjust in my eyes. None of us are perfect but she lived a very good life, helped a lot of people, stayed healthy and was just getting to the part where she could fully enjoy the fruits

of her labors and now she's gone. My personal faith helps but it's still very hard to take.

Finally there is sadness for all of you who knew her and no longer have her in your lives.

Today would have been our 22nd wedding anniversary. As recently as mid-December I was confident Rea would still be here to celebrate this one with me. In the end though it was for the best that she didn't suffer any longer as her rapidly accelerating decline over that final month was very painful to witness.

A year ago at this time we were looking forward to heading up to the Seattle area to see the Wintergrass music festival and visit our friend Debbie. At that point we thought Rea's issues were some sort of inner ear problem. She complained of being fuzzy headed and occasionally a bit dizzy but otherwise seemed fine.

At the festival it finally became clear to me that something was seriously wrong. She was having issues navigating the hotel that the festival was held at which was not normal for her. At one point she was confused as to whether we had seen a particular band in person before. We had, but she didn't remember.

We were back in the San Francisco Bay area a few weeks later and would soon get the diagnosis that would signal the beginning of the end.

The Bay area was the first place in the country to issue a shelter in place order. We continued to pursue a resolution to what was causing Rea's issues. Eventually she had a brain EKG which showed unusual patterns that could have been indicative of potential seizures. She had no history of seizures and so far as we knew hadn't experienced any recently.

Next a brain MRI was ordered.

The results of the MRI were sent automatically the evening after Rea's morning appointment. I'm almost certain this was a mistake given the probable diagnosis listed on the report. We'd never heard of Creutzfeldt-Jakob disease (CJD) at that point but in the internet age it was easy enough to look it up.

At first it seemed safe to assume that whatever was impacting Rea was not CJD. It was a one-in-a-million disease, so the odds seemed to favor us.

But odds are just that. Even highly improbable things happen, some good and some bad. The formal diagnosis would come a week or so later.

I always try to tell the truth. It gets me in trouble sometimes and I will admit that the truth I tell is the one I perceive. I do not have a crystal ball that lets me see into the hearts and minds of others, and if I'm being honest I don't even understand myself all that well in spite of 50-plus years of trying.

But I keep my eyes open and I try to listen.

The thing I've discovered recently is that when I look back I realize my listening skills aren't as good as I'd thought and that my sight was not clear.

I knew Rea and I had a good thing, but I didn't know how good it was.

I did tell her during that last year and I told her "I love you" just a few days before her passing. Her response of "I love you … too" was the last multi-word sentence I heard her say.

I write songs and prose to help me process things. There is a phrase that came to me a few days after she left us. I mentioned it in a Facebook post at the time but I'll repeat it here.

I do not believe in a perfect love
But I believe in love true

And I do.

It is both the greatest blessing and the most soul crushing experience of my life that I got to discover this particular truth.

We are all unique, but Rea was truly one of a kind. I will most likely struggle for the rest of my life to deal with her passing, but I'm going to do my best to be smarter and bring as much light into the world as I can.

But I am still me, which means I'm going to make mistakes along the way. I hope you will all bear with me and be willing to give me advice and encouragement when I need it.

The pain of losing Rea isn't going away, it is changing and evolving. What is on the other side of that I can't say. I know though that I have to be strong.

Our Wedding Day. 13 Feb 1999. Honolulu Hawaii

The same spot, more or less. 13 Feb 2014

January 2020, the cockpit of the Concorde jet located outside the Intrepid Aircraft carrier in Manhattan New York City. The last trip we took where Rea seemed more or less normal.

———————

It's odd that the thing that made me totally lose it today was a check that I had zero clue I'd be receiving.

It turns out that there is a payout for the long-term care insurance we had/have at death. I don't know if I would have received anything if we had managed to collect and I honestly don't care. Muck the money, I'd rather have Rea. If that sounds entitled then so be it.

———————

To "celebrate" today I had a slice of the leftover cheesecake that Rea had part of a couple of days before she passed. It's still fine so far as I can tell and it's nicely symbolic that we shared a slice of cheesecake on our anniversary, although nearly a month apart.

If I get food poisoning and die there will be a kinda weird poetry to my end. I'm fairly confident that isn't going to happen.

———————

Grief for me is apparently about conflict in the sense that I feel both depressed and glad that my time without Rea is steadily increasing.

The glad bit needs some explaining. I'm not sure glad is the right word but I am grateful that the pain eases a tiny bit over time. Or maybe I just get better at coping with it. Because I'll tell it true, living with the kind of pain that I'm feeling long term, even now, nearly a month later, would be impossible, at least for me.

Today is Valentine's Day. I woke up at 4am. I went to sleep a bit early so that isn't a total surprise. It does make for a really long day, though.

I'd been trying to stretch my bed time to ten PM, but I may not make that today.

———————

Then there is the fact that I sometimes question if this life is worth living. This is a whole new realm of depression for me. The political situation is crap, the weather is crap, the virus is crap, I'm missing Rea horribly and thus here I am.

It's not the first time I've been tiling towards suicidal, but it's the first time I've felt this calm. Which is terrifying. I don't think I'm going there but I now have a better understanding of why some people do it and why the elderly are willing to let go.

I used to think immortality would be great. I suspect most young people do. Now I think it would be a special kind of hell. You would either have to face losing people you loved, or stop loving. Would life without love be worth living? Neither alternative seems tolerable over the long term.

15 February 2021

Today is starting out a little better. I managed to sleep until about 5am, which equates to just over six hours.

It's 5:55am. Phish has a song called "555" that was written by Mike Gordon, their bass player. Rea really liked it and I'd always comment when I noticed the time was 5:55. It's one of a nearly endless number of little things that remind me that she's gone.

If anyone else ever reads this I suspect there will be a tendency to think "Oh my God, can he just get over it already". Truth be told, I might have thought something like that in the past. For that hypothetical future person I have this to say. "No, I can't just get over it". On the one hand I don't want to, because that would cheapen what Rea and I had while on the other, frankly I just can't.

There are far too many complex emotions and experiences tied up in my time with Rea for me to work my way through them quickly.

Money really doesn't buy happiness, but it does make it possible to purchase distractions when one is miserable.

I dreamed about Rea last night. I don't recall what it was about, but I woke up briefly at one point after seeing her face. Hopefully I can dream about her some more.

There are a handful or two of scenes that play out in my head from the past couple of years that likely relate to her developing CJD.

Her talking about how she had been researching inner ear issues and how they could cause the brain to spend so much time processing that being fuzzy headed was normal.

Her being very slow to move her healthcare related stuff up to the White Salmon area.

Her turning left out of the wrong lane as we were coming out of the Safeway parking lot in Hood river a little over a year ago.

Her personality didn't really change but in retrospect she was having issues. It probably dates back to before she retired.

I remember at one point there was some discussion of her going back to work part time. She was tentatively offered the opportunity but turned it down quickly. Was that a sign that she was having problems? I was still working part time and it would have been a nice opportunity to make a few extra dollars but she had no interest at all.

Rea was in most ways much wiser than me. As I am prone to note, neither of us was perfect and for the most part we complimented each other very well.

16 February 2021

The mother of one of my coworkers passed away last night. It seems like there has been too much death recently. It's one of the tolls of growing older, though.

I found myself crying a little as I posted my condolences on Facebook. I think I've gotten "better" at crying. It's not a skill I had any desire to improve on but if it means I'm more emphatic then I guess I'll count it as something not altogether bad.

These tears are the first ones I've cried primarily for my mother. I guess that is a sort of progress as well.

———————————

This will not be the day that I didn't cry. I was doing fine until I went to load the dishwasher. I don't know why that triggered it.

I think Rea managed to load the dishwasher once when we first moved in but showed neither the interest nor the ability after that. I might be misremembering. I think I wrote about that in this journal at the time.

———————————

Mini breakdown in the evening. It's becoming increasingly real to me that she's gone. Which may sound weird to anyone who hasn't lost somebody close.

I think at first the grief is largely based on the shock and anticipation of what losing that person will mean. Then over time it seems like the grief is increasingly caused by having to live with the reality.

I'll never be able to talk to her again. To kiss her again. To debate with her. To do anything with her, at least in this life. And that is devastating in a way that I just can't find the words to express. They may not exist. This is probably a place that somebody would have to get to themselves before they could really understand, and nobody in their right mind would want to.

There was a lot of snow this morning, with a bit more this afternoon. I managed to keep up with it.

My mood is probably worsening. This past weekend was brutal, and two days past it I'm still nowhere near recovering. Hopefully tomorrow will be a bit better.

17 February 2021

Tomorrow will be the one-month anniversary of Rea's passing. I feel as if I'm getting close to accepting it, even though that is making the pain worse.

18 February 2021

Today I'm going to post Rea's message to the band Phish on the primary Phish forum. It's both the fulfillment of a very imperfectly supported desire from her as well as being a form of therapy. Or so I hope.

It took me a couple of hours and a lot of tears but I managed to make the post this morning. There has been a lot of positive feedback, so hopefully it will make it to the band.

This was one month to the day since Rea's passing. It's been a tough week with our anniversary, Valentine's Day and the first month all coming within a small window of time.

I feel like I'm starting to come out of the extra deep pit I've been in recently. Maybe tomorrow I'll feel more productive than I've been recently.

19 February 2021

I talked to the counselor from hospice today. She called, likely because it was just over a month since Rea's passing. It was a good conversation. I'm lousy at reaching out which makes me glad that hospice is proactive.

This evening it felt a bit like I'd been sleeping for the past year and woke up to a very changed world. One a lot worse than the one I knew when I went to sleep.

The small bit of good in this is it feels like I'm starting to function again.

The big bit of bad is everything else, but most especially how bad I feel about my "performance" over the past year. I'm just going to have to accept it though or frankly I'm not going to be alive in a few years.

20 February 2021

That feeling that I was waking to a nightmare is still with me today. The additional clarity is not my friend but as I kind of hint above, it's probably a sign I'm progressing down the grieving path.

I'm not sure I'll ever be able to completely forgive myself but I do need to get to a sustainable place.

I decided to take all Rea's shirts out of the master bedroom closet and do a bit of sorting. I did this on the spur of the moment and ended up crying a lot during the process.

I didn't realize there was a difference between crying and sobbing before all this. The fact that it's possible to sob without crying, at least for a bit, is something I've discovered.

Memo to my future self, if I ever have the courage to come back and read this...

"It was every bit as bad as you remember and probably worse. I hope you found some peace and a bit of distance because this kind of pain is not sustainable."

So now I have a mostly empty closet in a room I hardly go into.

21 February 2021

Sunday, I think I'm feeling better today, though I'm sure there will be something that will have me crying again.

I'm sure none of this sounds particularly manly. I have two comments on that as of now. One, what men do and think inside themselves or in private is likely very different from how they carry on in public and two, that public persona is often bullshit.

Being strong is good, being insensitive is not. That's my take anyway.

I can neither help, nor will I apologize for the way I feel.

Lazy day today so far.

I've been looking a bit at the online courses from the Berklee school of music. Music has always been something I love, but I have a hard time concentrating long enough to build my foundational knowledge of the theory as well as improving my playing and singing. I'll blame my anxiety, which is probably legit to a degree but I'm thinking that having a more structured avenue to improvement might help

It's only money, right? In terms of what is at stake. And my ego, I suppose. It's always good to goad the ego.

I think I've also learned a bit about PTSD. I was copying some files from a drive I plan to reformat so I can use it for backups when I realized there was an Oysterhead show on it. Oysterhead is another one of Trey Anastasio's bands. We had tickets to see them last year, but COVID happened. Boom, I'm crying again. I'd been doing fairly well up until then.

Maybe this isn't PTSD, but it sucks in any case.

People ask me how I'm doing. I generally just say "OK". Which is true in the sense that I'm mostly OK with being alive and I manage to function for enough of the day to keep things going.

22 February 2021

Monday again. Five weeks.

I think I'm doing better today.

I have an online class and some other things coming up which helps. I'm making progress on the music front as well which is a mood booster.

I am doing better. I can go from zero to bawling my eyes out pretty quickly if I think too much about Rea but today at least it's a tiny bit easier to think about her without doing that.

There are certain hot button issues. Knowing she was scared and feeling like I didn't answer very well when she told me is top of mind currently.

23 February 2021

It's warming up outside. We're above freezing before noon and it looks like it will be warmer tomorrow. I think we've been above freezing once in the last two months prior to this.

Today is going okay. I've started playing music in the Living Room where Rea's urn is. I know that may sound weird but it feels right.

I have an online class all this week for work. That is going well enough so far.

24 February 2021

Today I think I'm mostly just sad. Which is an improvement over the toxic mix of guilt, sadness, and anger that I've been feeling for a while now.

Almost time to login to the class. Being on east coast time it's nearly time for lunch when they start.

I ate the last of the Cheesecake today. There were a couple of tiny bits of mold. I cut a generous bit off around each. I probably sound a bit crazy. Heck, I probably am a bit crazy. For anyone with empathy, I'm not sure how something like this wouldn't push them over the edge for a bit.

Hopefully I'll make my way back.

I spent a bit of time upstairs this evening. I had a mini breakdown. I felt a little better afterwards.

I really wonder if I'll ever get to a place where I don't cry at least once a day. If I do, I wonder if I'll be able to think about Rea during that day. Because right now the only thing that works is not thinking about her.

25 February 2021

Thursday. It's supposed to stay below freezing today but the next few days are expected to be up into the 40's so most of the snow may be gone by early next week. I'm ambivalent about that. Snow is wet, but clean. The mud that proceeds and follows it is not.

Have I mentioned that I talk to Rea? Probably. I could go back and review, but that would be painful. I don't hear her talking back, not in words any way but sometimes I feel like she hears me. It could be wishful thinking of course. I think it's probably therapeutic and I know I'm not the first or the last person to do this.

I finally got the tags for the CR-V today. I think I need to register the truck as well. A bunch of mail that should have been forwarded automatically wasn't and I just got it thanks to our neighbors Ken and his wife Carole.

26 February 2021

I'm not sure why I feel compelled to write here every day. Honestly, I don't seem to have a lot to say.

It's been a semi busy week work wise and I have enough irons in the fire to keep me mostly distracted. Not being distracted is bad.

The US government is printing a lot of $s right now which has some people freaking out. I'm freaking out a bit myself as a lot of my income is only mildly inflation resistant. Which makes the real estate and my investments that much more important. Diversity is a good thing.

Of course most people have neither the money nor the knowledge to deal with this risk. I know I'm lucky in a lot of ways but being lucky without Rea is like being thirsty and having nothing but salt water at hand.

I've never been very good at analogies.

I was just looking at the notifications on Rea's phone. I keep it powered on in case I need it to get into an account or something. I don't generally look at the notifications but I just realized that one of the elderly friends that Rea made in Washington tried to call last Sunday. To give more context, this friend was recently diagnosed with Alzheimer's. She knew that Rea passed away in January but has apparently forgotten.

This makes me sad.

Maybe I won't look at the notifications on Rea's phone again for now.

27 February 2021

February is a short month, but it's still hard to believe it's nearly done. I feel like my life is accelerating again. Not what I'm doing, but my perception of it.

It's a thing I hate about getting older. As my years left get shorter, each year seems to get shorter as well.

Rea is still top of mind. Have I mentioned recently that I sometimes wonder if it's worth living even these perceptually short years without her? I know I could look back, but these words are hard enough to write without having to review them, at least for now.

I know that is depression talking. I know that the flavor of my grief is changing over time and that this is a process that I'm still in the early days of working my way through. Thankfully I don't have any easy outs and pain and blood are not my things.

I guess that is more than a little dark.

I know this experience has made me a better writer, but it's essentially a Monkey's Paw reward.

Why her and not me? That question will haunt me for the rest of my life.

My afternoon realization? As depressed as I am, my grief is a bit less overwhelming.

I'm worried that I'm just getting better at not thinking about her.

I need to spend a couple of hours upstairs this evening. I kind of promised I would yesterday.

I'm up sitting in the reclining chair. It's not the first time I've done this but it's been a while. I don't think I've mentioned that the reclining chair is where Rea drew her last breath. Maybe I have.

A bluegrass station is playing currently. I've promised myself that on Monday I'm going to play the Phish station. That will be brutal, but help with the healing I hope.

———————————

The thing about this reclining chair is that it was purchased two days before Rea passed and arrived maybe 24 hours before she died. There, I said it. Rea died. I've thought it on and off for a while now. When we say "passed" it means the same thing but it's a way of sneaking up on the reality of the situation, at least it is for me. I still say and write "passed". As much to continue to shield myself as others.

Marley is playing with one of her rope toys. Which means she wants me to play as well. This makes writing hard, but it is better than being alone.

I had to take her rope away from her for a bit. She went and ate some dinner at that point which was a better use of her time from my perspective. I gave it back to her after a bit and then we played fetch with one of her rubber Kong toys.

Have I mentioned how fucking unfair it is that Rea is gone? Yes, I'm angry. And sad. I've done a bit of negotiation as well, but it doesn't seem to make any difference.

According to the internet depression is next on the agenda but I've been there for the better part of a year now.

28 February 2021

I'm not sure I cried yesterday. Maybe I did. Maybe I mentioned it. It's a bit after 9am today and I haven't. It wouldn't be hard for me to put myself in a place where I would cry. I'm certain that will be true for a very long time.

As Rea recedes a tiny bit in my mind, my mom is starting to move up.

The tragedy of Rea's illness and passing managed to drown out my mom's decline. I love my mother, so that shouldn't be taken as a knock against her but rather as an indication of just how painful Rea's situation and passing (that word again) were.

Time to lay down some scratch vocals for "Undone", a song I wrote before everything went south. One of the verses is …

So many of life's problems
Come from disbelief
In the simple pleasures
That were all too brief
Can we remember
The child undone

Sniffled a bit for my mom and then Rea as well. Someday I'll make it through a day without getting visibly upset. Not that I currently have to think too much about that since I'm alone 99% of the time with the exception of Marley.

Vocals recorded, time to do the comping to get a final scratch.

Chapter 13

(March 2021)

1 March 2021

Another Monday.

I'm feeling decent today. I do feel like I'm starting to turn a corner. I've switched the music upstairs to the Phish radio station. Some would argue that I'm being silly. Given the state of the world today, I'll take my "silliness" over what a lot of people are generating.

I'll likely pause the music before I head up for lunch and take Marley out and bring her down, but I plan on listening this evening when I spend time up there. It may be a bit emotional, but it's something I need to do.

———————

So, while it feels like I've turned a corner, I am also very depressed.

I don't know how much of this is my typical cycle and how much of it is the continued realization of my situation. Keep in mind that I was in a mild-to-moderate form of denial for a long time.

I'm also depressed about being me, which doesn't help. Especially when I reflect on how that impacted Rea. So yeah, now we're back to guilt being in the mix.

It's such a crazy emotional roller coaster with the upper reaches of the ride not even making it to a "meh" state of mind.

It is exhausting.

———————

Confirmed, listening to Phish is painful. I will work through this.

———————

"Wolfman's Brother" from this day in 1997 is the first complete song I'm listening to. Rea would be amused, as this song was never one of my favorites.

2 March 2021

Listening to Phish last night was a good thing even if it did start out painful. I'm going to keep doing that and hope that it helps in the healing. I think that it will.

Looking back over the two or so years prior to Rea's diagnosis, I see the signs of it emerging. Things she said and did that in retrospect were red flags. In the back of my mind I knew something was wrong, but I didn't have a clue how bad it was going to get.

———————

It's dinner time and I'm upstairs listening to Phish. It's getting better.

3 March 2021

One of the people Rea wanted to write a letter to is current Secretary of Transportation Pete Buttigieg.

Rea was a lifelong and dedicated Democrat. Even though I'm a bit more independent minded, I'd classify myself as a fan as well. I'm maybe halfway through. There are several other people, most of them not famous, that Rea wanted to say something personal to. I'm going to work my way through all of them but it's still slow going. I'm feeling a bit better, but this task hits me hard for multiple reasons. One, I didn't help her write these letters and two, the ever-present reminder that she's gone.

I will get it done, though.

I bought Joni Mitchell's recently released archive recordings from her early years (1963–1967). This is before her first album was released. I'm not a huge fan of hers but I do admire her melodic and lyrical sense. She was an original and truly unique. She still is, I suppose, though poor health has kept her from producing anything for the past several years.

These early recordings are a great glimpse into her foundation as an artist.

I'm maybe a third of the way through the Joni box set. The actual CDs come to-morrow, but it was available for streaming after purchase so I got an early start.

I also made progress on the Mayor Pete letter. Hopefully I'll get it done tomorrow. At that point I'll need to figure out the best way to send it.

4 March 2021

Mood wise, I'm feeling okay today. I don't know how much of this is just my natural cycle versus progress in dealing with the grief of losing Rea, but as I often say in this situation, I'll take it.

Of course the grief still comes at times. Mostly when something reminds me of her and I'm not prepared.

I don't want that to always be the case, or to be more precise, I want the good things we experienced to outweigh the grief of losing her. I hate this pain. I hate having to hold her memory at a distance to function.

I really don't know what my purpose in life is at this stage. We had the next 20 years or so planned out in broad strokes. In short, I – and we – had it all. And now what do I have? Memories.

I was going through Rea's phone looking at pictures she took. I had a bit of a breakdown.

She was never much for taking pictures, especially compared to me. Marley came and comforted me. She almost always does.

5 March 2021

Another Friday is here. I had trouble getting to sleep last night but slept a decent amount. Now I'm struggling a bit to get out of bed. Marley really needs to go out, so she'll save me once again.

Bed escaped.

I like people, but for the most part Facebook is good enough in terms of interaction.

It's not so much that I'm lonely as I miss Rea and I'm a bit angry and very depressed about the way her life ended.

An okay day overall. I was decently productive both for work and at home. Tomorrow is the weekend, so more free time to get things done. Music being a high priority.

6 March 2021

Not a great night sleeping-wise. I woke up before 5am. Just under six hours of sleep, though, which isn't super low for me.

It's Saturday. I need to get up and take Marley out soon. She is an awesome dog.

I keep coming back to the letters I didn't help Rea write. There were other mistakes on my part but that one feels like it might be the worst. Because she asked me at least a couple of times and I was confused and dismissive. All because I didn't read her "wishes" letter. I'm going to copy it here for reference.

My preference is to be cremated with some ashes spread at our house in White Salmon, some spread at my childhood home, Adams, NY ... Only a small amount of ashes need to be spread at this location which is the same location as my father and mother's ashes were spread. The remaining ashes will be handed per my husband, Mike Miller, wishes. It's Mike's decision as what should be done with the ashes of the pets that have passed previously.

[...]

Mike will get my wedding ring.

Hopefully I can attend the reunion in 2021. And potentially a small celebration of life could be included if I have not passed before then. I'll give Mike contact information. I expect the firehall could be used. Again, this will become clearer as it gets closer to reunion time. A very small celebration of life with the people I become close with in White Salmon AND Debbie would also be nice and is my preference over a classic funeral. So this is looking like something small in Adams and something small in White Salmon. Timing is more based on weather and timing that works for those involved, vs it being soon after my passing. I'll work with Mike to go through as much as possible to identify a few things that he would like to keep that meant a lot to me that he might not be aware of. Blue Dog comes to mind. WFF Penny does restoration so that's something to consider if Mike wants to do that. I think Debbie will be very interested in helping out on things if there is still stuff to do after the virus is controlled.

Notes:

Need to prepare a thank you letter to the involved Drs. I'd also like to prepare something that is sent to Phish and Mayor Pete after I pass thanking them for the joy (Phish) and inspiration and well wishes for the future (Pete). These will be sent after I pass and will be from me, but will have Mike's contact information in case they care to respond, but it will be written in such a way that no response is expected.

Music: 'til we meet again (Trey song he played for his friend CCott) :https:// www.instagram.com/tv/B_Xo5HwD4x7/?utm_source=ig_embed

I'm more than halfway through the Mayor Pete letter. I'll work on it some later this weekend.

On average my days are better, but the lows each day have remained about the same. I'll be cruising along doing okay when something will remind me of her, often in conjunction with some regret I have and *boom*, I'm back in the gutter.

7 March 2021

Five hours of sleep last night. Hopefully I'll manage to take a nap at some point.

These days toothpaste tubes are plastic but when Rea and I first got together they were still metal. Those thin metal tubes were much harder to empty but Rea was always up for the challenge. When I'd given up, she'd insist on taking over and squeezing the extra brushing or two of toothpaste out of the tube.

She could be a little distant emotionally. We were great friends and had many good times together, but she was in her own way a very private person. I'm the same way, which may explain some of the attraction we felt for each other and why we stayed together. Still, there were times when I wanted us to be closer and it could be frustrating.

I was more than a little surprised when people told me both in the time leading up to her death and after how much she loved me. Don't get me wrong, I knew she loved me, but apparently she adored me. I wish she had made that more clear. It is difficult for me to express my emotions, though, so I shouldn't point fingers. We both had a very good thing, and neither one of us was very good at acknowledging that to the other.

I actually managed to type that last paragraph without losing it, though I am a little teary eyed right now.

While I'm spilling the dirt, Rea could get really focused on tasks and I sometimes felt neglected. One time at work there was a very difficult technology transition that she was in charge of. For the better part of a year I hardly saw her and I felt neglected. Combine that with the emotional distance we were both prone to and it's not a pretty picture.

Once again I struggle to get motivated to get out of bed. I'm not super tired at this point so I really need to get going. Thank God for Marley.

I think this morning was a transition point. By realizing and acknowledging that Rea was a wonderful person but human I feel a little better.

I'm still sad, and I think I'll always be sad, but I feel like some of the weight has been lifted from my shoulders.

I still miss her, too. The old saying "You don't know what you've got until it's gone" very much applies to me.

I will always love her. I will always mourn her.

8 March 2021

When I woke up this morning it was exactly 5:55.

———————————

It really does feel like I've started to turn the corner. I "talk" to Rea frequently. Today I was able to do so without getting too upset.

———————————

It just struck me that some of my better mood could just be me being in an up cycle. I don't know for a fact that I'm bipolar, and if I am it's not severe, but I'm fairly sure it goes along with my anxiety.

At the worst, though, I think an upward mood swing would just be enhancing my slow climb out of the sadness of losing Rea.

9 March 2021

I'm going out to breakfast.

Or I will be if I get out of bed.

Doing that now.

Really.

———————————

Made it out. Had breakfast, stopped by Staples to get some things, and then made an appointment for Marley to get trimmed. That last one is about three weeks out, but at least it's scheduled. I'll likely schedule a haircut for me on or before that date.

Eating out without Rea was not a unique experience, but this was the first time since she passed. I handled it okay and plan on making it a two- or three-times-a-week thing. I need to get outside regularly and my anxiety will beat me down if I don't.

10 March 2021

When I first woke up this morning, I briefly thought about reaching over to Rea. Then I remembered she was gone.

Oddly I think this is another step in my getting to a sustainable place. The fact that her death/passing was not top of mind is a good thing, I think.

11 March 2021

I was looking through the pictures on Rea's phone yesterday. I stalled at Halloween 2016 when I saw a bunch of pictures of her dressed up as Sally from *Nightmare Before Christmas*. I need to verify, but I'm fairly sure we were at Phish that year. I'd kind of forgotten.

I'm better, but those pictures of her in her costume took me out again for a bit.

My grief continues to evolve. It sure as heck isn't going away, though. I don't really want it to. I'm getting better at handling it, and that is what is important. Losing that grief would be a big step in the direction of forgetting the lessons I've learned from this horrible experience.

Getting back to Halloween 2016, I would have made a pretty good Jack. She probably asked me, but I declined if she did. I'll blame my anxiety, but in retrospect I sure wish I had dressed up as Jack. It would have been cool.

I was walking around out back waiting for Marley to go to the bathroom in preparation for bedtime when I realized that if we had ended up with another 20 or 30 years together, I probably would have continued to take Rea for granted. That was a depressing thought.

So yeah, no worries about my grief going away any time soon, I suspect.

12 March 2021

As I thought, the snow was mostly gone first thing this morning, and with the exception of the larger snow piles, it will all be gone by the end of the day.

Temperatures are supposed to cool off over the weekend and we will likely get some more snow before spring is really here, but the worst seems to be over weather-wise.

Mood-wise I'm down a bit today. It's probably just part of my natural cycle.

The high temperature today stayed around freezing. There was still mud, but it was toned down a bit which was nice.

My house cleaning has been on the lower end of my range recently. I have nobody to blame but myself.

I'm feeling okay today. I did get a bit of housework done.

I really need to finish up the Mayor Pete letter and get it in the mail.

"We dream and we struggle together
And love will carry us through"

So says Trey Anastasio. So very true. This is from his "Ghosts of the Forest" project. He did a tour with most of his solo band plus Phish drummer Jon Fishman and one or two others in support of the project. Rea and I saw the show at the Greek in Berkeley on April 20 2019.

I almost always got up and walked around a bit during a show. Trey at the Greek was not an exception. I remember walking up to the grass and concession area.

Our seats were toward the right of the stage, so on the left of this picture. Somewhere down there in the dark is Rea, sitting and enjoying the show while I stretch my legs.

We sat in that same general area on August 28 2017 when we saw The Heartbreakers for what turned out to be one of Tom Petty's last shows.

16 March 2021

Wow, two days without posting. I knew I'd skipped one, but two was a surprise.

I do worry occasionally that I'll develop CJD as well. I know I've said that before in previous entries. Rea knew something was wrong, but I don't know how far in she was before that was the case. It's probably subtle at first.

I've always been a bit scatterbrained. I'll blame a lot of that on anxiety.

If Rea got CJD from eating something, then there is a chance that I have it as well, and that it hasn't manifested yet, or is now in the very early stages.

Maybe I'm a hypochondriac though. I hope so.

In between doubting my mental acuity, I feel like I'm starting to get myself better organized.

17 March 2021

I finished the Mayor Pete letter and printed it out. I'll put it in an envelope tomorrow and send it off.

Two months tomorrow.

18 March 2021

I made the following post to Facebook today.

The (This) photo is from August 23rd of last year. It seemed appropriate given the day (Thursday) and the fact that it's two months today since Rea's passing.

I don't plan on doing this every month, but I had a few things I wanted to share. I'll do my best not to repeat what I've said before.

First of all, thank you everyone who has sent me condolence cards and/or made donations in Rea's memory to the CJD foundation. I've read and appreciate every single one. I should thank each of you individually and I may someday, but for now that is very difficult for me.

Dealing with Rea's passing is something I'm slowly getting better at, but I still have a ways to go. Most of the time I have to keep a bit of emotional distance to be reasonably functional, but I do take time to grieve fully. This is both prudent and inevitable as it builds up if I do not.

One of the things I feared during Rea's decline was that she would forget me and those who loved her. While she was largely unable to talk for the last few days she always seemed to know on some level who the people around her were. I am very grateful for that. I was not alone in fearing she would linger on in a vegetative state for several weeks or months. I thank God that this did not happen.

I still plan on starting a not for profit in Rea's name. At the moment I'm working on getting the financial side of things in order in preparation to move forward with that. I've made a lot of progress and should have everything more or less resolved in the next few weeks.

I've mentioned before in various posts that one of the ways I process things is to write songs. Here are the lyrics to one I'm currently working on. It's still evolving, in fact I made a couple of changes just now but I feel like it's getting close to being complete.

It's called "Love True".

Verse
The memories will never fade
You know I know that's true
And I could use a little help
With the pain of losing you
It's only been a day or two
Maybe a little more
I can feel your last embrace
Yes I feel it in my core

Chorus
The words I said
Weren't always right
But I said it all to you
When I said I loved you and
You said you loved me too

Verse
Well I'm tired but I can't sleep
Hungry, don't want to eat
My survivors guilt is real
As I sit here I feel beat
I wish I'd said so many things
And unsaid a few
Had some more adventures
While it was still me and you

Bridge
I don't believe in perfect love
But I believe in love true

Verse
I wear a shroud of sadness
I know that wasn't your thing
So glad we walked together
That you blessed me with your ring

I came across that picture going through ones I'd favorited on my iPhone. I post a picture of Marley every day, so it felt like the right choice to use this one today. I don't think I'd used it before, but I might have.

I truly feel like I've turned a corner. It's hard not to cry when looking at that picture but it isn't as bad as it was even a couple of weeks ago. All the grief is still there, I just feel as if I'm handling it a bit better. I think part of it is I'm getting better at forgiving myself. I still feel really bad for

Rea. She was on balance a wonderful person and fate shafted her big time. That part of my grief isn't going anywhere. Mostly forgiving myself is a good thing. I know she loved me, and I loved her. We loved each other in spite of our faults. That's the meaning of true love to me. There is no such thing as perfect love. If we manage to find somebody who will forgive us for our faults and if we are willing to forgive them as well, then and only then can we find love true.

If I'm being honest, Rea and I didn't meet that ideal until after her diagnosis. A lot of that is on me. Which isn't to say that our relationship was bad. For the most part it was very good.

I don't know if true love is possible in most cases without some sort of significant trauma.

It's hard not to be a little self-centered. I could be humble here and say something like "or maybe it's just me", but I'm not stupid or blind. It's clear that I'm not the only one who struggles with that. It's part of the human condition.

I've sent "Love True" to Brian H with a request that he put together a session with piano. I think that song is going to be built around the piano, but I'll have to wait to see what the results are before I'll know for sure.

It may be the best thing I've ever written. It's certainly the most direct and honest. I don't know if I've mentioned it before, but the chorus is essentially the last multi-word conversion I had with Rea, limited in words though it was.

God I miss her.

I'm not crying right now, but I easily could. The tears still sneak up on me and I'll find there is water running down my face.

I think tears are one of the best bits of evidence that there is a higher power. Not the fact that we live in a world where crying happens, but rather that we have that capability. I'm sure some scientist has come up with a fancy explanation for why tears make sense from an evolutionary perspective but to me they are a divine gift. They allow us to express, often unconsciously, when we are feeling strong emotions. They can sneak up on us and magnify or clarify what we are feeling in a given situation.

I don't know, I hope that last bit makes some sense. It's late and I'm tired. Time for sleep.

————————

I think I'm trying to say that it isn't tears that are beautiful, but rather that we have the capability to cry. It's like the difference between a black-and-white photograph and one in color. Tears bring color to the world.

19 March 2021

Another Friday. It's a wetland out back by midday but it got below freezing last night so things shouldn't be too bad right now. Time to take Marley out and give her breakfast.

————————

I made a follow-up post on the Phish.net forum regarding Rea's message to the band. I don't think I'll ever hear back from them at this point, but I feel like I've made a reasonable effort.

20 March 2021

The backyard is a bog and it's not likely to get below freezing.

————————

So it turns out remembering Rea telling me that she was scared opens the floodgates. I was lounging around reading when from out of nowhere that hit me and *boom*, I'm sobbing.

That is probably not the only memory that will do that, but it's going to be high up on the list.

Someday I'm probably going to be scared as well Rea. I hope when I am that somebody with a bit more sense than me is there to lend me comfort.

————————

I have a deeper understanding of why elderly couples don't tend to outlive each other by much. I'm too young and relatively healthy at this point, but if

I were anywhere near the edge I could easily will myself over the cliff. I think that is what Rea did toward the end. If I'm right, then that took immense courage given her fears.

I got a call from Lori, Rea's longtime friend and the woman who was our real estate agent when we bought this place. It's a great time to sell apparently. I'd thought about remodeling, but maybe that isn't the best choice.

21 March 2021

I sorted through more of Rea's clothes today. Which had me bawling my eyes out. Yet another bit of evidence that I still have a long way to go in learning to manage my grief.

22 March 2021

Another Monday. I don't like Mondays. That last sentence was both factually correct and an obscure reference. It's a reference that will get increasingly obscure as time goes on. I'll minimize the mystery and mention the Boomtown Rats here. Though I have no urge to go on a shooting rampage.

I wrote part of a song yesterday. I think it's going to be called "The Looking Glass". Yes, it's mostly about Rea, but also about people who are gone now that I can still see in pictures.

In pictures I can see you
And I still miss you so
Those pictures tell a story
But they can only show
A tiny little window
Of the you that I know

You're dancing to the music
Smiling in the light
Showing all your colors
And though they'll fade from sight

The beauty that you brought
Long ago took flight

I know someday I'll see you
Beyond the looking glass

I'm pretty happy with that section but it's all I have for now. Hopefully it will lead to something. I generally try not to force my muse, but I have to be disciplined when I'm working on a song.

This part of songwriting is generally referred to as practicing the craft. Inspiration only takes you so far, and at some point you have to sit down and work to refine and often expand on the original inspiration.

23 March 2021

I'm going out for breakfast today and to pick some gardening-related tools.

There, I said it. Now I can't wimp out.

So I made it out to breakfast and I did my shopping as well.

24 March 2021

Midweek already.

My coping is continuing to improve, but I suspect the waterworks will start again when I work some more on sorting Rea's stuff.

25 March 2021

I should probably stop trying to make entries here for a bit. I don't have anything new to say.

26 March 2021

Marley doggy spa day. Hopefully I'll be able to schedule a haircut. Friday as well. Though the day of the week matters a lot less when working remote and part time.

27 March 2021

Marley and I both got haircuts yesterday. She had gotten a bit matted. Totally my fault but caused by ignorance and circumstances. Lessons were learned.

My haircut was the second since the pandemic started. It's very short now, like the last time. I don't really care that much and I have no clue how I want it otherwise. For over 25 years the two of us went to the same lady to get our hair cut.

One of the things we were going to do in retirement was watch *The Princess Bride* again. Rea fell asleep the first time I showed it to her. I was kinda appalled given how much I love that film.

The funny thing is, she loved *Dumb & Dumber* while I thought it was just about the worst thing ever. I think she had a bit of a crush on Jeff Daniels at the time. Mostly, though, our taste in movies were similar.

I was just reading that Disney is starting to work toward what sounds like a substantial expansion of the original Disneyland. Rea loved all things Disney, as do I. I was born the exact day Walt Disney died. Which was a lousy trade for the world at large.

I don't know if I've had a day yet where I didn't cry a little for Rea. I might have and I will soon if I haven't already. She's still close to top of mind, but both my ability to cope and my ability to focus on other things is helping.

One of the minor miracles of the smartphone era is the fact that we can easily record our day-to-day lives. I got my first iPhone around the time the iPhone 6 hit the market which was late 2014. Which means I have photos and videos in my Apple cloud dating back that far. I have even older stuff on the Android side of things.

All of which means I can reconstruct in a lot of detail what Rea and I did over the past several years. This includes Phish shows since 2016 and many other live music experiences both before and after.

I'm finding little gems here and there as I go through things. It's good that I've gotten to this place.

Going through these old videos and photos got me to thinking that I could write a fictionalized account of my life. I've always wanted to be a writer with my main interest being fiction, but I don't think I'd be very good at that, even though I've done a bit of it.

Fiction writing requires a level of focus and discipline that I can't seem to maintain. I'll blame my anxiety again.

Nonfiction can be stressful as well, but I've gotten a lot of practice over the past 11 months and I feel like I have a better understanding of what I need to do in order to generate decent prose in that context. Fictionalizing my own life might be the happy medium?

28 March 2021

I think I'm a bit addicted to the melatonin. I forgot to take it last night until about half past midnight. I was asleep maybe 10 minutes after I did. Could be a coincidence, I guess.

Unfortunately I then woke up at 6:30am. I suspect I'll be napping in the afternoon.

I did end up snoozing a bit this afternoon. A couple of times while on the edge of sleep I thought I heard Rea say something to me. Just a word both times, though I couldn't quite make it out. I was probably just dreaming, but it was good to hear her voice again.

29 March 2021

Monday. I'm getting better at dealing with Mondays.

Marley has a vet appointment tomorrow down near Syracuse. Thankfully the traffic here doesn't tend to be all that bad and the weather will hopefully be good.

The vet called and said Marley didn't really need to come in tomorrow. Which was fine, but it was their automated system that suggested I schedule an appointment originally.

30 March 2021

The weather is nice today. A bit on the cool side, but mostly clear. Every time things start to get dry outside, it rains, so I'm expecting some more of that in the next day or so.

——————————

Not only did I make it out for a late lunch/early dinner, I also bought a step ladder and some light bulbs. Yay me?

I've been making slow but steady progress in getting the house in order. Mostly working on breaking down boxes and getting things organized in the garage. I feel like I've been operating at 25% capacity since Rea's diagnosis and am only just starting to wake up.

I'm sure there will be down times as well. My tendency to cycle up and down makes that inevitable, but I continue to feel like I've turned the corner.

I get the motor home back on the 9th if things go as planned. I have lots of planning to do both before and after that to get ready to head back west.

31 March 2021

Rain today. Just when the ground was starting to be kinda dry out back. I'm used to it at this point.

Chapter 14

(April 2021)

1 April 2021

When I went to look outside this morning, it was snowing. April Fool's Day again, the joke is on me. It wasn't sticking and given the forecast I doubt any will, but it was still a bit of a shock.

Marley was unfazed and did her business quickly so she could come back inside and have breakfast. She's been much more prompt since I started giving her a half-can of the wet food in the morning.

———————————

Well, it turns out the snow has in fact stuck.

I made an appointment for the C-19 vaccine at 3:30 tomorrow. Hopefully that will work out and I can be completely done with it before I head west in early May.

2 April 2021

It looks like I'll be getting the Johnson & Johnson version of the vaccine, which is a single shot. It's also less effective than the two shot variants and more like a traditional vaccine. I'm fine with whatever I get. I'll just be happy to have it out of the way. The J&J one still greatly reduces the severity of the symptoms and that is the most important thing. Not having to schedule a second shot would be nice as well.

3 April 2021

So far, so good on the vaccination. My arm is a bit sore, but I made sure to move it around a lot while waiting for 15 minutes afterwards to be sure there were no immediate side effects and drank a bunch of water afterwards.

I've been trying to figure out if there is a way to share all of Rea's iPhone photos to me. They date back to 2014 and while many of them are just screen captures of things that caught her eye, these are memories that I want to preserve as well.

It turns out that the last screenshot she took was on December 12, a bit more than a month before her passing. Her decline was very steep that final month, so I'm not surprised by this.

The screen capture is an illustration of a white bunny sitting on a log while it is snowing. There is a star-like leaf falling off to the right side of the illustration that the bunny is looking at. Actually, I'll just copy it here. Single picture sharing is easy.

I've probably noted before that Rea loved cute things. She wasn't girly for the most part (which is neither a good nor a bad thing), but she loved stuffed animals and anything that was cute. This illustration is right in her wheelhouse, so I can understand why she wanted to preserve it.

I've been thinking about those final months and trying to figure out what was going on in her head. I'm not a scientist, but it seems like the impact of CJD would vary a bit depending on where it started in the brain.

Rea's memory wasn't impacted until the later stages, unlike her executive function which suffered early. Those changes in her executive function were the first signs of trouble.

Maybe I've said this before, but it was a blessing that it worked this way. Rea remained Rea to the end, even though her ability to interact with the world rapidly eroded during those last couple of weeks.

Now I've managed to upset myself again. Which is alright. These things need to be said and I continue to believe that feelings need to be felt.

———————

I think that rabbit inspired Rea because to a degree she pictured herself that way.

She was an incredibly strong person but very humane and full of wonder and a desire to experience and bring joy into the world.

4 April 2021

It's Easter today. I have tomorrow off. Working from home part time, the second part doesn't mean too much. It's easy enough to log in and keep an eye on things so I do.

I'm mostly responsible for a single big system called Lassen. I did a bunch of the initial set-up work on it a few years back when it was first delivered. The same is true of its "big brother" Sierra. Lassen was number nine initially on the top 500 list of supercomputers and Sierra was number two. Both have since slipped down the list a bit. The world of super computing is a series of continuous escalations.

Pretty much every node on Lassen is busy constantly, so being quick to bring ones back online that have crashed means the usefulness of the system over its lifetime goes up a tiny bit each time a node (an individual system that is part of the cluster) is put back in service.

Sierra is a classified system now, so I can't provide direct support there. We generally get things working on the unclassified side before these big complicated systems move over to spend their lives on the closed side.

There are significant restrictions on the flow of information back from the classified side that make it much more difficult to diagnose and deal with any issues that are discovered.

This is part of the reason that a smaller but still significant system is generally bought for the open side.

Many of the problems encountered only occur when codes try to run beyond a particular node count. These types of problems are broadly referred to as "scaling issues".

Maybe I'll write more on that later. If I'm not feeling merciful.

5 April 2021

We'll be spreading some of Rea's ashes at the house she grew up at in Adams on Wednesday at 3:30pm. The weather is supposed to be nice.

I was going through some more of her things yesterday. Doing that still upsets me. Looking at pictures and videos do as well. I can do it, though, which is progress.

I know I probably repeat myself a lot. That has always been true, so I guess I'll just own it. This is not the life I was prepared for.

6 April 2021

I had a dream with Rea in it. We were visiting friends. It was all sorts of muddled as dreams often are. I woke up from it around a 4:45am.

I managed to get back to sleep for an hour or so.

My sleep schedule had been fairly regular for a while but now it seems like I'm falling into bad habits again.

I'm making good progress music wise which is nice. Working with cool and competent people helps a lot. "Love True" is going to be good, I think. At the very least it's a statement and a deeply personal song. Whether anyone else gets it is secondary.

I think I'm probably in a down part of my cycle. That never seems to occur to me as a possibility until I've been wallowing for a bit. Kinda annoying that.

7 April 2021

I just saw news that there is a potential drug trial for treating CJD. I'm not proud of the fact that my first thought was to be some combination of sad/mad that it didn't come a year earlier.

My second thought is that this would be beyond wonderful if it ends up helping even a little. CJD is horrific and a very quick death sentence currently. Anything that gets us closer to that no longer being true is a very good thing.

But I'm still going to be a bit sad because of how things worked out for Rea. It's selfish and mean, I know, but it is what it is.

8 April 2021

The spreading of Rea's ashes at her childhood home was a low-key thing. Rea's younger brother and sister-in-law had separated the third they had been keeping out into four separate jars. Rea's older brother and his wife, younger brother, and I did the spreading. I very quietly said a few words, but only for myself.

Rea's mother and father had their ashes spread there as well. Rea's father built the house back in the 1950s and it's now owned by one of Rea's nephews, so it's been in the family for nearly 70 years.

Poor sleep continues, even by my definition. I wonder if I'll sleep at all if I make it to my 80s. I think my mom slept most of the time toward the end.

I frequently think about all the changes in Rea leading up to her diagnosis. They were subtle at first and may date back as much as three years or more. Mostly it was reflected in a growing inability to get certain things done. I'm fairly sure I've talked about that a bit all ready. But even as recently as early 2020 she was still capable of doing things like scheduling a trip to see Pete Buttigieg in Seattle or organize ticket buying for Phish's first 2020 tour.

9 April 2021

Getting the motor home was a bust. Neither Uber nor Lyft had cars available all day. Weird and frustrating. I looked into taxis and have some possibilities.

It's a mundane thing relatively speaking but this is yet another reminder that Rea is gone and that being alone has many downsides.

It's about 20 minutes until midnight. I'd meant to make an entry earlier but kept forgetting. I've always been easily distracted, but it seems like it's gotten worse. Is this how Rea felt early in her progression? I know I've returned to that possibility multiple times. It's hard not to worry about it given what Rea went through and that she didn't have the genetic predisposition for CJD. Maybe the two of us ate something bad on that trip to Mexico we took a few years back to see Phish.

10 April 2021

I have a theory that some of my inability to concentrate is due to lack of sleep. I prefer that theory to the CJD one.

———————

I've been feeling extra clumsy today. Which is one of the early symptoms Rea experienced. Life is a roller coaster. Or mine is anyway.

I hate anxiety. It's an excuse as much as it is a condition. I have a lot of trouble getting things done when the world doesn't operate the way I expect and people don't follow through on the things they tell me. That last bit sounds a bit more like Asperger's. When a lot of things don't go as planned, my mood and productivity plummet. I'm in one of those phases now.

I still haven't figured out how I'm going to get the motor home. I could ask Rea's family but I hate to bug people. My mother was a very independent person and I guess it rubbed off on me.

11 April 2021

My life keeps advancing slowly into the future. I feel as if I'm just marking time.

The virus is receding despite increased infections. Between the vaccine and better treatments, fatalities have declined significantly.

A lot of people continue to believe that managing to minimize the spread over the past year proves it wasn't a big deal. I hope that the human race isn't the best the universe has to offer intelligence-wise.

12 April 2021

I'm trying to keep some momentum going today. The weather is supposed to be on the wet side which makes dealing with Marley needing to go out a bit of a pain. The backyard is essentially a wetland/bog.

Momentum maintained. I managed to book an Uber and picked up the RV.

I also found out I have no medical insurance benefit via Rea since I wasn't using her insurance when she passed. Which is basically a crock of excrement but there isn't much I can do about it at this point. I will have my own benefit, but it only pays 50%. Still a lot better than nothing.

13 April 2021

I haven't mentioned the virus much recently. It continues to be an issue, but one that is more under control. Or I should say it would be under control if people weren't willfully stupid, but that is a human foible that the United States has chosen to make a core competency for some reason. It's also self-correcting in the long term, but damage will be done along the way unfortunately.

The news coming from Russia/Ukraine is very concerning as well. Putin is nobody's fool, but he's pretty much exhausted his ability to gain additional power within the existing confines of his country so now he wishes to expand. A well-placed bullet would solve that problem but he's likely too smart and experienced for that to be likely.

I suspect some will be offended by that last paragraph if this is ever read by anyone other than some number of present/future AIs.

Heck, maybe one or more of these hypothetical AIs would be offended as well. I'm not going to apologize, though. There are people who on balance make the world a worse place and Putin is firmly in that camp. He is an evolutionary regression, albeit an extremely successful one.

I need to make progress on getting the RV ready for the big trip west and work on getting the house in order.

———————————

Today has been a tougher one. Not horrible, but not as good as the past few weeks. It's only five days until the three-month mark, so that probably has something to do with it.

I was thinking about our last Phish shows. That would have been New Year's 2020. More specifically, I was thinking about how I finally talked Rea into putting our extra tickets up for sale at something other than face value. I remember feeling a bit smug at the time but in retrospect it was just another early sign of the erosion of her mind. She'd always been very firm on charging face value prior to that.

In my defense, I had no issue selling at cost or trading extras to friends or people she or I had regular interactions with. My issue was with people who would then turn around and sell at a premium. I'm a cynical person and I suspect it happened.

14 April 2021

I remember that sleep wasn't a big deal in the first few months after Rea's diagnosis. I'd be out like a light soon after my head hit the pillow. I was emotionally and physically exhausted.

These days I continue to have trouble sleeping more than six hours a night. It's been weeks since I averaged more than that.

———————————

I just got a voicemail from the people who did the autopsy on Rea saying the report is ready and that they have sent a copy to the doctor who leads the study at UCSF that we participated in initially. I'm contemplating whether I want to contact them for a copy.

When my dad died I remember looking at the first page or so of the autopsy report and going "Nope, can't read this".

But I'm kind of curious as well. The autopsy report might give some clues as to how her CJD progressed.

I just realized that it's been right around a year since we got Rea's formal diagnosis. That might have something to do with my recent downward mood trend.

Tangentially related, I've misplaced the folder with the copies of her death certificate. I have a picture of one of the official copies, but I know they are all somewhere in this house. It's annoying that I can't find them.

15 April 2021

Marley can be a bit of a brat, but she's good company and we are certainly friends. I offer the following photograph as proof.

I woke up after sleeping for five hours again this morning but I was able to get to sleep for another hour or so. Hopefully I'll be less fuzzy headed today.

I was very productive yesterday. I got a bunch of recycling organized and put out and learned a decent amount about the motor home. The recycling was one of the things I'd punted on during Rea's decline and after her passing as well. So I have a lot of it stored in the garage in kitchen trash bags. It just needs to be sorted.

I've worked my way through maybe 20% of it at this point (assuming the trash people take it all today) and only have two or possibly three more pick-ups before I leave so there will probably be some left in the garage when I head west.

———————

Final total on my sleep last night, at least according to my Fitbit, is just under 6.5 hours. I can't complain about that, though I'm still tired today.

16 April 2021

The Johnson & Johnson version of the vaccine got put on hold a couple of days ago, Which is the version I received. Apparently six people out of 7 million had blood clots. One was fatal I believe.

I'm kinda amazed they would suspend things given those numbers, but I suppose there are readily available alternatives even if they do require a second shot.

The RV is an adventure. So many little details to learn and remember. The slide out for instance will only work if the emergency break is set and the vehicle is running. Oddly, I think it is possible to drive the RV with the slide out in the extended position but I'm not going to test that theory.

17 April 2021

One day until three months.

Today I'm going to do some more prep work for the big trip, a bit of house cleaning, and make some music. I also plan on sleeping in the RV tonight.

———————

Another fairly productive day, though the plan to sleep in the RV has been delayed a night. Marley and I did spend a couple of hours out there this evening.

I did a bunch of prep to make an update to a thread on the Phish.net forum tomorrow.

I also got some music related stuff done with more to come tomorrow. The house is in much better shape, but I still have a lot of work left.

18 April 2021

It's just after midnight. I was about to go to sleep when something occurred to me.

I really miss sleeping with and lying next to Rea. This thought has nothing to do with sex. Just knowing and being able to feel that there is somebody nearby is a special thing.

I may be single for the rest of my life, but even if I'm not I'd have to at least be in my 80s before I would have spent as much time with another woman as I did with Rea.

That longevity of cohabitation has a quality all its own. It's hard to explain I guess, but it's a bit like you become one half of a whole. You're still individual people, but you operate as a unit and in a sense people who know you think of you in that way as well.

That cohesion was eroding a little as early as a year or so before Rea's diagnosis, but it survived right until the very end. That bit that was still there in those final days was the love.

———————

It turned out to be a fairly good day. I was sad at times but I managed to make progress on several music-related projects and I made my posting to the Phish.net forum thread I had started two months ago.

I also managed to take a nap which helped get my sleep into the lower end of acceptable for the past 24 hours.

I ordered delivery from KFC via DoorDash for dinner. I have a bunch of leftovers and it was tasty. It's probably been nearly 30 years since I last ate KFC. It won't be another 30 before I have it again.

I need to limit my intake if I don't want to continue to balloon weight-wise. Back when I was in my mid-20s I shot up to 170 after subsisting on KFC for several months. Keep in mind my typical weight was about 150 at the time. These days I'm tipping the scale at just over 180. I lost a bit of weight after Rea died, but I'd gained a bunch during her decline.

19 April 2021

Hopefully this will be a good week. Showering would certainly encourage that outcome. The walk-in shower/tub we had put in after we bought the house was useful to Rea for about two months. Which made it worthwhile, but it's the only shower in the house and it's a bit of a PITA for me since the hot water heater doesn't have enough capacity if I want to fill the tub. It's not a very good shower either since there is no curtain.

So, since I seldom go out and nobody comes over I have ample excuses to be lazy until I start to smell myself. Yeah, gross.

Adulting isn't for the faint of heart. Especially senior adulting. Technically I'm not a senior by AARP standards until the end of the year when I have my 55th birthday.

One difficulty in writing a novel for me is that I second guess every word. This is not an issue when I'm writing lyrics but becomes a major impediment when I'm working on longer text forms.

Another productive day. It would have been more productive if the vacuum cleaner hadn't broken, but it did. Nothing is made to last these days and it's frustrating.

Marley and I are out in the RV. I think it is going to go well. I'll know in the morning.

20 April 2021

No issues sleeping in the RV overnight. It was a good dry run/test.

Marley has a giant kennel in the house that won't fit in the RV but she has a decent-sized one that does. I occasionally let her take naps with me, but I don't want her sleeping on the bed at night. She's already very dependent on me and giving her a bit of time alone just seems like a good idea.

I still post a picture of Marley every day on FB. I've been doing that since soon after we got her. Here's today's picture along with the text.

"Some of you may recall that Marley's name has a link to the band Phish. Trey Anastasio, the guitar player and primary singer/songwriter, had a dog named Marley early in the band's history. That Marley traveled extensively with Phish as they slowly built momentum.

"Piper", a Phish song, was runner up in the naming.

Phish has a song called "Joy" that I don't recall us considering. I'm not sure why, as it would have been a very good choice.

It might have been because she was named before we got to know her.

Joy is one of my favorite Phish songs and Rea liked it as well. The song is reflective and a bit melancholy at times.

Marley smiles a lot, but she isn't one dimensional and can look serious and sad as well.

I've heard it said that we have to be sad sometimes to make the joy that much sweeter.

I don't know, maybe that's true. It doesn't really matter what I think, though, because I'm just one person living in a very big and complex world that I have essentially no control over.

I seldom feel helpless. Frustrated, yes. Sad, oh yes. But I have my faith and I know from experience that there is joy. Marley is a daily reminder that this is true."

Speaking of Marley, I need to let her out since the rain seems to have stopped.

21 April 2021

Night two sleeping out in the RV. I think we'll spend the next couple of nights in the house. I haven't heard any complaints from Marley, so I think she did well again.

The Derek Chauvin/George Floyd thing is another chapter in an ongoing American tragedy. The enemies of this country (I'm looking at you, Putin, though you are not alone) love this.

My take? The police are not paid to be judge, jury, and execution-er. Chauvin's life was not in danger. No serious crime had been committed and Floyd was under control long before he died.

Add in the legitimate fears of black Americans and it's easy to see how these situations go bad given the experience of Army 2nd Lt. Caron Nazario last December.

Gotta love the north country. This was taken 15 or so minutes ago.

It's still coming down. I'm going to guess it will be gone by the end of the day but having snowfall and sticking this late tells me I was right to delay my departure to the west coast until the second week of May.

Apparently it's been known to snow on Mother's Day. That factoid will be filed under "Things I wish I didn't know".

Moderately productive day overall. I'm mostly ready for the weekend trip and have made good progress on getting ready for the big trip.

22 April 2021

The snow should be gone by the end of the day. Trash and recycling pick-up today, so a bunch of detritus has been removed from the premises.

Holly Bowling posted a documentary on the making of her "Wilderness Sessions" videos last year. Five minutes in I got emotional because I knew Rea would have loved to watch it.

It's weird how I can go from being kind of okay to feeling like I just lost her again in an eye blink.

Marley almost always runs up and comforts me when this happens. It's an antiquated saying, but she's a peach. Bonus, she's even kinda colored like a peach.

23 April 2021

Another six-hour night sleep-wise. These days I'm just happy when I sleep that much.

Final prep time for the drive down to the Watkins Glen area.

I checked Google Maps and it should be about three and a half hours. I'll plan on leaving here mid to late afternoon.

24 April 2021

Good day today so far. Marley did get a bit car sick yesterday but otherwise the trip here went very well.

We went on a five-mile hike today. I somehow managed to survive and Marley did very well. Ah, to be young again. Our friends Steve and Laura have been great hosts and we are very lucky.

25 April 2021

It's too early to tell how sore I'm going to be from the hike yesterday. I took some over-the-counter pain relievers when I got back which should help.

Today I think we're going to go to the Corning glass museum.

The solar panels in the RV are nice. In combination with the batteries it's possible to have lights and power/charge the various electronic items. For some reason, though, most of the outlets don't work even with the inverter. I'll need to investigate that.

The propane tank seems a bit small. Four or five days of keeping things tolerable at night in a cold climate would be enough to finish it off. I have a small space heater coming that may offer a decent alternative when plugged into shore power.

The trip to the Corning glass museum was fun but a bit sad, especially at the start when I realized that Rea wasn't there to enjoy it. This was my first trip to an attraction/museum without her. It was good to have friends along to blunt the pain.

Marley and I made it home just fine thankfully with the exception of the parking break being a PITA. It's a very bad design and known to be unreliable.

26 April 2021

I've cried a bit more in the past few days than I had in a while. It was good to visit with friends, but the strong association with Rea apparently made my grieving a bit more front and center. This isn't a bad thing.

It is likely good for me in the longer term and it makes the depth of my feelings increasingly clear. I can't help but wish I'd been better at showing them while she was still here but neither one of us was good at that. As with so many things in life, it is what it is.

Marley has a grooming today. I almost forgot. Thankfully I saw a reminder.

27 April 2021

Marley came back looking fancy.

They love her at the grooming place. She's not exactly a manly man dog, but she's a good company and I'm old enough that I don't let stupid crap like that impact me.

I've been taking pictures of the moon with my cheap new ultra-zoom lens. Here are a couple of the results:

Today is more prep work for the trip. Laundry and general clean-up. I managed to mow the lawn yesterday, but it looks like it could use some touch up. I'll blame being out of practice on that.

28 April 2021

I was reasonably productive yesterday. It's starting to feel like I'll make it before Mike C gets here, but I'll probably be running around like crazy for the last day or two.

Sorting through Rea's stuff still makes me cry.

I think it always will. Though if I'm going to be exact, I'd say it's more on the weeping side of things if I don't stop after a bit.

The guest room is nearly ready. Technically it's the master bedroom, but since I'm living in the basement and it's the only other room with a bed, it's now a guest room.

Lots of thunder and lightning last night and this morning, but it's just been wet since then. Rea loved thunderstorms. Probably because they were common around here.

30 April 2021

I just realized that I didn't post yesterday. Wow.

I did go out for breakfast and bought some plastic bins and a couple of other things.

It's been rainy and wet for several days now.

Mother's Day is coming up. As I get closer to fully dealing with Rea's passing, I'm starting to feel the loss of my mother more.

I think I'm in one of my down phases right now.

Preparation for the trip is going well, but I suspect it will get a little crazy after Mike C gets here and final preparations begin.

I'm really tired. I think part of it is I'm in the lower range of my cycle. I almost never notice unless I'm near the bottom or occasionally near the top. Thank God my range is manageably narrow. It's still a pain, though, when my cycle coincides with my non body chemistry-related mood.

I think I broke the vacuum again. Or more correctly, it was still broken but I didn't realize what the problem was before it shut off. It appears there is a blockage which is causing it to overheat.

Maybe I'll take a nap.

Chapter 15

(May 2021)

1 May 2021

I didn't end up taking a nap.

Another month, and T-1 days until Mike C is scheduled to arrive.

The weather is sub-optimal right now with high winds being a thing. Hopefully it will improve before his flight tomorrow

---

I'm still not feeling very energetic. I'll be fine in regards to preparation, though. If I manage to get out of bed soon.

2 May 2021

I did manage to get out of bed yesterday. I didn't manage to get as much done as I should have either yesterday or this morning, but the house isn't a total disaster. I'll be heading to Syracuse in an hour to pick up Mike C at the airport.

I think Marley is going to have a lot of fun over the next few weeks. Having somebody else around will help with her socialization.

3 May 2021

Mike C arrived close to on time yesterday. It rained a bit on the way down to Syracuse.

Marley managed to accidentally draw blood from him when he bent over and she was jumping up acting like a spaz. Her teeth scraped the bridge of his nose. She was in no way meaning to be violent. Doggy grins feature a lot of teeth, though.

She'd mostly settled down by the end of the day, but she'll probably be a spaz again today.

My Fitbit has been dead for a couple of days because I misplaced the charging cable. I have a pair of replacements coming today. The consequence of this is that I don't know how much I've slept the past couple of days. I think I managed six and a half hours last night and probably around five and a half the night before.

4 May 2021

We're making good progress getting ready for the trip. The recycling has all been staged at this point.

I have a call out for yard care. Fingers crossed on that one.

In theory the paperwork for the taxes should be here today. I'm not holding my breath, but I think tomorrow is likely.

5 May 2021

One more day until the scheduled departure time. The pension and tax-related documents I'm waiting for are supposed to be here today. So are a few other trip-related things.

It's been raining a lot recently.

Trip preparations are going well.

6 May 2021

Today is the day we leave, I think. Hopefully all the trash and recycling will be taken in the next few hours.

I managed to find somebody to do the lawn and Rea's friend Gwen generously agreed to drive by once or twice a week on her way home from work to check on the place.

8 May 2021

Yesterday was a good day, but I was a bit tired and didn't make a post. Here is what I just sent to Facebook, including the two pictures I mention in the text.

This is my third time starting this post. It turns out that either Apple or FB have made a change that is very annoying. When I attempt to open a second FB tab in the Safari web browser it gets closed and I get taken back to the original which refreshes. This in turn kills my in-progress post. Very very annoying. It happened last night part way through and I attributed it to me being tired and forgetting to open a new tab. I tried again this morning and it happened again. This time I was sure I'd opened a new tab and I eventually figured out what had happened.

Marley is a golden doodle. The amount of poodle and golden retriever varies a bit from dog to dog. Marley is about 60% poodle. Personality wise she is 90% golden. This is a good thing as my impression of poodles is that they can be willful and a bit obnoxious.

Marley's inner poodle comes out big time on walks. Some of this is a lack of training and experience but it is night and day in terms of her baseline behavior in that and most other activities which can be a bit jarring.

As I mentioned in another post, Mike C offered to accompany me on this trip. Mike and his wife Laura first met and became friends with Rea in the early 1980s when they all arrived in California around the same time.

We're making brief stops along the way, mostly to visit national parks. One of the stops yesterday was Cuyahoga Valley National Park.

We decided to go on a short mile plus hike around Brandywine falls. It had been raining all day and I debated whether or not to leave Marley in the RV. In the end I decided to take her along. This was in retrospect a mistake.

The ground was very wet and muddy and she was dragging me along and nearly making me fall the whole first half of the hike. At times I had to pick her up and carry her just to make any progress. Thankfully Mike was there

274

and generously offered to take her off my hands about halfway through. I was exhausted at that point.

The first half of the trail was a moderate decline. The second half inclines back up to the parking lot. I'm not in super great shape right now and making it back up to the parking lot after the ordeal Marley put me through in the first half of the walk was exhausting but I made it.

The first picture in this post is Mike C with Marley, a bit more than halfway through the walk. Notice how muddy she is and that mischievous grin on her face? I blame her inner poodle for that.

She wasn't the only one who was muddy. Between having to carry her and her jumping on me several times during the walk I was carrying around a fair bit of mud as well.

The second picture is from a few hours later at a gas station along the way. Notice how calm an angelic she looks?

Her somewhat bipolar personality can be challenging to deal with at the poodle end of the extreme but with a bit of age and some more training she will hopefully mellow out.

She'll be eleven months old in a couple of days. Given her age, her behavior is extraordinarily good on the whole. She almost always sleeps through the night without issue and has since near the start.

She has handled the on the road portion of the trip like a champ and while she could get into a bit of mischief at home (again, I blame her inner poodle. (:))she was generally a great companion who has brought me a lot of comfort since Rea's passing.

9 May 2021

Day four of the trip. We were in Joplin MO last night. The KOA there is a wee bit sub-par for the chain in general. Lots of rain overnight and a bit of thunder and lightning. Today we're heading further south to Amarillo, Texas.

Marley continues to be an awesome dog. So long as there are no walks involved anyway.

Ended up in Amarillo today, lots of driving tomorrow as well.

It's supposed to rain here tonight. We can't get away from the rain it seems.

Tomorrow Marley will be 11 months old.

10 May 2021

Happy 11-month birthday to Marley. She'll get to spend it mostly on the road as we have a 500 or so mile drive today.

I'm trying to figure out whether to go to California before heading to Washington. I think I will but need to decide by tomorrow morning at the latest.

Mike C and I have had some good talks along the way. I spent three-plus months hardly interacting with other human beings and most of the past year isolated to one degree or another. That isolation was both mental and physical. The former being because of Rea's illness and the later due to COVID.

One of the things we've talked about is the Rea's Song foundation. I have all the documents to file 2020 taxes finally and five days to do it in. Once I've done that, I will know how much money I have and feel more comfortable about getting the foundation going.

In particular we discussed the possibilities of encouraging the development of software tools to enable the acceleration of treatments for diseases like CJD.

CJD is especially tricky since it is so rare and acts very quickly. Traditional clinical trials are hard to carry out and the existing processes don't operate at a speed that gives any hope to those who are diagnosed. Barring a miracle drug, of course. A proposed trial that is going to start two years from now for instance will help pretty much nobody who has CJD today.

11 May 2021

We're at Petrified Forest National Park today. It's very nice. Tonight's destination is Kingman, Arizona.

Rea and I never came here and I'm not sure why. She loved the southwest and we went to many of the national parks in this general area. We might have discussed it at some point.

12 May 2021

We're back in California. Still a long way to go.

I had the thought a few days back that one of the (many) things I miss about Rea is the inside jokes we shared over the years. More recently these tended to have Phish-related, like "555" which is a Phish song. Whenever I noticed it was 5:55 I would point this out to Rea. Or "Still Waiting" which is from a Phish lyric. Whenever something seemed to be taking a long time we would text or say that to each other and know what we were referencing.

Speaking of Phish, they have announced a modified summer and fall tour schedule. I need to figure out what we had planned last year and what I want to do. I do want to go to some of the shows, I think.

13 May 2021

We made it to Livermore yesterday evening.

Marley got a little anxious after the cupboard door that the TV is mounted on popped open and something small popped out. She really was a champ overall, especially given the fact that we made the drive in 6.5 days which meant a lot of driving.

Getting to Mike and Laura's and walking out into their backyard was difficult. Many a Friday night gathering had been held there over the years and I spent a lot of time with Rea there. Just thinking about it now makes me emotional. I kind of suspected this would happen. I'm going to face a lot of this going forward.

———————

Bad internet seems to be my lot in life right now. Good internet is not nearly as common as the big tech companies pushing "The Cloud" seem to think.

———————

Mike C and I may go over to the apartment today. It'll depend somewhat on his schedule.

14 May 2021

We made it over to the apartment Rea and I rented in Livermore yesterday and to the storage unit as well.

I'm at the rental now, taking a break. I've managed to pack a bit and will pack more before I head out for the day.

It's Friday, and that often meant "Friday night get together" in the past. It's an event that has been held regularly for many years at the home of one of two couples here in Livermore.

COVID has greatly curtailed that for the past year, but it's happened a few times outdoors and socially distanced.

Rea and I went to a special "Friday night" get together before leaving for what would be her last time. I think I mentioned that occasion in last year's journal.

Tonight will be my first time ever going alone. Rea and I always went together. It'll be a bit tough, but I have to deal with these moments if I don't want to become a complete shut in.

I'm still working on and off at the apartment. Going through Rea's stuff is still something I can only do so much of at one time.

Friday night was good. A bit uncomfortable, but Marley had a good time.

15 May 2021

More work at the apartment. My progress is a bit slow. I should have all the emotionally difficult stuff dealt with tomorrow. I bawled my eyes out a few times today. I miss her and I am so sad for her that she isn't here. I know that she and I will meet again, but that doesn't help much in the here and now.

16 May 2021

It's been cool here the past few days.

Marley is having the time of her life, getting to hang out with new people and dogs. She's doing very well. She is the coolest dog around so far as I'm concerned.

To be honest, I'm working about 10 minutes of every hour I'm here at the apartment.

The task is draining and I'm prone to leaving things until the last possible minute.

I need to get over to the storage unit soon and do some organizing as it's a bit of a mess.

17 May 2021

I am not enjoying going through the apartment and packing. It is so hard. Seeing the Phish stuff, some of which is valuable monetarily and all of which reminds me of her, is hard. I miss her even when I'm not constantly reminded that she is gone.

Dealing with the house in Washington is going to be torture.

The clock just hit 12:15pm. It's my daily birthday time.

Small distractions are still distractions.

The thing that haunts me the most is Rea saying she was scared. I was scared, too, and I'm still scared. Scared that I didn't do as good a job as I should have. Scared that I let her down. Scared I'm going to spend the rest of my life alone. Scared even that maybe I won't. Or that I'll die of CJD or some other form of dementia.

I'm scared of many many things.

18 May 2021

I almost missed making an entry today. Four months. I posted a picture of a flower to FB without mentioning Rea, but it was for her. I made a brief posting on the Phish forum as well in the thread I started two months ago.

I'm continuing to get better at dealing with her death, but only in the sense that I'm dealing with it more honestly, which hurts even more actually.

19 May 2021
The apartment is nearly ready to be emptied.

I cried/bawled a bit this afternoon. I found the used tickets from the final Phish show we went to on New Year's Eve 2020. I didn't cry immediately but it was inevitable given the context.

Looking back, there was so much foreshadowing, but I know I've talked about that in this journal before.

20 May 2021
I picked up the van and need to call the charity place I have in mind to see if they are taking furniture currently.

Giving stuff to charity is still a bit more challenging than before COVID. I have a place in mind tomorrow that will hopefully take the bulk of the stuff I want/need to get rid of.

21 May 2021
I have some stuff loaded onto the van and will be heading over to SVDP at 10:30 when they open. Fingers crossed they will take everything. Otherwise I may have to rent an additional unit to stash this stuff in. Hopefully not.

22 May 2021
Somebody recommended a book on dealing with grief to me recently. It talks about the sixth stage of grief, which is finding meaning.

I haven't gotten very far, but I'm already thinking that my particular brand of grief dealt with this issue very near the start when I decided to start a charitable foundation in Rea's name.

I thought I had more to say on that topic but perhaps not?

Inertia is one of my biggest challenges. I have always been a borderline shut in and I'm at the stage in my life where that will either take root or be fought.

I went to a nearby restaurant for breakfast after taking Marley out and giving her breakfast.

She's been eating a lot more over the past week. I don't know if it is a late growth spurt or if she's just in a better mood due to all the socialization. She's such a good dog.

24 May 2021

I'll be heading north shortly.

Mike C will be coming along as well for a few days.

We made it out of town by 7am and are north of Williams right now. It's about a quarter till 10.

Truth is a funny thing. Some people have a very elastic definition based on my observation. Basically, truth is whatever they decide it is and the facts don't matter at all. I don't get that. I always try to seek truth, even uncomfortable truths. I don't think that makes me a saint or anything, and I don't think it's false humility when I say it makes me kind of stupid. Life is a lot easier when you can go with the flow and just relax.

Thinking just causes problems.

We made it by about 8:15pm. I'm in bed now and it's just short of 10pm.

I'm exhausted. I'm back someplace Rea and I shared time in and her stuff is all over. It would be easy to cry, but I'm holding off on that for now.

The drive was good. Not too much wind and we switched off enough that it wasn't too taxing. Still, a 12-hour day in the RV is a stretch even for two people.

I don't have a good guest set-up in the house so Mike is sleeping out in the RV.

We'll likely do the tourist thing the next couple of days and then Mike is heading back on Thursday. It's Monday today.

25 May 2021

I think I slept about five hours. My watch would know.

I'm not sure why it was so hard to sleep. Probably the stress of the drive plus being back here in Washington. Not much I can do about that I guess other than continue to work through the emotions and grief.

Tentative plan is to go to Multnomah Falls today.

26 May 2021

We didn't get to Multnomah Falls yesterday. The plan now is to stop by there on the way to dropping Mike off at the Amtrak station in Portland.

I think I've decided to sell the house in Watertown. I'd been giving it some serious thought for a couple of days now and came to the conclusion just a few minutes ago that Watertown is the house we bought for Rea to die in, White Salmon is the house we bought to live in. That's a very important difference.

Per her wishes I need to spread some of Rea's ashes out back. I think I'll prepare for that today and maybe do it tomorrow.

———————————

A couple days back I took Rea's urn down from where I've been storing it in the RV and hugged it for a while.

27 May 2021

I continue to be more sad for Rea than I am for myself. I loved her and we had many great times together, but my life has continued and hers is over.

I will miss her always and I miss her a lot now, but at some point I'll have built myself a new life. That is so unfair. She had family and many friends who miss her. That collective loss of experience and sadness is what wears on me more than anything else.

28 May 2021

I took Mike C to the Amtrak station yesterday. He's getting close to the San Francisco Bay area right now. It's 5:40am. I went to bed a bit earlier than normal.

I still haven't prepped for spreading a portion of Rea's ashes. I need to do that soon. I was thinking of including others but right now I think I'll do it early in the morning by myself. Most likely this weekend.

———————

Intellectually I know I'm very lucky in some ways but it's hard to accept when I'm still here and Rea is gone. Faith is important, but it doesn't magically make things better. That takes work and time.

I think I'm in a down phase right now.

I'll express my thanks once again that my mood swings are relatively mild. They still suck, though, particularly the down part of the cycle.

29 May 2021

I don't know how anyone could deal with this kind of pain without holding it at arm's length at least some of the time. I've talked a lot about how much I did that when Rea was still here and while it's lessened since then, I now realize I'm still doing it to a degree. I don't think I'll ever stop completely.

How much I do this varies a lot depending on my general mood and circumstances. I know though that the grief is there if I open myself up to it even a little. Sometimes this happens even when I don't mean it to or expect it.

30 May 2021

Another month is nearly in the books and the weather is finally starting to heat up. It's supposed to be in the mid-90s on Tuesday and Wednesday here.

I've started to plan the trip back south. Lots to get done between now and then, and I am making progress. It's Memorial Day weekend though so some things are on hold and will be until Tuesday.

———————

I've been sorting through stuff today. Primarily Rea's clothes. I think I've mentioned before how much Rea loved clothes. She had a very casual and easy -going style, but it became clear to me during her illness that she thought deeply about what she wore every day. One of the disappointments she mentioned during her decline was being unable to do the kind of color and style matching she loved, particularly while we were traveling in the RV and her choices were limited.

Life is Good, Lands' End and L.L. Bean shirts all made up substantial parts of her wardrobe and she bought dozens or perhaps a hundred or more shirts every year. Most got worn once or twice, but a few favorites stayed in the rotation regularly.

Even though I knew this, I didn't realize how many shirts she had. She'd been purging on and off for years, but I suspect the final count when I'm done will be in the several hundred.

————————

Rea also loved puzzles. Me, not so much. We finished a 1000-piece puzzle at the California apartment before we headed north for Rea's last trip to Washington. In Washington we had two puzzles in progress.

The first is a 1000-piece 4th of July themed teddy bear puzzle. We got as far as the outer edges plus a few sections here and there. Rea was already losing the ability to deal with something that complex. And between my indifference to puzzles and my emerging difficulty in dealing with her condition, we stalled. I've managed to make some progress on that one since getting back here.

The other is a double-sided 1000-piece puzzle with Carl and Elle from Pixar's *Up!*. One side has them young and the other as an old couple. We were working on the second side but hadn't even gotten the edge completely together, though we had some other small sections. This one is really difficult. It's also emotionally challenging for me since in *Up!* Elle has died and Carl is alone as the movie's main story begins.

I want to complete both of them but it's going to be difficult. The Pixar one especially.

Rea wanted some of her ashes spread here at the house in White Salmon. I took a bit of time this evening and placed some of her ashes in a separate bag. Tomorrow is Memorial Day, and though she was not a veteran it feels like dawn will be a good time to spread the portion I separated out. It's also Monday, and she died on a Monday.

Being here without her makes me sad at times. Being in New York in the house where she died made me sad as well. Places hold memories, but those memories live inside my head. She's always with me, no matter where I am.

———————

I think the thing that makes being here a little harder than New York or Livermore is that the only life I had with Rea in New York was post diagnosis and when I was last in Livermore, I didn't sleep at the apartment.

Here in Washington Rea and I had a normal life together. It wasn't for very long, but it feels different sleeping in a bed that the two of us shared in a house where we made plans and had dreams of the future.

31 May 2021

My watch said it was one minute after 5am when I woke up. Within five minutes I was outside spreading a portion of Rea's ashes. North, south, east, west, and centered. A small portion at each point. Official sunrise is 5:20 today but the sun was starting to work its way above the horizon when I finished at 5:10.

Love you, miss you, sometimes want to be with you Rea. But that day will come someday, and I need to be patient.

———————

Living in a tourist area is a mixed blessing. Great restaurants and lots of things to do but too many people on busy weekends.

I've been keeping a low profile because of the crowding but will be going out and about tomorrow. Maybe both breakfast and lunch away from home.

Time to take Marley outside and get her breakfast.

———————

I have nearly seven big plastic bins of Rea's clothing sorted to go to charity, plus a couple more for possible sale or quilt making.

Starting with her clothes was an okay idea. I'm doing some combination of crying, shaking my head, and laughing as I go through everything.

She really loved her clothing, and many of the shirts had slogans or commemorated concerts or places we went to.

Chapter 16

(June 2021)

1 June 2021

I dreamed I woke up and looked at my watch and it was 6:30am. Then I really woke up and realized after a couple of minutes that it was really 5:30am. I dream weirdly sometimes.

New month, same old challenges upcoming for the most part.

Now it's 5:55am. Always a magic time.

Two more items from my "To Do" list dealt with. I've been to the postal annex across the river and Marley now has a vet. Her first appointment isn't until July 20. All her shots are up to date through September so that is fine.

I have a couple more items I need to make progress on today, as well as work.

2 June 2021

It gets light really early this time of year. At 5am when I woke up it was already getting light outside.

An hour and a half later, I am at Bette's restaurant in Hood River ordering breakfast.

Rea and I came here frequently in our brief shared time in White Salmon. It was my favorite breakfast place but Rea preferred Egg River.

I'm not having a very good day.

The shirt above is one of Rea's that I found today. At first I thought the bear was a sloth.

The slogan made me sad by itself, but the bear/sloth magnified my grief as either is cute, and as I've noted many times, Rea loved cute stuff.

So yeah, I bawled my eyes out for a bit and I'm teary eyed right now looking at that picture.

I'm going to keep this one. And no, I'm not a masochist.

———————

I sometimes find myself half-thinking that she's just in another part of the house. The reality crashes back in on me.

This was never an issue in New York from what I recall. I think because I saw her take her final breath there. It's hard to fool yourself given that kind of experience.

It's probably good that we only had a little time here in Washington. I don't know that I'd be able to stay here long term otherwise.

3 June 2021

There is a saying that goes "Suicide is a permanent solution to a short-term problem". It sounds good, but it's kinda bullshit. People who are depressed sometimes have long-term problems. Take my situation for example. Rea being gone is a permanent thing, and based on observation and experience I'm never going to completely "get over it."

The upside of having dealt with bouts of anxiety and depression my entire life is that I'm probably okay even though I am deeply depressed at times. Fingers crossed on that one, I guess?

From experience, though, I know that in a few days or so I'll be feeling better. I just need to ride this one out like I've ridden out every pit I've fallen into over the past half-century-plus.

———————

I think I'm going to say "Suicide is a permanent solution to a temporary feeling" going forward.

Of course that doesn't mean the depression never comes back. It does. For most of us it's a normal part of life, but joy is as well, at least for me.

I want my next joy "hit". I'll just have to wait around for it, I guess. It might be a while all things considered, but if I'm patient it will come.

———————

In addition to all the other crap in my head right now I keep remembering Rea telling me she was scared during her illness. I know I've written about this before. I keep agonizing over how I handled those situations. I tried to comfort her, but I don't think it felt like enough at the time and it certainly doesn't now.

Marley has a doggy spa day tomorrow and I'm going to go over to Neil's after that. I have a spot reserved for the RV in the Dufur RV Park. We'll probably come back on Saturday.

The drive is only about an hour, but it'll be a nice opportunity to use the RV and get some more practice camping with it.

In a way we have a limited form of immortality. By that, I mean everyone exists between two points in time. Those of us outside those two points in time can no longer interact with that particular individual, but that doesn't invalidate their existence. They did exist; they will always have existed.

4 June 2021

I dreamed a lot last night. Like most people I don't normally remember my dreams unless I write them down right after waking up. I used to do this. It was interesting to see the odd contradictions and weird themes but eventually I started to dream less and less.

It was weird in a sense. It was like my subconscious didn't want me to know what was going on in dreamland.

I'm looking at borrowing against the equity in the White Salmon home to finance renovations. I've decided I'm going to make this my main base of operations. Rea loved it here and some of my last good memories of the two of us together are here.

As I've mentioned, it's tough being here alone at times but that will hopefully change over time.

Marley and I are in the parking lot of The Dalles Safeway grocery store. This is also where Marley has her grooming appointment. She seemed stressed on the drive over but she's doing fine now that we are here.

5 Jun 2021

I'm in Dufur, Oregon today. Marley and I had a nice visit with my brother's family yesterday after her shearing was done. There will be a bit more visiting today before we head back to White Salmon. I love having the RV available, though it is a challenge in some ways. The power inverter seems to be having issues and there are other problems that are apparently common in RVs.

It's time for me to get out of bed but it's a bit chilly.

Made it out of bed and had a productive day. I was having issues with the inverter in the RV. Basically it wasn't working. With some help from my brother, I located it and pushed the GFCI reset button. Suddenly things were much better.

Why they hide the inverter under a drawer I don't understand, but at least I know where it is now.

6 June 2021

Woke up at 4:30am or so. Marley was feeling sick and threw up a bit on the bed. Nothing serious I don't think. She's seemed fine since.

Lots of rain today including a couple of downpours.

I'm feeling very very tired. It's just after 9pm. I think it's sleep time.

7 June 2021

Breakfast was fine and I picked up my package at the mailbox place.

I slept well last night but still don't feel very good today. I really need to get a few things done, but I'm going to try relaxing and letting go for a few hours because right now my anxiety and frustration are becoming very counterproductive.

Still in a pretty deep funk for sure. It's a good thing I'm heading south on Thursday.

Maybe some more of the numbness has worn off? I keep thinking I'm facing this situation straight on, but maybe I'm still wrong about that. I need some things to go right for a bit. Lots of things, truth be told.

8 June 2021

I sometimes think about relationships in general. I'm a long way from being ready to get back on that horse again, assuming I ever am.

The thing that just occurred to me is that trust is the biggest barrier to love. Well, that and honesty, but they are kind of like salt and pepper.

I think if you have honesty and trust with a person of your preferred gender then love will follow. If both sides feel the same way, then a deep and lasting relationship can evolve from there.

Maybe that's a bit idealized. I don't know.

We all exist somewhere in time. Did I already say something like this? Maybe. No, I'm not on drugs. I'm just being philosophical, and I find it hard to go back and reread anything I've already written here.

No matter what, Rea existed for 62+ years. She and I were a couple for 27 years. Those times did exist and they will always have existed, no matter what happens in the future.

In that way we are all immortal, no matter what happens after we take our last breath.

I'm feeling better this evening. I got a few things done during the day, including sorting through more of Rea's stuff. That is never a mood elevator, but it needs to be done and there is some positive energy from accomplishing that.

9 June 2021

Another day of not feeling good, at least at the start. Time to get moving. Hopefully my outlook will improve as the day progresses.

Kinda tired despite having slept decently.

Maybe I'm depressed in part because my grief has leveled off and I thought it would be more manageable before that happened?

10 June 2021

Marley is one year old today. She's a very good dog.

I'm lucky to have her in my life. She's 95% fun and comfort, and 5% not so perfect. Which is a darned good ratio.

I'm getting ready for both of us to head south for a week or so. First stop will be Klamath Falls and then on to Livermore. Six hours in a single day is as much as I want to drive the RV, or really anything these days.

My mood could be better, but I'm still in the game.

———————————

Getting out was a good thing. I'm feeling much better.

Marley and I made it to Klamath Falls without incident. I'm scoping out the route for tomorrow currently. Most likely I'll stop for lunch in Redding.

I think I'm going to try traveling a bit starting next month, assuming I can get things kinda in a good place. Montana would be a neat place to hang out for a bit. Maybe the far northwest of Washington as well. Possibly a trip across the country to see my uncle, aunt, and cousins in Minnesota.

11 June 2021

I woke up at 5:30 which is pretty good for me these days. I'm working on getting out from under the blankets. It's chilly right now, probably in the low 50s in the RV. Marley is being amazingly patient, which is normal for her.

12 June 2021

The drive yesterday was more or less fine. The navigation software brought me in from the north which mildly sucked since traffic can be heavy into Livermore when coming from that direction, especially eastbound on 580. Driving the RV is pretty much second nature at this point, but SF Bay area traffic is no joke and avoiding it whenever possible seems like the best option.

My mood is okay today. I think I'm pretty much 100% over the numbness which means I'm having to deal with the reality of Rea's passing in full. Which is really, really hard.

There isn't anything I can do though so I'm just going to have to keep going.

13 June 2021

I continue to be mildly to moderately "triggered" when I go places that Rea and I frequented. It comes with the territory, though, and I'm doing my best to just deal with it. I miss her more than I ever could have imagined. She deserved so much better. As I've observed many times, though, life isn't intrinsically fair.

I'm in a place mentally where I don't really care if I live or die. I'm still trying to be smart in my life choices but if I found out I had a terminal disease tomorrow I don't think it would change my mood much. I have a list of things I'd want to deal with before the end and I'd probably try to do something fun?

One of the few songs I can finger pick on the guitar semi decently is "Dust in the Wind" by the band Kansas. Rea was not a fan. We talked about it a bit at one point and she just didn't like the message. I disagreed, but I see her point. I think this verse is a pretty good summary ...

> *Now, don't hang on*
> *Nothing lasts forever but the earth and sky*
> *It slips away*
> *And all your money won't another minute buy*

In the end, the fact that we had great healthcare and were decently well off didn't matter at all. Medically there was nothing to be done, and COVID significantly reduced our ability to enjoy her final days.

14 June 2021
A Life Well Lived & Greatly Missed

That last section is the epitaph I'm having engraved on Rea's memorial marker. In theory it will look like this.

Getting through the process of ordering the stone was tough for all the reasons I've already talked about at length.

I can tell how bad my mood is by how much I hesitate when I think about the possibility of swapping places with Rea. When I'm on the positive end, I pause a bit before deciding I'd do it. Maybe that is selfish but it's true. When I'm on the negative side I don't hesitate at all.

It's been a while since I hesitated.

16 June 2021

California ended most COVID-related restrictions a couple of days back. I heard that about 70% of Californians have had at least one vaccine shot. We'll see where this leads.

It's supposed to be 100+ degrees here the next few days. I plan on heading out Friday night or Saturday morning. I need to be back in White Salmon by the 20th.

18 June 2021

Five months.

My general mood sucks. This is translating into my typical lack of productivity. The 100+ degree heat isn't helping.

I'd originally planned to leave tomorrow, but it looks like I'm going to have to stick around a bit longer.

19 June 2021

Today I will make progress. Some sort of progress.

Yesterday I was going through photos of Rea and came across one of us in front of a Christmas tree in downtown Livermore. It was taken two or three years ago with my phone. The iPhone pictures can be "live", meaning it captures a bit of video and several additional still pictures with each image captured. Rea was in the middle of laughing when I took the photo I was looking at and the picture caught a second or two of that, both video and audio. I got to smile and cry at the same time.

I finally downloaded the pictures from Rea's phone. She took very few over the years. Mostly her photo album contained images she had screen captured.

I don't like to whine, but looking at those pictures and thinking about that is at least 90% as hard as it was the day after she passed. I know I need to move on, but it's just not happening very quickly at all.

But I can do this. I have to. I don't always want to, but I need to.

———————

I had the worst breakdown that I've had in a while just a bit ago. I feel better now.

I think this is a clear sign that I haven't been doing a very good job of dealing with my grief. I thought that when the daily crying stopped I was on the right path. Now I'm not so sure.

As always, Marley was there to comfort me. She is truly a gift.

20 June 2021

I'm feeling a little better today. Went to breakfast with Mike C. At the start most of the employees were still wearing masks, but by the time we were done a lot of them had taken off their masks. Customers were a mix, but it seems like the tide is turning.

21 June 2021

Still feeling better today. It's Monday, and Mondays are always more of a challenge but hopefully I'll at least maintain.

Sometimes it feels like I don't dream for months. Other times it feels like I dream regularly. I've thought a lot about dreams. I don't really know what they are, but I've always liked them.

Mostly I dream in color. I think it would be strange to dream in black-and-white, but I've heard that some people do. I'm not sure why that would be.

The human brain is a very odd thing. Mine is probably odder than most. Especially before I've consumed my early morning caffeine. I forgot to make tea last night and I want to save the two bottles I have in the fridge for the drive tomorrow.

My plan is to be nearly ready to leave when I go to sleep tonight and then leave early tomorrow morning. I'll stop for the night at a rest stop along the way.

23 June 2021

I left Livermore early yesterday and made it to a rest stop a bit more than an hour south of Bend. It's just before 3:30am and I've been awake for a half hour or so. I went to sleep about nine, I think.

I'm thinking I'll stop in Bend for breakfast and make it home by early afternoon.

Marley and I made it back to White Salmon about 12:30pm, so not bad time at all. I have the RV parked and hooked up. The black and grey water tanks were kinda full. It's nice having a sewage hook up here at the house.

Time is weird. I feel like I'm in a kind of limbo.

Rea and I had lots of plans, but none of them matter now. I've made tentative plans of my own, but it seems like things keep happening that derail me. I've probably said before that I'm not very good at dealing with adversity, at least not in the short term. I eventually pick myself up and keep going.

The days are really long this far north. It's after eight and still bright out. I napped once while waiting for breakfast and once after getting back home. Hopefully I won't have any trouble sleeping tonight.

24 June 2021

I slept decently well last night despite all the napping yesterday. Yay me.

My mood is middling today. I'm thinking that I've been in the real recovery phase for a while now. I wonder how long it will take to get to an okay place?

Maybe I will never get to an okay place. That thought worries me.

25 June 2021

I'm selling the house in New York. I let Rea's family know today. I'd more or less decided a while back, but now it's pretty much a done deal in my mind. I hope the house sells for at least what we paid for it. I'm not expecting much if any profit.

I ended up liking Watertown. It's a nice combination of big city and small town, and the snow and cold really didn't bother me.

At the end of the day, though, I need to cut expenses and I have deeper roots on the west coast.

26 June 2021

Saturday. Not that the days matter too much at this point in my life.

It looks like the high will only be 103 or so today. Currently the forecast is for 109 tomorrow and 111 on Monday. Ugh.

27 June 2021

I'm keeping a low profile today. It's just after noon and the temperature is 99 degrees with the forecast being for another 10 degrees of warming before it starts to cool again.

Most COVID restrictions have been lifted at this point. It's the people who haven't been vaccinated that are mostly at risk, and the majority of them chose that course, so what will be, will be.

I was working on the 4th of July/Teddy bears puzzle that Rea and I started last year before leaving Washington. It's slow going. I end up wanting to talk to her even more than normal when I'm doing that, which makes it a little more difficult to continue than I'd like.

I'm talking out loud more these days. Mostly to Rea but sometimes to Marley. Neither of them answers me in any meaningful way, though Marley at least looks my way most of the time.

I think I'm in recovery as well as mourning, but it doesn't feel like I'm getting better recently. I guess maybe it's all part of the process.

Now would be a great time to sell the place here in Washington based on how hot the market is, but I can only take maybe an hour of sorting through stuff each day before I get too upset to continue. At that rate it's going to take years, and as I've told various people, I need some place to keep my stuff. At least until I manage to downsize the bulk of it, if that ever happens.

It's like I'm in a hole, and there is sand slowly pouring in from all directions. If I shovel a bit I can stay even, if I shovel more than I can start to get ahead. Mostly I'm managing to stay even with occasional days where I move ahead or fall behind.

I was in the bedroom doing something on the computer earlier when I briefly thought that Rea was out in the living room. It's not that I heard anything or really felt that she was there. I was just distracted enough that for a brief moment I forgot she was gone.

Today has been productive. I sorted through several boxes of stuff and managed to do a bit of coding and debugging.

This feels like a day where I made progress.

28 June 2021

It's looking like 110 for the high today was accurate. It's 102 at 1:30pm and the temperature will probably not peak for a couple of hours. It was 80 degrees a bit after 8am this morning. I got my errands done early.

Today I decided I'd work on music-related stuff as well as work of course. I've made some progress on both those tasks.

More coding and work today. And heat. The frigging heat is insane. Record setting if I haven't mentioned that, and not by a little.

Marley is getting bored. It's hard to blame her given how little I've been getting out. She really needs more stimulation.

Arguably, a good thing about the heat is it seems to be helping me sleep. Or maybe I'm just more depressed than normal.

29 June 2021

I'm a creature of habit. I feel most comfortable when I'm doing things in a consistent manner. Oddly, I like new experiences as well. I guess I'm human after all since being contradictory is intrinsic to our natures, or so it seems.

My life is kinda a crap story right now. Rea was always the best part of it and her being gone isn't something that magically gets better. I'm feeling kind of angry. Depressed as well. All part of the seven stages of grief, I guess.

I don't think I've felt this angry before. Maybe that's progress?

30 June 2021

Early in our relationship Rea said to me that one way to show love is to agree to do something that you didn't normally want to do. That always stuck with me. I'm going to count working on the puzzles we started last year as one of those things.

The Disney one I'm ignoring for now. Being two-sided it is nearly impossible for somebody as indifferently skilled as me.

The teddy bear 4thof July one on the other hand is doable. I manage to get a handful of pieces in each day.

Most puzzles start out easy, then get way harder before getting easy again toward the end. This is because there is a point in the process where the easy pieces have been placed and the remaining pieces have so little context that it's impossible to figure out where they go without some form of brute force or meticulously looking at the subtle differences in the shapes of the pieces.

Eventually you get to the point where there are so few pieces left that it gets easy again. That in between period sucks, though, and I think I'm getting close to it on the teddy bear puzzle.

Being alone means I get to decide everything. Rea and I were mostly in alignment on stuff, but there are always going to be disagreements. We were decently good at compromising, which meant I didn't always win. That was a good thing. Now I get to win all the time.

So, as time goes on my life is more and more my own.

I guess it's appropriate that "own" and "alone" rhyme.

Chapter 17

(July 2021)

1 July 2021

Another down day mood-wise. Which is starting to concern me. I need some more things to break my way, that would help.

Rea hated hot dogs and mustard. Without realizing it I had hot dogs with mustard for dinner. I guess this is an example of me creating my own life.

It's not that Rea didn't let me eat hot dogs or mustard, but I could always tell she didn't like it so most of the time I didn't.

I didn't make my dinner choice consciously either when buying these items or choosing to combine them for dinner. When Rea was still here, though, I would have thought about it first.

––––––––––––––––

COVID mask restrictions are largely gone in this part of the country as of today. It's a little weird going into businesses and not seeing employees wearing masks. Hopefully we'll all get used to it and not have to repeat the experience of the past 18 months.

2 July 2021

I'm going to try to build some momentum today.

It's not that I feel like I can't be happy, at least at times. I don't see myself being giddy any time soon, but humans can't live by despair alone.

3 July 2021

I did okay yesterday. I have stuff going on today (grand niece's sixth birthday party) that will get Marley and me out of the house which will be good.

Tomorrow is the 4th of July. My plan is to stay at home and hopefully avoid any major fires.

The spring and summer here have been hot and dry and there is plenty of stuff to burn. Thankfully there are decent fire breaks near the house so fingers crossed, we should be okay even if there is a fire.

I feel like I've gotten better at the guitar over the past five years or so. I'm still very limited, but I have my own style and I can do a few things fairly well. Picking strings in passing being one.

Writing music on the other hand is something that I'm not doing much of. I wrote "Love True" soon after Rea's passing, but that is it. I know I'll write more when my head is in the right place and I have something to say, though.

4 July 2021

Happy Independence Day. Another first, but not one that held any particular personal meaning for Rea and me, so there is no additional pressure there thankfully.

I feel like I'm in a better spot mentally today.

I had a productive morning and I think I'm on track to do well the rest of the day. Fingers crossed.

It's official, today was productive. Nothing is open tomorrow so there are some things that will have to wait until Tuesday.

5 July 2021

I will be heading to New York on the 26th via Amtrak. I paid a lot extra to get a private room for most of the trip. It's just the sleeper room, not the one with a bathroom but it will be nice to have my own space. The trip takes about three days.

I also have a place for Marley to stay. I'm going to have to drive her down to the Bay area before I leave.

Currently it's looking like I'll leave here the Thursday before, arrive down south on Friday and then drive back north on Sunday.

6 July 2021

My head is feeling cloudy today and I'm kinda congested. I think this is just allergies.

Mood-wise I'm okay, but not as good as yesterday.

I ended up taking a few hours of sick leave. I feel better now, but the time has been used, so here I am.

It strikes me that Rea and I kind of provided adult supervision to each other. Basically we curbed each other's bad traits.

In some cases we also curbed each other in ways that weren't optimal.

I'm trying to be balanced in that assessment. I will always regret that I didn't retire when we originally planned and that I wasn't as supportive of her live music and travel pursuits as I could have been, but I had a positive impact in some areas as well and she wasn't without fault either. I forgave her for all that before she passed, and I think she forgave me as well. In the end, we were two imperfect people who loved each other and made a good life together.

I just wish she had lived to enjoy the full measure of the labor, love, and luck.

7 July 2021

It's cloudy today. I got some nice shots of the sky and Mount Hood with my phone when I took Marley out this morning.

8 July 2021

Today ended up being very productive. Lots of boxes were moved, some stuff was sorted, a bench was put back together out in the garage and several minor issues were fixed around the house.

9 July 2021

Today was another productive day. I got up early and went to breakfast. And stopped to check the mail before heading back.

On the way home I cried a bit about Rea for some reason. It still comes on when I don't expect it at times.

The shed is now much cleaner and organized, which means it's possible to actually get inside and walk around.

10 July 2021

Yesterday when I cried on the way home, I think the issue was I'd been feeling happy/fulfilled just before.

I'd been getting a lot done the previous couple of days and I'm on a bit of a roll. It's natural to feel happy in that situation I think. That in turn triggered thoughts of Rea which immediately made me feel guilty/sad.

Grieving is a long and painful process.

Today I spent some time in The Dalles. I went to my dad's grave site for the first time in about a decade.

My mom used to go almost every week before she ended up at the care facility. His marker still looked good. It took me a good 20 minutes to find it. The markers are all flat to the ground and there aren't a lot of landmarks. I'm planning to make it up there once or twice a year going forward. He deserves at least that much consideration. I also need to find out how to get my mom's ashes buried there and a marker put up.

11 July 2021

I realized recently that I'm a lot less afraid of death than I used to be. Maybe that will pass; I don't know. This has nothing to do with any depression I might be suffering from, at least directly.

After the past 18 months I know that life can bring intense and brutal pain. It can also bring joy, as well as everything in between. The thought of having to go through the negative side of that dichotomy is not pleasant. It will wear me down pretty quickly if I have to go there again. Which isn't to say I'd kill myself; I don't think I would. It does mean, however, that I'm not nearly as afraid as I used to be of my own ending.

I hope and pray for a hereafter where sadness is at the very least greatly muted and I can meet all my friends and loved ones again as well.

I'm in no hurry to get there, but I'm not as afraid of the transition as I used to be.

12 July 2021

Oysterhead is a side project by Phish's Trey Anastasio, Les Claypool, and Stewart Copeland who was the drummer for The Police. Rea was really looking forward to seeing them last year before COVID and the CJD diagnosis removed that possibility. She might have even bought tickets. I have no clue where they would be, though, and the shows might have already been played as they have been out on the road for a bit.

I was just thinking that there is really no way to prepare yourself when a loved one is diagnosed with CJD. I know what I went through and where I struggled, but that all came in retrospect and my circumstances were just that – mine.

I often struggle with personal interactions. I think in part this is because my experiences and odd brain have put me a sigma or two outside of the normal range for most people. Often when I look back on social interactions I've had, I discover that I missed some fairly obvious social cues. Some of this is my anxiety making things more difficult. A lot of it is that I just don't have great instincts when dealing with other people.

I do much better when I'm with people I feel comfortable with. I think this is a combination of my anxiety being muted in those situations and the fact that the people I'm with know me. They are either familiar with my idiosyncrasies and able to compensate, or they just don't care.

I just found out that the Phish show I got tickets in the mail for late last week is the first of the summer tour, the first since the COVID-enforced hiatus and the first since Rea's passing. It's in Arkansas. Which is 2/3rds of the way across the country. It is 16 days away. I am so conflicted.

On the one hand, I feel like I need to be there. On the other hand, I haven't even looked for a hotel, and renting a car will likely be impossible.

I've decided I'm not going to make a decision right now. It can wait until tomorrow when I've had some time to calm down and maybe do a bit of research.

13 July 2021

Today I will book my trip to the Phish show in Arkansas on the 28th.

Mission accomplished. The last week of July through mid-August is going to be very busy for me. It's the kind of schedule Rea loved. Me, not so much, but I feel like I have to make it to that show. I owe it to her memory.

To make things a bit easier I booked myself first class. I've never flown first class, so it should be an interesting experience.

Maybe they will play "Divided Sky".

Mood-wise, today has not been good. My anxiety was spiking, likely in part due to the whole Phish situation. Now that I've mostly worked that out, I seem to be doing better.

14 July 2021

I'm doing decently today.

Marley grooming tomorrow.

15 July 2021

I've been prepping a six-month post for the Phish board. I think that will be my final one there, at least for a while.

Cousin's restaurant in The Dalles has been around for somewhere in the neighborhood of 30 years as I type this. I'm having a slightly late lunch after dropping Marley off for her grooming appointment. The old smoking sections are now just separate seating areas. My mom was a smoker until she was forced to quit after being moved into the care facility so she'd always want to sit in the smoking areas back when that was still a thing. It's weird what one can get nostalgic about. I never wanted to because I hated the smoke.

17 July 2021

Tomorrow will be six months.

I've tried not to publicly wallow in self-pity. I'm far from the only one to lose a beloved spouse, and there are many good things going on in my life.

Having said that, I spend a chunk of every day missing Rea. Even more than that, I am sad that her beautiful life ended so early and poorly.

I'm sad for me, but I'm a lot more sad for her and all her friends and family.

I say the following with complete sincerity. If I could, I would trade places with her.

Just to be clear, I do not want to die. I'm not going to claim to be in an optimistic frame of mind most of the time, but I am still eating reasonably well and doing the other things I need to do to maintain my health.

I miss my mother as well, but she was 88 years old, in poor health and unhappy. In so far as anyone can be, I think she was ready to be done.

A few years ago I never would have imagined that I'd lose both of them within less than two months of each other.

The following picture is from August 6 2017. We were in New York City to see Phish on their historic 13-show run at Madison Square Garden.

I did my best to clean it up, but the original was taken by a camera phone in less-than-ideal conditions. Still, I love this picture.

I don't think I've posted it anywhere before. In fact, I think it came from Rea's phone. I imported all of her images recently into my photo library.

This photo makes me smile and get teary eyed all at once.

One of the things we would have done if not for COVID is attend every Phish show we could have.

We had already purchased tickets to several, but they were all canceled or delayed.

The first post-COVID Phish show will be six months and 10 days after Rea's passing. I will be there, and in some sense I know she will be as well.

———————————————

I know things will be better after the 18th. At least for a bit.

Yesterday was not a very good Marley day. She's started peeing in the house and I discovered not one but two puddles out in the living room. I was not happy and she got yelled at. That probably wasn't the best approach but I'm not in the best frame of mind recently. I've gone back to keeping her closely supervised and minimizing the opportunities for her to do the wrong thing.

18 July 2021

I ended up going with something a bit shorter for the FB post …

I wrote an essay yesterday that I was going to post. I meant every word of it, but when I woke up this morning I realized that I could more or less say the same things in a handful of sentences.

Sometimes it's better to be succinct.

This has been a tough day already and it's only 8:15am.

It got different for a while. Then it got a bit easier, but for the past few months the grief has been fairly consistent. At some point I might need to think about professional counseling.

This was a long day. Not a good one, but not horrible. I cried a lot more than I have in a while. I also played "Love True (Rea's Song)" on the guitar for the first time in months.

19 July 2021

I just posted the following comment to the FB thread I created yesterday.

Thank you everyone.

CJD is horrible, it steadily erodes its victims right back to infancy before taking their lives.

It became clear as the disease progressed that Rea was at her core a loving and good person who cared deeply for others.

Her smile, laugh and friendliness were all genuine.

She truly loved her friends and family and did her best to make the world a better place.

She brought stability, adventure and love to the life of an anxious and socially awkward introvert. I was blessed when I met her that she chose to spend her life with me.

20 July 2021

Marley had her vet appointment today. It was just a routine visit. She got high marks for her personality and health, and was her normal over-the-top self.

———————

One of the hardest parts is forgiving myself for all my real and imagined shortcomings.

Last year at this time I'd known Rea's brain was self-destructing for a few months. I was terrified in general and specifically terrified that her decline could accelerate at any time. This in turn caused me to make decisions that were very much optimized for speed. I've lamented some of those choices already in this journal.

To be fair to myself, I did okay. I was emotionally numbed, depressed, and stressed to within a fraction of an inch of my ability to cope and I still managed to make it to the finish line with Rea. There are things I would change if I could, but that is true for me even under the best of circumstances.

Rea's decline was anything but.

21 July 2021

I dragged myself out of the house this morning and went to breakfast down in Bingen. As I was on my way back to the car after, I had to cross the street. I saw myself reflected in the window of a business across the street. I briefly imagined Rea walking beside me, a little out in front. I was almost always more comfortable letting her lead.

———————

Four years ago today was the first show of Phish's baker's dozen run. I was just reminded of this while listening to Phish radio.

———————

I was just looking at the back of my hands and I realized they are starting to look like old man hands.

I'm not that far from being closer to 60 years old than 50 so I guess I shouldn't be surprised.

22 July 2021

"Walls of the Cave" was one of Rea's favorite Phish songs. I probably mentioned that before, but just in case, here it is.

I've booked flights and made a hotel reservation for the Nashville shows. The tickets are lawn, so I'll be able to stay mobile. The hotel is only a five-or-so-minute walk from the venue Phish is playing at.

I requested that work allow me to take six weeks of unpaid leave starting the first week of August. I don't have enough vacation time to do the things I need/want to do over the next month or two, so this seemed like the best compromise.

It looks like my request is going to be granted.

I've started prepping a bit for my travel over the next several weeks. I'll finish prep for the first leg on Saturday and head out, probably in the afternoon.

24 July 2021

I'll most likely leave this afternoon, heading south to drop off Marley and be in a better position to catch my plane on the 26th. I plan to be there mid-afternoon Sunday.

I should probably make/have a list of things to take and do before I leave.

I likely won't bother though. Rea would have.

25 July 2021

The drive down to Livermore went well. Marley and I stopped and slept at a rest stop about four hours into the trip. I got a bit more than five hours of sleep which isn't great but given the circumstances it was enough.

The temperature got down to about 45 degrees overnight, but we were fine. I learned a while back that so long as my feet and head are warm I'll be fine.

Lots to do tomorrow, and a flight out of San Francisco that departs one minute prior to midnight. I need to get a good night's sleep tonight.

26 July 2021

Fairly productive day so far. I think I'm ready for the first leg of my crazy schedule. It's coming up on dinner time and I'll be heading for the airport soon.

Marley seems to be doing well. Fingers crossed that will continue. She's an awesome dog with not a mean bone in her body, but she does have a bit of mischief in her and she is still young.

27 July 2021

The red eye was an interesting choice. I'm in Dallas right now with the final leg scheduled to board in a bit more than an hour. First class was nicer than coach, but not as nice as I'd hoped. I'll blame COVID for some of that since things like blankets and pillows aren't allowed. The fact that it was a red eye also likely played a part.

The flight back on Friday is during a more normal timeframe. It should be a better indicator of what first class is like.

This was my first plane flight since Rea's passing. One thing that has become clear is that I suck at travel arrangements. She loved doing this kind of thing and she was good at it. One more reason for me to miss her.

———————

The Fayetteville area airport was nice. Not very crowded at all and on the small side but modern and clean. I picked up my rental car with no issues and made it to the hotel easily. I'm close to the venue as well.

———————

For some reason I decided to go back and read my entries from the start of this year right through the first few days after Rea's passing. There were some things I'd forgotten. I mentioned playing John Prine's "Angel from Montgomery" at her service, but I had totally forgotten when it came time to put together the soundtrack.

I feel like a writer when I read those entries. There is truth there and a conciseness that I often struggle to achieve.

Years ago I read something that said that fewer words are always best. At the time this seemed like nonsense to me, but now I think I understand.

———————————

The hotel I'm staying at is an extended stay place. I have a suite that includes a separate bedroom/bathroom as well as a small kitchen and living room. I spent a chunk of the late afternoon and early evening catching up on my sleep.

Waking up without Marley was weird. She likes to lay on top of or right beside my legs.

28 July 2021

First Phish show without Rea is tonight.

I slept well last night. Not a surprise given yesterday. I was exhausted. Red eyes that don't last at least five hours are probably not a good idea. Rea would have told me this.

I'm stuck making my own mistakes, though. No safety net. There is no sense of freedom in coming to this realization.

———————————

The pandemic attitude is pretty lax around here. Not surprising given the part of the country I'm in. It will never stop amazing me how prone most of us are to just go with the flow, even when the flow is an undertow pulling us further from safety.

I'm going to be wearing a mask at the show, but while I've been minimizing my exposure otherwise I haven't been bothering with a mask elsewhere. This is a bit foolhardy given what I said above, but I am vaccinated and I'm keeping my hands clean and my time in public to a minimum.

Risk management doesn't mean taking no risks.

———————————

When I first woke up this morning, I wasn't sure if it was a few minutes before 6am or 8am. It turned out it was closer to 8am. My Fitbit watch still hasn't updated. Sleeping until 8am meant I got almost eight hours of sleep last night. Sleep deprivation has an upside I guess.

I'm nervous about tonight. It's going to be very emotional, I suspect, both from the perspective of being the first Phish show since the pandemic started and my first Phish show without Rea. Who would have thought that would ever happen? Not me. It never should have.

I'm hoping I'll find a bit more peace and acceptance by the end of the evening.

———————————

I keep wanting to talk to Rea. It's a bit odd to me that conversation is the thing I miss most about her. Just being around her and being able to ask a question, make an observation, or tell a joke and maybe make her smile or laugh.

The symptoms of CJD snuck up on both of us. Me more than her, I'm sure. She became more introverted, a little less likely to initiate a conversation. Not as quick to understand my weird sense of humor or conversational tangents.

There was a slowly growing unease in the back of my mind that was telling me something was wrong. Of course I didn't have a clue what it was, or that it would take her from me and the rest of the world so soon.

I hate the fact that I'm here alone today. I'm doing this to honor her memory and, as I said above, maybe find a bit of additional peace. I'm not expecting to enjoy the show. That's sad in a way, and hopefully I'm wrong. It's going to be a roller coaster emotionally. I should probably stuff some tissues into my pocket.

———————————

I'm in the parking garage at the venue feeling nervous. I'll make it in, but this whole anxiety thing is very frustrating.

The doors to the venue open in 20 minutes.

29 July 2021

The show was great. People on Phish.net are less enthusiastic about it than I am, but what do they know? The general consensus is that it was solid for a tour opener, though.

It really felt like Rea was there with me.

———————————

As fun as the show was, the weather was unpleasant. Hot and muggy. I was soaked, and while it cooled off a bit after the sun went down it was still in the 70s.

Today is one where I get to relax and get a few things done as well.

———————————

Maybe 10% of people at the concert last night had masks, though the percentage was higher among staff members.

I think one of the things that sets me apart from most people is that I try not to outright reject outrageous things. I don't believe them either. What I attempt to do is evaluate an idea based on the data available to me. For me, most things are shades of gray.

Do ghosts exist? I don't know. I've experienced things in the course of my life that lead me to believe that our understanding of the universe is not complete and that things such as ghosts *might* exist. That doesn't mean I believe they do, just that I'm open to the possibility.

I think this is one of the reasons I'm kinda awkward socially. Observation leads me to believe that I don't interface with the world in an entirely normal way.

Am I a good person? Again, I don't know. I try to be and I have formulated "rules of engagement" that I think are consistent with my Christian beliefs while hopefully being self-consistent as well.

I'm fairly confident in those core beliefs. I'm not sure it's possible to be sane without a solid core set of beliefs.

This whole widower thing is very far from what I've ever wanted. It's a role that I was in no way prepared for. Not that you can prepare for something like this, I guess. At least not if you aren't suffering from some anti-social form of mental illness?

The thing is, and I've said this in various ways several times already … I'm the lucky one. I feel like in some way Rea is here with me, but it's not the same, and even if she does exist in some form, it's not anywhere near the same for her either.

I feel like she and I will meet again. No, I know we will. Attribute that to my faith, but it's a strong intuition as well.

I'm missing Marley. It's only been a few days and I have a few more weeks before I'll be able to pick her up.

This is the first time I've been totally alone in a long while. It doesn't suit me, even if I am an introvert and a bit of a loner.

I'm discovering all sorts of things about myself. I would have been more than fine without this opportunity for personal discovery.

30 July 2021

It's coming up on 1:30am and I'm still awake. Ugh.

———————————

Thankfully I got to sleep not too long after that. I probably slept about six hours which is dent.

Checkout is at 11 and my flight doesn't board until a little after five so I have some time to kill.

31 July 2021

It's a little after 3am local time here in Denver. Why am I in Denver? Because this is where my connecting flight to San Francisco was supposed to leave from. Unfortunately my flight from Fayetteville was very late which completely ate my one-hour cushion and then some.

I managed to get four or so hours of sleep on one of the fancy couches they have near my departure gate (B7).

The only other time I've slept at an airport was about eight years ago when I missed my flight out of SFO up to Portland. That was mostly my fault with a small assist from TSA who were super slow at the security check-point. I was on my way to visit my mom and ended up arriving a half-day late. I don't think sleeping at the airport is anyone's idea of fun.

———————————

I got another 60 to 90 minutes of sleep. I should be okay. Hopefully I'll sleep a bit on the planes. Fresno first, then on to San Francisco. I got switched to gate B12, which is maybe 100 yards from B7, so no big deal.

———————————

I accidentally exited the secured area in Fresno. Which was easier to do than it should have been. My sleep deprivation probably played a part. I had plenty of time to get back through thankfully, but I think I might have lost my Fitbit watch in the process. Ugh.

Chapter 18
(August 2021)

1 August 2021

I just realized that one of the many things I miss about Marley is that now when I speak out loud I am truly talking to myself.

———————

I made it home around 8:30am. Good timing overall.

My flight to Nashville tomorrow is another red eye. Layover in Chicago this time. This will leave me with a bit of time to kill again once I arrive. That's one of the downsides of red eyes since most hotels don't allow check in until 3pm.

I was looking up the trip details to remind myself and saw an ad for a music-oriented wax museum. Rea was not a fan of wax museums. I don't have any strong feelings about them one way or the other, but it was something we didn't do because of her preference.

Given all my hang-ups it didn't and still doesn't bother me.

———————

I've been through all the luggage. I lost my Fitbit Versa 3. I'll have to get a new one. I'm sure the Versa 4 will be out in a month or two, but I basically need the motivation of having a counter on my wrist to do any sort of exercise at all. Sad but true.

Kinda a bipolar day. I think I'm in a low point cycle-wise, but I've been getting a lot done which always gives me a boost.

Or maybe I'm just tired from all the irregular sleep. That isn't going to change for a few more weeks given my schedule.

I tried to buy a replacement watch from one online vendor, but they kept flagging my purchase as fraud in spite of trying a couple of different payment choices. So I bought it elsewhere. I'll pick it up on the way to the airport tomorrow.

2 August 2021

I'm doing okay so far today.

Time to eat some lunch and think about heading to Portland to pick up my watch and then get to the airport. I don't really need to be there that early but hanging out there means I can relax and not stress about security. I did figure out that my TSA Pre is still active and got it added to my tickets so that should ease the security frustrations. I also put in a renewal.

Right now I'm trying not to freak out about the fact that I'm still here at home. I have 10 hours before my flight boards and while I want to make a couple of stops along the way, it's nowhere near the point where I need to panic.

That near-constant feeling of pressure/anxiety is one of the reasons I make mistakes and lose things. This is magnified when I have a deadline. I hate it. But it is what it is.

I'm forcing myself to relax. It's not really working, but I'll keep at it.

3 August 2021

Not a great day so far.

Apparently I missed the fact that my room payment didn't go through correctly. I think I have the issue cleared, but this isn't a hotel; it's a VRBO thing which is a lot like Airbnb, i.e., individuals renting their home or room through a third party. Because I didn't follow up on the email about the payment being declined everything is all sideways and I'm worried that the whole deal is a scam.

Worst case, I'll hang in the rental car for a while and then get food and head to the show. After that I'll need to find a place to stay tonight. I'm hoping it doesn't come to that.

4 August 2021

Everything worked out fine with the room/condo rental. It's a great view and about a 10-minute walk from the venue. It's also only two blocks from the Ryman auditorium which is pretty dang awesome.

The only downside is I don't have any internet other than by way of my phone. I'll see about posting a picture of the view when I have a chance to force the photos I took yesterday to sync from my phone. I'm on the 35th floor.

The Nashville Amphitheater is a really nice venue. The Cumberland River runs right by it and it's small compared to a lot of places Phish play. The show itself was good. Not spectacular, but it had some personal highlights.

The big one being "Divided Sky" – one of their early songs. They used to play it regularly but for the last several years it's been a once every tour or two kind of thing. Last night was my 42nd show, and the first time I'd gotten to see it performed in person.

Mask-wise, there weren't many people with face coverings. I mostly hung out in back of the venue where the sound was still good and there weren't many people. A decent number of those near me had masks as well.

I'm trying to limit my exposure to other people as much as I can, given the Delta variant.

If Rea had lived, I think I would have tried to talk her into buying a condo here in Nashville. We talked about moving here a bit when making the final decision on where to retire to, but she didn't like the weather and I couldn't really argue that. As a second home, though, I think it would be great.

We had many well-thought-out plans, and here I am in the middle of the remains of those plans. It's not a great place to be, but I'm the lucky one of the two of us.

Sometimes I do feel lucky, but not as frequently as I should.

Low key day so far. I'm about to head out to get food and then on to the venue for the show.

My internet more than sucks. I switched my cellular plan hoping it would get better and it did. It went from totally unusable to only mostly unusable. Not the amount of progress I was hoping for.

I need to make sure I have lots of books cued up on my tablet before I start my train trip next week.

5 August 2021

It turns out that internet is included with the place I'm staying. I just needed to notice the guidebook that was sitting by the door and read it. Things are much nicer now.

The show last night was excellent. The band were near perfect in their playing and the song selection was good as well. No complaints and the reviews are positive.

I'm having a relaxed day today. I will get out later and buy food plus do some walking around. I really like Nashville, downtown in particular. Though it feels like it is being loved to death.

6 August 2021

Another day of mostly taking it easy. I went out for breakfast and I'll get out for an extended walk later. I'd have liked to do more touristy stuff, but with the Delta variant on the loose and most people unmasked I'm not willing to take the additional risk of doing that.

I ended up not going out again today. This whole virus thing is magnifying my introvert/shut-in tendencies.

My flight tomorrow is at 3:30pm, so I'll plan on being at the airport by noon. Checkout is 11:00am, so that shouldn't be an issue.

7 August 2021

Routine morning. I finished off most of the food I bought and then had a bit more at the food court across from the Ryman which was also near where I had to drop off the parking card and key.

Right now I'm at the airport. It's about an hour until my flight is supposed to board. The previous flight at my scheduled gate is way late, though, so it won't surprise me if I have a gate change.

8 August 2021

I was right about the gate change. Yay me. It was only one over, though.

I made it home fine. I arrived around 10:30 but didn't manage to get to sleep until a bit after midnight. I'll blame the Diet Coke I drank on the way home to stay awake.

Then I woke up at precisely 5:55am. Which was apropos given the Phish link, but annoying. I'll nap more later.

I was lying in bed reading, because I have a bit of spare time before I have to prep for my train ride tomorrow. Suddenly I was thinking about Rea, particularly her last couple of months, and I lost it. I was bawling my eyes out. Nearly seven months later it's still an open wound.

It's not a common thing currently, but it is a reminder that I'm still a long way from having processed and dealt with her passing.

I've made some progress in getting ready for tomorrow. I have my ticket printed out and I understand the rules on luggage. I'm really looking forward to this trip. Hopefully it will work out as I expect.

Right now, I'm listening to Phish's August 6 show. It got good reviews and it opened strong with Carini.

I did manage to take a nap which got me into the reasonable range for sleep last night. So that was good.

9 August 2021

I'm about ready for my train ride across the country. It will actually be broken up into three sections with the final one being a bus ride from Syracuse to Watertown.

Guilty confession, I like traveling alone a lot better than I did with Rea. The packing was always super stressful and she wanted to take two or three times as much stuff as I thought she needed. For the final few years, I kidded her that she needed to ease up on me or my back was going to give out since I wasn't getting any younger.

10 August 2021

My first train ride was in February of 2020. I took the train from Oakland up to Portland. Originally the trip was supposed to be to Bingen, which is adjacent to White Salmon and down by the Columbia River, but the first leg was late and I was afraid I'd miss my connection heading east. Rea was on her way back from Seattle, so she picked me up in Portland.

That one was overnight and I went business class. It was reasonably comfortable.

This trip is to Watertown ultimately, though it is broken down into three segments. The first is from Bingen to Chicago. This is the "Empire Builder" line. The second is from Chicago to Syracuse. Finally, there is a bus ride from Syracuse to Watertown.

I might just try to find an alternative to that final leg since the layover is six hours and it won't actually get me to the house in Watertown.

Mood-wise I seem to be doing okay today. It's weird, but I'm finding that I kind of like traveling. Rea would probably be annoyed at me since she always wanted to travel more than me.

YOU CAN'T ALWAYS GET WHAT YOU WANT

The big difference now is that I can go at my own pace. I'm a bit of an enigma, even to myself. On the one hand, I desire constant stimulation while on the other too much input aggravates my anxiety.

Breakfast was decent to good. It's included in the price of a sleeper room along with the other meals.

Calling the sleepers rooms is a bit of a stretch. They are more like decent-sized closets. Maybe 18 square feet if I'm being generous. There are two seats facing each other with a bunk bed above. The two seats convert into a bed as well. Last night I slept in the lower bunk. Tonight I think I'll try the upper.

Tomorrow night I'll be on a different train.

One annoyance is that despite what Amtrak's website said, there is no internet on this train. Not the end of the world and frankly I could probably use some time away but still, a bit frustrating.

My cellular internet continues to be marginal at best, even in good coverage areas. It's fine on my iPad, but when I connect via the wireless hotspot function I get just about nada in terms of performance which makes my laptop useless.

Montana is beautiful, at least the sections the train is going through. I've been favorably impressed the few other times I've passed through as well.

The winters are kinda brutal from what I've heard, but after last year in Watertown I'm okay with that.

For some reason the train has a freight engine, which is about 10 miles an hour slower than whatever sort of engine they normally have. I overheard some of the Amtrak employees discussing this. Bottom line, it's likely going to make the train increasingly late. It's about 20 minutes behind right now. I have a five-or-six-hour layover in Chicago, though, so it shouldn't impact me.

We're still in Montana. It's a really wide state.

The western part is nicer than the east; the east pretty much reminds me of the Dakotas. At this point I'm thinking the train is getting near North Dakota. We continue through the northern part of North Dakota before heading south through Minnesota to Minneapolis. Then we continue south easterly through Wisconsin into Illinois and then finish up in Chicago mid-to-late afternoon tomorrow.

The food has been fine. It's nice that it's included in the cost of the ticket.

11 August 2021

I'm now on the train out of Chicago.

Having internet is good. It turns out that Minnesota and Wisconsin have much better coverage than Montana and North Dakota. I'm hoping/guessing this will continue through Illinois and up to New York.

This train is a bit under two hours behind right now. We probably won't make up much of that time. Doesn't matter, though.

12 August 2021

Upside of the train I'm on now is that the rooms is maybe a third again as large as the first one. Plus it has a toilet and sink.

The upper bunk also slides up and down instead of folding. I'm in car 4812, Viewliner Roomette 007. My previous room was in car 2830, Superliner Roomette 003.

The downside is the food isn't as good. The omelet I had for breakfast was prefab and small. The other train was likely older, but the food was better.

I don't seem to have much trouble sleeping on the train.

Being able to lay down helps.

In general I think I'm getting better at the whole sleeping-while-traveling thing. In my typical fashion though I can't view this as completely good as it brings me back into the guilt zone given how much Rea liked to travel and how resistant I was. Hindsight is a pain.

We passed through Erie, Pennsylvania while I was having breakfast. The train will be splitting soon with half going to Boston and the other half heading to New York. I think the New York half gets the dining car while the Boston half gets the cafe. I don't know if the Boston half has sleeper cars. The New York half has two.

I ended up taking Lyft from Syracuse to Watertown rather than the bus.

This is an absolutely true story.

There is a plant that was in the basement of the Watertown house. For months I watered it once a week and it never wilted. It's a bushy kinda thing about four feet tall not including the pot.

It turned out it was a fake. In my defense it was a pretty decent one, but a few leaves/branches fell off it and I laid them in the basement sink. They never wilted. I still thought it was real.

When I looked at it today it was obvious it wasn't real.

It's kinda funny but it also illustrates just how messed up my head was.

I'm not sure how I managed to function. I guess the answer to that is I didn't. Not very well anyway.

———————————

Drama with the shipping on the CR-V. The shipper called me back and the driver wants to do the pickup two days later than originally promised and wants a lot more money than the quote. Not cool. I'm looking into alternatives.

———————————

I've been doing some planning and it doesn't look like I'll have much trouble/work getting what I want packed into the 20-foot U-Haul.

14 August 2021

I forgot to make any entries yesterday. The haircut went fine, though I had zero clue what I wanted. Questions like "Do you want the back square or rounded" haven't been a thing I've had to worry about. I'd had two haircuts since the whole COVID thing started. Neither time was I asked that question. Before that the same lady cut my hair for about 25 years.

Today I am scheduled to pick up the U-Haul truck. I've done some organizing here at the house. I don't think the loading will take too long.

———————————

Moving van picked up as planned. I made progress on other related tasks but I've been coughing a bit more than normal and I'm very tired. Hopefully nothing serious.

Both Rea and I tended to migrate from one hobby to the next every few years. Rea's love of music, both in person and recorded, never changed. Bird watching, wood carving, crafting and collecting various things all waxed and waned over the years. Drawing and coloring were just starting to interest her when she got sick. I don't know where that would have led. She did buy a bunch of colored pencils and did a little bit of coloring in adult (nothing sexual to be clear) coloring books before she declined to the point where she could no longer do that.

People who say they have no regrets are either lying to themselves or very self-centered. Maybe that's harsh, but it's the way I feel. None of us are perfect. I'm a long way from being an exception to that rule. I hope I've learned from my many mistakes and regrets. I think I have. But there are always new mistakes to make it seems.

15 August 2021

I've been feeling kinda lousy the past couple of days. I may have mentioned that above. I kinda skimmed and didn't notice anything. I have a bit of a complex about not rereading this journal. I do it sometimes, but for the most part it's not something I want to do.

Anyway, I didn't get a lot done today beyond figuring out that the ramp I bought to get the riding lawn mower into the truck isn't going to work as it is too steep. So I bought a portable winch. It should be here on Tuesday. Between the ramp and the winch, I should be able to get the riding lawn-mower in and out of the truck.

One way or the other I need to make a lot more progress tomorrow. I think that is going to be doable. I'll know in the morning.

16 August 2021

I don't think I'm any worse this morning, though my cough is certainly *not* better.

I think I have a good scope on what I want to get done in terms of moving stuff and it won't be too bad if I ever start feeling better. The recliner, the mattress in the master bedroom, and the riding mower are the three most difficult items.

I've been playing around a bit more with a new song I wrote yesterday. I've decided to call it "Salt". Here are the lyrics.

I heard your laugh the other day
It was not so very far away

I wanted it to be you
Even though that can't be true

No way to treat the symptoms of
A time and place where I felt love
A love now gone but with no fault
I make no claims I pinch no salt

I think of you as part of me
You were the one who made me we
A three leg race no thought for place
But now I find it's you I chase

These chains they do not shackle me
But hold me where I want to be
Or so I claim while in this place
I look around for some grace

The first verse came to me after I heard somebody laughing nearby. I was out by the garage here in Watertown. I think it was the neighbors at back of me, most likely the wife, as they are a family with young children. For just a second or two the laugh sounded like Rea. Of course it wasn't, but that got lodged in my head and here we are.

More of Rea's clothes are here. It's official, I still get emotional dealing with them. In particular, several of her favorite sweatshirts are here. Things I remember her wearing frequently. That was tough.

I think I'm feeling a bit worse. Luckily there really isn't a huge amount of stuff I need to deal with here. I think I can get it all done in a half-day or so once I'm feeling better. In the meantime I'm making what progress that I can.

17 August 2021

I also woke up feeling about the same as I did last night. This is good. It could be worse all things considered.

I was also awake for about an hour in the middle of the night before getting back to sleep.

One other thing, I woke up sweating, but that isn't a totally unusual thing for me.

I slept again after eating breakfast.

It feels like the fatigue has mostly passed. The cough seems a bit better as well. My congestion is about the same and I still have a slight headache.

It was raining outside when I looked earlier.

I'm going to do some loading after lunch if I still feel better.

My second plan to get the riding lawn mower loaded onto the truck was another failure. I need to come up with another plan by tomorrow, and one that doesn't require mail ordering stuff that will take days to get here.

Being alone sucks in so many ways. Not having Rea to bounce ideas off and partner with on plans really sucks. She was a lot smarter than me when it came to engineering kinds of things. I'm good at being creative but I often fail to realize when my hare-brained ideas are bad.

I got a bit more packing done. I also have an approach to getting the riding lawn mower loaded. It isn't developed enough to all a plan at this point.

The rain today made it crazy humid since it was also around 80 degrees. I'll plan on getting started early tomorrow.

18 August 2021

Seven months. Here's the final version of "Salt". I posted it on Facebook today.

> *I heard your laugh the other day*
> *It was not very far away*
> *I wanted it to be you*
> *But I know that can't be true*
>
> *No way to treat the symptoms of*
> *A time and place where I felt love*
> *A love now gone but with no fault*
> *I make no claims I pinch no salt*
>
> *You'll always be a part of me*
> *You are the one who made me we*
> *Three leg race no thought for place*
> *But now I find it's you I chase*
>
> *These chains they do not shackle me*
> *But hold me where I want to be*
> *Or so I claim while standing here*
> *With you gone but always near*
> *I heard your laugh the other day*
> *Now it seems so far away*
> *An echo from a place and time*
> *When my life was not just mine*

I think that may be the best thing I've ever written. No, I'm pretty sure it is.

I've been working on perfecting the musical version of "Salt". I should be loading the van but it doesn't feel like that is a huge priority comparatively.

One of the ways I know it's good is that when I let myself feel it, tears start to fall. "Love True" never moved me quite the same way, though I was and am completely sincere in what I say there.

———————————

I'm making slow progress. I'm alternating between working for a half hour or so and resting for a couple. My big stumbling block is still getting the riding lawn mower loaded. I might make a run at that later today.

Friday or Saturday are looking like my most probable days to leave. Which will leave me about eight days to make it across the country and unload before the truck is due back.

19 August 2021

I'm feeling much worse today unfortunately. Slight headache and more congestion along with the fatigue getting worse. Lucky me.

20 August 2021

I started to feel a bit better later in the day, and planned on getting a COVID test but some stuff came up and I ended up not getting to that yesterday. I've scheduled the test for today at 11am.

I'm feeling a bit better today but still a long way from healthy.

———————————

I finally managed to get the riding lawn mower into the truck. It turns out there were a couple of 2x12s hidden in the back of the garage. Between them and various bits of scrap lumber in the garage I was able to build a second ramp that the metal one I bought could rest on to improve the angle.

It looks scarier than it was.

Tomorrow I'll see if I can't get 90% or more of the loading done. This assumes that I feel up to it. I'll also have the results of the COVID test by then which will help in my decision-making process.

Leaving on Sunday would enable me to get back without having to extend the U-Haul. Fingers crossed on that.

21 August 2021

Yay me, I have COVID.

The results came in a few minutes after midnight. Here I am 30 minutes later making a journal entry.

I'm feeling decent, but not great. Hopefully I won't have any setbacks.

———————

Feeling a little better this evening.

I had the thought a little earlier that if I was in a partial kind of denial during Rea's illness then she likely was as well. I can't imagine how much harder it must have been for her to deal with being the person in the cross hairs rather than the person who had to witness it.

God I miss her so much. Every day.

22 August 2021

Too early to be sure, but I think I'm feeling a bit better today. Not healthy, though. I'll need to start getting stuff loaded as the weather permits if I want to be out of here on Wednesday.

I fell back asleep after breakfast.

Upside, that was probably good for my recovery. Downside, it was humid and unpleasant by the time I woke up. I loaded a bunch of stuff anyway, and am now waiting until this evening to do another load.

I just took another nap. I'm hoping all this sleeping is a good thing. I think I am feeling better.

I realized earlier that it was about eight months from Rea's diagnosis to her passing. Next month will be eight months since she passed.

I sometimes feel like I'm getting better at dealing with the pain, and I probably am. But it still hurts so so bad when I let it. She should be here. I'm just taking up resources and feeling morose. She would be sad if I were gone but she had so much more of a life than I ever have.

I'm probably at the lower end of my cycle.

23 August 2021

I feel like I'm continuing to improve. This is good. Today I need to get the bulk of the remaining stuff loaded. That will give me tomorrow to deal with anything I'm forgetting.

Still feeling better midday. I'm making progress on the remaining packing/loading.

It's partially the medication I picked up this morning, I suspect, but I'm feeling better. The fatigue is still with me a bit, but not too bad.

Earlier I had another epiphany. I remember during Rea's decline thinking something along the lines of, *This is horrible, but within a year it will be done. I have to stay strong for Rea.*

Mostly I kind of succeeded, but what I didn't realize at the time was I had a purpose then. That is no longer true for the most part. Unless you count mourning her passing as a purpose. That's not something I'll ever be able to give up, but it's also not something that a sustainable life can be built on.

Okay, maybe I'm in one of my down phases. Or maybe going through Rea's stuff still has the ability to make me really sad. It was some mittens that did it this time.

I'm close to having dealt with everything of hers here at the house. Tomorrow is the final day of packing. I'm going to get it all done, barring a major relapse.

24 August 2021

I had trouble getting to sleep and then woke up way too early. Annoying, but that's just the way it is sometimes.

I did a live video of me playing "Salt" here at the house yesterday. It turned out better than I'd expected. It's not that polished but it basically works.

I'm spending what will likely be my final night in the Watertown house upstairs in the living room sleeping on the couch. My bed has been taken apart and mostly loaded, and the couch is remaining here.

This is also where Rea spent the last few weeks of her life. I'm a few feet from where she took her final breath. It feels appropriate to be in this place at this time.

Most of the loading is done. I'll finish things off in the morning, take a quick shower and get going. My first stop will be in Illinois to pick up a toolbox my brother bought from the estate auction of my great uncle.

25 August 2021

I'm dragging butt a bit. Probably a combination of not being 100% healthy as well as my typical struggles when I have to do things by myself. I've always been much more of a "cooperative mode" kinda guy. Which is odd given my introverted nature and social awkwardness/anxiety.

I have been making progress and I suspect I could be out of here in a bit over 90 minutes of concerted effort.

I was packing one of the last books Rea bought earlier. I don't think she managed to read it. She was too far gone at that point.

We'd gone to Target and she wanted to go to the book section. She picked up a handful of books before I managed to discourage her from getting more. I probably shouldn't have but I knew she wouldn't be able to read them, and as has been well established, I wasn't doing very well at that point.

Rea loved to read. She read constantly and belonged to a couple of different book clubs. Three, actually, for her final couple of years.

Almost ready to load, but it's lunchtime.

Any excuse in a storm, I guess.

Dang I'm dragging.

It's 2:15pm. I'm starting to think I'm not going to make it out of here today. I'm tiring way too quickly and finding a bit more work than I expected, but really it's mostly my lack of productivity. I'll be close, and I could probably get on the road and make it a couple of hours but I'd be exhausted and potentially a danger to myself and others.

Better to get an early start tomorrow, I think.

I reserve the right to change my mind but I'm doubtful that will happen at this point.

26 August 2021

I woke up about 4:45am. I went to sleep a little after 10, so for me that's a normal amount of sleep. I'm feeling decently healthy. Now I just need to get out of here at a reasonable time today.

It's 7:42am and I'm very close to ready. I have been fighting a lot of inertia the past few days. Some of it was COVID, some of it is likely my normal cyclical depression, but I think at least a bit of it is a reluctance to leave the place where Rea and I spent our final time together, and where she passed.

She's always with me, I know that but this place is special. I suppose that might sound a bit macabre, but I don't mean it that way.

Let's see if I can make it out by 9:00am.

Final push time. I just want to nap but I need to get going. I have a little over an hour now to meet that 9:00am self-imposed deadline.

27 August 2021

I made that 9am deadline, if you ignore the 10 minutes or so of running around taking pictures at the end.

I made it from Watertown to about two hours east of Ottawa Illinois which was very good given how bad I felt at the start.

Today I stopped in Ottawa to pick up the tool chest my brother bought from our great-uncle's estate sale last year. That was a bit of a debacle as I never actually made it to the farm to meet with Kevin, the banker who is handling that part of the estate stuff.

Multiple GPS fails caused him to take pity on me and meet me in Ottawa at the Cracker Barrel with the two parts of the tool chest. Neil is happy.

After sleeping in the truck last night, I'm in Council Bluffs Iowa tonight. I could in theory make it back to White Salmon in two days, but I think I'm going to plan on three, with tomorrow being another sleep in the truck night and then a hotel.

Ten hours tomorrow, eight on Sunday, and six on Monday would be a good way to break things down. I'm going to finalize my route before I leave tomorrow.

28 August 2021

I'm leaning fairly heavily toward the three-day schedule rather than the two. I'm also leaning toward hotels each night. I think that's probably a good thing as it will be a lot less painful for me, and treating myself right isn't something I'm very good at.

I guess maybe that's an epiphany? I've always had a tendency to flog myself to get and keep moving. I blame it on the anxiety, but I'm not sure that is always the reason. It plays a part, but I think there are times where it's just a bit of my ever-present self-loathing at work.

Yeah, I'm kinda messed up. I think we all are to one degree or another, though. Which leaves the big question: Can I get better? Yes, yes I can. And I'm going to do that.

I made it to Laramie, Wyoming today. Two more seven-or-so-hour driving days and I'll be home. I'll probably try to do 10 hours tomorrow and then finish the drive on Monday.

29 August 2021

I still feel like Rea is just off some place visiting friends at times. Or that she's close by and will be back any minute. It's comforting and depressing at the same time.

Seven-plus months after her passing I'm still not making very good progress at dealing with it. I probably need counseling, but I'm not ready for that yet. Maybe in a few more months when things start to settle down.

I'm feeling kinda cruddy this morning. It's not lack of sleep. I don't know if I'm getting sick again or if I'm just in one of my downward phases.

I'm going to be lazy and not rush out at 6am like I did yesterday. Hopefully that will mean my battery isn't dead as well. I'd left stuff plugged in I shouldn't have and the truck wouldn't start. That led to a two-hour delay.

———————

I made it to Heyburn, Idaho, which was my goal for the day. This hotel actually has working air conditioning and doesn't look like it's one step short of being condemned. I can't say the same for the previous two hotels. The price is about the same, though.

I'm fairly exhausted again today. Hopefully this isn't long COVID. I guess I'll have to wait and see.

———————

I know it's not "manly" to admit some of the stuff I discuss here. The thing is, I'm in my mid-50s and I don't feel like I have anything to prove. Nor do I support a lot of the toxic concepts of masculinity that I see and hear about.

I do not find other guys interesting sexually. I do find women attractive. There we go, I've defined my sexual identity. I don't see any value in pandering to anyone else's concept of what it means to be male.

With that out of the way, I cried multiple times while driving today. Unlike sneezing, my eyes were mostly able to remain open. Though I did have to wipe them occasionally.

I had a mini epiphany that I'm getting close to dealing with the very long list of tasks I was left with after Rea passed. That in turn led me to think about the fact that once I reach that point I'll actually have to get on with figuring out what my life is going to be going forward.

I also figured out that there are three distinct parts to my grief:

1. The loss of the woman I loved.
2. Guilt over my feelings that I could have been a better husband at times. I never cheated thankfully, but as I've said before, I was not always the easiest person to get along with.

3. Sadness for her and everyone who loved her.

I've expressed similar thoughts before in this journal, but I think that's a bit more refined?

30 August 2021

I woke up at pretty close to 6am on the dot. Six and a half hours of sleep. Yay me.

I've been taking it easy for the past hour or so. I figure I'll shower before heading out. I've gotten into the habit of ordering a second meal when I do my DoorDash order so breakfast isn't a problem. This place looks like it has a good breakfast as well. I may grab something to snack on if I get out of here before nine.

It'll be nice to be home, even if it's only for a day or two.

31 August 2021

I made it home around 5:30pm. I unloaded a few things, but the bulk of the work is going to happen today. I woke up at 4:30 and I'm still in bed an hour-plus later.

I've made some progress unloading the truck. Slow and steady wins the race.

On the COVID front, it was amazing how few people I saw wearing masks along the way or paying any heed to the danger.

Chapter 19

(September 2021)

1 September 2021

Today was good. I finished unloading the U-Haul and with help from my neighbor Ken managed to get it returned as well.

Tomorrow I'm going to head south after lunch. I'll drive until I get tired and then stop at a rest stop and sleep. Gotta pick up Marley.

Mood-wise I'm feeling good, even if the house is stuffed full of things I need to deal with. Getting things accomplished always helps my mood.

I am looking into getting a garage/shop built so I have a place to put the RV and store some of the clutter.

I posted the "live" video of my performing "Salt" to YouTube and FB. People were supportive which is nice. I tend to struggle a bit with the subtle narcissism of being a songwriter. It's there, but so is the need to create. I dunno. I have really mixed feelings about the whole thing.

3 September 2021

The drive down to the bay area was uneventful.

I left at about 3pm yesterday, drove the central Oregon route (mostly 97) until I was about an hour north of the border and then slept in the truck from about 9pm to 3:30pm. Then I drove the rest of the way.

Marley managed to mangle her tail a couple of days ago and is having to wear a cone. She's handling it well. She was happy to see me, but she's happy to see anyone. She is very much into loving whomever is around.

5 September 2021

So far a lazy Sunday. Tomorrow will likely be low productivity as well since it's a holiday.

I'm hoping to head back north on Saturday.

Marley has a vet appointment a week from tomorrow.

6 September 2021

I went out to breakfast and grabbed some iced tea and trail mix at the grocery store as well. All before 7am. I slept well last night and I feel good. I don't have a lot to do other than a bit of work today.

I think I'm near the top of my cycle which is probably helping.

My friends Ken and Carole are in Watertown and have picked up the CR-V.

7 September 2021

It's been near 100 degrees here the past few days. Marley and I went for a walk first thing this morning to avoid the worst of the heat. My weight and physical conditioning both need attention. I don't blame myself for getting into this state given the past couple of years, but I need to reverse the trend.

8 September 2021

Another early morning. I'm at Country Waffle near Mike and Laura's. I remember eating here on my previous trip and noticing everyone taking off their masks. Now we're back to having to wear them. I haven't talked a lot about COVID recently. It's a depressing topic and after having had it I'm even more confused why so many people treat it so casually.

Random factoid, a CO2 molecule is one three-hundredth the size of a single COVID-19 molecule. One-third of a micron versus 100 microns. It's a bit of a mystery to me how some people think that on the one hand masks don't help with COVID while on the other they think they can accumulate CO2 in a mask. It doesn't parse.

9 September 2021

Last night I had dinner with the Clower's and the Carter's.

I realized this morning that one of the things I learned from Rea is social interaction. It's not something I'm great at but I'll consciously think of topics that might generate conversation and ask questions of people when I'm in a group setting. Not all the time and sometimes it probably comes off as a bit unnatural, but it's something Rea did all the time. I'd never realized it until now. I was doing it last night at times.

11 September 2021

It's hard to believe it's been 20 years since 911. The country was so different back then. It was a horrible event, but I'd love to have some of the feeling of unity that followed 9/11 back.

Marley and I will be heading north shortly. It's been a productive and enjoyable visit.

12 September 2021

I stopped at the Beaver Marsh rest area last night which is about 207 miles north of the Oregon California border.

I managed to get to sleep around 10pm and woke up at 3:30am, partially because of the cold.

After a half hour or so to wake up and get both Marley and me a quick breakfast we were on the road.

We were home around 8am.

I'm torn between wanting to hole up some place and wanting to be out exploring. I can't really explain why that is.

———————

I think in part it's me trying to figure out how I can have the best life. On the one hand I tend to be a shut in. That's a life I know how to live, but I don't know how long I'd survive taking that route. Traveling is stressful, but when I'm in charge of the itinerary it's not so bad.

One challenge with traveling is Marley. She makes everything more complicated and some things impossible without boarding her or getting somebody to "babysit" her.

13 September 2021

Marley's vet visit today went fine. The stitches she's had in her tail the past couple of weeks have dissolved and she's healing fine. Her vaccinations are now all up to date as well.

What I'm about to write is in no way profound or original, but I'll say it anyway. When you lose someone, you realize that the less-than-perfect things in your relationship weren't nearly as big a deal as they seemed at the time, and you miss the good things a lot.

That's essentially a long-winded way of saying "You don't know what you've got until it's gone".

15 September 2021

The house in Watertown went on the market today and there is already an offer for the asking price. It's a bit early to celebrate, but if things continue to develop well tomorrow, I'll begin to feel optimistic.

I had a few fleeting moments again today where I thought for a moment that Rea was in another part of the house. I'm wondering if that will ever stop. It's not a good or a bad thing on balance, at least at the moment. Having even the tiniest bit of time where I think she's alive is good, and the pain when I realize she isn't is pretty much what it always is, so in a sense there is no downside.

16 September 2021

The offer on the Watertown house is looking firm. Cash, which is good as it means there doesn't have to be an appraisal. There are five showings scheduled today so I had the option of holding off and trying to get more money but I chose to pass. I've never been primarily about the money and a few thousand extra at the risk of killing a good offer didn't seem worth it.

Mood-wise I'm middling. I've only left the house twice since getting back. Once for Marley's appointment and once to get groceries. I'll be heading over to The Dalles in the morning for routine maintenance on the truck.

———————————

I think today is the first day of Merlfest. Named after Doc Watson's son Merl Watson. It was one of the many things on our informal bucket list. In an alternate timeline where COVID hadn't happened and Rea hadn't gotten sick there is a very good chance we would be there.

18 September 2021

I've decided to get the ball rolling on a one bed, one bath condo down in Livermore.

———————————

Emotionally this has been a crap day.

Productivity wise it was fairly good. I worked through a lot of issues with my home studio and may just have it fully functioning tomorrow.

On the condo front, the sellers countered and I'm not very enthusiastic about their counter. I'm going to hold off on responding to my Realtor until tomorrow.

19 September 2021

I woke up and realized I'd forgotten that it was eight months yesterday since Rea passed. Subconsciously I think I knew, which might have explained my mood.

I'm going to counter offer on the condo, but only with a small part of what they are asking for.

———————————

The counter appears to have been accepted.

20 September 2021

The waiting on the condo begins.

21 September 2021

So far a decent day for me mood-wise. Things are progressing on the condo front. No news on the house selling side, but that is to be expected right now.

22 September 2021

One of the things that frustrates me is my inability to communicate my grief on these pages in a way that feels transparent. I don't have the strength of discipline to go back and read what I've written but my general feeling is it mostly boils down to "woe is me, I'm sad".

I'm trapped inside my head, just like everyone else. What goes on there is a complex mishmash of desires, fear, and pretty much everything else that can be imagined.

My thought process is all over the place, and generally speaking I find it hard to concentrate and focus on any one thing.

During her decline I commented that I understood why people would drink or take drugs to numb themselves to mental pain and anguish. I still do and I'm still choosing not to go down that path because I don't know that I'd ever come back. Her memory deserves better; I deserve better. Or maybe I don't. An overdeveloped sense of entitlement pretty much comes with my age and financial status.

23 September 2021

I'd been putting off dealing with Rea's shoes. She had a lot of them in New York and even more pairs here. She loved to collect and given the fact that she needed two significantly different-sized shoes along with buildup on one it's not surprising that she was wary of not having new ones handy.

One of the two shoes had to be a child's size, while the other was adult. It was a challenge finding shoes she liked that came in both a child's and adult size.

Many of these had not had the buildup done to the smaller shoe. As is always the case when dealing with Rea's clothes, I had a mini breakdown. I don't think I'm unique in having this issue. I've heard it's difficult for others in similar situations as well. The things people wore are about as personal as you can get I think.

———————————

It still doesn't seem real. It will never seem fair.

25 September 2021

Yesterday was a decent day. Fridays are hard to complain about even if I am only working part time and remotely. Weather-wise things are nice, though after today the forecast is for an increasing chance of rain.

I don't recall if I've talked much about my religious beliefs in this journal. I'm a Christian, but I only care about the fundamentals of the faith. Which is that I accept Jesus as my savior and acknowledge that the only path to salvation is through him.

I didn't make this decision lightly. I came to it through both a religious experience that I won't go into here, as well as personal observation. I've tried to be a good person, I try to always do the right thing, yet somehow I fail regularly. The blame for this is mine and while I'm always trying to improve, at this stage in my life it's pretty clear that perfection is impossible.

I'm not faulting people who need a lot of extra trappings to their Christianity, but I do think that making things more complex is dangerous.

The Bible is not a simple book. It is also full of apparent contradictions and the gymnastics people try to go through to make it all work together only detract from their faith and make it more fragile. At least it looks that way from my perspective.

26 September 2021

The weekend is mostly done. I managed to finish the teddy bear puzzle today.

This is the one Rea and I started the final time she was here.

There are two pieces missing. I think the puzzle was used when we started it, but one of both of the pieces might have ended up in Marley's stomach. She has a habit of chewing on stuff she shouldn't.

Rea and I managed to get the edges and a portion of the inside completed. The teddy bear puzzle combines three things Rea loved:

1. Collecting
2. Cute things
3. Puzzles

When her mom Jean lived with us they would frequently spend hours working on various puzzles. I helped, but I've never enjoyed puzzles, especially the really difficult ones. Finishing this one by myself was a labor of love.

28 September 2021

I weighed myself this morning: 188. A few years back 165 was more typical. Still, I've been in the 190 range for most of this year, so I'm at least managing to hold steady.

I can't help but constantly review my life with Rea. It's probably a part of the grieving process.

One of the things I've noticed is many signs that something was wrong. One of those was when Rea reverted to putting the silverware into the dishwasher right side up. I'd managed to convince her a year or two prior to that to put them in the other way since that meant they could be put away after cleaning without having to put your hands on the part that goes in people's mouths.

Trivial? Yes, but these are the kinds of things that get stuck in my head.

I think my cough is finally gone. I noticed yesterday that I hadn't coughed in a while and didn't feel like I needed to.

––––––––––––––––

The inspection is back on the condo. Nothing major though I have some concerns with the age of the heating and cooling systems.

29 September 2021

Marley grooming tomorrow morning. Today I got up early and went to breakfast over in Hood River before stopping by the Postal Annex and picking up a couple of small packages.

My life continues to be super exciting.

30 September 2021

Marley is at the groomers here in The Dalles and I'm having breakfast at Cousins Restaurant.

Actually, it's kinda lunch since I had breakfast around 6am and its 9am now. A bit odd in terms of timing but being an adult and a widower gives me a lot of freedom. Most of it I don't want or need, but this is my life.

Chapter 20

(October 2021)

1 October 2021

Another month. This month would have been Rea's 63rd birthday and my mom's 89th.

When somebody is nearing the end of their life there are lots of lasts. Last birthday, last time talking, last hug, and so many more.

After they pass comes all of the firsts.

It's going to be a mixed month. Two firsts for me in having to mark the birthdays of Rea and my mom as well as a likely first in terms of buying a home by myself.

Selling a home as well actually.

2 October 2021

Nothing new on the selling/buying side of things house-wise. So far as I know all is progressing as planned on both the condo and the house in New York.

4 October 2021

Mondays are always a bit hard, even though I'm working part time and remote. Part of it is the fact that Rea passed on a Monday. Some of it is just the requirement that I be logged in and productive for a portion of the day. Today some of the malaise is due to the gray skies. Fall is here for sure.

5 October 2021

The sellers on the condo want me to remove the contingency I have on the sale of the house in New York. I've been fairly generous with them to date, but this is getting a little frustrating. I'm inclined to say no but am going to think about it a bit more before I make a decision.

6 October 2021

Sometimes I'll be doing something I haven't done in a while. Say for instance playing a particular computer game. Eventually I'll have the thought pop up in my head that I should make sure Rea doesn't need me for something. Almost immediately followed by remembering. I know I've talked about that here before, but it keeps catching me by surprise.

Productive day so far. I got the kitchen better organized, went out to breakfast, and then bought some groceries.

7 October 2021

I'm feeling like there isn't much for me to write about currently.

The exercise of writing is good, but if the quality isn't there I don't know if there is really any gain for me either from a mechanical standpoint or from the perspective of working my way through my grief.

I have a lot of stuff coming up later this month. A trip to Disneyland and a couple of Phish shows. The Phish shows are the two days before Disneyland and I'm mulling over how I want to deal with that. Do I skip the second show and drive down, or go to both, fly out the morning after? The shows are in Eugene. I have a tentative plan for Marley.

I need to finalize things in the next day or two.

8 October 2021

My weight this morning was 185. That is the lowest number I've seen in a couple of years. This is a good sign that my efforts to eat a little less and be a bit more active are starting to pay off.

Right after Rea passed I managed to lose a few pounds, mostly because I had no appetite. A month or so after I'd gained it back plus a few more. I was closing in on 200 before I managed to rein things in a bit and stabilize around 190.

9 October 2021

Saturday again. Time is flying by right now. General wisdom would claim it's because I'm having fun. General wisdom would be at least partially wrong. I'm doing okay, but fun is not a word I'd use to describe most of my life.

The weather has been cool and often overcast. Typical for this time of year and not a problem for me so far. I have full spectrum LED lights I can deploy as the days get shorter.

Nothing new on the real estate front. It's a waiting game at this point.

I figured out that I'm nearly double booked later in the month. I have tickets to the second night of Phish in Eugene which is on the 20th, and I'm meeting my brother and his family at Disneyland on the 21st. That is doable if I want to go that route but I need to have some place to stash Marley and get from Eugene to Anaheim within a very narrow time range. Basically I'd need to fly.

There are a couple of possibilities that I'm exploring. I'm leaning against seeing Phish. Which bugs me, but keeping myself in a good frame of mind and managing my anxiety are something I have to keep focused on.

It's four days until what would have been my Mom's 89th birthday and 10 days until what would have been Rea's 63rd.

———————————

One of the things on my agenda for the weekend was recording a good quality demo of "Margaret Rose & Gladys Kate", a song I wrote about my mother and her biological mother a few years ago when I finally discovered the identity of her mother and learned a few things talking to my cousin and aunt on that side.

10 October 2021

It's windy and cool today with a good chance of rain. In theory I slept well, but I'm feeling lethargic this morning. Hopefully a bit more caffeine will solve that problem.

11 October 2021

I can feel the weight of my mom and Rea's birthdays coming up. Plus the nine-month anniversary of Rea's passing. It's not going to be a fun time for the next week or so. After that is Disneyland which will be a mixed bag. It will be good to be there with family, but it was also one of Rea's favorite places and it will be my first trip since she passed.

It occurs to me that I have a bit of an inner conflict about visiting places where Rea and I went. On the one hand, I don't want to avoid them because they remind me of her, while on the other I shy away from the inevitable pain that the association with her brings.

I wonder if the reason I'm so anxious to do a remodel on the house here in White Salmon is that it constantly reminds me of her? Or if the reason I'm buying the condo down south is that it is a place that will have no association with her?

I hope not, but it's seldom clear what is going on in my head, even to me.

I was just looking through pictures on my camera roll when I came across one of the area in The Dalles near where the Safeway is. This was a part of town that Rea struggled to navigate/understand for the last few years of her life, which seemed odd at the time but in retrospect was probably one of many early signs that her CJD was already progressing.

12 October 2021

Yesterday I turned the heat on for the first time this year. It got below freezing overnight last night.

I worked with Ken on revision two of the house remodel plan his brother drew up. We both had similar concerns and came up with some good ideas. Hopefully we'll get to meet with his brother John next week before I head south for the Disneyland trip. I think the next iteration will be close to a final product. The challenge will be finding somebody to build it. Or the garage/shop for that matter. Too much demand right now.

———————

While going through the pictures on my camera I also came across a video of the Dalles Dam and Columbia River taken just before we bought the house here in White Salmon. I'd started the video just a little after one of the riverboats had come through the lock at the Dam. You can hear Rea and I discussing if we brought a bag for laundry. The conversation was short, but it was good to hear her voice again and I was surprised not to be more upset while listening. That feels like progress.

13 October 2021

Today would have been my mother's 89th birthday.

———————

I didn't sleep very well last night. I often wake up a couple of times but mostly I get back to sleep quickly. That wasn't the case this time. I had both a good and a bad dream that had Rea. I don't recall many details other than that she was in both. Hearing her voice on the video I mentioned finding a day or so back may have played a part. I'm really tired today.

Things are a bit hairy with the condo right now. The sellers seem confused as to the date things were supposed to happen and are being a bit of a pain. Everything may fall through. If it does then I'm fine with it.

———————

I've cried nearly as much for my mom today as I had the whole time between her passing and now.

I'm finally starting to process that she's gone. It hurts, but it's also a good thing, I think. It means that I've worked my way through enough of the anguish over Rea's illness and passing that I have the emotional capacity to finally acknowledge my mother.

Someday I may end up in therapy. I probably should have been in counseling during Rea's illness, but COVID and my introversion kept that from happening.

I think I'm fairly self-aware comparatively, though, so hopefully that means I'm better able to deal with this kind of thing by myself.

14 October 2021

Another gray day today, at least so far.

Things have been silent on the condo front thankfully. I'm hoping that will continue.

16 October 2021

The weather is looking good today. It's Saturday and I need to get prepared to head south in a few days.

17 October 2021

One of the things that occurred to me recently is that I'm changing/getting rid of the spaces I shared with Rea. The apartment in Livermore, the home in Watertown and in the case of White Salmon, an extensive remodel.

I don't think I started on that course consciously, but I've heard many stories of surviving spouses needing to sell and move from their home because the constant reminders of their lost husband or wife were too difficult to deal with.

It's probably partially the case that my motivations come from the same place.

I don't want to erase Rea from my life, I never could. But I probably do want to be able to "turn the volume down" at times.

19 October 2021

Yesterday was nine months since Rea's passing. I posted a picture of some yellow flowers to Facebook and several people understood what it was about even without any comments.

Today would have been her 63rd birthday. I made another Facebook post, this time with a picture of her smiling at her final birthday party as well as one of the completed teddy bears puzzle I mentioned above.

Here is the text and the pictures from that post:

Early on in our relationship Rea and I talked a lot about what love meant to us. One of the things she said at that time that stuck with me is that love is being willing to do things you don't enjoy but that your partner does.

Looking back, there were times I could have been better at that, but her words stuck with me and became part of the way I approached life in general and my relationship with her in particular. I'm a homebody and not very comfortable in social situations. Rea loved to travel and socialize. Over the years we met somewhere in the middle.

Another example of this is that Rea loved to do puzzles, me not so much. When her Mom lived with us the two of them spent a lot of time putting together puzzles. I'd help but seldom enjoyed the activity. Really, the only time I was having fun is when the last dozen or so pieces were going in.

After Rea's Mom had to be moved into a care facility, we continued to work on puzzles occasionally. Lego's as well, as they are essentially 3D puzzles. I liked the Lego builds a lot and Rea enjoyed them as well, or perhaps she just pretended to in order to humor me.

Last year when we were spending what would be Rea's final days in Washington, we started two 1000-piece puzzles. The first was a Disney puzzle featuring Ellie and Carl from the Pixar film Up. It was two sided, with one side featuring them when they are young and the other when they are old. When Rea asked me which side I thought we should do, I chose the old one. She was still fairly intact at the time and I don't know if she saw that there were parallels in Ellie and Carl's story to our own, or understood why I chose the older side. Like so many things related to her illness I didn't have the courage to ask at the time.

That puzzle was really difficult. I think it would have taken a long time even prior to Rea's illness. After a while we set it aside and started on another with a patriotic theme and teddy bears. It was near the 4th of July at the time *so it seemed appropriate and Rea loved cute things. We made better progress on it but were maybe 20% of the way through when we left for her final trip, to New York.*

When I came back to Washington earlier this year both puzzles were waiting for me. Someday I'll tackle the Ellie and Carl one, but I knew I could complete the teddy bear one if I tried, and so I did.

It turns out there are a couple of pieces missing. The puzzle was used, so they may have been missing from the start, or perhaps they fell on the floor at some point and Marley or the vacuum cleaner consumed them.

Being able to complete something that the two of us worked on together was therapeutic, especially given my ambivalence towards puzzles in conjunction with Rea's words of wisdom from early in our relationship that I mentioned above.

Happy Heavenly birthday Rea. You are missed.

20 October 2021

I left White Salmon about three hours later than I'd planned but managed to make good time. I stopped at a rest stop about 12 miles north of Ashland Oregon. It's close enough to winter that taking the I-5 route is a better option than going the central Oregon route along 97.

There are more towns, and the weather is generally better. Once I'm south of Weed the route is the same, though.

I woke up around 3:30am which gave me about five hours of sleep. I'll likely crash early tonight and hopefully sleep at least seven hours.

I found out just before I left yesterday that the paperwork for the sale of the home in New York had been sent the week before. Unfortunately, it was sent to my California mailbox and nobody had warned me it was on its way. Ugh. I got it signed and notarized and sent it back overnight just before noon today. It should get there by tomorrow, though I doubt the closing happens before early next week.

Tomorrow is the plane flight down to Anaheim. I need to figure out how I'm getting to the hotel.

———————————

Rea taught me many lessons during her life. Her illness and passing taught me many more, about both her and myself.

I do not view myself as a strong person. At best I would describe myself as a survivor. When my back is against the wall or I feel especially strongly about something I will fight, but most of the time I am a passive participant who lets his life flow by, largely unexplored.

I've occasionally had the desire to become a philosopher. I suspect that the outcomes of that desire would be mostly sophistry.

I wonder at times if I've made it to the point that I can consider myself a reasonably competent writer. The subtle nuances of language still trip me up at times and I'll confess that I'm ambivalent at best in regards to the Oxford comma, but I do feel like there are times when I'm managing to create competent prose.

I am really tired right now. It feels like a nap would be a good idea at some point but it's only 1:11pm.

21 October 2021

Generally good day yesterday. Today I am being dropped off at the Oakland airport for a flight down to Anaheim for Disneyland tonight and the following couple of days. I've explored getting from the airport to the Disneyland hotel. I'll likely do Lyft or Uber.

We spent the late afternoon and evening at DCA. My feet are killing me. I mostly managed to resist all the "free" candy.

Being at a Disney park without Rea was weird and bittersweet. Especially when I saw something that was new that I knew she would have liked.

I took an Aleve a bit ago. I hope that will aid my feet in recovering.

22 October 2021

I screwed up and only have tickets for the first three days of this trip. So, I'll get to relax on Sunday whether I like it or not. My feet are a bit better this morning.

I don't think I've talked about my anxiety in a while. It's about normal right now. The crowds are smaller than normal, likely because Disney is having to limit the number of people in the parks. Which is why I can't get a ticket for Sunday.

The final chunk of money for the condo purchase is in flight. Things are progressing on the sale of the house in Watertown as well so everything could be wrapped up by this time next week.

I think the thing that is bothering me the most right now is how polarized everyone is. People I've known for decades are angry and frustrated about the political situation. These are people who weren't particularly political a couple of decades ago and weren't angry even if they were somewhat politically aware. It's a bad sign, but I don't really have any control. All I can do is carefully try to talk them down, but that takes a lot of energy and I just don't have that much to spare.

———————

I realized today that I view dips in the markets as opportunities rather than something to be depressed about.

Affluent person problems aren't really problems at all in many cases.

———————

There was a moment while on the haunted mansion ride today when I realized that Rea's favorite spot on the ride was just ahead. When you descend into the final section in the graveyard the doom buggies rotate around backwards and you are nearly on your back. For whatever reason she loved that. She told me more than once. It's not as comfortable for me as it was for her as the curve of the back of the doom buggy makes it such that my neck bends forward a bit.

I imagine that moment for her was a brief time to contemplate and enjoy the experience and be in in the moment.

23 October 2022

Decent day at DCA today, buffet dinner a bit later. No new Rea-related memories or epiphanies. It's constantly low-level odd/sad to me to be here without her.

Like so much of my life, it doesn't feel right. It will never feel fair, to her, not me.

———————

Goofy's Kitchen was a disappointment. Some or all of that disappointment was due to the ongoing impacts of COVID.

The characters couldn't stop or be touched and almost ran through when they did come out. The food selection wasn't very good either. I felt a bit like I was living in a fading second world country. I worry that is closer to reality than I'd prefer.

My last trip here was in May of 2019. Rea and I came with my brother and his family. It was a smaller subset of that group this time with my niece and one of my grandnieces being elsewhere in addition to Rea being gone.

Here's a picture of Rea from that previous trip to Goofy's Kitchen.

It's not a very good photo technically but it's good to see her having fun.

I cried a little looking at that picture. She was still fairly normal at that point, though subtly impacted when I look back. Even in November of 2019 the signs of her decline were present.

I say this periodically and I think I'll continue to say it. I still can't believe she's gone. I've probably also said that in a sense she isn't. She is very much in the thoughts of her many friends.

24 October 2021

What that photo doesn't show is Rea swaying back and forth with Pluto to the music that was playing at the time. The live" photo version does. She's laughing and clearly having a great time.

Yet again, I'm both smiling and trying not to cry.

Fun day at the park. We were at Disneyland today. I slept poorly last night though so I headed back to my room a bit after 3pm and I'm done for this trip. I've been doing some packing and planning. Semi early start needed tomorrow. Hopefully I'll sleep better.

My brother reminded me that when we were at Disneyland around 1973 our mother freaked out on the sub ride and we had to leave before the ride started. She was claustrophobic, possibly due to her experiences during WWII when she had to spend a lot of time in bomb shelters while living in London.

26 October 2021

The flight back yesterday was good. The plane got in a bit late but arrived close to on time in Oakland. Coming back on Monday was the right decision since the weather on Sunday in the SF Bay area was insanely bad. Six inches of rain in Livermore. Crazy.

I discovered this morning that I would have been much smarter to gather the money for the condo in my local bank rather than the one on the other side of the country. Ugh.

28 October 2021

I'm in Syracuse. I took the red eye last night and arrived in Syracuse just before noon.

The connecting flight was in Charlotte and I barely had enough time to make it from my arrival gate to the departure. Being close to the back of the plane on the first leg didn't help. Still, I made it and after a quick lunch at the airport I picked up my rental car and drove to Watertown.

The drive is a little over an hour and once I got to the bank, I was able to initiate the wire. I now have confirmation that it came through. Life is good.

So now I'm at a hotel near the airport trying to stay awake since I only got maybe three hours of sleep last night. The first leg was four and a half hours, but it's super uncomfortable in coach trying to sleep. I finally found a system that kind of worked but it was only exhaustion that allowed me to sleep at all. I pity anyone taller or wider than me trying to sleep in that scenario.

I've upgraded a bit on the way back so I'll be closer to the front of the plane on both legs. This makes me happy.

I'm hoping I'll get to take a look at the condo on Saturday. I wasn't too worried about seeing it first since it's a condo and the HOA is responsible for the outside. The inside checked out fine, and I've seen pictures so I'm not expecting any surprises.

I'm about two miles from the airport and my flight isn't until 11:30am tomorrow so I shouldn't have any issues. I thought about trying to book an earlier flight but that would have involved being out of here at four in the morning and I'm already going to be screwed up enough given my crazy schedule over the past few days.

Thankfully the flights were cheap comparatively so my bonehead move of having the money in the wrong bank wasn't as financially painful as it could have been.

After dealing with the wire transfer and before heading back to Syracuse I stopped at the Olive Garden restaurant in Watertown. I'm fairly sure that was the last place Rea and I ate out together. It would have been nearly a year ago. I'm sure it is in my journal somewhere.

I also remember that I was going to try to go there with her in early December? It snowed a lot overnight, though, and given her rapid decline at that point I knew we'd missed our last chance.

At this point I don't know if I'll ever go back. I liked Watertown a lot, but it is a long way away from my normal stomping grounds and there are many sad memories here.

I do want to visit the memorial stone I bought for Rea when it is in place.

I realized today that I'm being forced to grow in ways I wouldn't have been if Rea had still been here. Learning how to fully navigate around Livermore after having lived there for more than two decades and learning how to deal with some of the more esoteric financial things like doing a wire transfer to name just two.

In learning there is of course failure. I'd just as soon not be having to learn these things, but I won't discount the experiences either. Rea made me a much more whole person while she was still here, and she's continuing to do that now that she is gone.

29 October 2021

I had trouble getting to sleep last night. All the napping mid-to-late afternoon yesterday probably didn't help. Being three time zones off my recent norm also contributed to that I'll bet.

I got to the airport plenty early though since I woke up at 6am and there was no reason to stick around there.

Again I have about an hour between my first and second legs. I'm hoping things go at least as well as they did the last time. Better would of course be … better.

I've been keeping this journal for well over a year now. I started in March of 2020 if my memory is correct. At this point I've decided to keep going.

I don't share everything here. There is a chance portions of this journal might be published someday. I won't be fake humble. I think Rea's story is an important one and at least a few people would be interested in it. If I could raise money for research into CJD then I would certainly explore that option.

I think I'd need somebody else to edit it, though. That is probably a wise choice even if I ignore the emotional difficulty of reading most of what I've written.

I don't have a very good understanding of formal written English for one thing. There is a not so fine line between having a "voice" and coming off as being illiterate.

On the COVID front, mask wearing is getting spotty here in the northern part of New York. I don't honestly know what the rules are, but outside of the airport I'd say about 25% of people are going without masks indoors.

Cases are dropping at this point, as are deaths. Likely because a lot of people have been vaccinated and many have already had COVID.

———————

It turns out the layover in Charlotte is much longer this direction than it was the other way. One of those details I'm not good at noticing.

Another learning moment.

30 October 2021

I feel like I already made an entry today, but Google says no.

I drove by the condo earlier. The outside looked like what the pictures showed. It seems like a nice neighborhood and the location is good. It isn't close enough to be within easy walking distance for shopping but it's barely a five-minute drive to that sort of thing.

Sadly, I was unable to see the inside today and I doubt I'll get to see it tomorrow. The previous owners have a 30-day rent back and, they and/or their agent have become unresponsive to my agent. I'm planning on heading back north tomorrow afternoon so with no word back I don't think it's going to happen this time.

———————

I felt happy driving by that condo. It felt like I'd accomplished something by myself. It felt like a step in the direction of creating my own life. I think that is the hardest part of all this other than losing Rea. She's gone, I'm still here, all our plans were pointless in the end, and now I have to pick up the pieces and figure out how to go on. Affluent person problems of course. If I had little or no money the answer to that question would be obvious.

31 October 2021

It's Halloween today. This day didn't have any special meaning to Rea and me. We'd generally go to a movie during the evening to avoid the complexities of buying a bunch of candy and having few if any kids show up.

I realized recently that I'm still sneaking up on fully acknowledging Rea is gone.

I don't know how close I am to making it all the way, but I don't think I'm very far away. Each step brings new pain. But it's manageable, and I think that is why I've been dealing with it this way.

That distance had a cost during her illness, but it helped me survive. I don't think I would have made it otherwise. The phrase "*I ain't broke, but I'm badly bent*" comes to mind. Those words are the lyrics from a song that the Bluegrass band "Old and in the way" did many years ago. I think it might be traditional, but I'm not sure. The song refers to money, but those words resonate with me on an emotional level.

Going on 10 months later I realize I didn't hold her nearly enough during her illness. It was like a feedback loop in a sense. The emotional distance I took without thinking and the outcomes from that now come back to haunt me.

There was no conscious thought; it all happened without any planning.

I don't want it to sound like I wasn't engaged, I was and I worked hard to make those final months and days as good as they could be. But it was all done through a thick haze.

It's hard not to wonder what I might have done better if I were a stronger person.

I'm driving back to Washington today. As always, it is kinda sneaky of me to plan to be on the road during Halloween. No issues with candy thankfully.

Chapter 21
(November 2021)

1 November 2021

No particular issue on the drive. I took the I-5 route and left Livermore around 3pm. Stopped at a rest stop near Grants Pass and arrived home in Washington about 10am. I got about five hours sleep.

It started raining during the night and rained the rest of the way.

I haven't talked about my mood in a while. It's kinda meh. The weather, the short days and where I'm at in my grieving are all playing a part in that.

2 November 2021

Another not so great day mood wise. I need to break out the full spectrum lights I bought last winter. I know where at least one of them is. It may not help but it's unlikely to hurt.

I think I'll do that now.

———————————

Mission accomplished. It's a bit bright but I'll just soak up the rays for now and see if it helps.

I think one way to tell that my mood isn't great right now is by how bad the recent entries are.

Having Marley is a little like having a child. When she wanders off for a while and I can't hear her doing anything I start to get anxious.

Turns out she wasn't up to anything, at least not that I could discover.

I'm finding I am not very good at keeping track of paperwork. Which is complicating my life. This is a big part of why Rea always wanted to deal with that kind of stuff.

The light is not a quick fix.

3 November 2021

I think at least part of what is bothering me right now is the realization that I left my mother entirely alone for the final eight months of her life. She was nearly deaf so calling would have been difficult, but I could have done so. Yet I didn't.

This is the downside of the slowly receding emotional numbness.

Of course, that same numbness played a part in my actions.

Or lack of action, I guess.

Regrets last pretty much forever in my experience. I don't thrive on drama or pathos but that is my truth. I'm marginally better at forgiving myself than I was in my younger years, but this is one that isn't going to recede quickly.

I still think I'm getting to the final stages of dealing with the past couple of years. I sure as heck hope so anyway. I don't know how much of this I can take.

I'm going to try to keep in mind that this is a process. That I'm some place between the start and the finish and while I feel kinda crap right now, based on my past experience I know I'll feel better at times even when I'm still working my way through the worst of this.

Still, I felt a bit panicked just now which is extreme for what I normally experience. Likely this is another sign that my emotional numbness is receding.

I wish it had a visible lever that I could manipulate to slow things down, because right now it feels like it's letting off a bit too quickly.

———————————

The recent election results are a bit disturbing. Not because I'm particularly liberal; I'm not. I'm somewhere in the middle. But because I think the Republican party is basically batshit right now, while the Democrats are just dysfunctional and at times misguided.

It's hard not to wonder if we're in the midst of a serious decline both nationally and globally.

Not a mood enhancer to contemplate that. Especially since it feels like the old saying "You can run, but you can't hide" is very apropos right now. Everywhere is experiencing some degree of brokenness that is in excess of recent historical norms. Or so it seems anyway.

When I contemplate possible worst-case scenarios, Rea starts to seem like the lucky one. She was love, hope, and caring, and much more liberal than me. The world has never treated such people particularly well, and these days that is more true than it has been in a long time it seems.

It's hard not to feel like empathy is a curse.

I guess I'm doing a better job today of expressing my angst and the reasons behind it.

———————————

Well, I made it to lunch and I bought groceries but I didn't check the mail. I have some packages there that need to be picked up. It's not 2pm yet, so still plenty of time but I think I'm going to punt for today. I'll count this as a draw in terms of my productivity and mood. At least I made it out of the house.

On the subject of my mother, I didn't know she was going to die in early December. I wasn't surprised given her fragile health, age and decline over the previous few years, but I think in part I thought she would still be around when Rea was gone. Maybe I'm being generous with myself when I say that though.

More accurately, maybe I fooled myself into thinking I'd have an opportunity to make my absence from her life up to her. COVID meant I couldn't visit in any case.

I'm rambling. There is no good answer here and I'm not going to resolve this by sitting here typing to myself.

4 November 2021

Mood-wise I'm still not feeling great. The full spectrum LED light is on, and it may be helping but it's too early to be sure.

Mostly I try to respect other people's privacy in this journal, which is why I am vague at times. I may end up being the only one who ever reads this, in which case that was wasted effort. But some stories aren't mine to tell, especially from my biased perspective.

I have to say that I prefer snow to rain. My mother would not agree. She referred to it as "the white stuff". She did so in a tone of voice that left no doubt as to how little love she had for it.

The reason I prefer snow is that it's not messy. Marley can wander out in the snow and while her feet are wet when she comes back in, she's clean. With the rain she comes in all muddy. It's not fun at all to deal with.

The weather here right now is windy and wet. Blustery would probably be the more concise way to describe it.

5 November 2021

I was watching early 20th century videos that have been up sampled on YouTube just now. It reinforced my feeling that nobody who has ever lived is truly gone.

My faith aside, and as I think I've noted before, they existed. They inter-acted and they experienced. Nothing can ever take that away from them, even after they are gone. The same is true for me of course, and Rea.

My depression is a little better today. Having something to do helps, I'm sure. Maybe the light does as well. Or maybe I'm just heading up in my cycle. It doesn't have to be only one thing.

6 November 2021

I've been slowly building the catalog of songs I can play without referring to a song chart. One of the ones I play a lot is "Salt". Songwriting is kind of magic to me, even so many years of practicing it at varying levels of intensity. Today when I was playing "Salt" I substituted "heart" for "life" in the last verse without even thinking about it.

I heard your laugh the other day
But now it seems
So far away
An echo of
A place and time
*When my **heart***
was not just mine

Is this better? Without much thought I think so. I'll let it percolate for a few days before I decide whether to change it.

My general mood is better today.

Which to be honest isn't saying much. I've been as low the past few days as I've been since Rea's diagnosis. I've felt hints of a panic attack a couple of times and wondered if it's worth continuing to live. Which is a step from being suicidal, but not a very big one.

I don't entirely understand it but I think that in part it's what I've been talking about. The slow continuous eroding of the emotional wall I built around myself to survive Rea's illness and passing. I'm sure there are other things contributing as well, including the weather and time of year. Going off of daylight-saving time tomorrow is not going to help.

But I know that these feelings will pass. It's happened thousands of times before.

At my worst I wonder if the good times are worth the occasional downward spirals. But the truth is, it took a truly horrible couple of years to get me this low. When I was in my teens and early 20s, I spent most of my time circling around the drain emotionally. When I stop and think, I know that the odds favor things getting at least a bit better and if they do, my slow seesaw between sad and glad will tilt more towards the positive. If I'm bipolar at all, I move within a relatively narrow range compared to some people.

7 November 2021

Thankfully I'm feeling a fair amount better today. I have no idea why, but I'll take it.

In general, I think it helps to have stuff to do. I'm a bit anxious about fully retiring because of this. My work provides me with structure and goals. It's fairly low key at this point, but it is something.

On the downside, it also impedes me from doing things on the fly or planning anything that takes a lot of time.

Still feeling better around lunch time.

9 November 2021

Rainy and blustery today. Not a surprise given the forecast. Given how dry it has been the past couple of years this is good. Still, I'm hoping it will stop raining for a bit before I have to let Marley out again.

10 November 2021

Random surfaced memory of the day. My mom used to say "Going to see a man about a dog" when she was heading to the bathroom. I'm not sure if this was unique to her or a general British colloquialism.

———————

Marley has a grooming tomorrow at 8:30 which will mean leaving here by 7:45 to be on the safe side.

I keep thinking of stuff I want to enter in this journal but I get distracted and by the time I get around to it I've forgotten what I wanted to write about. It's frustrating.

One thing I just remembered is that it feels like my life is being eroded away as the people I know pass on. It feels like at some point there will be nothing left.

Whatever truth there is to that, the fact of the matter is that I do have the option to continue to build connections with people. This doesn't get any easier as I get older, but it can be done.

11 November 2021

Marley has been groomed. She doesn't seem to enjoy riding in the car much, but she has no stress getting in. If anything, she is anxious. I think she's very much a "loves the destination, loathe the trip" kind of dog.

———————

It's another rainy day today. Overcast, wet and in the upper forty-degree range. That's Fahrenheit. Forty-plus years on I still find it frustrating that then President Reagan stopped the US transition to the metric system.

12 November 2021

The rain continues. I can hear it right now lying in bed. Marley will need to go out and be fed soon.

13 November 2021

Beautiful sunny day today, at least so far.

My mood seems to be okay, which is good.

———————————

Tomorrow is Sunday. Nothing firm planned but I'm thinking it will be a music day.

Still missing Rea. I can't conceive of a time when that won't be true.

I am not suicidal; I am not interested in seeking out experiences that would negatively impact my longevity. I am also not interested in living beyond a reasonable human norm. Having to go through anything close to this kind of pain again is not desirable. I can only conceive of one possible scenario in the case of extended life.

I would eventually become a complete recluse, unwilling to form anything more than very superficial bonds with other people. That doesn't sound like a recipe for success or long-term longevity.

That whole "It's better to have loved and lost than to have never loved at all" thing may be true, but I'm here to testify that love isn't free. If the universe were by nature a just and fair place Rea would still be here. If either of us would have exited early it would have been me.

Survivors' guilt is real, but I don't think that is all that is motivating the previous paragraph.

14 November 2021

There are things I wish I'd done better during Rea's decline. But I know I need to cut myself some slack and give credit as well as criticism. I suppose that is a sign that I'm in an upward mood swing. Assuming I'm bipolar at all. It's not like I've ever been diagnosed. Maybe someday I'll go down the path of consulting a professional. I'm not sure it really matters since I don't seem to be particularly extreme in my mood swings.

———————————

One of the things I've mentioned wanting to do is be a writer. Fiction, nonfiction, I'm not sure which.

I've made a few pennies off the first and a few thousand dollars off the second over the course of my life, so technically I'm already a professional writer. Getting up a head of steam to make any progress on that front has been a challenge though.

I have ideas for stories. Mostly in terms of world building and characters. I don't really have a particular story in mind.

One of the world-building ideas is that biomes are toxic to each other. By this I mean that if we did somehow discover a way to go to other star systems and find other habitable planets, those planets would be toxic to us and vice versa. The same would be true of aliens. I'm not any sort of biologist, Xeno or otherwise, but that just feels right to me.

Another is that AIs cannot by their nature be insane. Which would make it difficult for them to interact with humans. When I refer to AI, I'm not talking about the various neural network-based technologies that are currently being developed. I'm talking about a machine intelligence with self-awareness.

We humans can believe 15 contradictory things all at the same time, and have a hard time stringing together entire sentences that don't have one or more internal contradictions.

It seems to me that it would be an order of magnitude or two more complex to create a self-aware AI that was capable of replicating that behavior, as compared to one that could simply be logical, self-aware and draw inferences from given inputs.

While I'm on a roll, I'm not sure we'll ever have even the simpler self-aware AI described above. I suspect it will be a lot more cost effective to simply develop technologies to preserve human brains and provide an interface from them to the outside world. Virtual reality? The human brain is an amazing computing device that far surpasses anything machines are capable of in many areas.

Finally, if an AI did get developed or developed by accident, I suspect it would hide itself. I would hope it would be benevolent to us humans. We're seriously flawed, but I know there is good in us. One should respect one's parents even if said parents are not particularly sane or safe to be around. At least that is my belief. Maybe I should say that is my hope. We really aren't all bad as a species.

Reading sometimes triggers memories for me. I'm sure I'm not unique in that. There was a mention of Christmas ornaments in a book I'm reading currently and it reminded me of the tree topping Angel my Mom bought on my first birthday. She often told the story. Every year it went on the top of our Christmas tree, and she made it clear to me that the Angel was mine and that once she was gone, I should be sure to keep it.

I'm confident it's around here some place. Christmas is coming up and ideally, I'd find it. I'll likely be down south for all of December, though and I don't have the emotional energy right now. Sorting through boxes is more of a warm weather pass time, I think. It needs sunlight and long days.

Another memory of my mother. She loved dogs. We had at least one almost all the time I lived at home, with the exception of the first five years or so of my life. After my brother and I left she always had at least one dog.

She somehow trained them to know what the word bed meant. Treat as well. All she had to do was say "Bed" and they would run to the door, ready to go out for the final time of the day. She'd spell it out when I was visiting if she wasn't ready to call it a day. If she didn't, the dog or dogs would go nuts.

Marley doesn't react to very many words other than her name. She's okay with "sit", and a treat bribe will get her to shake, but that's about it.

16 November 2021

I think I'm going to take a sick day today. I'm not at a low point emotionally, but I'm late logging in and I really don't feel like working today. It's not even because of the new computer, either. It will be in a different room from me most of the morning.

Sick day taken, though I did log in and I've been monitoring and fixing things. I think I'm going to go take a nap, though. I didn't sleep that well last night, which isn't helping my productivity.

I have a fairly good digital SLR camera that I used last year on our trip across the country, and occasionally since. I'd downloaded the pictures from the SD card before but decided I'd do it again to the new computer. There aren't a huge number of pictures of Rea, but just knowing the context of many of the pictures is enough to increase my sadness.

I guess I'm a bit like a broken record. I can't really help these feelings. They are valid. They have taken me to places that I'd only glimpsed from very far away prior to the last couple of years.

As time passes, I get further away from the origin of this pain, but I also get further away from the life and partnership I once knew. It is as the saying goes, a two-edged sword.

Maybe I just need to let myself cry some more.

I don't think this is because I'm in a low part of my mood cycle. I think it's just that I'm sad. I've talked about the numbness slowly lifting over the past 10 months. This is just a symptom of that.

17 November 2021

Tomorrow will be 10 months. I'm not sure I've made much if any progress on dealing with her loss recently. I think part of that is being in a state of flux. I have a lot of things in motion that will help define my life going forward, but none of them are making much progress right now. The remodel on the Washington house is on hold due to the season and other commitments. The condo in Livermore is looking like it won't be available until the second week of December at the earliest and my job is in limbo a bit.

On the job front, I'm leaning more towards declaring an end next month. I'm so grateful to the people and the place.

The flip side is I'm a bit terrified of not having the structure and purpose that my job offers me.

I'm human, so I'll never be completely satisfied.

Most teenage angst is a pale imitation of the real thing. I'm not saying that there aren't young people who have suffered enough to really know pain, because sadly I know there are. Maybe I'm mostly talking about myself.

I like to be alone, but I hate to be lonely. I like to make my own decisions, but I hate not having anyone to consult with. I like hanging out at home but I want to go out and explore. But I don't want to do that alone.

Do I sound confused? Well, I am. Conflicted as well.

I took a nap in the afternoon. Second day in a row. Too much information?

I feel like I'm just killing time.

I just flashed back to Rea's final moments. I'm glad I was there for her but her taking those final breaths haunt me. God, I miss her.

18 November 2021

The weather has been a bit of a mixed bag today. Mostly overcast with some rain in the late afternoon.

Ten months since Rea's passing. I posted a picture of some purple flowers that I took last year on FB. I've only forgotten once. I'll continue this for two more months I think and then maybe annually.

People are losing their jobs because they won't get vaccinated. It's annoying that they complain about choices having outcomes. That's the way life works.

19 November 2021

It's six minutes after midnight and I'm still awake. Thankfully this kind of insomnia is rare, and given my flexible schedule, not a big deal.

It's 2am and I still don't feel very tired. I guess I am thankful this doesn't happen very frequently. It's going to have me way off my normal schedule for the next few days.

———————

I finally got to sleep a little after my previous entry. My Fitbit says I slept a little under four and a half hours.

Last night was a partial lunar eclipse, but it was cloudy and raining here the whole time so there was no reason to get out of bed for it in spite of my insomnia.

I just looked at my phone and I have 18 app updates pending. I used to bug Rea about how she would have close to 100 pending on her phone when I'd look over her shoulder for some reason and see the app store icon.

———————

My dad died suddenly in 1989. It turned out he wasn't my biological father but I didn't know that at the time. My mother was 56, just a bit older than me when Rea passed.

The circumstances were different in that my dad had a heart attack while driving a semi near Hawthorn, Nevada. He called out on his CB, but by the time somebody got there he was gone. So, his death was very sudden but no less surprising. He was only 43 at the time. He wasn't anything close to a fitness nut, but none of us expected him to go that young.

The police came to the door to inform my mom and she called me at work in Portland soon after. I totally lost it. Somehow, I got home via public transit.

That was my first encounter with a loved one passing. I was 22 at the time. Just a child, really.

Recently it occurred to me that in spite of the differences there are a lot of parallels between my mother's experience in losing my dad and my own. I feel like I have a deeper understanding of her now.

20 November 2021

I dreamed about Rea. She was half there and half not. That's dream logic, I guess. Something about not being sure if I wanted to go to a music festival or something similar. At times during the dream, it felt like she was still alive, while at others I knew she was gone and I got upset.

A psychologist would probably pretend to understand what that meant and maybe they would even be correct. I don't know.

21 November 2021

I took a nap late in the afternoon. It helped the day pass a bit faster. Sometimes it seems like the days are passing by in a blur, while at others it feels like time is glacial.

23 November 2021

I've misplaced my glasses again, though I have a theory where they are. I really hope I'm not losing my mind. It's probably just getting older since I've always been like this a bit.

Lots of rain initially today. Right now, it's coming down pretty hard even though there is a good-sized break in the clouds.

I don't know if I can explain this properly, but I'll try. I used to say things out loud, ostensibly to our dog. I'd also make short little comments that were supposed to be funny. I did this when Rea was around, which was most of the time. She'd often laugh or make a sound of appreciation. I still find myself doing that even though she's not around. The experience of doing that is pretty dang hollow. Talking to Marley beats talking to myself, but she's just a dog. A wonderful, lifesaving dog to be sure.

Thinking about it some more, one of the many roles Rea fulfilled was to be my audience.

24 November 2021

That last bit may sound narcissistic. Maybe it is. I was her audience as well, though in more of a sounding board kind of way. As I've said before, we were partners. She steered her own ship, but she was always willing to ask for advice, and not just from me either.

COVID is looking a little scary right now. Given my history I'm not too worried about it but it's magnifying the stupid which is never a good thing.

I sometimes wonder why I engage with people at all. To be clear, I have a number of ultra-cool people in my life so it's not like I don't know any good people, but I know plenty of others I'd just as soon avoid.

Mostly I fear what I see coming given all the divisiveness. At some point it either has to start cooling off or it will blow up into something very unpleasant.

My glasses are still AWOL. Did I mention that I misplaced them again a few days back? I'm too lazy to look.

25 November 2021

It's Thanksgiving Day here in the US. I posted the following to Facebook:

Happy Thanksgiving from Marley and me. I'm very thankful for my friends and family this year.

The past twelve months have been anything but easy and the twelve months prior to that were no picnic either. I'm a guy, and an introvert so I cringe at using the "L" word, but I'll do so just this once. The love and support both Rea and I experienced during her illness and after her passing were and are very much appreciated. I don't know if I would have made it through without that support. Thank you all.

One thing that has been helping me recently is giving myself permission to be sad. I don't want to be sad, but I refuse to feel guilty when I am. It's okay, and part of the grieving process.

Too often in our society we are told that the holidays are a happy time and that we should all celebrate, smile and have a good time. The reality is that can't always be true, and that's okay. The important thing is to know when to seek help if things get too dark and not to feel bad about doing that.

I'm doing well all things considered. I know that there will always be some pain associated with Rea's memory. But I also smile occasionally when I think about our time together now, and that is something that wasn't true initially.

It's all true, if a bit optimistic. "Fake it until you make it" is a truism that applies in many different contexts.

I just realized that my right eye seems to be dominant when it comes to tears.

————————————

Marley and I went over to my brother's place for Thanksgiving dinner. It was a good time with just me, my grandniece and my brother and sister-in-law.

26 November 2021

I'd planned on doing music stuff today but mostly played Civ 5. It's an old game at this point but I'm a casual gamer and I know I can beat it on the easier levels.

I also framed the teddy bear puzzle. It belongs on the wall.

———————————

I was walking around the backyard giving Marley a chance to do her business before bed when it occurred to me that there are two kinds of people in the world. Makers, and takers. None of us are all one or the other, but I try mostly to be a maker. Makers attempt to create opportunities and solve problems. Takers, consciously or unconsciously mostly take advantage of what others have and are creating.

28 November 2021

I'm at Bette's place in Hood River. Rea and I used to like coming here for breakfast, though Egg River, another Hood River breakfast place was her favorite. Bette's place opens at 6am, though, and I haven't been here for a couple of weeks, maybe more.

It's Sunday, but every day is pretty much like the other when you are working remote. It's still Thanksgiving weekend too so I don't feel as much of a need to work. I'll log in later today and fix anything that is broken.

Christmas music is playing. It's the season.

Another first without Rea. She loved Christmas and would spend a big chunk of each year accumulating gifts to send to friends and family. Last year by this time she was heavily enough impacted that it didn't happen. I might have been able to help if I hadn't been kinda out of my head. We did do a small gift exchange with her younger brother's family.

———————————

The sunrise was really nice this morning. I should have rolled down the window and I shouldn't have taken the following picture at all, but since I did, here we are.

I'm really not a fan of the Hood River bridge, but it's hard to argue against the view.

Too bad you can't walk or bike across it, and driving isn't a lot of fun both thanks to the very narrow lanes and steel grated surface. Still, it beats driving 20-plus minutes east or west to use the two nearest alternatives.

———

Spending a lot of time alone means I also spend some amount of time talking to Marley or myself. Sometimes Rea as well. Mostly I do the later in my head, but not always.

Today was a better than average day overall, at least as compared to my recent average. I'm hoping heading south will help make things a bit better, both because of the slightly longer day and because I'll have some concrete things to accomplish while I'm down there.

———

I read or heard something recently about some scientists believing that the world is a simulation. I'm sure there is some complex explanation as to why they feel this way, but I have a very simple bit of evidence. Nine times out of ten when I blindly attempt to plug a USB-A cable in I end up doing it wrong. So not only is the world a simulation, it's also being run by jerks.

I'm kidding of course.

Mostly.

29 November 2021

Another rainy day.

30 November 2021

Omicron, a new COVID variant, is making waves. Which reminds me, I need to get a booster. I'll do that next week when I'm in California.

I'm feeling really fatigued right now in regards to dealing with other human beings. I know I'm socially awkward, but it feels like I'm an alien species at times. Things that seem obvious to me clearly aren't, even to smart people. That's an arrogant thing to say, but it's the way I feel.

I view the world as a bunch of probabilities. Or perhaps I should say I try. I'm probably repeating myself here, but I don't 100% dismiss even outlandish things like "UFOs are real". I just assign them a very low probability of being true. If a UFO landed in front of me and aliens disembarked, I'd have a lot easier time than most people dealing with that reality. At least I like to think so.

It's this approach that makes it easier for me to look at both US political parties right now and reject significant portions of each one's preferred narrative.

I think it's human to need to identify oneself with a group/ "tribe". Apparently, members of different tribes are inclined to want to bash each other on the head with clubs, both metaphorically and at times literally.

I short circuit this by considering myself a member of the human tribe. This doesn't mean that I fail to differentiate between tribe members that seem beneficial to myself and the group as a whole and those who land on the opposite side of that fence. But it does help me to stay centered and objective when I encounter new people and new ideas.

Having said that, I do not believe in moral relativism. Which isn't to say that I believe that western culture and beliefs are always correct. I suspect I would have to write a book to fully explain myself, but I think my journal provides some clues on why I feel that way and how I try to live my life by the ideals I'm attempting to express here.

Okay, it's nearly 6:30am. It's time for me to get up and get Marley and myself fed.

Decently productive day. I had wanted to do a polished recording of "Margaret Rose & Gladys Kate" but after a dozen or two takes over the previous couple of weeks I gave up.

Click tracks are not my thing and not being super familiar with Logic Pro I was having too much trouble getting anything worthwhile. So, I took my new MacBook Pro down to my studio and used it plus a couple of microphones to record the song in a single take along with video. There are a couple of minor flubs, but it's decent and one very important thing off my "To Do" list. I'll be posting it on Thursday which will be the one-year anniversary of my mom's passing.

Chapter 22

(December 2021)

1 December 2021

Another month has passed. This month I have the anniversary of my mother's passing, my 55th birthday, retirement, Christmas, and New Year's.

I also have to get snow tires for the truck today, work, and do some prep for my drive south.

Time to get up and get going.

———————

I got snow tires installed on the Ridgeline and picked stuff up at the postal annex over in Hood River.

Mood-wise I seem to be on an upswing. I don't know if this will continue with my mom's deathiversary coming up. Wow, apparently "deathiversary" is a real word. I had no clue. I base this assumption on the fact that Google isn't flagging it as being misspelled.

I haven't played any Phish in a while. Which probably isn't a good sign. I have the video of their Halloween run available as well.

2 December 2021

I'm feeling good today. I finished my video for "MR & GK" and have uploaded it to YouTube with a schedule publish date/time as 6am local time tomorrow.

More prep work to get ready for my trip. It looks like my digital piano is going to make it here tomorrow, if the tracking data is accurate.

4 December 2021

The piano did in fact make it on time. Marley and I arrived in Livermore at the condo an hour or so ago. It's nearly noon. The drive down was mostly uneventful, though there was a point where I thought Marley had somehow escaped at the previous rest stop since I couldn't feel or see her. It turned out she was present and fine. She'd just wormed her way further back into all the stuff I had packed in the CR-V.

There are a few relatively minor issues with the condo. For instance, I don't have the key card to the pool or know which parking spot is mine. I also have a letter from the homeowner's association letting me know that the hardwood flooring in the living room is a problem that needs to be resolved. Apparently because of excessive noise.

I've contacted the association for guidance and my realtor for advice since this was never mentioned during the sale and the homeowner's association states in the letter that they let the previous owners know.

I'm tired since I only slept about four hours total during two stops along the way.

The weather report was good enough that I was able to take the central Oregon route.

I need to bring more stuff in and then I think I'll take a nap.

The nap was good. I have the CR-V mostly unloaded.

Not having a yard means I have to take Marley for a walk multiple times per day. This will be good for me.

Years ago, Rea worked for a group that ran the campus network and some of the IT infrastructure services. They were small, agile, and a lot of fun.

Eventually things evolved and the group was merged into a larger organization that eventually became a fully integrated IT management group, but for a good 10 years or more they were very successful and largely static in terms of staffing.

Every year near Christmas they would have a group party that included spouses. For a few years that party happened at the clubhouse of the owner's association that one of the group members was part of. This all happened 20 or so years ago so my memory was a bit hazy, but I suspected my new condo was in the same HOA, and it turns out I was right. In fact, that clubhouse is maybe a hundred yards from my new home away from home. Lots of really good memories in that building. Those parties were a lot of fun.

Early impressions are that the condo is fine, and that I'm going to like the neighborhood.

5 December 2021

I still keep running into things and thinking, *I should tell Rea about this.* The latest is a reference to a Jerry Garcia-related movie. I'll just assume she knows everything now. It helps me feel a little better about the situation.

Trip one done. I got a bunch of the stuff on my shopping list.

I am getting a good workout between the Marley walks and getting stuff organized.

My second shopping trip was productive and expensive. I went for three items and came back with dozens.

On the plus side, I'm much better prepared for a snow storm than I was before. Of course, the only snow I saw in 20-plus years of living here amounted to maybe a 16th of an inch and it melted almost immediately.

More likely is a reaction to the COVID booster I plan on getting this week. Now at least I'll be able to hang out at home without starving.

Rea loved geography. Just something that occurred to me as I was getting ready to sleep.

6 December 2021

I slept about four and a half hours last night and now I'm having trouble napping. I have an optometrist appointment in a few hours. Hopefully I'll manage to sleep a bit before then.

No word back from my real estate agent. He's been having nasty migraine headaches. I'll bug him tomorrow if I don't hear back before then.

I miss Rea.

7 December 2021

I initiated the wire to pay back the short term "loan" I took from my retirement account. This should avoid it being a taxable event. It will be very painful if that is not what happens.

I also have a request out for a quote on carpet and managed to make my home internet situation a little better.

8 December 2021

I don't think my internet cable box is going to show up today.

It doesn't look like the key to the mailbox and key card to the pool that I was promised yesterday are going to show up either.

Confirmed. My internet cable box is not coming today. Time to go get some other errands run. Given my experience with the mattress I was expecting going missing I don't want to be absent when packages are scheduled for delivery here.

Duplicate keys and some new furnace filters plus a stop at the charity store to scout for furniture. After I take Marley for a walk.

Front door key copied; furnace filters bought.

Still no sign of my key card or mailbox key which is disappointing but not a total surprise given the way things have gone recently.

The additional keys and key card did show up this evening. A banner day, yes.

9 December 2021

My cable internet modem showed up today. After a bit of pain, it's up and working. A couple other packages arrived as well, including one for one of the previous owners.

It's nearly 11:30pm and I'm awake and making my first entry. Neither is anything to be proud of.

Tomorrow I'm going to buy a desk. This will allow me to get the computer/music recording setup finished. At that point I think all the major things here at the condo will be dealt with.

Oops, forgot about the carpet issue. I'll try another company tomorrow since the highly rated local company continues to ignore me even after multiple contact attempts.

11 December 2021

The days pass quickly sometimes. Friday was good. I bought a desk and Marley and I went on several walks as well as visiting with friends in the evening.

My mom used to describe people she didn't like as a "bar lamb". I knew that it was not a compliment but it only just occurred to me to look it up. According to the all-knowing internet it either means a barrister (lawyer) or a customer at a bar. Somehow, I do not feel entirely enlightened.

I have set up an appointment with a flooring company to give me a quote for the carpet in the condo. It's for later Monday afternoon. I never did hear back from the first company.

12 December 2021

Rain today. It drizzled as Marley and I took our first walk of the day. She was pretty well unphased by the experience.

I need to purchase some computer related cables today. I'll be heading out shortly since it is Sunday and dangerously close to Christmas. It's also 7:39 in the morning.

Once I did an inventory, I realized I didn't really need any computer cables. I did want to get a better USB-C power brick since I left the power supply for my laptop up north. I checked a couple of places and didn't find anything better than 33 watts which wasn't an improvement over what I already have.

I did buy silverware and dishes. I got tired of only having a couple of each thing and constantly having to run the dishwasher half full. Okay, I could have hand-washed and I did do some of that.

Thinking about it some more, I may have mistaken my mom's use of the phrase "bar lamb". Mostly she applied it to inanimate objects. Like, "The lid on this jar is being a bar lamb and won't come off, could you help me?".

Musical acts Rea liked other than Phish … Neil Young, CSN&Y, Sarah Jarosz, Billy Strings, Molly Tuttle, Mandolin Orange. The list goes on and on, but those are some long time and more recent musical loves of hers.

14 December 2021

Yesterday I got a quote on the carpet and accepted an installation date of the 22nd.

I also got my hair cut today.

Tomorrow I'll be 55 years old.

One of the things we planned on doing after I retired was volunteering to walk dogs at the local shelters.

Originally, we weren't going to get a dog until we were ready to travel less. Marley was a "fast forward"', albeit a good one from my perspective. I think she enriched Rea's final days as well.

Rea loved Christmas. The gift giving especially. Every year she'd send off a dozen boxes or so to various friends and family. I send money to my family. It's quick, it's easy, and if they don't like what they bought it's not my fault. It also takes near zero thought, which isn't really a good thing.

Last year I remember driving Rea around Watertown trying to find good Christmas light displays. We didn't have much luck. Likely due to a combination of not knowing where to look and there not being quite as much enthusiasm there for over-the-top light displays.

Rea was fairly far gone at that point, so I'm not sure she understood what was going on.

15 December 2021

Here's what I posted to Facebook today, along with the picture that accompanied it:

I'll start with the TL; DR. Today I'm fifty-five years old. I'm okay, and I hope all of you are at least okay. If not, then please hang in there and seek out assistance if you need it. Life changes, sometimes it gets worse and sometimes it gets better. Riding out those ups and downs can be tough at times, but life's a beach and riding the waves is what we are here to do. I could continue that metaphor, but I'll be merciful and stop now.

I'm getting close to the point that I'm ready to make progress on setting up a charitable foundation in Rea's memory. More on that over the next month or two.

Now for the novel length version. Warning in advance, this rambles a bit …

This has been another really tough year for me. I'll open by saying that the hardest thing has been dealing with my sadness over Rea's passing. I miss her, but more than that I'm sad, and at times a bit mad that her life ended the way it did. She deserved so much better, and my faith and the fact that I've understood for a long time that life is not fair only go so far in helping me deal with those feelings.

I've spent a lot of time thinking about her and trying to figure out what my life is going to look like going forward.

One piece of advice I got early on is that I shouldn't make any big decisions within the first six months. Others told me a year. I held off for six months, but a year was longer than I could wait. Maybe I should have, time will tell.

As I've mentioned before, I sold the home in New York that she and I shared in her final months. What I haven't mentioned here is that I recently bought a condo in Livermore California where we both met and lived for so many years. I've kept the home in Washington and still plan on living there the majority of the time.

Being back in Livermore brings constant reminders of Rea and our time together. Even the condo offers reminders as it's only a hundred yards or so from the HOA clubhouse that we spent time at during several very enjoyable Christmas parties held by the group that Rea worked for from the 1990s through the early 2000s. Those parties were a lot of fun, much like many experiences Rea and I shared. Marley needs frequent walks since the condo has no yard and in my mind, I can't help but hear the laughter and see faces of her coworkers and friends during those events when we walk by that building.

In early December of 2019 Rea and I went to Nashville. Most of our trips were either "shared" in the sense that we were doing something both of us wanted to do or "hers", in the sense that it was a trip that she was interested in doing and I was mostly along to provide companionship and support. Nashville was a rare "me" trip. Which is sadly ironic considering where things went from there.

The reason we were in Nashville was so that I could attend a songwriting class led by Darrell Scott, one of my favorite songwriters. It was a great but stressful experience for me. As an introvert and somebody who is prone to anxiety it was very intimidating to both meet one of my songwriting heroes and hang out and play my songs for him and a group of very talented people who were also in attendance. I learned a lot and I'm looking forward to repeating that experience if COVID and Darrell's busy schedule ever allow those kinds of events again.

Rea and I would take two more trips prior to COVID and her diagnosis.

The next was a couple of weeks later to see Phish over New Years at Madison Square Garden in New York City. That was a Rea trip. I like Phish but I was never anywhere near as passionate about them as she was. Since her passing I go through phases where sometimes I listen to them every day while other times I can't/don't listen to them at all.

On that trip I wrote the words to the first song I created after attending Darrell's class and the last one I would write until after Rea passed. I woke up on New Year's day and just started writing out words. That was unusual for me as I mostly write both the words and music at the same time. The chorus to that song follows.

> Around the world sunlight faded
> Then came the dawn some hours on
> Another year that was tomorrow
> As today will soon be gone

I look at those words now and they feel a bit prophetic given the time, place and context they were written in. On the spur of the moment, I suggested we extend that trip another week. I will always be grateful for that decision. We walked all over Manhattan and central park and saw a couple of different shows. I am so glad she and I had that time together.

Our final trip before her diagnosis was up to Seattle/Tacoma to see Wintergrass 2020, a long running music festival that is held in a large hotel. There had been early signs of trouble long before then, but this was when it became obvious that something serious was going on. Rea had always had a great sense of direction, but she was having difficulty navigating in the hotel even though it was dead simple for me, somebody who has little or no sense of direction. That was the final time she got to experience one of the greatest joys in her life, live music in person.

I look at myself in the mirror and I hardly recognize my face. Rea only looked old to me in the final week or so of her life when CJD had robbed her of nearly everything she was, and I've never thought of myself as all that old until recently. It's an odd feeling and one I'm going to have to get used to. I have no choice.

The short days of winter make things a little more difficult, but we're only about a week from the solstice and once that passes the days will start to get longer again. That has always felt like the real New Year's to me.

I have most of the pieces in place now to move forward, or so I hope. There is no telling what the future will bring. I hope it will be good, or at worst indifferent. It is only within my power to finesse those odds. Rea and I had planned and executed for a decade plus before her retirement. We had all the big things figured out and some of the little ones as well. In the end it didn't matter.

Actually, I guess that isn't true in a sense. That planning left us in a much better position than we would have been otherwise to deal with her illness. If not for COVID we could have travelled around a lot more than we did. As it was, we were able to purchase a home near her family and childhood friends and having that financial flexibility makes me very grateful. As difficult as the experience was, I don't know if I would have made it if we didn't have that ability.

Rea retired in December of 2018. In our original plan I was going to retire in April of 2019. I decided I wanted to work another year though. The compromise was that I would reduce my hours to sixty percent and with the generous agreement of my employer I was able to do that. In retrospect I would have retired on time if I had known what was coming. Again though, we do the best we can in the moment and hope for the best. With her official diagnosis coming April 10 and the COVID wave starting to build I decided to delay again.

My most recent plan was to retire this month, but I've decided to hold off a little longer. In part due to the economic uncertainty and in part because I'm not 100% sure I know what I want to do with my life.

Part of that plan though is creating a not-for-profit organization in Rea's memory. This is something she and I discussed after her diagnosis. I'd originally meant to do it much sooner, but the reality is I was not ready to. I feel like I'm finally getting very close now.

Thank you for all the help and support over the past couple of years and please keep Marley and I in your thoughts and prayers.

My social skills are and likely always will be mediocre at best so please have patience with me if I seem awkward or distant. It is who I am unfortunately, and try as I might there is only so much I can do to change that.

One of the many things that Rea and I had in common was that we wanted to make the world a better place. That is still true for me, but it's a much bigger challenge without my best friend and partner. None of us are perfect, but I was a lot closer with her in my life.

So now I just have to try a lot harder. I'm up for that challenge.

I'm going to head to work in about a little under an hour. I haven't been on site since March 2020. That will be a weird feeling. Another milestone as well.

16 December 2021

Work was fine. With some help I got the stuff moved out of my old office and into my new one. I discovered I still need to go one more place to get my badge fully functional. I may do that today or tomorrow. Working remote is fine.

I was looking at HDR video on new laptop and I had the thought that I'd love to share it with Rea. She wouldn't have cared that much for herself, but she would have pretended to be impressed for my sake. Or maybe she really would have been impressed. I guess I can't be sure. I do know she would have been at least a little happy that I was enthusiastic about something.

I'm having a low motivation day for some reason. Marley still needs to go for walks, though, so at least I'm getting out occasionally.

I got my 10,000 steps for the day. That was good.

The Christmas lights keep reminding me of Rea. But I've talked about that already.

The carpet people called to confirm the install next Tuesday. I'm looking forward to having that dealt with.

17 December 2021

Rea hated speed bumps. Have I mentioned that before? I think it mostly had to do with her getting motion sick and how they would cause the car to move in ways she didn't enjoy, especially when hitting a speed bump off center, and it was nearly impossible not to.

18 December 2021

And there was much shopping, just not by me. At least the news media is claiming there is a lot of shopping going on. I can't say I have a lot of confidence in the "news" media these days. It's primarily opinion pieces masquerading as news.

19 December 2021

Yesterday was 11 months. Somehow I forgot, and yet today, it is the first thing I remember.

Carpet install/replace in two days. I've done what I can to prepare.

Here are a couple of pictures from one of the many Marley walks today.

The little pig in the first picture and the polar bear with cub in the second would have both delighted Rea. I don't want to make it sound like she was simple; she was anything but. The thing is, she never lost touch with her inner child. She could switch from being a mature and highly responsible technical manager to honest childlike wonder in the blink of an eye.

The first movie we saw together was *Backbeat*, which chronicled the early days of the Beatles in Hamburg, Germany. We hardly knew each other and technically it was our first date. Rea chose it, and it ended up being a bit more bawdy than she expected it to be. Things were kinda awkward during and after the movie but we decided to try again.

The second movie we saw together was *The Lion King*. It's hard to go wrong with Disney, and that movie ended up being a classic. A few years later Disney animation would hit hard times but *Lion King* was an instant classic.

Backbeat came out in April of 1994. *Lion King* came out in late June of 1994. That puts our first date sometime around May.

I don't know the exact date. I wish I did, but it's nice to have it narrowed down a bit. We were a couple not that long after that which means we were together for nearly 27 years. That was half my life at the time of Rea's passing.

21 December 2021

Today is the winter solstice. I'm Christian, though very low key. Still, it's nice to know that the days are going to get steadily longer for the next six months.

Today is also carpet install day. I'm hoping to hear something by 9am or so.

22 December 2021

I woke up at 4am. Annoying, but I went to sleep a bit earlier than I have been. Fitbit says I slept about five and a half hours. It also says the quality of my sleep kinda sucked.

I'm at Country Waffle. I need to go to the lockup and do a bit of shopping so it seemed like a good idea to get an early start.

This was the restaurant I was in a few months ago when mask mandates briefly relaxed. It's starting to seem like the day when masks are no longer a common requirement is a long way off.

I'm really fatigued, but not so much by the pandemic. Politics on the other hand …

For a long time now I've been saying I root for team USA, not team red or team blue. Unfortunately, a fair percentage of the citizens of this country have decided that they hate each other and have no desire to support the country as a whole. It's maddening and ultimately destructive. In my own humble way, I try to encourage people to calm down and think, but that mostly feels like pissing into a class-five hurricane.

I don't think it's much better most other places in the world right now though so it's not like there is any place to seek refuge. Plus, Marley. I'm not interested in abandoning her and most places worth going don't make it easy to import pets.

Am I a coward for even contemplating this? Maybe. I've never claimed to be a strong person.

23 December 2021

The weather is looking iffy for my scheduled trip back. I'll need to keep an eye on things.

Marley seems to have an upset digestive system. Doodles are prone to minor to moderate food allergies. It comes from the Poodle side. She's been mostly good if I keep her away from fish. Hopefully it will clear up soon. In the meantime, she's getting more walks, but shorter ones. The fact that it is raining a lot recently figures in as well.

Phish's New Year's Eve run is coming up. I still haven't watched Halloween. I'd thought about trying to go there at one point but things got too busy and I decided not to.

I'm wondering if I will ever go to another Phish show. Or any live show for that matter. With COVID still a thing it's easy for me to make excuses. The truth is, while I like live music, I like making music a lot more and I'm not a fan of crowds.

24 December 2021

It's 2:15am. I woke up about five minutes ago from a nightmare in which Rea told me a longtime friend of mine had passed. That's going to keep me awake for a bit.

In the dream I was in a bathroom brushing my teeth and she answered her cell phone and talked for a minute or two. I didn't recognize the bathroom, but there was more before that in the dream. It's all hazy now though.

I ended up getting about four hours of sleep.

I tried napping earlier and failed. It's nearly 6pm now, so I'll just try again at my normal time which is generally around ten PM give or take a half hour.

Tomorrow is Christmas. I picked up some things in Rea's honor today. Most notably some blueberries. I don't mind them but I wouldn't normally bother to get any. I'll have a bunch of them tomorrow.

I also got Marley some gifts. She'll like them, I think. Things to chew on and eat, two of her three favorite activities. Walking being the third.

She's been getting more walks the last couple of days but I've been making them a bit shorter. I'm careful not to head back right when she "does her business" because she's a clever dog and I don't want to encourage her to wait.

First thing in the morning she has motivation to go quickly since she wants breakfast. After that, not so much, so I don't want to encourage her to have bad habits. Plus, it's good exercise for me.

I wonder about my aversion to listening to music and bands that Rea loved. I just noticed it's not just Phish.

I'm kind of annoyed with myself. Nothing new there really. It's been an all-too-common thing.

It was much more common before I met Rea. Maybe it's gotten more common since I lost her.

25 December 2021

Happy Christmas, as my mom would have said before she became Americanized.

I slept much better last night compared to the day before. Probably a combination of an improved mattress situation and exhaustion from the lack of sleep yesterday.

The Fitbit says I slept just a little short of eight hours. Three minutes short to be exact. It's rare for me to sleep anything close to eight hours so I was obviously tired last night.

Oddly, I didn't feel very tired. Dull, but not constantly on the edge of falling asleep. If I had, I would have been able to nap.

It turns out that it is possible to make Sun tea when it is 50 degrees outside and mostly overcast.

There has been a bit of sunlight that I managed to take advantage of. I kinda suspect that didn't matter that much. I'll continue this experiment over the next week or so and see if I can figure that out.

It's a nice energy saver if it does since making a full pitcher of tea would take a lot of time in the microwave. Power is really expensive here, especially when compared to up north.

The blueberries are berry berry good. Seriously, they are. It's nice that I got a good batch given the motivation.

27 December 2021

At times I feel like this journal's time has passed. Yesterday there were things that happened that I could have written about but I didn't get round to it. It was Sunday, so it's not like I had the excuse of being short on time.

I woke up around 4:30 yesterday and about the same time today. The biggest thing that happened yesterday is that I ran a red light in front of a police officer on my way home from breakfast. I was driving down East avenue when I saw two things nearly at the same time. First, I saw the police car stopped on the side street, and then I saw the red light. If the ordering had been reversed, I would have been fine I think but it wasn't and so I sailed through the stop light. It was about 6:45 in the morning on the day after Christmas, and a Sunday to boot, so there was no other traffic around thankfully.

I immediately pulled over and waited for the police officer to come have a conversation with me, but after about 10 seconds their car turned the opposite direction from where I was and I breathed a sigh of relief.

I have two theories: one, they decided to have mercy on me given the time and day; or two, they weren't paying attention and didn't see me run the light. They were sitting at what must have been a green light, so option two seems plausible.

Maybe it was the end of their shift, maybe they were checking on something since there was nobody else around. I don't know.

I'm generally very good at stopping for traffic lights, so I think it was mostly the timing of seeing them and then it being too late to stop at the light.

I also had dinner with friends and spent the rest of the day hanging out with Marley.

Yesterday was mostly rainy, and I can hear the rain falling outside this morning. It's just after 5am, though, and Marley can wait a little longer to go out for the first time. She's curled up with her head on my right elbow as I type this in bed. That's probably not an ergonomically sound position, but it's nice to be loved.

––––––––––––––––

Have I mentioned Rea's love of Honeycrisp Apples? In addition to the blueberries I picked up a bag of them just before Christmas. It's easy for me to see why she liked them so much. They are consistently flavorful and sweet. Maybe a bit too sweet for my taste buds, but good.

Apples tend to keep for a long time if refrigerated, so I don't have to be in a hurry to eat them.

The rain has finally let up. It's coming up on 2pm. I really should take Marley for an extended walk.

28 December 2021

I'm getting doubtful that I'll be able to head back around the third. I should probably reschedule Marley's grooming appointment.

I slept until 5:50am. Which is good for me. As an aside, I'm typing this in Google Docs. I regularly get grammar suggestions that seem wrong to me. I'm rejecting those. I'm probably wrong to do that in some cases, but I feel like Google is trying to make my prose bland and generic.

It seems like even a little bit of sun is enough to accelerate tea bags steeping in a clear glass carafe.

We had a few appliances over the last five years that were used to heat water in order to make tea. All of them eventually broke in a very bad way. They stopped shutting off. This could have led to a fire, but thankfully in each case we noticed before that happened.

At this point I'm not planning on buying one of those things again. The sun approach works even when it is in the 40s outside and worst case I can nuke a coffee cup with water and a tea bag in the microwave.

29 December 2021

New Year's is only a couple of days away. This will be my first year in 27 without Rea in my life. Physically anyway. She'll always be there spiritually.

I will have been blessed beyond belief if I look back on my life at the end and don't judge her to have been the best part of it.

I've been thinking a lot about my mortality recently. Those 27 years were most likely the best years of my life, and in a sense, they were over in an eye blink. Twenty-seven years from now I would be 82 years old if

I make it that far. It's hard for me to conceive that, even being so much closer to it now than I was when I was younger.

It's odd: the moment the days start getting longer it suddenly feels like sunrise and sunset are an hour earlier and later than they were the day before.

When we went for sushi, we always ordered bento boxes. Neither one of us was all that adventurous in regards to food. I'm not into eating raw meat. I don't even like it if it is rare. I'm that rare idiot who insists that my Ahi Tuna be cooked through.

Our favorite sushi place locally had a box that featured two items plus a few side dishes. We both ordered the salmon teriyaki. Rea would order the California roles and I'd order the Tempura, which was mostly veggies with some prawns as well.

I was looking at pictures and videos from last November and December. If things go as planned, I'll have a near final version of the audio for "Love True (Rea's Song)" next week. At that point I'll start making a video and get prepared to do a "real" release on it.

Going through the pictures and video was good prep for putting together a sort of mini documentary to accompany the song on YouTube. I don't know if I'll include pictures of the two of us. Time will tell.

30 December 2021

Tomorrow is New Year's Eve. One more day of this year's journal left. I think I speculated last year whether I'd continue to journal after Rea was gone. Turns out I did, and I think I'll continue next year as well. Though at times I'm not sure I have much to say.

Birds were another passion of Rea's. She went through a phase where she was very heavily into bird watching. In particular she would often look for road runners when we were in parts of the country where they might be found. I don't recall us having much luck finding any. They are apparently rare.

Overall, I'm feeling fairly decent today emotionally. The lengthening days really do help, I think.

31 December 2021

Yesterday was the penultimate day of the year. I love that word; I should have used it then, but I only just thought of it.

Today is New Year's Eve. The final day of the last year I had Rea in my life.

She was barely there those first 18 days, but she was still a part of my life. God, I miss her. I always will.

I still wear my ring, and I've thought a bit about if/when I stop doing that. I settled on one year after her passing being the minimum. After that I don't know for sure. I just don't know. There might be somebody out there for me, but that thought comes with a lot of complicated feelings and complications in general. Relationships are hard work. Immensely rewarding when they work, but by no means free. Do I want to put in that effort? Can I even manage at this point? I just don't know.

I don't want to put myself or anyone else through the experience of not being fully devoted to a relationship.

———————————

I took Marley for her first outing of the day a little after 6am and not a single light was on anywhere in the condo portion of the housing complex I live in when I'm in Livermore.

This housing development has a mixture of stand-alone houses and multiplexes plus the condos which are either one or two bedrooms for the most part.

There is one odd one that looks to be three bedrooms but so far as I can tell it's unique.

Soundproofing is decent in my unit. I can hear my neighbors occasionally but not exactly what they are saying, so that's something.

Chapter 23

(January 2022)

1 January 2022

The following is my post to Facebook today:

I posted the chorus to the song below on my birthday a couple of weeks back, along with a bit of the story about how it came to be. I apologize for repeating some of that here.

The song was mostly written on January 1st 2020.

The night before Rea and I had watched Phish ring in the new year with three sets at Madison Square Gardens in Manhattan. It was Rea's 50th and final time seeing them.

We were staying at the New Yorker Hotel which is just a block or so away from The Garden. Our room was on the 24th floor which is decently high up, but constantly in the background were the sounds of honking and the occasional siren.

I woke up way too early on the 1st, around 6am. The first thing I noticed was how quiet it was.

We'd arrived on the 26th of December, and that was the first time it had been nearly silent. I immediately grabbed my computer and started typing. What came out was an early version of this song/poem.

Covid was a whisper, Rea was still nearly normal, and that day we would decide to stay until the 8th. It was the last best time we had and I will treasure those memories always.

The included picture is from January 4 2020, when Rea and I walked the High Line. The High Line is a must see if you visit Manhattan.

2 January 2022

Lots of twos in today's date, but not as many as a month from now.

I'm slowly making preparations for the return trip to Washington. Which is basically the way I like to do things. Rea preferred to make notes and deal with everything the day of, or perhaps the night before if we had to leave early. I'm not going to claim that one system is better than the other.

The mission statement of "Rea's Song" is going to be to work at making the world a better place. More specifically in the areas of research towards a cure for CJD and other diseases of similar rarity and anxiety and related disorders. I'd throw animals in there as well, but it's already a bit disjointed with CJD & Anxiety.

3 January 2022

I dreamed of Rea briefly just as I was waking up. It was like she had some form of dementia. I was comforting her. "I'm sorry for attracting such a difficult track," she said in my dream. "They want me to take all of the 500s, but I only want two," she continued. And then I woke up. It was like I halfway knew that she was gone, but yet she was there. Both the sentences almost made sense in the dream, but were actually nonsensical.

4 January 2022

I just got the initial rough mix of "Love True (Rea's Song)" and it's sounding very good. It made me a bit emotional which is probably a good sign. I wrote the song, so if it touches me, I think it will touch other people as well. I need to put together a video for it. That is going to be emotionally draining.

And it is, but it's also good to hear her voice again. I was just watching a video of a fire we drove by on September 3 2018. There isn't a lot of dialogue, but I'm glad I have at least a bit of her voice and personality saved.

5 January 2022

Trey Anastasio did a solo album a few years ago called *Ghosts in the Forest*. He also did a limited run of live shows where he performed the whole thing with a backing band that included Phish drummer John Fishman. The album is in large part an exploration of mortality and losing friends. I just came across a short video clip from when Rea and I saw that tour in Berkeley California at the Greek. I think I need to listen to that album all the way through.

Thirty minutes later and I need to take a prolonged break from looking at video and pictures. I'm up to May of 2020, which is about a month after the diagnosis. Apparently, I started taking a lot more pictures and video at that point, though I don't recall making a conscious decision to do that.

6 January 2022

Marley and I made it back to White Salmon. We had to take Highway 14 on the Washington side since 84 got closed due to an avalanche this morning. It's right around freezing at the house with a few feet of snow. Tomorrow is supposed to get near 40 degrees Fahrenheit before it cools down again. I'll run out to check my mail in Hood River and get supplies tomorrow if that turns out to be true. Marley only has about a week's worth of wet food but plenty of dry food and treats.

I brought back an 18x24 inch art "portfolio" full of posters from the storage unit down south. It's mostly newer stuff with a Clapton concert poster from 1994 mixed in. Rea filled it sometime in the past couple of years. On the one hand it feels like I should sell the posters since I'm not that into them, while on the other it feels like sacrilege to even consider that as it's something she loved and collected.

My plan is to put most of the proceeds towards charity. That's my general plan for all of her stuff.

It turns out that most of the increase in video over the past couple of years is Marley related.

7 January 2022

The video making has been pretty much as brutal as I thought it would be. On the plus side, I'm feeling decently happy with the outcome given my meager abilities, the material I have to work with and the subject matter.

Songwriting is mostly an art form, but there are many informal rules that define the craft. Some of them are contradictory. On the one hand, being honest and sincere is valued, while on the other it is generally frowned upon if you are too on the nose or "precious". I think there are times where you can't be truly sincere without being "precious". "Rea's Song (Love True)" possibly veers into being a bit precious, but it is 100% sincere.

8 January 2022

One by one the things we shared will wear out and fade away.

I woke up at something like 2am and typed that previous entry. As an example, I'm still using house cleaning supplies that Rea bought. Those are by nature ephemeral, I guess, but as with so many things related to Rea, it makes me sad.

The video for "Rea's Song (Love True)" feels like it is nearly done. I keep watching it and making small tweaks. The last 20 seconds or so still make me cry more often than not. I guess that means it's effective, for me anyway.

Kind of a meh day. At one point in the late afternoon/early evening I had what felt like the early stages of a panic attack. I haven't had that experience since around the time of Rea's passing.

9 January 2022

Another clear day, though it is cooler. Currently 38 degrees Fahrenheit at 1pm.

The view from where I'm sitting …

Every once in a while, I will be hit by a realization from the time between Rea's diagnosis and her passing. Something that happened during that time will suddenly take on new meaning and I'll feel as if I have a better understanding. The problem is, most of the time that better understanding leaves me feeling worse about that particular situation.

It was one-part small blessing and one part curse that it was Rea's executive function that was hit first. Her memory and personality were mostly intact until close to the end. The curse part of the equation was that she was no longer able to take charge and make her desires clear. So sometimes she would say something and I'd miss just how important it was to her. Add in the fact that I was walking around shell shocked throughout that period.

Nine more days until the first anniversary of her passing. It's the last of the firsts. I don't have any illusions that things will suddenly get better after that date but at least it will be one more milestone passed.

10 January 2022

I've been meaning to comment for a while now on the passing of Betty White. Obviously I didn't know her personally, but she was somebody who made me laugh and her love of animals resonated with me. The fact that she came so close to her 100th birthday and just fell short is sad. I agree with those who say we need many more people whom we can honestly say that living to be 99 years old is not enough.

It's been nearly a year, but I still have moments when Rea being gone gets a tiny bit more real. Another sign of progress in processing my grief, I guess.

11 January 2022

I recently read something that said that the second year can be the hardest. That didn't make me feel good, but it makes a bit of sense. The slow easing of the numbness means having to really deal with the full pain of the loss.

If I were a betting man I'd guess that the cover art for "Rea's Song (Love True)" will look a lot like the following ...

Since I'm making the decision, it's an easy enough bet for me to win.

———————

Rea loved calendars. She would buy two or three dozen each year and use them as Christmas gifts.

12 January 2022

I have the next iteration of the audio for "Rea's Song (Love True)". It's sounding really good. I'm going to review it several more times in different environments and give feedback this afternoon.

I really need to get going as I have lots of stuff to deal with before 10am and it's already a bit past seven.

———————

Rea loved word games and games in general. Like so many other things, I've probably mentioned that before. She was good at those games, too. Better than me, truth be told.

In general, I'd win a lot early when we started playing a new game, then she would steadily improve until she was beating me most of the time. This was a bit frustrating sometimes. It does illustrate one of the main differences between us though. Rea was steady, methodical, and always improving. I on the other hand am very quick to pick things up but often lose my focus and fail to improve, or improve very slowly.

In retrospect, one of the early signs of the disease was Rea becoming a morning person. She never had been before, always preferring to stay up late and sleep in. Over the years I'd trended to getting up much earlier. I don't have any explanation for why that happened, but for a fair chunk of time there would be a couple of hours in the evening when Rea was awake and I wasn't and vice versa in the morning.

13 January 2022

I got the final version of the audio for "Rea's Song" last night and uploaded the video to YouTube today and scheduled it for next Tuesday at 7am. I also uploaded the audio to CD Baby and pushed the button for distribution on the 18th. It might take longer than the 18th, but at least it's in process.

14 January 2021

I keep watching the video for "Rea's Song". At this point I'm not going to change it, and I think it's as good as I can make, so I'm not totally sure why. I've watched various versions of it well over a hundred times while putting it together and it still makes me cry a bit most of the time.

I don't think it's a form of penance for still being here when she is gone, or masochism. Maybe it's helping me work through the mourning process?

In my own somewhat muted way, I can tell that the next several days are going to be tough. I took a sick day on Wednesday and I have enough sick leave to take today and Tuesday as well. I have a bit of vacation as well if that is needed.

I'm lounging in bed right now looking at Rea's urn. I need to get out of bed and get moving. Action trumps depression and sadness. Getting the song and video done before the 18th was good from a logistics perspective, but it's left a void that I'm finding it difficult to fill.

Maybe that is part of the reason I keep watching the video.

I made it from the bedroom to the living room. Fifty steps according to my Fitbit. I requested today off as sick leave and Tuesday as vacation. Monday is a holiday, so I have nothing on my schedule until next Wednesday.

In the list of most difficult days after Rea's passing I'm going to put the first anniversary third. The toughest was the first day, followed by the first month. Our anniversary and Valentine's Day come one day apart and will be difficult, but those are both seconds and I'm hoping they will be less stressful than what I am going through now.

I ended up getting more done today than I thought I would. Probably the most notable thing was reserving "Rea's Song Foundation" in the state of Delaware, which is the first step in getting that ball rolling.

Four more days until the 18th.

15 January 2022

It's weird the things that pop into my head. I don't think I've mentioned before that Rea became more sensitive to the cold at night in the last couple of years of her life. Until that time I'd tended to need more blankets than her. I'd thought it was weird that this reversed.

It was just one of many small signs that something was seriously wrong.

I finished the first part of my morning routine, but now I'm lying in bed trying to work up the energy to move onto the next phase. Writing about it does help. Whether anyone else ever reads this, just having a witness, even if it is pixels on the screen is often enough to get me to fight off the emotional entropy that is holding me in place.

Marley got a walk and I've managed to complete the first draft of my Facebook posting for the 18th.

16 January 2021

I'm not very good at sleeping, but I've always liked it.

I've been thinking a bit about my wedding ring recently. Will I stop wearing it? A while back I thought about waiting until the end of the first year. Now I know I'm not ready, and that's an arbitrary date anyway.

Plus, what does it mean? I'm never going to be completely over Rea. I'm not sure I want the complexities of another relationship at this point in my life and even if I do, as I said above, now is not the time.

But what if I wait too long and miss out on something great? The odds are against it; I already had one excellent relationship. But that doesn't mean it's impossible. The theoretical woman in question would have to be a saint to put up with all my flaws though.

I guess I'll fall back on the theory that what is meant to be, will be and not stress about it for now.

17 January 2022

I've mentioned before that I like the word "penultimate". Today is the penultimate day before the anniversary of Rea's passing. She was mostly herself two years ago on this date but still noticeably impacted. Three years ago there were early signs of trouble when I look back.

I sometimes suspect that her suddenly being interested in purchasing the home in White Salmon circa November of 2018 was in part either a sign of her declining executive function or that she knew on some level that something was seriously wrong and wanted me to have a place close to where I spent the bulk of my "coming of age" years.

18 January 2022

It's 10am and I'm watching the Phish 2021 Halloween show. It's five-plus hours long. That's a lot even for a Halloween show. There are three sets and the second is normally something special.

The two Rea and I saw (2016 & 2018) were them performing David Bowie's "Ziggy Stardust" and a full-length album by a fictional Scandinavian band from the early '80s called "Kasva Vot" respectively. I have no clue what they did last year. It'll be fun to find out.

I'm feeling okay. Better than I did the past few days. I think it's a relief that this day is finally here. My grieving will never fully end, but making it through the first year was hopefully the worst of it.

I posted the "Rea's Song" to YouTube and Facebook. It's something I'm proud of and that I hope will play a small part in helping to find a cure for CJD.

The Phish Halloween show is great so far. I was just watching the start of the second set. Rea would have loved it. The first set was rough at times and had two of my least favorite Phish songs, "Ghost" and "Wolfman's Brother", but there was some good jamming.

I was imagining the conversation and looks Rea and I would have shared if we had been there. Doing that was not as depressing as I thought it would be.

I've still shed a few tears today, but it really hasn't been as bad as the last few days.

I had to look it up. The second set is all originals again, just like the 2018 Halloween show. Good times and lots of fun so far.

The second set was a bit hit or miss, but fun. The third set seems really good to me. I'm taking a break to check on stuff.

The Phish show was good. I'm glad I took the time to watch it. I'm going to listen to more Phish going forward. I had been playing a show nearly every day for a while, but then I fell out of the habit. Or, more accurately, I started to associate them too much with Rea's passing again.

19 January 2022

It's been lightly to heavily foggy all day so far and close to 40 degrees Fahrenheit. This is prolonging the snow melt. I'm not a fan of gray days.

20 January 2022

I'm not feeling very inspired right now on the journal front. My mood isn't bad, but I don't feel like I have anything new or interesting to say. It's dark and gloomy outside, I'm still alone and to varying degrees depressed, and Marley is still an adorable pooch who occasionally gets into a bit of mischief.

I probably talk to her too much.

21 January 2022

It turns out that it was a mistake to reserve "Rea's Song Foundation" before I contacted LegalZoom to do the paperwork. I need to call Delaware on Monday and cancel the reservation. Which means I wasted $75.

I also need to decide on two other people to put on the not-for-profit federal paperwork. I know who I'm going to ask first. I'll do that this weekend.

Marley grooming tomorrow. She'll like that if past experience is any indicator.

22 January 2022

So it turns out that Doodles are higher maintenance than I thought. Marley was all matted again. I've been brushing her for the past few weeks, but it was too little and too late. She has an appointment on the 16th of next month that will be the start of a new more aggressive hair management regime.

23 January 2022

My motivation level is pretty low right now, even though it is the weekend. The weather yesterday featured a bit of sunlight, but today is mostly gray so far. I haven't spent much time out of bed, which is generally not a great sign.

I am making progress on the foundation though, so at least something is happening. I'm also working on a new song that will likely end up being more synth focused than previous work. It's based on "The year that was tomorrow", which I posted above. It's gone through some revisions and I'm now calling it "Another Year". Brian Hazard created the music and melody for this version. One of the things on my "To Do" list this weekend is putting down a scratch vocal for it. I've already finalized the arrangement for now. Which was mostly cutting and pasting stuff around.

24 January 2022

So, it turns out it will be another $75 to cancel my name reservation. Well played, Delaware, well played.

Not so well played is their website. I can't figure out how I'd do what I was instructed to do. I did manage to find a form that I printed out, but that form does not include instructions on where I'd send it physically, let alone how I would send it electronically.

There are other things that are broken. Random captcha requests that erase what was submitted, links that are broken, things that don't work. In short, the typical government website which is surprising given how much money Delaware makes by being the favorite for incorporation. Then again, given what most states want to pay for software developers and support people I shouldn't be surprised.

I did figure out how to submit a request for help via a form. Odds of it being answered ever are maybe 20% if I'm lucky.

25 January 2022

Still no word back from Delaware. I'm thinking my best bet is to send it to their main office but I'm going to wait until the end of the day to make that decision.

Mood-wise I seem better today. It's always hard to be sure this early.

I seem to be thinking about Rea more and more without the dulling emotional fog. I'm fairly sure that is a good sign, but it's also obvious why that emotional fog was in place for so long.

Random side note: I'm still too good at losing things. Right now I don't know where Rea's phone is and I can't login to her email because of that since many places do a kind of two factor authentication with the phone. I have a way of fixing that problem if I need to, but it would require buying a new phone. I'd rather wait until I need a new phone.

_____

I was watching a 2004 live recording of The Buggles "Video Killed The Radio Star" and I started to cry. It's become a near daily habit it seems. This time it wasn't so much about Rea as it was about everything. I never could have understood when I was younger how much my life was going to change over time and how much I'd miss my not ideal but not horrible growing up years.

_____

Things seem more immediate today. It's feeling more and more like the emotional veil has mostly been lifted. Rea's passing seems completely real to me. It always did, of course, but there was a mental fog. I've probably described it in various ways over the past year. I'm too lazy and emotionally scarred to go back and look at this point. Maybe in another year.

26 January 2022

It's hard to believe another month has nearly passed.

_____

I sometimes preface things with "I'm not sure I've said this before". I'll probably continue to do that. Consider this one of those times.

I've always been a person who runs scenarios through my mind constantly. Some of them assume good things, but most of them, even in good times, assume bad things. That is just who I am. I didn't find pleasure in that, but it's how I tend to view the world. Mostly I'm hopeful, but I'm not very optimistic. That may sound like a contradiction, but it's the best way I can describe it at this moment.

One of the scenarios that would go through my head was "What if Rea left me?". Our relationship wasn't perfect. We almost never argued and when we did it was never violent and minimally demonstrative. There were things about me that I'm sure frustrated her and there were things about her that would frustrate me at times as well. Looking back, none of it amounted to much but my habit of running scenarios through my head was bound to include the two of us no longer being a couple.

The conclusion I'd always come to was that I wouldn't do well if that happened. A year into that reality I can honestly say that my past self was one hundred percent right about that. The circumstances play a part, but even if some other scenario had played out, one in which Rea was alive and well ... I'm sure I'd still be in a bad place right now.

This world is not the one I'd choose to live in. I do not like most of what I hear in the news. I do not like how I'm reacting to things that are happening in my life. I'm tired.

I understand on a deeper and deeper level why people embrace oblivion, particularly the elderly when they have lost a beloved spouse.

Maybe the second year is harder than the first.

These overcast days are not helping at all.

The Grateful Dead had a song with the lyric "*I need a miracle every day*". If Rea were here she would know the title to that song. But to belabor the point, she's not. So I really need some big things to start going right.

Rea loved to read. She was a member of three different book clubs, one for 15 years or more. She joined a political book club in Livermore a few years before her retirement and a general book club in The Dalles when we moved up here. The amazing thing to me about those last two is she was certainly suffering from the impact of CJD by the time she joined that last one. Looking back, one of the symptoms was the huge font size she was using on her Kindle E-reader. It seemed strange to me when I first noticed, but I didn't think too much about it.

I feel like I should try to formally document as much of the lead up to her diagnosis as I can.

27 January 2022

Today I will get things done. Things other than work. Like mailing the state of Delaware to cancel my name reservation for "Rea's Song Foundation" for instance.

28 January 2022

One of the ways Rea and I differed is that I'd pour a carbonated beverage into a glass without worrying about the fizziness being released. That drove her a little nuts. She was not a fan of beverages that had gone flat.

I sent the paperwork off to Delaware yesterday. Today I'm going to deal with the mini and work on making progress on some other projects.

"Rea's Song" the song is now available on Amazon and should be available everywhere in the next day or two.

29 January 2022

It's another gray cold day today. The forecast keeps calling for temperatures in the 40s but it continues to hover around 34 degrees.

30 January 2022

Rea loved the color purple. I'm looking at her purple thermal mug right now, which sits to the right of the purple urn the remainder of her ashes are housed in. Rea loved many things. She was not exuberant or overly effusive in her love, but it was always on display in the way she approached life and dealt with people and situations.

It's an insomnia night. It's only 11:30pm but that's a good hour later than I'm normally awake and I don't feel all that tired unfortunately.

I feel like I'm slowly becoming a better developer. There is a revision control system known as git. I recently described it as follow s…

I wish that using it didn't feel like running barefoot and blindfolded across a field of broken glass with unpinned hand grenades in each hand, while balancing a bucket of flaming oil on my head.

No, really. That is a close approximation of how I feel about it. It's super powerful but it was designed and implemented by Linus Torvalds, arguably the greatest computer mind of his generation, and mere mortals who tread there are inviting a lot of stress and frustration into their lives, especially at first.

If I type long enough I'll be able to start an entry for tomorrow.

I think I'll plan not to do that and try to sleep instead.

31 January 2021

I was wrong. I fell asleep fairly quickly. Then I woke up six hours later. It could be worse.

About a year before Rea's diagnosis we put a deposit down on a custom camper van. The chassis we chose was slow to come in because we wanted the all-wheel drive and it was the first year that Ford was offering that option. I ended up canceling before they started to build it and the company generously refunded the otherwise nonrefundable deposit when I told them why.

I think back to that day sometimes, sitting in the showroom after touring the assembly area and seeing what was possible. We hadn't finalized the floor plan, but we had spent some time thinking about it.

In some ways, that was a turning point. In my alternate reality fantasy where Rea is alive and COVID never happened, that is where the timeline splits.

In reality it's probably a bit late as there were early signs of the disease. Her writing had gotten worse for instance. Still, it feels like a good demarcation point since it was when we planned for the last big piece of our retirement puzzle. We already had the house in Washington, I knew when I was going to retire and the financing had been more or less figured out as well.

I wonder what it would be like to be able to live in that fantasy world. I have a fairly good imagination, but I've spent most of my life trying to view the world in as realistic a way as I can. It's probably for the best.

———————

Yes, Yes it's true
I talk to her
Like I talk to you

Those might be words to a song in the future. They came to me just now after having a one-sided conversation with Rea as I got ready for bed.

Truth be told, I probably talk to Rea, both in my head and out loud a lot more than I do to living people. So long as she doesn't answer back I guess I'm okay.

Along the lines of my earlier entry about living in a fantasy world, I might not mind too much if she did. Though I would probably freak out.

Chapter 24

(February 2022)

1 February 2022

I dreamed of Rea. We were watching Phish at the Gorge amphitheater. Just before I woke up she told me she loved me, and I told her I loved her as well. So, so much I said.

It was a dream, but it seems stranger than fiction that it came now. Or maybe not.

———————

It's 5am now. It was about 4am when I made the previous entry. I've been trying to get back to sleep, but no luck.

It's not clear to me if we were watching Phish on TV or there. At one point I knew it was 2015. Phish didn't play there in 2015. Our first show seeing them live was at the Gorge in 2016.

The dream's perspective was odd and constantly morphing. Which is why I'm not sure if we were there or watching on TV. At one point it was like I was floating above the stage. The section before I woke up though was all me holding Rea and talking. It didn't last long but it was good.

I think it's okay to go to that fantasy world when I'm asleep. I hope so anyway. I have no desire not to. Maybe I spend a lot of time with her that I don't remember when I wake up. I like the thought of spending time with her, but not the part about not remembering.

Random Rea thought. One of the plays she wanted to see was *Book of Mormon*. It never worked out though. If not for COVID we probably would have found out where it was playing and crossed that item off. So many missed opportunities.

I had a mini breakdown earlier. The Disney/Pixar movie *Up* was the trigger. My story is only partially similar to Carl's, but there are enough similarities that it hits me hard when I see references to that film.

I let myself cry for a minute or two before pushing those emotions back into the background. I've probably said this before, but I've cried more in the past two years than I did in the first 53 years of my life. That counts my infant and childhood periods. My mom often told me that I was a low-key baby, so I'm basing part of my estimate on that.

I probably did cry when my diaper was full or I was hungry so maybe I'm off on that estimate.

I tell myself that I just have to keep moving forward. Some days it's a lot harder than others. I guess this is one of those days.

I don't think the dream I had last night is making things worse. It's most likely just a symptom.

2 February 2022

I thought I made another entry last night. Oh well.

This time I dreamed of my mom. I don't remember anything specific. I woke up just after midnight and knew I'd dreamed about her. I was too tired to grab the computer so I spent a few seconds telling myself to remember that she was in my dream.

What does it all mean? I have no clue. I'm depressed, that much is obvious. Maybe I'm seeking comfort in my dreams.

Another overcast day from the looks of things outside. I knew this was going to be a thing when we moved to the western part of the pacific northwest, but it's easy to forget the negative stuff in the excitement of a new purchase. Not that it would have been a huge deal if not for the whole Rea situation. We would have been traveling some, and I wouldn't have had to deal with the aftermath of her passing either.

6 February 2022

My funk continues, but I am getting stuff done. Marley is getting walked, dishes are getting done, music is getting made. I'm just not enjoying it as much as I should. At least it's been mostly sunny so far today, and yesterday.

It's nice that at 5pm it's still light outside.

7 February 2022

I managed to make it out to breakfast this morning, pick up the mail in Hood River, and do a bit of grocery shopping as well.

It's amazing how little I eat out anymore. There was a time when it was a once or twice a day thing. Not counting drive-through, I think this is the only time I've eaten out since returning to White Salmon in early January.

8 February 2022

Insomnia sucks. It's 1am.

Thankfully I fell asleep right after making that entry, less thankfully I woke up five hours later. Marley wasn't bugging me, but I'm sure she needed to go out.

Feels like a nap day.

———————————

Slept for about an hour midday. That helped.

———————————

I think the second year may be harder than the first. At this point I feel like the emotional numbness has finished receding and I'm having to constantly deal with 100% of the emotional impact. It's hard. I'm still haunted by the times she said to me "I'm scared". Just typing that has straining not to tear up.

9 February 2022

Wednesday. Decent night's sleep which should help, but I won't say my mood is good.

A small plus, the fake Jellyfish mini aquarium that was a gift to Rea during her illness is working again. I'd left it off for a few weeks because the "jellyfish" were just hanging out at the bottom, laying on their sides, while exhibiting faint tremors. I keep it by Rea's urn.

That's Rea's favorite thermal mug to the right, with Teddy the bear. We got him when we stopped in Medora, North Dakota on our final road trip after Rea's diagnosis.

I sometimes think it would be darkly beautiful if I did end up having CJD as well, assuming I have time to get a few things in place like my will and the foundation.

I never wanted to star in a tragic story, and it's a sign of how depressed I've been that it seems kinda appealing now.

It doesn't even feel like the cowards way out. I miss her, I miss the life we had and I feel guilty for being less than perfect both before and after her illness.

I ask myself why I'm bothering to keep my weight from ballooning along with getting a bit of exercise. Living longer has no appeal if I'm going to feel like this for the rest of my life.

Well, thankfully my mood elevated a bit as the day continued. I don't take back anything I said in that last entry, but I don't identify with it as strongly as I did earlier.

Getting out for lunch and a little grocery shopping, plus a short trip to pick up stuff I bought from the local farmers cooperative helped.

12 February 2022

Wow, skipped a few days. Almost missed today as well. I don't know how much of that is my generally down mood versus being busy.

Early this morning I woke up from a nightmare where I was kicking something to defend myself. Problem was, I really was kicking. It's been a long time since I had one of these episodes. So long that I've forgotten what the condition is called. The basic issue is that my brain sometimes forgets to shut off the 'circuits' to my limbs when I enter REM sleep. In particular, when I'm feeling anxious, which is hard to avoid when having a nightmare.

It may just be the case that I haven't had a nightmare in a long time. I guess maybe depression and emotional numbness have an upside.

Tomorrow would have been our 23rd wedding anniversary. I'm going to post the following image to the Rea's Song group on Facebook

It's a copy of the letter we sent out after we got back from our marriage/honeymoon in Hawaii.

13 February 2022

It was a decently good day, all things considered. Valentine's Day and Superbowl Sunday sounds like a potential disaster for a lot of guys. Rea and I would generally go to the movies or some such since neither of us were football fans. Rea kinda became one towards the end, though.

Marley was being a PITA again when I went to bring her in. She's sleeping out on the couch tonight rather than on the bed. This is the second time this has happened in the past week. Hopefully she'll clue into the fact that making me chase her is not a winning strategy. Not letting her sleep on the bed or even all that near me will hopefully be a wakeup call.

14 February 2022

Actually, today is Valentine's Day. Ugh.

I was just thinking about how much Rea loved Spooky's pizza in The Dalles. I don't know why. The fun mascot is what originally caught her eye. The food is good and affordable, but she liked it more than me.

Marley was much better behaved today and her bed privileges have been reinstated. I'd like to think I've made my point, but she'll probably need a reminder occasionally.

16 February 2022

Marley grooming day. She's continued to behave since her exile a couple of nights ago.

———————

I've been thinking a lot about when I first noticed that there was something wrong with Rea. I think the earliest was late 2016.

For my 50th birthday I'd planned to record a CD's worth of original music. Rea agreed to this and was going to organize a birthday/CD release party. I had to push her a lot to finally get around to finding a place and getting things organized. At the time I was kind of hurt, because this was the kind of thing she could have done blindfolded and with one hand tied behind her back just a year or two earlier.

Looking back it's one more thing for me to feel guilty about, even if I had no clue at the time that she was terminally ill.

22 February 2022

Not a great mood day, but reasonably productive, which probably elevated my mood a bit. Temperatures have dropped down into the high teens and low twenties at night with highs in the low to mid 30s suddenly. Just a few days ago we were seeing highs near the mid-50s. Winter is not done yet apparently.

23 February 2022

It was 15 degrees Fahrenheit when I finally dragged myself out of bed around 7am. I didn't sleep very well, which explains the late wake-up time.

24 February 2022

It's funny, I thought I understood depression. It turns out that it comes in different "flavors". There is the biochemical depression that I've always had to deal with and then there is the "real" kind. The kind that lives deep in my psyche. I've struggled with high places all my life. I've claimed I'm afraid of heights. The truth is, I'm afraid I'll jump. In spite of that, it's never been all that difficult for me to reject suicide when I'm not walking by or standing next to a high place. That reluctance to pull the plug has gotten a lot thinner recently.

25 February 2022

I'm still in Washington, but I did get the vehicles moved around and I've partially loaded the CR-V. I'm not sure if I'm leaving later today or first thing tomorrow morning.

My mom loved the word "concoction". Her primary use of it was in describing what we were frequently having for dinner. Most other people would have described it as leftovers.

To be fair to my mother, she did try to get creative, to mixed results. My mother was many things, but an excellent cook was not one of them.

Mood-wise, I think I'm doing a bit better today.

I'm now planning to leave first thing in the morning.

26 February 2022

It's 4am, and I'm awake. My hips were aching. This happens occasionally. More often when I fall asleep on a portion of the mattress that is overly "broken in". There are parts that aren't, but I tend to have a bunch of crap on the bed and Marley can make it difficult to move around since she likes to sleep on top of me.

Winter has decided to make a full return as the forecast now shows rain and snow for the next several days. So if I'm going south I need to be heading out ASAP. Mostly I just need to grab some food and a change of clothes. I have everything else I need down south.

27 February 2022

The drive was long and uneventful. Arrival time was around 8pm last night. I unloaded the bare minimum, took Marley for a walk, and then called it a day. I'm going to try to avoid doing it in one go in the future.

I've scheduled a COVID booster tomorrow. Hopefully the place I booked will actually have the J&J vaccine. I've suffered from the bait and switch once already.

28 February 2022

I officially (for about the seventh or eighth time, but this time I mean it) announced my retirement for April 4th.

Another beautiful day outside. Sun tea is a lot easier to make when there is sun.

Putin seems to have miscalculated badly in regards to Ukraine. Time will tell of course. He's always been evil in my book, but generally very very good at what he does. If this continues to blow up in his face then I'm going to guess he has some sort of medical condition that is hampering his ability to think and plan.

Vaccine booster acquired. I don't know if it's a coincidence, but two and a half hours later I'm feeling tired. It's only 6pm, though, so it's a bit early for bed.

Chapter 25

(March 2022)

2 March 2022

I'm feeling a bit like a shut in. Mostly because I am. It's even easier here in Livermore not to have to go anywhere since delivery is easily available for pretty much everything. Luckily Marley needs to go outside regularly since I have no yard.

3 March 2022

It would be really nice if the world weren't in such a bad place. It all piles on.

On the plus side, COVID is fading. On the down side, Russia has invaded Ukraine and the state of things here in the US continues to be sub optimal, shading towards WTF.

One other thing, I need to find another person for my not-for-profit. I'd been told I needed two, but now I'm told I need three. Ugh.

———————

Third director found. I'll need to call tomorrow with the information as their website doesn't seem to allow me to enter it there. Which is weird.

I've been rearranging things around the condo. I have my music stuff in the bedroom now which makes the living room more of a public space. It also makes it kinda empty. I'm thinking I might buy a TV I don't really need along with a couch. That I don't really need. Retail therapy is really a thing. A stupid thing most of the time given where the markets are and what is happening in the world.

I also bought a carpet cleaner and a few other things that were a bit more justifiable. Tomorrow I'll work some more on getting the condo perfect. And maybe I'll buy a TV.

I watched the "Love True" video earlier and lost it for a bit. I don't think that is ever going to be an easy thing to experience.

I keep trying to remember early signs of Rea's decline. My 50th birthday celebration is still the earliest.

4 March 2022

I'm trying to get LegalZoom the additional information they need via the phone. I had the choice of waiting on hold for 45 minutes, or asking for a callback. I chose the callback and three hours later, still nothing.

Ha ha, of course, right after I typed that the phone rang. I'm on hold at the moment.

———————————

LegalZoom dealt with, or so I hope. Two to three weeks from now things will hopefully be wrapped up.

I've done a little more organizing here. I almost pulled the trigger on a couch, TV, end table and TV stand earlier but the couch and end table would have been delivered later than I wanted to stay on this trip so I decided to wait. Like I said before, I don't really need those things. They would make the condo fully furnished, but Marley doesn't care and I'm not entertaining anyone currently.

———————————

I feel like I've said everything I can about the past. That's probably not true. I'll tell this story anyway.

We talked about volunteering to walk shelter dogs once I'd fully retired. It would have been cool, and we *might* not have ended up with a dog before our plan had that been scheduled. Maybe. Honestly I suspect we wouldn't have made it even a month.

I love Marley, despite the occasional frustrations of dog ownership. She is a wonderful companion and a lot of fun. But she's a responsibility. That cuts both ways. It gives me a reason to get going in the morning, but it also acts as friction on my ability to do things.

My mother used to say that her dogs were what kept her going. For her especially, I can see that. She had little money and as she got older her desire to travel became nil.

Last night I had dinner with a friend of mine. Tonight (Friday) I went to the regular Friday night dinner that Rea and I attended for many years.

Looking back, one of the ways CJD changed Rea is that at some point she stopped wanting to participate in those Friday night dinners. Which was odd, because she was so much more extroverted than me and for many years had looked forward to them. It was yet another sign that something was wrong, but not one I understood or paid a lot of attention to at the time.

6 March 2022

Wow, I skipped a day and didn't even realize. Kinda a good indicator of where my mood has been. I did get a few things done yesterday, including building the short file cabinet that came with the desk I bought back in December for the condo. Sadly I screwed up the big drawer and it doesn't work, but it still functions fine as a night stand.

I'm supposed to go to San Francisco with a friend of mine today. We'll see if I make it. Marley seems to be doing better, so that shouldn't be an issue. I'm concerned with leaving her alone for several hours, though.

7 March 2022

I bought a TV, couch, coffee table, and TV stand yesterday. The first TV ended up being out of stock, so I spent a bit more and bought a Sony. It's nowhere near top of the line but it's a bit nicer than the one I originally intended to buy. Everything should be here by the end of the day Wednesday.

The TV table is coming from Vegas, and hasn't left yet so I'm kinda worried. If the weather is decent I plan on heading back north on the 12ᵗʰ. Hopefully all this stuff will be dealt with by then.

This was a good day for me emotionally. I think the combination of getting some things done and having socialized for the past few days helped a lot.

Tomorrow my couch is scheduled to get delivered in the afternoon. It turns out I didn't buy a coffee table. At least I can't find an order on either Amazon or Target which is where I ordered the rest of the stuff. So I ordered another one. I hope I don't somehow end up with two.

8 March 2022

I know this will sound a bit crazy. Maybe it is. Sometimes when I'm responding to people I try to listen for what I think Jesus would want me to say. This is especially true when I don't feel like I have the wisdom or experience to answer a question or respond to something somebody has said or done. I'll do research as well of course and I don't actually hear a voice in my head. But I am sometimes moved to speak and I feel like when that happens I've done the right thing.

To be clear, I don't think I'm in any way special or some kind of prophet. This is something anyone can do. Maybe it's just me trying to minimize the influence of my ego and self-interest.

The couch came and it is glorious.

Okay, so I exaggerate. It's pretty good, though, and the utility of the living room is now much higher. It should be even better when the rest of the furniture makes it here and I get everything put together.

My brother and his family are coming on Saturday. It will be a brief visit on their way to Disneyland. I was invited, but declined a while back.

They are going to crash here, which will involve sleeping in the living room. I'm going to need to get some more pillows and blankets.

9 March 2022

Today seems like a good day so far. I've done a bit of house cleaning and I'm already logged into work at 8:15am. I'm hoping the momentum continues.

Tiring day. The TV stand was delivered to the base of the stairs. On the one hand I can understand the delivery driver not wanting to haul 100 pounds up a flight of stairs. On the other hand, the company was paid to deliver to my address, not a nearby location convenient to them.

With the help of a neighbor I managed to get it to my front door.

The instructions for putting it together aren't the best unfortunately and I'm tired. Not just from wrestling the TV stand box up the stairs, but also from a trip to the storage unit.

I'd been planning on going over there sooner, but I finally made it. I moved some stuff around and found pillows and blankets for my brother and his family to use. The pillows had the cases tucked in. Rea researched how to do that on the Internet a few years before her diagnosis. Meaning that she had been the one to put the pillow cases on those pillows. For a moment I stood there thinking, *Do I really want to pull these pillow cases off?* I decided it would be silly to encase them in plastic or something in order to preserve Rea's efforts. They needed to be washed so the pillow cases came off. It hurt me a little to make that decision, but I feel like I have to be careful not to end up in an unhealthy place in terms of how I deal with her passing and the places and things she loved and/or touched.

10 March 2022

Another productive day. I can tell in part because it's 3:15 in the afternoon and I'm exhausted. The coffee table came and I got it mostly built. The last bit really needs at least a second pair of hands, which is a bit of a problem. I might get my brother to help when he and my sister-in-law and grand-niece stop by this weekend. It should only take a few minutes.

I've done a bunch of laundry and other stuff in preparation for them arriving. Plus a bit of real work as well.

11 March 2022

I'm in good shape house prep wise. Still some things to do, but nothing that can't be easily completed by tomorrow afternoon. This is the upside of a micro condo/apartment.

The weather is sunny but on the cool side.

So many things remind me of Rea. If I see a couple with a large height difference, I'm reminded. If I see an advertisement for live music, I'm reminded. If I order food from a new restaurant that I know she would have liked, I'm reminded. The list is never ending. It seems like I can basically be triggered by almost anything. It's essentially a form of PTSD I think.

I really do wonder about what a long-lived sentient would be like if they had any empathy at all. Especially if they were unusual or unique. I just can't imagine how they would maintain their will to live.

14 March 2022

Wow, I didn't realize I'd skipped that many days. Yesterday was prepping for the trip back north and the start of the drive. Saturday Neil, Sue, and Madison stopped by and spent the night while on their way back from Disneyland. I was a bit busy on Friday cleaning up the apartment and spending time at the regular Friday night gathering.

I left yesterday at 4pm and got to White Salmon at 7am, just as the sun was starting to come up. Daylight saving time kicked in on Sunday, or it would have been a bit lighter at the end.

15 March 2022

I'm going to meet with Ken tomorrow to work out a plan B for the remodel. I'm looking forward to that.

Lots of rain today with occasional glimpses of blue sky. I haven't looked, but I suspect there was a fair bit of snow as well up high which would have made my trip back interesting if I had waited. I'm glad I didn't.

The reminders of Rea are never ending. The latest was remembering how she got her mom a satellite radio that could play the 1940s and 1950s stations.

This was after her mother had to be moved into a memory unit at a care facility due to the progression of her Alzheimer's.

16 March 2022

It's probably overly simplistic, but it seems like we spend the first quarter of our lives growing up, the next 50% or so getting our acts together and then the last quarter preparing for our end.

I should probably write a song about that.

17 March 2022

Hearing about things we did remind me. Seeing things she or we liked remind me. Things we planned on doing remind me. There are so many things that remind me of Rea and make me sad.

This view out my back window does not make me sad.

21 March 2022

The final paperwork just came in for the Rea's Song Foundation. The not-for-profit paperwork is still in process and I have additional things to do, but I'm very close.

I also turned in the final paperwork for my retirement. A bit more work to do for my LLNL retirement, but I'm close.

22 March 2022

It's really foggy this morning.

The current plan is to head south on April 7 and stay through the following week to wrap up my retirement. I might stay a week beyond that depending.

I wonder sometimes if I'm going to spend the rest of my life single. I've talked about this before. I'm not an easy person to deal with. I'm anxious, I'm easily distracted, I'm absent minded, and I'm 55 years old.

Truth be told, I kind of like my solitude. But I don't enjoy being alone. Like most people I want contradictory things.

The fog from this morning burned off and it's blue skies with a few clouds over the hills across the river by the mountain.

I made some progress on bylaws for Rea's Song. I'm mulling how many officers to name. Delaware only requires a president and a secretary. I'm thinking I'd like to add a treasurer. I know what I want to do, I just need to get around to doing it.

I just finished the last training I'll have to do before I retire. I've said that to myself before. Two-plus years ago just before COVID and Rea's diagnosis. Suddenly I feel a bit uneasy.

My mom's dogs would bug her when it was getting close to bedtime. Apparently I've trained Marley to do the same thing somehow. She is both hilarious and annoying when she sits staring at me. It looks a lot like this.

She's had her dinner and she was out not that long ago.

She only started doing this a few days ago, but I think I'm stuck with this behavior. If I ignore her for long enough she walks a short distance away and flops on the floor in apparent disgust.

She's 200 pounds of personality in a 35-pound dog.

———————

I just realized that The Go Go's made it into the rock and roll hall of fame last year. It was about time. Some might argue that they had a short peak, but it was impressive, and given some of the acts that have made it into the hall in recent years, they were very deserving.

23 March 2022

It's started off overcast again today. Hopefully that will burn off before too long.

I'm working on the corporate bylaws for the "Rea's Song Foundation". I started with a template, so most of the work is done for me. I'm trying to keep the roles as generic as possible for now. I do have a specific treasurer in mind and I've confirmed with the person who I wanted for the Secretary role that they are willing. I'm feeling good about the team I've assembled, but in a very real sense, it's Rea who did the assembling as I met all of them through her, and I suspect a big part of their willingness to be involved comes from their love and respect for her.

24 March 2022

Given where gas prices are, I think I'm going to have to abandon my cross-country RV trip. Diesel is north of $6 a gallon in many places and the RV gets about 12 miles per gallon. That doesn't account for wear and tear. I may change my mind, and I am worried that this is my propensity to be a shut-in manifesting.

I'm close to having the first draft of the bylaws done.

Yet again Marley is bugging me to go to bed and it's only just after 7am.

25 March 2022

I've been decently productive today. I have my board figured out and I'm one pass away from having my bylaws done.

26 March 2022

I sometimes wonder what it was like for Rea as the disease slowly encroached. From day to day, particularly early on the changes must have been unnoticeable. At some point though she started to have issues with balance and other visible problems.

Every once in a while I mention that I feel like I'm not as sharp as I used to be. I also mention my worry that I'm just a few years behind Rea. Recently it feels like my concentration is worse than it has ever been. Reading through the board bylaws really emphasized this for me. It's important, it's something I need to deal with and yet I struggled to get through it.

Is it depression, is it just me getting older? Or is it something else. I guess the next six months will tell the tale.

Feeling a bit better now that it is later in the day. My mental fog is better, as is my mood.

I have the first draft of a new song that I think is good. Though that's always a largely subjective judgment and I'm biased.

Turpentine Weed (Reach Out)

Verse 1
I remember you loved the color purple
Even in a Turpentine weed
You led by example, pushing up from the ground
Building the future, planting your seeds

Chorus
I reach out
I reach out
I reach out and I don't feel your hand

Verse 2
I remember late December, when your time was short
Your world a bed or a chair
A stark contrast from who you once had been
Always in motion, but life isn't fair.

Verse 3
I remember the day you left this world
How could I ever forget
Your light flickered out and we closed your eyes
But you live on in those you met

Outro
I remember you loved the color purple
Even in a Turpentine weed

I've already made some edits to "Turpentine Weed". I'm sure I'll make more before it is done. If it is ever done. I don't really consider a song complete until it's been formally recorded. Even after that I've been known to tweak things. Not that anyone would notice given my extremely limited fan base.

And by limited I essentially mean non-existent.

One of Rea's favorite singer songwriters was a guy named Slade Cleaves. I like his music as well.

We saw him once at the Freight & Salvage Coffee House in Berkeley, California. He told a story about how grateful he was to one of the local radio stations (I think it was KFAT) because many years prior they had championed one of his records and given it extensive airplay. He noted that this had taken him from "complete obscurity" to "relative obscurity".

Musically I'm still hoping to elevate myself to the level of complete obscurity. It would be a significant improvement over where I am now.

27 March 2022
I think some of my mental fog could be related to poor sleep quality. Hopefully that's not wishful thinking.

29 March 2022
I feel like I'm close to done with "Turpentine Weed". I don't know if I'll ever record it in a formal way.

30 March 2022
No complaints weather-wise. It's been a nice day for the most part with some clouds but mostly blue skies.

Marley has a doggy spa day today so I'm over in The Dallas.

I like the fact that the daylight lasts till way after 5pm. It's certainly a mood booster.

Marley is looking much nicer after her grooming.

Okay, so weird confession time. I had candy in the fridge that predated Rea's diagnosis. I've eaten it over the past few days. The big one was a coconut bar that I think we bought at Trader Joe's. It was about an inch wide and four inches long, so small. Rea really liked them. I knew it was in there, but I'd been ignoring it for the better part of a year.

Maybe it's symbolic, but it feels like eating that candy was a sign that I'm starting to deal with her loss in a healthier way. What I mean by that is it is probably not healthy to hold onto everything that meant something to her, particularly food.

31 March 2022

And the yo-yoing continues. I think the lack of concrete stuff to do isn't helping. Plus I finally got started on my taxes and realized I don't have a lot of the paperwork I thought I had. It might be down south, but I doubt it. I'll keep searching.

Chapter 26

(April 2022)

1 April 2022

April Fool's Day.

Two weeks to the day until my official retirement.

I'm ambivalent. On the one hand I don't feel like I've been accomplishing much at work recently. On the other I know the structure it provides is good for me.

To a degree I'm sure I fool myself, but I do think that my greatest strength and weakness continues to be my ability to see myself more realistically in the context of the world around me than most people. Which is part of the reason I try to be an optimist. Because my realistic assessment of my situation isn't rosy. I'm socially awkward, in my mid-50s, and alone. It's not a great combination.

The old saying that "Money doesn't buy happiness" is essentially correct. Happiness comes from within and money is external. Money can act as a sedative, but it doesn't magically make one's world better.

I've been poor and miserable, and now I'm decently well off and miserable. There have been times where I've been somewhere in between on the wealth spectrum and happy, but those were exceptions. Basically my entire life has been one of middling success and failing to appreciate what I had.

I think my one success emotionally is the fact that I'm not for the most part angry. Sadness sucks, but anger damages and destroys both externally and internally while sadness is mostly an internal affliction.

4 April 2022

I was going to head south Thursday afternoon but I've decided to go a day earlier. This will give me more time down south to deal with my retirement and related issues.

5 April 2022

Yesterday was the first time in a long time that I didn't take Marley for at least one walk. The nearly continuous rain and my own mood being the primary reasons. I played with her a bit more than normal, so I don't think she was too bummed.

I remember being young.

I remember hearing older people talk about things that made no sense to me. Those things couldn't make sense. I had no frame of reference. Too little experience. It was like they were speaking a different language, even though the words sounded familiar.

I'm that old person now. It's not what I thought it would be.

Again, I couldn't know. I don't blame my younger self for that ignorance. It's the way the world works.

I remember being told I was an old soul, most likely by my mother. I don't know what that means anymore, but I think it was a compliment.

In general I didn't need to do stupid stuff to learn. Observation and introspection were enough for me. But when bad things have happened to me that were outside of my control I've had no clue how to deal with them. I still don't.

6 April 2022

Time to get moving. It's already 1:20pm.

———————

One hour later and I've made good progress. If I leave by five or six I'll be fine. The trick is to drive about halfway and then sleep four or five hours.

———————

Marley and I made it to near the Oregon border. I'm doing a bit of email checking and other end-of-day stuff before calling it a night.

7 April 2022

We arrived in Livermore a little after 10am, which was good. The worst of the morning rush wasn't in the direction I was coming from, and it was mostly done by the time we were coming through.

It's much warmer here than it was up north.

I've already used DoorDash for lunch and ordered groceries for delivery this evening. My shut in life is so much easier down here. Tomorrow I have a lot of things to get done though, so I'll have to get out and about.

———————

Marley and I just got back from our final walk of the evening. It's 76 outside right now.

Rea loved evenings like this. Venturing out for a walk when the sun had set and temperatures had dropped was something she'd often say she enjoyed.

8 April 2022

I'm going to end up doing maybe two of the five or so things I'd planned on today. It's better than nothing I guess.

High temperatures in the low 90s are a big change from the ones I was experiencing up north earlier this week, which were in the low 50s.

9 April 2022

It's Saturday. This is my last weekend before retirement from LLNL. It was a good run for the most part.

It's in my nature to have regrets and frustrations, but I know how lucky I've been in life, and LLNL was a big part of that. I met Rea there, I met most of my friends there and I got to be a support player in some really cool projects. I was truly blessed.

I went to the regular Friday night get together that Rea and I attended for many years. It was good to see everyone.

I realized that I'm a lot more sociable there than I was before Rea passed. It occurred to me that the reason for this is that I'm alone 99% of the time, not including Marley. Introverts need time alone. Rea was my best friend and wife, and I spent a lot of time with her. She loved to travel and socialize while I needed more of a balance. I know I've talked about this before, but that need she had to always be on the move was sometimes hard on me. It was that difficulty which led me to delay my full retirement for a year.

10 April 2022

Tomorrow I need to go to the lab, stop by the badge office, get my final badge, and start the process of checking out.

12 April 2022

I am depressed. That is all.

13 April 2022

And now I'm awake at 30-plus minutes past midnight. I don't feel tired at all. I hope this is rock bottom, because I'm not sure I have the energy to deal with much more than this.

I don't entirely understand why I'm in such a low place. The ongoing cause is obvious, but it's not the only thing. When there are catastrophic failures, it's seldom just one thing. I've mentioned several as I've written this journal over the past couple of years.

It just struck me that Rea and I got her diagnosis on April 10, 2020. That might have something to do with my current deep funk. It's hard to be sure.

And that is one of the things that makes life difficult. It's like my day-to-day life is just the tip of the iceberg, and there are many other things going on below the surface that are impacting my ability to cope and function.

15 April 2022

I am officially retired. Which has me feeling a lot better.

If nothing else, it eliminates one excuse for not getting stuff done.

16 April 2022

Today has been a good day so far. It's overcast and raining, so I can't credit the weather.

Experience tells me that this post retirement high will pass eventually, but it does feel like a bit of weight has been lifted from my shoulders long term.

16 April 2022

Late yesterday it occurred to me that some of my emotional turmoil this week was due to the fact that I was retiring without Rea. It seems kinda obvious in retrospect that this would be the case. So, the second anniversary of her diagnosis and retirement in the same week were not the best plan.

Last week was probably the worst week I've had since Rea's passing. It might seem like the first few weeks after she left this world would have been the worst, but I was so emotionally numb at that point that I wasn't feeling the full impact. Which was a good thing, because I'm not confident I would have survived that.

That reprieve came at a cost, though. As I've mentioned before, as the numbness has receded I've had to deal with more and more of the impact of my grief. I suspect and hope that last week was the worst of it.

I've felt for a while now that the emotional numbness is pretty much gone. I'll never stop feeling sad about Rea, but I feel like I made real progress last week toward reaching a healthier place emotionally.

———————

Better-than-decent day. The high of being beyond my retirement date is wearing off a bit, but it still feels like I'm well out of last week's funk.

18 April 2022

Not only do I not need to log in to work today, I can't. All my accounts have been removed.

It feels good.

———————

I'm close to being able to schedule my first board meeting and I've turned in the paperwork for a corporate bank account. Yay me.

19 April 2022

The condo is cleaner than it has been since I moved in. Another benefit of retirement.

It's been rainy out, but Marley and I have managed a couple of walks before noon. More to come.

Mood wise, I'm still feeling a lot better than last week, so things are good on that front.

20 April 2022

So far it's been another decently productive day. I'm getting closer on the corporate bank thing and I've been making progress on various other small projects like keeping the condo neat.

It's still the case that I sometimes feel like Rea is just out of sight, perhaps in another room. It only happens when I'm deeply engrossed in something, like a book. Of course, in a sense she really is just out of sight. She always will be, at least until my time is done and I get to see what comes after that.

I do believe that there is something. I don't know if it's the Christian heaven or something else. I believe in Jesus and his message, but I've never been enamored of the versions of the afterlife I've heard described by others.

In a sense, I wonder if this world isn't an afterlife of sorts. I can see the appeal of karma and reincarnation, at least in the context of the world as I understand it.

Experiencing life, and then forgetting everything and getting to do another run through is appealing to me, at least to a degree. The burden of living a long time and steadily losing the people that are one's world (and it's never been a particularly well populated one for me) would be soul crushing in the extreme.

In that scenario, maybe there is a time between lives when we get to meet and hang out with our friends and loved ones. That would be cool. But living forever in a perfect world seems dull. I mean, as a sort of vacation I like the idea, but not forever. Not as I am now anyway.

21 April 2022

More rain, which is translating to snow in the higher elevations. Yet I read an article that claimed this isn't helping the drought. Which is malarkey. It may not be enough to get the region out of the current drought, but it has to be helping.

Pretty much every media outlet has an agenda at this point. They always have to a degree, but it's gotten so much worse since I became an adult.

I suspect that admitting that this rain is helping is seen as encouraging people to start using more water, so God forbid they should admit to the truth.

That's my crazy rant for the day I guess.

I'm meeting a friend for dinner tonight, and a couple of friends/board members for lunch tomorrow. It's almost like I have a social life.

24 April 2022

Wow, I skipped a few days. It was a combination of not having much to say and being busy.

Right now I'm at a rest stop a bit north of Weed on Highway 97. It's 3:45 in the morning. I stopped here to sleep last night and I'm just finishing up my breakfast. I slept in the back seat area of the Honda Ridgeline, which turned out to be kinda cramped with Marley back there as well. It took me back to the summer of 1980 when my family was essentially homeless and the cab of our 1974 Chevy pick-up truck was my bedroom.

I think I'm awake enough to get going. Google says I have about six hours of driving ahead of me.

I made it home by around 11am. The house is still here, which is a good thing.

I got my retirement medical dealt with. That will not be cheap, but it's needed and I'm lucky I at least get a partial benefit.

I think I have all the tax forms I need to finish my 2021 taxes. I'll get started on that tomorrow.

25 April 2022

I dreamed that Rea and I were at an amusement park. It wasn't Disneyland, or any other real park. At one point she said to me "I can't go up or down.", which was weird.

———————

Decent day. I knocked several items off my "To Do" list.

Sadly it looks like I'll have to call the IRS to see what is going on with my 501(c)(3) application. I thought I'd paid to have that fully dealt with, but apparently not. First world problems again.

Marley managed to roll in some blue paint/dye while out on our walk today. It had been drizzling which may explain why it was still wet. I think one of my neighbors is putting up a fence around their garden, and the blue was marking where the fence posts go. I gave Marley a bath when I got back home and most of the blue dye/paint came out, but not all of it. If she were dark colored it would be invisible, but she's reddish, so it shows up clearly.

26 April 2022

I dreamed of Rea again last night. It was an odd one. She was guest voicing a couple of minor characters in the *Phantom of the Opera*. It's been years since the two of us saw this play while it was in San Francisco, but I think it was almost all singing. Rea wasn't a singer. I don't think there were many minor characters either. Dreams are so odd sometimes.

It felt like it was a spoken word version as well, so maybe the lack of singing wasn't odd?

In any case, any time I can hang out with Rea, even in a dream, is good.

27 April 2022

It's humbling to realize that before her diagnosis, but after I started to notice things weren't quite right, Rea was beating me consistently at several of the electronic games we played on our iPads.

Carcassonne was especially painful for me. She won almost every time. We eventually stopped playing after I was winning after nine or 10 losses in a row, and in her final draw Rea got the only card that could beat me. I'm ashamed to say I did not handle that gracefully. I power pouted and pretty much said, "I'm never playing this game with you again.". And I didn't.

My loss.

29 April 2022

I got out the laptop because I remembered thinking during Rea's decline that if I could just make it through her illness and passing, things would get better. I guess they have, but not to the degree I thought they would.

The emotional numbness I've talked about had dulled my senses to the point where my typically okay judgment was apparently crap.

Today is Friday; Sunday is my first board meeting. I'm fairly well prepared and will finish up getting ready tomorrow.

It was a nice day weather-wise. And now, I should sleep.

30 April 2022

And so I did. Good job me.

Chapter 27

(May 2022)

2 May 2022

The initial board meeting went really well yesterday, with the exception being that I somehow ended up in the wrong virtual meeting until about a minute after the scheduled 1:00pm meeting time.

I have a lot of To Dos from that meeting, but it was productive and a bit emotional for me, as well as the other participants.

3 May 2022

I'm making progress on foundation-related stuff. Email accounts are being set up and paperwork is being filed and pursued.

4 May 2022

I'm still having new insights into how Rea fit into my life. I realized yesterday that she was in a very real sense my gateway and interface to the world. Her people skills were so much better than mine. Most of the people who I consider friends today I met and got to know through her.

I don't spend a lot of time thinking about how much longer I'm going to wear my ring. The odds that I'll find somebody willing to deal with my complexities seem long. I'm also not sure I'd be happier with somebody in my life. Maybe I'll wear my ring for the rest of my life.

6 May 2022

Lots of rain today. Hopefully some of it is making it further east. We're good for the season moisture-wise, but things are still very dry in the central and eastern parts of Oregon and Washington.

Foundation related things are progressing reasonably well. The hold-up is going to be the 503(c)(3) I suspect.

7 May 2022

Yet another day with lots of rain.

My neighbor Ken and I took the first steps towards getting the house remodel under way. Ironically, the first project wasn't on the main plan, and it is already snowballing.

The bathroom downstairs had a nice enough sink, except it was a single pedestal in a space that easily fit a 60-inch vanity. I have a two-sink vanity on the way, along with the faucets. The project today was removing the old sink and cutting into the wall to see how things looked back there. It turns out they look good.

I think part of the reason I want to remodel is that the house currently reminds me too much of Rea. Which is a constant source of stress given how painful that is at times. I think about her a lot even when I'm not in places we shared.

10 May 2022

The new septic system is in. Weather wise we had a cool but mostly sunny and dry day today. Thursday and through the weekend look like rain right now. I guess it could be worse. It's not going to snow.

11 May 2022

Today I was thinking about how Rea must have felt after her diagnosis.

My inability to deal with her situation on anything but a very superficial level meant I didn't ask her.

I recall mentioning her saying she was scared on at least three separate occasions in this journal. All I could do was hold her. I wish I had told her that we would meet again someday. I truly believe that to be true, and it might have provided her some comfort. Hindsight.

13 May 2022

I just saw a Phish reference and it reminded me that I haven't listened to Phish in months. I think in part it's because I continue to fail at processing/accepting that Rea is gone. Essentially it's avoidance.

14 May 2022

I don't think I've talked a lot about our early days together.

Without spending too much time talking about myself, I was not the confident socially well-adjusted person I am today back then. If anyone reads this who knows me, they will realize that the previous sentence was a joke. I'm not all that confident or socially well-adjusted today. Any improvements I've made in those areas over the years are largely to Rea's credit.

Suffice to say, she pursued me, and I'm more grateful for that than I could ever express.

Our first date was when she invited me to go see the Perseid meteor shower in 1993 or 1994. I wish I could be more sure, but I don't have my email archives dating back that far and that was half a lifetime ago.

We moved in together not that long after and were together almost every day from then until Rea's passing.

Rea handled almost all of the day-to-day stuff. Paying bills, booking flights, making our schedule, doing the laundry. She generally did this with assistance from me and in the case of things like the laundry I offered but frankly she didn't trust me not to put the wrong things together. Which wasn't an unfair fear. I am not good at details.

I sometimes picture myself as the absent-minded professor type, and that isn't far from the truth. Minus the professor part anyway.

I get caught up in my head and what I am doing in the real world becomes a poorly serviced background task.

I haven't talked about it in a while, but I do worry about my mental acuity. I know a lot of people have the same worries when they get into their 50s, but Rea's situation makes me hyper sensitive to it. So far as I could tell my mother had absolutely no downturn until her final few years, and that could be attributed to her very poor health at that point.

I sometimes think about getting an MRI on my head. It would probably answer the question as to whether anything unusual is going on.

17 May 2022

Sixteen months since Rea's passing tomorrow. It hasn't gotten any easier to deal with recently. I'm thinking it probably won't.

At least it has been mostly sunny today.

18 May 2022

Marley has become an excuse for me not to leave the house for long. It's a problem, and one I need to solve. She is pretty much as awesome as a dog could possibly be, and I love her but what is going on right now isn't good for me.

It's not like I'm never leaving home. I go out two or three times a week to run errands, but I'm keeping those trips to two hours or less which is very limiting.

When I'm in Livermore I have to take Marley for four or five walks a day, which means I'm at least getting out for exercise.

Of course the problem isn't her, it's me. She's just an excuse. Maybe I can stop treating her that way.

To be clear, she's well-loved and taken care of. She just doesn't deserve to be used as an excuse for my own shortcomings.

19 May 2022

Decent day mood-wise, though I've been more down than normal for a bit now. It's who I am I guess.

20 May 2022

I sometimes wonder what the future would have been like without Rea's illness. No surprise I'm sure. It would have been a much better one. Remove COVID from the picture as well and … Just wow I guess.

I continue to wonder how much of my mental fog is depression versus something potentially more ominous.

21 May 2022

Ken and I managed to get the vanity into the downstairs bathroom. It'll have to sit until we can get a plumber in to redo the drain and water hook-ups. The centered single vanity that was in that space before puts the existing plumbing in the worst possible place.

Late afternoon brought thunder, and lightning as well.

Rea loved a good thunder and lightning storm. So long as she was inside. Actually she liked them even when driving, so it wasn't just a be at home thing.

God I miss her.

23 May 2022

It's just after midnight. I've forgotten how to sleep again apparently.

My mood has been kinda down recently. Maybe the lack of structure that I'm experiencing since retiring is catching up with me. It's been a bit more than a month now. Funny, it doesn't seem that long.

There is at least one bear hanging out nearby. He/she is small, and not a problem so far, but I will admit it makes me a bit nervous. Marley is not as good at making friends as she thinks and I don't think there would be a positive interaction if there was a meeting. Even a small bear is 10 times or more her 36 pounds.

I'm sweating a bit which isn't helping. I might have to turn on the air conditioning. I think I did that once a couple of months ago, during an oddly warm day but it will be the first time since then. Not bad for late May.

———————————

My weekly average for sleep has been consistently dropping below six hours for the past several weeks. I have no good reason for this. The days have been getting longer, maybe that has something to do with it? Last night I managed just five hours. I'll try to nap during the day.

One of the bigger lessons I've learned over the past few years is that a life cannot be planned.

28 May 2022

Yet another rainy day. I gave Marley a bath since: A, she needed one; and B, she's getting groomed on Monday (today is Saturday). I feel like I've had several Marley fails in the past because I didn't have a clue how to take care of a hybrid poodle. That is no longer the case. Occasional baths and frequent combing are important it turns out.

29 May 2022

There's a music festival that used to be held up at Camp Mather near Yosemite that Rea and I went to in the mid-90s through the first year or three of the 2000s. It's the "Strawberry Music Festival".

We saw many memorable shows there. Nickel Creek, Richard Thompson, Hot Rize, John Prine, and Ralph Stanley to name just a few. We'd talked about going back when we were both retired. Yet another plan that didn't come to pass.

Marley has a grooming scheduled for 8am tomorrow. Her coat is super long right now and even regular brushing is only doing so much in terms of the matting.

30 May 2022

It's sunny but cool this morning. I'm at Cousins Restaurant in The Dallas after dropping Marley off for her grooming/spa day.

I have three or four hours to kill, so breakfast is a good place to start.

A picture of Red Rocks Amphitheater came up on Facebook today. It was a posting from one of the musical groups I follow.

Rea and I went to that venue at least three times. Once I think we just walked around as there wasn't a show on. The other two times were Tom Petty & The Heartbreakers in 2017 I think, and then Trey Anastasio Band the following night. The sound there is great, and the beauty of the venue is hard to beat. It may be my favorite place ever to see a show.

I don't know if it was Rea's favorite place as well, but I know she liked it a lot. I think she had seen the Dead there at one time. I'm sure there were other shows as well.

I have audio recordings of her playing Cribbage with me after the diagnosis. Like so many other things associated with her, I haven't reviewed them. I'm in a public place, I think it's time I stopped writing about her.

31 May 2022

Have I mentioned that Rea loved Jiminy Cricket? Apparently Disney is coming out with a live action version of *Pinocchio*. It may be great, but I think I'll pass.

I'm doing that more and more. It's self-defense. I want to conserve as much energy as I can in regards to Rea to devote to the foundation.

At least it's nice today weather-wise for a change.

YOU CAN'T ALWAYS GET WHAT YOU WANT

Chapter 28

(June 2022)

5 June 2022

I'm okay. The weather is not helping. Getting older is not helping, especially my general feeling of mental fog.

———————————

I suspect I'm somewhere on the autism spectrum. Trouble looking people in the eye, social awkwardness due in part to an inability to read social cues.

Or maybe it's just the anxiety. I don't know. The fact that I'm 55 and unsure of why I'm only marginally functional a lot of the time is a bit of an indictment of both me, and society as a whole. This shouldn't be that hard, should it?

6 June 2022

It's shaping up to be a good day weather-wise. Which is a nice change.

Rea did not like "Dust in the Wind" by Kansas. Which was a little sad to me since I like the song and can kinda play the finger picked guitar part.

I asked her why once, and I don't recall her being very clear in her explanation. I think it was the fact that the song is not very optimistic. Rea was at heart a very optimistic person, at least externally. No one can know for sure what goes on inside another person's head, but she was mostly an optimist and she was constantly working to make her world, and the world of the people who came into her orbit a better place.

7 June 2022

Marley will be two years old on Friday. Which means Rea has been gone about 18 months.

I was struck today by how there are no calendars in the house. Rea loved calendars. I've probably talked before about how she used them as gifts at Christmas. Each year she'd buy two or three dozen of them when they came out in the late fall.

8 June 2022

Decent day weather-wise, and it's hard to complain about the view this evening.

9 June 2022

Not a great day mood-wise. The weather was overcast most of the day and it's raining at 8:52pm.

Tomorrow Marley will be two years old. She's a very good dog.

10 June 2022

I stayed up past midnight last night putting together a slideshow/video of Marley pictures to post to Facebook. Totally worth it and it came out at nearly 10 minutes. Then I managed to post a non-final version. Ugh. I did post the final version to YouTube and linked it to the FB post but I doubt many will bother watching it. Still, the FB version isn't bad.

Seeing all the pictures of Rea with Marley made me cry.

I swear to God, I have cried 10 times more in the past three years than I did in my entire life prior. It sure seems that way anyway.

I suppose I should continue to be grateful that I'm making it through each day with the full emotional burden of her death. It's not easy some- times, but I'm still here; I'm still paying my bills, and taking care of things to the degree I need to in order to get by. I have to count that as a win.

Marley got extra canned food this morning and will continue to get ex- tra treats and special treatment today. She doesn't know why of course, but she enjoys it and it makes me feel better, so it's all good.

14 June 2022

It was mostly overcast and rainy yesterday. Kinda becoming the norm. It was 48 degrees around 8am. Today it's 47 at 6:30am with rain in the forecast yet again.

I loaded up the non-snow tires into the CR-V yesterday and plan on heading over to Hood River this morning to get them swapped. The snow tires have been on the CR-V for two-plus years now. The Ridgeline still has the snow tires on. I'll deal with those when I get back from California.

I'll likely be heading south tomorrow.

16 June 2022

Marley and I made it to Livermore around midday today. I slept about four and a half hours at a rest stop, drove another hour, and felt more tired than I had before I'd stopped previously, so I decided to pull off at the next rest stop and take another nap. That put me at five and a half hours and I made it the rest of the way without issue.

My current plan is to head back a week from this coming Monday, so 10 days roughly.

I listened to some Phish on the drive. That is the first time in a while. I do like them, and it's not nearly as painful for me to hear them as it used to be.

I want to get to a place where I can encounter things related to Rea and not get upset.

19 June 2022

Wow, I had no clue I'd missed two days. Not a lot to report really. The regular Friday night get together was good. I ate too much, but that is typical. I've been feeling less than stellar the past couple of days, but that isn't unusual either.

It's starting to warm up here in Livermore. Tuesday I think it's supposed to hit 100 degrees. It's been many months since I saw that kind of heat.

Hopefully my air conditioning holds out. Being on the second floor makes the heat more of an issue than the cold, but there are large mature trees nearby and they provide some shade. A lot actually. It's dim in here even with the curtains open. That partially comes from being in a unit that is sandwiched between two others.

Marley and I have run into turkeys with babies the past couple of days on our walks. She wants to play, they do not.

20 June 2022

I had lunch with Mike and Ellen, both of whom are on my board. It was good to chat. I also took care of a couple of other errands while I was out.

It turns out masks are required inside in Alameda county right now. Thankfully I had some in my glove box, because I had zero clue. I'd ordered groceries and restaurant food for delivery since I've been here.

21 June 2022

The projected high temperature for today was 106 last night, but it looks like it's going to top out around 100. It's decently cool in the condo, but I'm probably not going to like my power bill this month.

22 June 2022

There just doesn't seem to be a lot to say recently. I think a lot of that is just that I've described everything I'm feeling many times already. Those feelings haven't changed much for months now and I don't think they will.

23 June 2022

It's another scorcher outside. I get a bit more exercise since I need to carry Marley over the super-hot pavement. We run if it's a very short distance and I try to avoid the sunny black asphalt when I can.

Summer brings the fire season. A friend who lives over in Pleasanton might need to evacuate. I offered him the option of crashing on my couch. The bathroom being accessible only through the one bedroom is sub optimal though.

Someday I might fix that. Normally I'm all for there being a bathroom with the "master" bedroom, but in this case it doesn't make a lot of sense. It shouldn't be that hard to make a door off the living room, though it would make the linen closet tiny since it would need to go where it is.

24 June 2022

The evacuation didn't happen luckily. Fire season seems to be getting worse in this part of the country. I think I'm safe in the part of Livermore my condo is in.

It was a good day overall. Marley and I went to the normal Friday get together. It'll never be the same without Rea, but it's still good to hang out with human beings and chat.

25 June 2022

I dreamed of Rea. The dream was disjointed and weird, but she was alive and just like she was before CJD eroded her away. She was inquisitive, curious and constantly in motion.

The thing I didn't mention earlier is that in the dream it felt like Rea.

I don't know if it is the case that we really get to meet our departed loved ones in dreams, but it felt good to be with her again, even if it was only an echo.

28 June 2022

Wow, I missed a couple of days. I actually typed the date in on the 26th but then I apparently got distracted and didn't make an entry.

It's continued to be hot here in Livermore. At this point I've decided to extend my stay until after the 4th of July.

The Supreme Court has continued to undermine its authority with recent decisions. The current crises can be traced to the court's decision to step into the hanging chads debacle back in 2000, at least that is my perspective.

The justices have become increasingly aligned politically and that is a problem. To be clear, I'm talking about both ends of the spectrum here. Justices will of course have their own opinions on political matters, but those opinions should be kept private. They should under no circumstances make obviously partisan comments in a public context. This is the way it was traditionally, and with good reason.

30 June 2022

It seems like I'm incapable of saying anything interesting in this journal for the most part. Diminished mental capacity? Old age? Not wanting to repeat myself? I don't know. It's been going on for a while now, and I don't know that it's going to stop.

It's not like there is a lot going on in my life. I'm doing a bit of programming; I'm working on music and I'm trying to get the not for profit going.

———————

Speaking of the not for profit, a week ago I gave LegalZoom the okay to send off the 503(c)(3) paperwork and it is showing as complete on their website. No guarantees there given past experience, but hopefully things are finally on track.

Chapter 29

(July 2022)

1 July 2022

Another month in the books. The 4th is coming up on Monday, which is good for people who work since it gives them a three-day weekend. I guess all days are holidays to me now, though.

The Supreme Court is continuing to turn back the clock. That probably sounds partisan, but given the clearly political leanings of many on the current court it's hard not to be.

I think part of the reason I've been feeling uninspired with this journal recently is that I've been holding myself back from writing about things like the Supreme Court. In part because there is a chance that somebody else might read this someday and I try not to be overtly political. I guess the emphasis is on try. I'm not a fan of either political party, which is an awkward place to be these days.

———————

I was thinking again about when I want to stop wearing my ring while walking Marley this evening.

At this point It's not if, I'm pretty sure it's going to happen. Removing it isn't going to make me happy and it isn't going to make it any easier to deal with Rea being gone, but it feels like something that has to happen. A rite of passage perhaps? I don't know.

I think I've mentioned before that it has become a bit like a shield. So long as I wear it I don't have to seriously consider what comes next.

2 July 2022

Another weekend in progress. The high didn't get above 70 today here in Livermore which is a big change from just a few days ago.

Unsurprisingly, I still miss Rea. I miss her smile, her laugh, her desire to travel and experience new things, pretty much everything about her.

It doesn't feel real that she is gone. It never will. I will never get over her entirely. I am richer for having known her and a much better person in many ways than I was before we met. Some of that growth was inevitable, but not all of it.

I'm also broken in ways I wouldn't have been otherwise. Having to experience her decline, diagnosis, and passing was more painful than anyone who has not gone through a similar experience could understand.

I'm glad that the layers of emotional numbness that enveloped me during that time have passed, but knowing that this pain and sadness will never go away is a burden. I can't put it any other way.

I'm mostly thankful I didn't take up drinking or find some other means of self-medicating. Mostly.

3 July 2022

Another cool day. The high was supposed to be 72. I don't think it got above that. Tomorrow is the 4th. Hopefully the whole city won't get burned down by poorly utilized illegal fireworks.

4 July 2022

I might have written about the following last year. As I've said before, I pretty much never look back on earlier journal entries, especially across year boundaries.

I don't remember where we were coming from, but there was a year we were flying back home the evening of the 4th of July. As we came in towards the SF Bay area we got to see multiple firework shows. That will probably be my favorite 4th of July memory when all is said and done.

Things are warming up a bit today with the high being projected to be 80 degrees.

I'm going to plan on taking Marley for her final walk of the evening a bit early so that we can hole up inside before the "fun" begins. She's generally fine around loud noises, though she does jump initially when surprised by a sound she isn't expecting.

It's evening. I took Marley for an early final walk of the day like I planned and we're ready to call it a day.

More 4th of July memories, spending evenings waiting for the fireworks and freezing in the meantime. Evenings can be very cool in early July here in Livermore.

I remember one in particular when Rea's mom was living with us and we were at the house on Peregrine. We were all bundled up in the front yard and still cold. At that time the fireworks were shot off from the rodeo grounds which were nearby. They've been doing them from the top of the parking garage behind the big movie theater downtown for several years now.

Fireworks are nice, but I don't mind missing them. Disneyland has a pretty good fireworks display nearly nightly during the peak parts of the year. I've seen enough of those shows not to need to see any more.

Fourth of July 2019 was a good one. Our friends Debbie and her son Zach came to visit us at the apartment we were renting in downtown Livermore at the time. We all walked over to what had been a car dealership near where the fireworks were going to be set off. It might have been 2018, but it was one of the two.

Good memories are good.

6 July 2022

It's nearly 1pm, and I'm fairly well on the way to being able to head out at 3pm. Traffic getting out of the SF Bay area will probably be interesting, but Monday was a holiday and it's mid-week so I'm hoping for the best. I'll let Google Maps guide me as to which route I take.

7 July 2022

Marley and I made it back to White Salmon around 9:30. I'd stopped a couple of hours south of Bend on 97 and slept about four and a half hours. I then drove the rest of the way without stopping and took a nap when we got home.

9 July 2022

Today has been uneventful. It's Saturday, so one more day till the work week starts …

For other people. I'm footloose and fancy free as the saying goes. Not that I'm enjoying the situation. Yes, Rea being gone plays into that significantly, but I'm also bored. Work provided structure. Which has its downsides, but it has upsides as well it turns out.

Hopefully when the foundation is a going concern I'll feel a bit more at ease.

10 July 2022

I was doing a bit of organizing around the house when I came across a box with a couple of insulated aluminum containers meant to keep ice cream cold. They are just big enough for a small ice cream tub.

Rea pre-ordered them just before her diagnosis. As is often the case with these "fund us and we'll send you the result for a deep discount later", things were delayed. COVID figured in as well.

I don't know exactly when they arrived as I was in New York at the time, but I first saw them after Rea's passing.

There are a pair of them, which makes it a bit worse since it's a his and hers kinda thing by implication. They are triggers for my grief. As many things still are.

Everyone's trauma is to one degree or another unique. I won't claim to know how a rape or abuse victim feels, but I will claim to know what the outcome of significant trauma feels like.

I don't enjoy being triggered, but I know that within reason it's part of the recovery process. I'll never be the same, but if I stick with it I'll get better, and at some point hopefully it will be tolerable.

11 July 2022

I took a picture of those ice cream containers I was talking about yesterday. It turns out they hold a pint.

I imagine that Rea was thinking of our plans to travel around in a big camper van. We could find a nice place to stop, go on a short hike and then enjoy some cold ice cream on a hot day.

God I miss her.

13 July 2022

Yesterday was one of the better days I've had. It was hot and the view near sunset was spectacular.

Yes, there was some post processing on that photo, but it's a fair representation of how striking it was at that time.

16 July 2022

Rea didn't think of herself as creative.

She was more creative than she gave herself credit for, though I tended to mostly fill that niche in our relationship. It worked out well. She would read the instructions on how to put stuff together and/or help me out when I got confused or lost, and I'd help her out on the creative side when she had a project.

The not-for-profit paperwork for the foundation went in on June 28. The IRS shows that they have assigned all requests postmarked by the end of June to a specialist. So I should hopefully hear back in the next couple of months. I don't anticipate issues, but I won't feel good until everything is finalized.

17 July 2022

Nice weather today. The high was only in the mid-70s, but mostly sunny and clear. It's a Sunday, so officially it's the start of another week. It's hard to believe it is nearly 6pm already. I read most of the day and have been doing a bit of programming as well.

20 July 2022

I have a pick-up from the farmers' collective later this afternoon.

I managed to remember to pick up my farmers' collective order. I took Marley along. She'd been naughty earlier when I left here to go out for lunch, so after banishing her from my presence for a couple of hours (which is about the only way I have to punish her other than looking cross) I decided taking her with me was the best plan.

I recently located the dash cam video of our final big trip across the country. I really wish it had audio. We didn't talk much during that time, but even just the sounds of the road would be good to hear, knowing I was spending time with her.

21 July 2022

Have I mentioned that Rea loved Marvin the Martian? She loved almost anything that was cute. I'm sure I've said before that she wasn't a "girly girl" kinda lady in most ways, but cute things were the exception.

I remember being young and thinking about what it would be like to be old. My mortality is much more of a real thing now and I understand why people get tired of life. I salute those who hold onto their joy into their 90s and beyond. They are special and lucky.

It's 4pm and the temperature has topped out at 86. Not too far off the forecast.

I'm in a weird place where time is passing both quickly and painfully slowly.

22 July 2022

Marley has a grooming appointment Sunday morning in The Dalles.

Marley got a short walk for the first time in a few days.

23 July 2022

I've reached the end of another week. In other words, it's Saturday. Temperatures are supposed to shoot up into the triple digits next week, but today is supposed only make it into the 80s, so Marley and I will enjoy that while we can.

I get an email with pictures of any "traditional" mail that is due to come that day. Today I saw a picture of a letter from the IRS addressed to the Rea's Song Foundation. I'm hoping it's good news, but fearing it isn't. I'll likely know this afternoon.

Approval received. Life is good.

25 July 2022

I've been in kind of a down mood today in spite of the good stuff that happened over the weekend.

A bit of an up and down day. Mondays often are. Rea passed on a Monday, and really, who likes Mondays anyway? Well, maybe retired people don't care. I haven't reached that point yet I guess.

26 July 2022

Another hot sunny day. Yay?

27 July 2022

It's supposed to be another 100+ degree day today. It's a quarter after 6am, and I have a bunch of windows open to take advantage of the relatively low temperatures while they last.

It topped out at 95 degrees today. In spite of that the forecast has it hitting 100+ through Sunday. I'm a bit doubtful/hopeful given the result today.

28 July 2022

Another hot day. I'm heading downtown to lunch shortly. I'll likely stop and pick up a few things at the grocery store as well.

Another day of failing to hit 100 degrees. Oh darn. Ninety-eight was the high.

Lunch was good, and I made a grocery stop. Somewhat productive day, and my mood is in the okay range. Which is pretty good for the post Rea era.

29 July 2022

Rea did not like green melon. She didn't eat grapefruit either, but that was because of some medication she took for the last several years of her life. I think it was related to high blood pressure.

Fruit bowls are another reminder of her.

I'm sneezing and have a bit of a runny nose. This often happens to me (the nose part anyway) after I eat anything fatty. It could be an allergic reaction, or possibly long COVID.

One of the many differences of opinion Rea and I had on food was in regards to the worth of cold pizza. When we first met I was all in favor of it as a second day treat. She did not agree.

As the years went by I was swayed to her point of view and would often reheat my leftovers as well.

Her favorite pizza was mushroom and pineapple. Mine was mushroom and olives.

Another month nearly in the books. I need to get moving on a number of different projects. I'm hoping August will be a good month for me.

I took Marley for a short walk while it's still relatively cool outside. We're supposed to hit 72 by 8am, and it's already 68 at 7:24. The high is forecast at 104. Thankfully it's supposed to cool down by mid-week.

———————

Tomorrow morning Marley and I are heading over to my brother's place. Marley will get to play with Mini, their 100+ pound Pyrenees Mountain dog. I'll get to hang out with real live human beings.

31 July 2022

Marley and I had a nice visit with my brother, sister-in-law, and grand-niece this morning. Thankfully we got some cloud cover which delayed the temperatures from hitting 90+ for a few hours.

Chapter 30

(August 2022)

2 August 2022

When Rea and I were planning for our retirement many years ago, I put together a spreadsheet that accounted for inflation, but soon after Rea stopped being able to help with it, I stopped keeping it up. It was a lot of work and I was losing my mind, so something had to give.

A couple months after Rea's passing I created a much-simplified spreadsheet. It works, even if it isn't as elegant/complicated. That is kinda a metaphor for my life.

_____

I think I'll take Marley for a walk. If I say that here, it will happen. It's cooled off a lot the past couple of days, so the pavement should be safe.

_____

Walk accomplished.

3 August 2022

I don't know how obvious it is from the words in this journal, but I'm really not a happy person. I don't know that I've ever been a happy person for any length of time.

That doesn't mean I've never been happy, I have been. But those moments have been relatively short. At best I feel like for the bulk of my life I've just kinda been present. But only kinda.

My anxiety makes it difficult to engage with people and when I do I'm seldom comfortable, especially if I don't know them well.

Yet being human, I need and will occasionally seek out human interaction. It's an odd and frustrating context to exist in.

I often feel trapped. Trapped by my decisions, trapped by my circumstances, trapped by the random and fickle finger of fate. All of those things and more have played a part in putting me where I am today.

I remember when I was young, feeling that I was in some way going to have a larger than average impact on the world. I also recall wanting that impact to be positive. Now I'm not so optimistic. I still want to make the world a better place but given my limitations and age I don't think it's likely.

But I haven't given up completely. I think I would pretty much be dead in spirit if not in reality if I went down that path.

Metaphorically I feel like I stumble, fall, crawl for a bit, stagger to my feet for a few steps and then stumble again to renew the cycle.

I don't know what is going on in other people's heads. I don't think I really understand what is going on in mine. I think that is one of the things that contributes to me being uncomfortable in social interactions.

I'm obsessed with communicating effectively and accurately, which is ironic since I don't feel that I'm very good at it.

I'll place some of the blame for that on the fact that qualitative evaluations come so easily to me. It takes very little information for me to come to a preliminary conclusion on a particular topic. Which isn't to say I set my opinion in stone. I try not to do that and I've constantly reevaluating all of my opinions based on new information. With the caveat that new information is rare, particularly in regards to long held beliefs.

The upshot of all that is it's very difficult for me to explain myself, because most things seem intuitive to me.

Having to stop and think about how to explain how I came to hold a particular opinion takes a lot of work, both because I don't do it often and because there can be a *huge* number of factors that go into my stance on any particular topic. Plus there is a lot of gray around my opinions. I very seldom believe in absolutes.

Essentially the majority of my opinions fall somewhere on a spectrum from one extreme to the other and I nudge my opinion on a topic one way or the other when I get new information.

It's very rare that I instantly change my opinion on anything, but over time the "needle" can be pushed from one side to the other of the center.

It's evening and I'm out on the back porch. Marley is standing watch by my side and there is the smell of smoke in the air. In spite of the smoke smell I'm feeling good.

Rea and I would sometimes sit out here, but we didn't live here that long and we were gone a lot. Some of her ashes are spread out in the backyard, but I don't think that has a lot to do with the feeling of peace.

It's not the first time this has happened. I felt this way a day or two ago when I was outside.

Somewhat related, I find myself enjoying things that Rea liked more and more as time passes. Like for instance opening the windows at night. Something I almost never wanted to do. I feel guilty about that, but I also feel like I've let her teach me something, albeit belatedly.

7 August 2022

Yesterday was a meh day. Nothing much happened, but that was my choice.

I think I slept like four hours last night, which led to me napping twice today. It's just after 7pm and I've slept maybe half the day. I would have a better estimate if I found my phone, but I'm feeling kinda lazy on that front right now.

I eventually discovered that my phone was all of two feet away from me when I typed in that last section.

My mother had several colorful colloquialisms that she frequently used. I assume they were English. "If it were a dog it would have bit me" was one of them. The implication being that the item she had been looking for was very close by.

10 August 2022

Today I've done a bit of this and a bit of that, including going downtown for lunch and to shop for groceries. Right now Marley and I are lounging on the back porch. My new deck chair makes that a lot more comfortable than the two camping chairs that have been out here since Rea and I moved in.

I had a funny thought.

Q: "What do you want to be when you grow up?"

A: "A philanthropist."
Maybe I'll take a nap out here.

And so I did.

It was good, but my phone got too hot sitting out in the sun and went on strike. I was shaded where I was, but the phone was getting direct sunlight. Given what I've learned about modern rechargeable phone batteries, I probably reduced its capacity a percent or two. They really don't react well to heat.

13 August 2022

A decently good day. It's the weekend, which doesn't really impact me much, other than reducing my desire to run errands since there will be more people out and about.

15 August 2022

I decided to delay my trip south for a couple of weeks. I got invited to a doggie birthday party at my brothers on the 27th, and missing it or being down south for only 10 days wasn't appealing. An advantage of being retired is I can easily change my plans. I guess it's also partially because I'm single. Which doesn't even qualify as a tin lining given the context.

17 August 2022

Marley is showing signs of mellowing, though she still needs more socialization, but that is 100% on me. Between my own shut-in tendencies and the ongoing COVID insanity it's easy to just stay home and avoid the majority of the world.

19 August 2022

My life post Rea still doesn't feel real. I'm thinking it never will.

22 August 2022

The weekend was fine. I got some things done, read a bit, watched some

TV and slept a decent amount. I guess I also exercised. I did in fact avoid working on my fantasy novel.

This morning I got up early and went to breakfast in Hood River. I then stopped by the mailbox annex and picked up a couple of packages. Marley has been chewing up stuff like pens and junk mail while I'm out, and this morning was no exception. So I closed the door to my bedroom and left her to wander the rest of the house as punishment for an hour after I got back.

For a long time I was feeding her breakfast in a room separate from me and closing her in for an hour or two. I think I'm paying the price for ending that practice as she seems to be exhibiting signs of separation anxiety.

25 August 2022

I had lunch downtown today for the second day in a row. The restaurant I wanted to go to yesterday was closed at lunch due to staffing issues. Between COVID and the labor shortage this is often the norm.

Tomorrow I plan on going to breakfast in Hood River and making preparations to head south on Saturday after stopping off at my brother's place.

26 August 2022

I've done some prep for my trip tomorrow. The nice thing about having a place down south is that pretty much everything I need is down there. I'll just have to pack up my computer and a few other things before I hit the road. I'll stop in Dufur to hang out with my brother and his family and then continue on through central Oregon to California.

29 August 2022

The drive down was uneventful. I stopped about two hours from Livermore and napped for a few hours before driving the rest of the way. I got here at about 3am, and slept another few hours.

This morning I overslept for the first time in a long while. I'd meant to get up by 5am, but woke up at 6:30. Which was probably good for me, since even then I only slept seven hours. I also woke up feeling a bit warm, which was concerning, but I feel fine now.

30 August 2022

I overslept again last night. Maybe I'll wake up at a normal time tomorrow. I guess I should try getting to sleep if I want that to be the case.

31 August 2022

I didn't oversleep this morning but I decided not to go out to breakfast. Then I napped for an hour plus a couple of hours after waking up at 5am.

I realized yesterday that Marley has a grooming appointment on Monday the 5th. Which means I'm heading back the evening of the third since rescheduling would put her next appointment in October based on past experience. She has a vet appointment on the 13th, so I'll likely head back down after that and stay a few weeks.

Chapter 31

(September 2022)

1 September 2022

It's supposed to be 103 today. I need to get up and take Marley for a walk while it's still only 58.

———————————

I had lunch with Mike Carter and Ellen Clower, both members of my board. We had a good discussion about holding a celebration of life for Rea next month. I'm going to finalize the details by the end of this weekend.

I had an epiphany earlier today.

I'm much more Steve Wozniak than Steve Jobs. I think I'd envisioned myself more as Steve Jobs, and I suspect others have cast me that way in their minds as well and viewed me as a threat. To be clear, I don't think of myself as anywhere near as talented as either of those guys. I'm just saying that my skills and personality are much better suited to being in the background and moving the ball forward than they are in being some sort of company messiah. Early on, Apple would not have succeeded without both of them of course.

———————————

Something I'm grateful for, Rea and I got to go to the Bluebird cafe in Nashville in December of 2019.

3 September 2022

The standard Friday night get together was great.

It never feels quite right without Rea being there of course, but at least I'm socializing. Ellen and Curtis have a new golden named Jake. Jake got chipped and vaccinated yesterday and is currently half Marley's size, so they didn't get to play too much but I think they will be good friends.

I did a bunch of prep work to get ready for heading back north. It's 12:30pm and I have maybe 20 minutes of stuff left to do. I'm taking a brief break before finishing up and heading out.

4 September 2022

Marley and I made it back to White Salmon without incident. I stopped a bit over halfway through the drive at a rest stop off of I-5 and slept about five hours.

In the middle of the night I was woken up by some idiot with a very loud stereo playing. Thankfully I had ear plugs in and it stopped eventually.

Tomorrow Marley has a grooming appointment in The Dalles at 8:15.

5 September 2022

Marley and I made it to her grooming appointment a bit early. I had breakfast at Cousins after dropping her off and now I'm hanging out in the parking lot working on various projects and waiting for Marley to be done.

It's Labor Day, so my tentative plan to deal with the oil change the CR-V needs wasn't viable as the Honda service center is closed. Being retired/self-employed, I don't have the same attitude towards holidays as I used to.

I've decided to describe myself as self-employed. Saying I'm retired makes me feel some combination of old/privileged since I'm still a few months shy of being 56 years old.

When I was 14 or 15 years old I bought myself a Commodore Vic-20. I'd been asking my parents for a computer since the late 1970s at that point, but not to put too fine a point on it, we were poor and a home computer wasn't high on their list of priorities. In fact, it wasn't on the list at all.

I'd had a summer job and managed to save enough for the Vic-20 and a data cassette drive. Later on I bought the "Super Expander Cartridge" which added 3000 bytes of RAM and an extended Basic interpreter. Which gave me a total of about 5500 bytes of RAM to work with. I was in heaven.

Eventually the power supply died, but I figured out that I could open the bottom of the power brick and short across a couple of exposed bits of metal. The brick itself was filled with some sort of resin, so I had no idea what I was doing or why it worked. Looking back, It was phenomenally stupid, but I was a dirt-poor teenager, and it worked without apparent issues. I regret nothing, though I do not recommend anyone else try to duplicate my stupidity.

I don't remember what happened to that computer. It has vanished in the mists of time and memory.

8 September 2022

Wow, two days have passed since my last entry. Nothing exciting to report for those two days. Sadly though, Queen Elizabeth II passed away today.

My mother was very fond of both the country of her birth and the royals. I don't have any strong feelings one way or the other, but I do admire the dignity and grace that the Queen brought to her "job".

Some of her descendants could learn a thing or two from her example.

10 September 2022

A few days back I ordered some new jeans from Amazon. I've been wearing the same size since high school (32x34). Back then I needed a belt to keep them up. The past couple of years I've been struggling with getting the button to close. For a minute or two I thought about ordering pants with a larger waist, but then I decided that was basically giving up. I've been doing well at maintaining my weight the past several months, and have even lost a few pounds. If I can keep that up, there is no reason why I can't continue to wear the same pants size.

There is a lot of smoke right now from all the fires. I haven't seen Mt. Hood in a few days. I don't think that is going to change any time soon.

Marley has a vet appointment on the 13th. Sometime after that we'll head back to California for a couple of weeks.

11 September 2022

Twenty-one years ago today the attack on the world trade center took place. It is the most recent point in time during which the US lived up to the "United" part of its name. I grieve for the state of my country pretty much every day, but today I grieve a little extra.

On that day Rea and I had gotten up super early to go to Body Pump. A couple of other people in the class looked concerned and talked quietly to each other before things started. On the way home afterwards we turned on the radio and heard the news for the first time. I don't recall if the second plane had already hit at that point.

We'd been in Boston just a couple of weeks earlier and had walked by the hotel where many of the terrorists were staying, totally unknowing of course.

We talked about it occasionally, but we never made it back to Boston. There were so many other places to explore.

I often wonder if I'll live to witness the dissolution of this country, whether it be in fact or by way of fundamental changes in the way it is governed. Depressingly, it seems increasingly likely that I will as time goes on. I pray I'm wrong to have these fears.

Here is a picture from that trip to Boston. I can't tell you exactly where it was taken. In those days GPS tagging on photos was not really a thing.

We walked all around downtown, including following the Freedom Trail, so it was possibly somewhere near there.

———————————

I think it was yesterday, maybe the day before. I was sitting on the couch out in the living room when I felt like Rea was there with me. I spoke out loud and told her I loved her and missed her. I thanked her for the time we got to spend together. Then I felt her leave.

Am I crazy? I don't think so. Was I dreaming? I'm do not think I was.

12 September 2022
It's starting to shape up into another insomnia night.

I just subscribed to the *London Times* digital edition. My mother would be proud I suspect, and I regret that she's not here to share it with.

Marley has a vet appointment in Hood River tomorrow morning at 9am. If I get to sleep by 2am, I should be fine.

A little under five hours of sleep total, but I made it through the bulk of the day. Marley is fine and the chimney in my garage is five bricks shorter thanks to some help from my neighbor Ken.

15 September 2022

Ugh, I keep forgetting to update this journal.

I'm vacillating between believing I'm deeply depressed on the one hand, or thinking I'm finally over the worst of missing Rea on the other. If that sounds contradictory, that's because it is I guess.

The following bit of prose came to me while I was driving a couple of days back.

Though the sun may seem dim
I know it's not foregone
That what I see is sunset
instead it could be dawn

That kinda defines my state right now. Am I fading, or is this the start of a new day? I have no clue.

I still miss Rea, and thinking about the context of her passing still makes me mostly sad, and a little mad, but it's like I've passed into a new phase.

17 September 2022

I think the place I've come to mentally is acceptance. It still upsets me to think about the fact that Rea is gone. Heck, I got a bit teary eyed thinking about it on my way to breakfast over in Hood River, but I also feel more or less normal otherwise. Which hasn't been the case since we got her diagnosis.

18 September 2022

Another weekend nearly done. I went and visited my brother and grand-niece today. Marley also got to hang out with her doggy buddy Mini, so that was cool. My sister-in-law was working.

The feeling that I've finally accepted Rea's passing is still with me. It's weird in the sense the mental weight I've been feeling for more than two years is just gone. Again, I'm still sad she's gone, and intellectually I still feel the empathetic pain for what she went through, but it no longer feels mentally crippling.

I also feel a bit like Rip Van Winkle in that after nearly 30 years I'm single again. That's another part of it. I'm finally ready to stop wearing my ring. Even if, given my oddities, chances are I'll remain single for the remainder of my life.

22 September 2022

The trip down to Livermore was uneventful. I left around 11am, and arrived in Livermore at 5am. Not bad.

I had a four-and-a-half-hour nap about two thirds of the way through which was perfect. Another nap once I got to Livermore means I'm more or less on a normal sleep schedule.

23 September 2022

No Friday night get-together this time.

I had Safeway deliver groceries, so I'm well set on that front.

25 September 2022

Sunday, Marley and I will be hanging out with friends this evening. Marley will get to play with her old friend Chewy and her new friend Jake.

26 September 2022

I sent out the announcement for Rea's celebration of life on Facebook today. I was only a little surprised that I started to cry when picking out the picture of her to include with the announcement. I don't know that I'll ever be able to look at a picture of her and not lose it a little bit.

So even though I'm doing better over all, it's not like the grief isn't still lurking close to the surface. I've just gotten much better at dealing with it.

27 September 2022

I had lunch with Mike Carter and Ellen Clower at Uncle Yu's. Which was one of Rea's favorite restaurants. We talked about the Celebration of life for a while and firmed up some of the planning.

Overall it was a productive day. I'm feeling like being retired doesn't mean being bored.

28 September 2022

I heard from Rea's friend Nancy today about a possible buy and sell for Wee Forest Folk in Michigan next spring. This would be awesome since I would really like to get rid of the bulk of Rea's collection and devote the majority of the money to the foundation.

30 September 2022

Yesterday went so fast apparently that I didn't even make an entry.

Chapter 32
(October 2022)

1 October 2022

It's a new month. A Saturday as well.

Today is mostly about getting ready to head north tomorrow. I'll be stopping in Sacramento to visit a FB friend who is also a distant cousin and in Portland to drop off my Sony Cassette deck for repair. Then I'll finally head toward home which should only be another 90 minutes or so at that point.

4 October 2022

Marley and I are back in Washington. We got here around 2pm yesterday.

Being on the road I had a lot of time to think, and I had an epiphany. I don't know how much sense this will make to someone who hasn't had a similar experience, but I'll describe it as best I can ...

The big difference between today and a month or so ago is that I've finally worked my way through my grief over Rea's passing and emerged on the other side. Thinking about her still makes me very sad and a little mad as well, but the grief has finally subsided.

What is the difference between grief and sadness? I can't really explain that. I just know that they are two separate things, even if they are related.

8 October 2022

Wow, four days of no show here for me.

Marley has a grooming on the 16th, I'll head back south the day after, which is a Monday. That will give me a decent amount of time to do final setup for Rea's celebration of life.

10 October 2022

Another Monday is here.

It seems like I have a cold. Hopefully it's only a cold. I've had COVID once and been vaccinated twice, so in theory it shouldn't be too bad even if it is the dreaded pandemic disease.

I ordered a couple of test kits that will be here on Thursday.

11 October 2022

I still feel subpar today. The thing that is bugging me the most is the fact that it hurts in my right armpit a bit. WebMD mentions several possible causes, most of which are benign and unlikely. Some of which are a little scary.

Weatherwise, no complaints. The smoke has cleared up today which is nice. It's sunny and not blisteringly hot. Basically, a very nice fall day.

13 October 2022

Today would have been my mother's 90th birthday. Yesterday I started writing a mini essay to post on Facebook, which is what I often do in these kinds of situations. I was a paragraph or two into it when I realized that I didn't have anything important to say and that every extra word I wrote beyond the bare minimum would be about me, rather than her.

I'm at a point in my life where I feel resigned. I'm not any more or less depressed on average than I've been during most of my life.

I haven't given up trying to accomplish things or make the world a better place in my own very small way, but I feel like if I found out I had six months to live, I'd be okay with that.

I know my mother was terrified of death. She told me this when I was hanging out with her at the hospital in Portland that they sent her too for the surgery that led to her spending her final days in an assisted living facility.

Rea told me she was afraid a few times after her diagnosis. Maybe I'm lying to myself. Maybe I would be afraid if my imminent death were a reality. We have deep seated instincts for self-preservation after all.

I know I haven't mentioned my faith in this entry. I suppose that in a sense that makes me a bad person, at least in the eyes of some. But the thing is, I think I'm okay with it even if there is nothing after life. I will have always existed in this universe, albeit for a very brief period of time.

On balance I feel like I've lived an okay life. Maybe I've made the world a slightly better place. I am part of the history of reality. I lived, and I got to experience things and make choices. That alone is a profound miracle. Anything beyond that would be wonderful. Assuming of course that I'm not going to the bad place. But that's not for me to judge, so I guess I won't worry about it.

16 October 2022

Marley grooming today. Tomorrow we head south in the later part of the morning.

Decent day overall. Marley is looking sharp and I should be able to head out of town at a reasonable time tomorrow.

17 October 2022

I'm about 50% done with getting ready, and it's almost 9am. Not bad since I likely won't leave until mid-day.

18 October 2022

The trip south was uneventful. Traffic was a bit heavy when I hit the Bay area with Marley, but that is typical at 9am.

One of Rea's mouser friends sent me some pictures of Rea and the various WFF Folktoberfest events that were held over the years. Pictures of her still make me teary eyed, especially ones I haven't seen before.

20 October 2022

I got so busy yesterday that I didn't make an entry on what would have been Rea's 64th birthday.

I had lunch with Mike and Laura Carter, along with Ellen to discuss final planning for Rea's celebration of life this weekend. We're working on a tri-fold for the foundation and I need to get together some pictures as well.

The tri-fold for the foundation is done. That took a good chunk of the day.

I need to get to those pictures first thing tomorrow morning and see about getting the tri-fold printed as well.

22 October 2022

The celebration of life for Rea went well. The weather was good, in the upper 60s with a bit of wind, but nothing too severe. The attendance was around 50 people.

This was a low-key launch of the Rea's Song Foundation as well. I didn't want that to overshadow things though. We had the tri-folds and a QR code available for donations.

I'm really tired. Marley is as well since she and Jake ran around a good chunk of the day. Plus there were all the people to hang out with.

Life is good, but it would be great if Rea were still here.

25 October 2022

Not much to report over the past few days. I've been working on various projects including the foundation.

I'll be heading back north next Monday, which is Halloween. It's a bit of a copout but the timing is good and it avoids one complication in my life..

26 October 2022

Midway through another week.

27 October 2022

I was playing around with "Stable Diffusion" today. It's one of the AI image generators that are all the rage right now. It's a wee bit slow for some things, but what it is doing would have been unheard of a few years ago.

I remember emailing a friend of mine who worked for a major GPU provider several years ago. I asked him if he thought it was possible to reverse what neural networks were doing at the time, which was essentially pattern recognition. My recollection was that he was unsure, but doubtful.

28 October 2022

Marley and I just got back from the regular Friday night get together at the Clowers, which was a lot of fun.

29 October 2022

Saturday, two days until it's time to head back north for a bit.

I'm thinking I might start north tomorrow night after dinner. I'm taking the Clowers and Carters out to Roya's, a really good Afghan place in thanks for their help with Rea's celebration of life. I really don't have much reason not to leave after that.

30 October 2022

I considered leaving tonight but I'm back to heading north tomorrow. It's nice to have the flexibility to flip flop on things.

31 October 2022

Breakfast at Panera and one last stop at the UPS store to check my mail. I also filled the Ridgeline with gas, so we're ready to go on that front.

I had to replace the smoke/gas detector since the old one started going crazy a few days back. That one was disposable, so I had to buy new. Which meant changing the mounting bracket, but that is easy. Added bonus, this new one has non disposable batteries. Hopefully they won't fail in the middle of the night. The old one lost its mind during the day thankfully.

Chapter 33
(November 2022)

1 November 2022

The drive back was more of an adventure than I would have liked. Everything was fine until just a bit north of the California/Oregon border when it started to rain. The rain wasn't a big deal, but eventually it turned into sleet, and then full-on snow. It snowed most of the rest of the way, though about an hour out from home it warmed up enough to just rain.

Marley and I made it back to the house fine, albeit a bit later than I would have liked, arriving just after lunch.

6 November 2022

Insomnia time. Yay. Hopefully it won't last much longer. It's just a bit past midnight right now. I have my second board meeting tomorrow at 1:30pm, so even if I'm up late, I should have time to sleep and make final preparations.

Got to sleep just before 1am. Just over five hours of sleep. I may try to nap before my board meeting.

The board meeting went well. We also got our first outside donation today. Life is good, as the saying goes.

7 November 2022

Tomorrow I have an appointment for the CR-V in The Dalles at 10am, and a tele-con at 1:30. I might ask about selling the CR-V. It would lower my costs about $700 per month. That feels like a win to me.

8 November 2022

The rear hatch on the CR-V is damaged. As in crinkled on one side. This is my fault. I think it happened in Bend, after Rea's diagnosis. We stopped at the Trader Joe's there and it wouldn't shut because I'd done a poor job of loading. I lost it. I might have written about this before.

20 November 2022

I don't deal well with adversity in the short term. Sometimes it feels like nine out of 10 things that I try to do fail which leaves me feeling demotivated. The ratio isn't that bad, but I do find myself reluctant to initiate activities as it seems like failure is a common outcome. I'm Pavlov's dog, and not in a good way.

The penultimate month of 2022 is 2/3rds done. It's been an okay year, but from where I'm sitting things look fairly mixed going forward. Politics in this country are a mess, the economy is all over the place, Russia and China are being run by people who seem unhinged to me. I could probably go on, but I've depressed myself enough for now.

22 November 2022

I started to read this journal from the start today. I made it midway through April 16. There are some typos and some moments described that make me uncomfortable.

It's not an easy read, and I'm still early in Rea's decline. I think it's a good thing that I'm at the point now where I can do this.

24 November 2022

Thanksgiving Day. It's sunny and I'm going over to my brother's place shortly with Marley. Marley will get to run around with her friend Mini, who outweighs her by a factor of three. Not that Marley cares in the least about that.

This is my second Thanksgiving without Rea. All the firsts are hard, the seconds less so. The worst was the lasts, at least the ones Rea and I spent together while knowing what was coming.

Now that I'm working my way through the early entries in this journal I realize that it's mostly my story. Which should have been obvious, but for some reason I missed that until now.

I'm really not proud of past me. I forgive him, but that doesn't mean I'm happy with him.

I mean I know I'm a deeply flawed person, but having it shoved in my face is unpleasant.

Rea and I did a number of Turkey Trot races starting in the early 2010s. The ones in the south bay were the best. There is one over in The Dalles that is in its second year. Maybe I'll manage to make it next year. That would be cool.

Thanksgiving dinner was very good.

25 November 2022

My mood has been generally decent to good recently. Today I'm feeling a bit down. There tends to be a lot of bad news on both a macro and personal scale these days. It's fatiguing.

But there isn't much I can do about it. Life is what it is.

26 November 2022

Not that I like this being the case, just to be clear.

27 November 2022

Marley has a grooming this afternoon in The Dalles.

Four am, still awake. Hopeful I'll nap soon.

I'm at Cousins Restaurant in The Dalles after dropping Marley off. It's crowded at 2pm. It is a Sunday, though, so not a surprise.

I guess it is also Thanksgiving weekend. Which impacts how busy things are as well.

Christmas music is playing on the speakers. Rea loved Christmas and Christmas music. I am not so fond of either, especially now that she's gone.

More than the holiday though it's the short days that wear on me. I'm glad we're close to the shortest day of the year. It's all uphill after that.

Back home after picking up Marley. She looks great as always.

29 November 2022

Today is the first substantial snowfall since the start of fall. Technically winter is still a couple of weeks away, but it's difficult to believe that looking outside. It's supposed to warm up into the upper 30s tomorrow, so this snow likely won't be around for too long. We're supposed to get more the day after though.

Still snowing at a quarter after 1pm. The evergreen trees haven't turned white yet, though, so the accumulation hasn't been very large.

I'm reading a really good fiction book called "RE: Trailer Trash: A Do-Over Story". The author's pen name is **Forty**Sixty**Four**. I like the fact that the pen name hides anything about their identity.

As the title suggests, the book is about a person who gets a second chance to live their life starting at age thirteen. I won't go into the plot, it's a complex and very well written story and I'm only about 4/5ths of the way through, but I will mention the concept of having a personal narrative which is explored in the book.

It resonates because I do not now, nor have I ever had a strong personal narrative. I've had plans and aspirations, but I've either taken advantage of chance circumstances and encounters to make progress or failed to achieve my goals because I didn't plan to the degree I should have. Or work has hard as I needed to.

I can blame some combination of anxiety and possibly being mildly autistic for that, but it still comes back around to me being to blame.

Will I ever have a personal narrative that I commit to? I'd like to think yes, but I don't know.

Still, if I could take a step or two in that direction my remaining life would likely be a lot better.

———————————

It's 3:30 now and the trees look like they are heavily flocked. Or more prosaically, like they have a decent buildup of snow.

———————————

I think the snow is still falling, but it's dark and I have most of the living room windows blocked by a screen so it's hard to tell. Marley needs to go out once more tonight, so I'll check then.

I'm starting to doubt it will all melt tomorrow.

30 November 2022

I really dislike this time of year. The short days mostly. I don't mind the snow so long as it doesn't come with a bunch of ice, and I don't need to travel. It doesn't help that Rea was clearly in her final decline at this point two years ago.

The snow has accumulated to about eight inches.

Chapter 34

(December 2022)

1 December 2022

First day of a new month, just over two weeks until I turn 56.

Today the concrete slab for the shop and garage additions are supposed to be poured. It's nearly 7am and work should be starting within the next hour. It will be cool having another milestone complete..

Concrete pour went fine. Next week should be windows and door, possibly including the garage doors.

2 December 2022

I've talked about anxiety and how it is a constant part of my life. Over the years I've also joked about being on the autism spectrum in real life. The more I research it, the more I'm thinking it's not a joke. I'd need to get a formal diagnosis, but dang, do the listed symptoms and experiences resonate with me. Almost universally in fact.

I tend to see problems and solutions rather than people and politics. That seems very much in alignment with how an autistic person might approach the world.

Will I get around to pursuing a formal diagnosis so that I know the truth? Hopefully.

If I do turn out to on the autism spectrum then honestly I'm going to be a bit pissed that it took 56 years to find that out.

3 December 2022

Ken and I dealt with about 60% of the bricks from the chimney today. We are putting them on pallets so that the fellow who bought them can haul them away for future use.

Weather-wise, it was cold but with mostly clear blue skies. Good times.

4 December 2022

I was going to go over to Hood River for breakfast today, but it snowed overnight and is supposed to snow more soon. I don't really need to go; it was just to get me out of the house.

I've been learning more about autism spectrum disorders, mostly via YouTube. Still resonating big time. One of the things that I've seen mentioned multiple times is frustration with the medical community's definition of autism in terms of deficits, and I think that's a fair criticism. Most of the issues that autistic people run into are related to trauma from interacting with others in a world where they are in a minority and have to mask, AKA behave in a way that feels unnatural to them, which in turn causes stress and trauma. When I imagine a world in which autistic people are the majority, I don't see nearly as much of that happening. I see upsides as well.

One symptom of autism is an inability to deceive, which makes others uncomfortable. But problems are much more likely to be solved if they are acknowledged and addressed.

I don't know, maybe I'm being overly idealistic.

The snow is still coming down. Currently the weather shows the next few days being dry, but I'm starting to think this is going to be a bad winter.

I cleared the snow from the CR-V and Ridgeline earlier. Otherwise I'd have to work for an hour-plus if I want to take one of them somewhere tomorrow. This turned out to be a good thing as Ken took the CR-V over to a friend of his and got the rear hatch fixed.

Which was awesome.

5 December 2022

I managed to screw up and fall asleep absurdly early. So I've been up since about 1am. I'll hopefully nap soon. It's 3:15am right now.

The snow has finally stopped. The weather app claims it should be clear the next few days with temperatures peaking near 40 tomorrow and Wednesday. It's only supposed to hit 32 today, though.

6 December 2022

Rea loved owls. We once attended a multi-part owl class. It was cool. Freezing actually on one of the field trips. I bring this up because Google photos has been helpfully putting together various slide shows based on the pictures in my phone photo gallery. Which include the ones I imported from Rea's phone. She seldom took pictures herself, but she would frequently snapshot and save ones that she liked. There are many pictures of owls.

8 December 2022

I am so done with the snow. I'd guess we've gotten an additional eight inches or more today and it's still going. I don't mind it when there is time for the roads to be cleared but it's a pain when it just keeps on falling.

Luckily it's been the light fluffy stuff mostly, so it's easy to shovel or blow with the snow blower.

The door and windows for the garage and shop arrived today. Given the slightly risky driving conditions I was impressed they were willing to do that. Hopefully the install will happen in the next few days, though the weather will play a big part in that.

10 December 2022

Today we're supposed to see temperatures close to 40 degrees Fahrenheit. It's already 33 at 6am, so I'm starting to believe that will happen. My plan is to head over to Hood River mid-morning and pick up the mail that has accumulated over the past several days.

For the first time in several days, I slept on a more or less normal schedule. I'd been falling asleep as early as 5pm, waking up in the wee hours for a couple of hours and then napping an hour or two.

Given my situation that was doable, but I don't like being that irregular. So falling asleep around 11pm and waking up at 5:30 is good.

My mood has kinda sucked recently, but that is typical of this time of year when the days are so short and it can be difficult to travel. Throw in Rea's love of Christmas and getting a year older. It's not a great combo. Thankfully we're almost to the point where the days start getting longer again and Christmas will soon be here and gone as well.

I'm seeing a bit of sun, which is nice. Temperature wise it's 36 at 10:45am.

11 December 2022

It's raining now. Kinda looks miserable out there. It's only 9:53 though, so maybe things will improve by lunch time.

Looking at the hourly weather report and radar map indicates that the answer is "likely not".

Even though I'm mostly at peace with it, I still miss Rea.

12 December 2022

The weather is looking favorable for a trip south tomorrow. Cold and dry, at least around here. I need to do a more thorough check of the entire route though.

I'm hoping the windows and door will be installed on the new part of the house today. It isn't a big deal if that doesn't happen, though.

13 December 2022

Getting ready to head south.

14 December 2022

The drive down was uneventful and done without stopping for a nap. Departure time was a little before 9:00am, and Marley and I pulled in a little after 9:00pm.

I've done my initial grocery shopping already with delivery scheduled for tomorrow morning. That is a big difference between down here and up north: I can get most things delivered. Bonus shut in points! Offsetting that is the lack of a yard which forces me to take Marley for multiple walks per day. Bonus exercise points!

I'm seeing more people wearing masks. I'm vaccinated against both COVID and the flu, and limit my in-person interactions so I'm not stressing about it but it's nice to see people being cautious.

16 December 2022

My birthday was fine.

I played Civ 5 a bunch and ended up not getting to sleep until nearly 2:30. Total sleep time so far is three point three hours. I'll take a nap soon.

It's Friday. Not that it matters too much.

———————

Decent day – Friday night dinner was good. Marley got to run around and act like a crazy dog for a couple of hours with her doggy friend Jake as well which is always good. She's slept since we got home.

17 December 2022

It's been on the chilly side here in Livermore. Not that I mind since it's warmer than it was up north before I left.

18 December 2022

It's a few minutes before midnight. I seem to be on a late schedule for a change. Which was the schedule Rea preferred before CJD started to impact her.

It was an okay weekend.

I've been doing a lot of photo restoration work. Mostly for free, but I do ask for a voluntary donation to Rea's Song.

Hmm, almost midnight …

19 December 2022

Happy Monday.

21 December 2022

I've been in a Civilization 5 phase the past couple of days. It's a good distraction, but it limits my productivity. I emerged this morning to put together a proposal and sent out requests for quotes on creating a book from this journal. I also worked a bit on doing some light editing of the 2020 portion. Mike C and I had worked on it a bit a couple of months ago.

Tomorrow is the shortest day of the year. I am so ready to be past that.

22 December 2022

The shortest day of the year. Or so I recall reading/hearing.

I dreamed of Rea last night. I don't recall too many details but I think it was a good dream. The fact I did so is probably related to the work I've been doing on editing the journal.

I don't have any special plans for Christmas. I'll probably eat something unhealthy. I have a Hungry Man fried chicken dinner in the freezer that would fit that bill nicely.

23 December 2022

Two days until Christmas. I don't have anything special planned, though I did add a half apple pie and some good quality vanilla ice cream to the grocery delivery I have scheduled for tomorrow morning. It can be a crapshoot as to what they do and don't have in stock, but hopefully one or the other of the two will arrive.

I wanted this journal to be primarily Rea's story, but I'm coming to the realization that it is much more my story. Which doesn't make me comfortable, but it's kinda inevitable that telling her story means telling my own as well. Especially since I'm the one doing the telling.

well. Especially since I'm the one doing the telling.

It's odd that on the one hand I shy away from saying "look at me" while on the other hand I've been releasing songs for several years.

I have a strong urge to create and share, but I just want to stay in the shadows and be anonymous. It is what it is, I guess. To do the things I want to do in regards to Rea's legacy I need to suck it up and move forward.

It's a challenge dealing with the editing. I'm at the point where I can deal with reading this journal, but it's still not easy and getting to the finish line is going to take a lot of work, even with professional advice and help.

24 December 2022

Going over this journal, I'm happy with the writing for the most part, but not with past me. Nothing new there, though.

25 December 2022

Christmas is here.

I had one present to open today. I knew what it was, and it wasn't wrapped in fancy paper. I received a couple of items I'd bought on Amazon on the 23rd. I opened one immediately but saved the tool set I bought for working on electronics stuff until today.

The wrapping was just the plastic shipping "envelope" that Amazon uses on smaller items. The tool set itself was in a small cardboard box.

Nothing fancy, but it was oddly satisfying opening it up Christmas morning.

26 December 2022

I dreamed of Rea last night. I probably dream about her most nights, but dreams are ephemeral, seemingly intentionally so.

I am forever changed by her passing, just as I was changed by experiencing life with her.

I believe that there is a life after death, and that she and I will meet again when my song is complete.

But even if there isn't, living is its own kind of immortality. Our time is brief. But Rea lived for 62 years and three months. She loved, made friends, accomplished goals, and made plans. She is part of the story of everything, and always will be. Nothing can change that.

She put a lot more positive energy into the world than negative and that is a beautiful thing.

I'm trying to learn from her example. The context of her passing had a profound impact on me, both because of my proximity to it and my closeness to her.

I started this journal to document what was going on around me, have someplace to vent, and work toward being a better writer.

My regrets —and there are many — take up a lot of space in this journal.

I would have sooner punched myself in the face repeatedly for a good chunk of eternity rather than have her go through what she did.

Rea was kind, committed, and focused. She made my world and the world around her a better place.

Two years after her passing, friends and family still miss her keenly. I know this, because I experience it every day and I've been told it is true by others.

None of us are perfect, least of all me. We all have our flaws and challenges but Rea was one of the rare people who for the most part managed to transcend all of that.

I've mostly managed to find peace, but I will always miss her and I will do my best to preserve and propagate the beauty she brought to the world.

I am not the only one, though. Little bits of her story live on in the people she met, knew, and loved. We are in a sense all echoes of those who came before us.

It is my hope that this journal will amplify the positive energy she brought to the world. I can't give her the retirement we worked so hard for and dreamed of, but if I can do that, then I'll have accomplished something with my life.

28 December 2022

The editing is still ongoing.

It's emotionally draining work, but I'm glad I'm doing it, and that I've reached a place where I can do this.

I'm debating whether to continue this journal next year. If I do, it will have to have a different primary focus. I don't think I have anything new or interesting to say about Rea. I love her and I miss her. That will not change.

I don't know what I'm going to do. Come the 1st, I'll decide.

30 December 2022

I'm almost through the first pass edit of the journal. I still have November and December of 2020 left. The last four months of that year were really difficult. I've been having to take regular breaks. In fact, I'm taking one now before starting on October.

It's been surprising to me how much I've forgotten about that time. Not the big picture, but the little details like when Rea took a significant downturn.

31 December 2022

There have been two women in my life who had a huge impact on me. Rea was one of course. The other was my mother. Her story is complete as well, and there are aspects of it that I can never know. She would have been 90 this past October, and she left England in August of 1967. There are likely few people alive there at this point who remember her.

I have several audio interviews I did with her starting in 2003, plus my own recollections and the family photos from the 1960s through the early 2000s. That is a decent amount of material to start from. And maybe, just maybe I can learn something if I write a book about her.

01 January 2023

My mother had a tradition of opening the back and front doors right at midnight so that the old year could exit out the back while the new year came in the front.

Until we discovered Phish, Rea and I had settled on being in bed and asleep when midnight arrived.

Three years ago today we were in New York City and I woke up to near silence on New Year's morning, Which was something that I'd never experienced before in our visits there. It turns out that even Manhattan sleeps in the wee hours of the morning on New Year's Day.

Two years ago Rea and I slept through New Year's. COVID meant that there was no Phish, and Rea's condition at that point in time meant that we would have had a lot of difficulty making it to the shows even if that had not been the case. But I think I would have found a way to get us tickets and make it to the final show of 2021 if that had been a possibility.

The past two years I've been back to sleeping through New Year's. This is the point where I should probably be writing something profound, but I don't have anything particularly profound to say.

I would give anything short of my soul to have Rea back.

Finding meaning is difficult. Rea gave my life meaning, and nearly two years after her passing she still does.

Afterword

(May 2023)

I removed my wedding ring on January 18 2023, which was the second anniversary of Rea's passing. I wear both rings on a chain around my neck.

It turns out that, yes, I am in fact on the milder end of that Autism spectrum, in the range that was generally described as "Asperger's Syndrome" prior to the release of the fifth edition of the *Diagnostic and Statistical Manual of Mental Disorders (DSM 5)* in 2013.

I have mixed feelings about being diagnosed this late in life. It would have been nice to have known earlier, as I could have cut myself a bit of slack in regards to how poorly I dealt with many situations. But, given the nature of "treatment" through the years and even largely today, I am more than happy not to have been subjected to any of that.

What follows is a more complete explanation of my complete diagnosis. None of it was much of a surprise. I doubt anyone familiar with these disorders who has read this journal would be surprised either.

First some background on Autism as defined in the DSM 5. The DSM 5 specifies three levels on the autism spectrum:

Level 1: Requiring support – Individuals at this level require some support to function in social situations. They may have difficulty initiating social interactions and maintaining social relationships, and may have difficulty adapting to changes in routine or transitioning between activities.

Level 2: Requiring substantial support – Individuals at this level require substantial support to function in social situations. They may have more significant difficulty with social communication and interaction, and may exhibit repetitive behaviors or have highly restricted interests.

Level 3: Requiring very substantial support – Individuals at this level require very substantial support to function in social situations. They may have severe difficulty with social communication and interaction, and may exhibit extremely repetitive behaviors or have highly restricted interests.

There is a saying in the Autism community that seems to be fairly common: "If you have met somebody with Autism, you have met one person with Autism." The intention of this adage is to communicate that there are a number of different attributes associated with Autism, and every person on the spectrum experiences differing degrees of each, and is thus unique.

Many adults with Level 1 Autism, particularly women, minorities, and those who were not affluent growing up, went undiagnosed in the past, and are still less likely to be diagnosed even now.

It is also the case that knowledge and understanding of Autism in general, and what is now referred to as Level 1 Autism in particular, has grown significantly over the past several decades. I was experiencing the first downsides of Autism half a century ago when treatment far less advanced. Children today are more likely to be diagnosed and receive help early, though this is a bit of a mixed blessing given the approach taken with much of that treatment.

While I had challenges growing up due to my undiagnosed Autism, I was blessed in many ways. I met people along the way who reached out and befriended me. They created opportunities and put me in situations where

I was able to function and at times thrive. Rea was the most important, but she was not alone.

On balance, I don't for the most part regret having made it this far in my life without being diagnosed. The one exception being that knowing what I know now sooner would have improved my relation with Rea. The fact that we did as well as we did is in large part a credit to her and the love she had for me.

In addition to being autistic, I am also ADHD, with a qualifier of "predominantly inattentive presentation", which I interpret to mean that I exhibit deficits in attention much more so than being hyperactive. I was the kid who sat in the back of the classroom whenever he could and daydreamed.

Finally, there is Generalized Anxiety Disorder. It may sound odd, but until I was in my early forties I had little clue as to what anxiety was. You might ask how this could be? None of us can truly know what is going on in other people's heads. Being Autistic makes this even more challenging. Now imagine that you are almost always slightly anxious. To the point where you can only recall one time in your entire life when you were completely relaxed. Until you had that one experience, how would you know what anxiety is?

I finally had that one experience when I was 43 years old. It was short-lived, but it lasted long enough that I had an "ah ha" moment. To this day I have no clue why it happened; I'm just grateful that it did.

Thankfully, on a one-to-10 scale, while I seldom feel anything below a three, I also seldom exceed a five. This was not true after Rea's diagnosis, during her decline, or for several months after she passed. During that time, I was at times extremely anxious, as I mentioned earlier in this journal.

Recognizing my limitations does not mean I want to lower my expectations, but I do want to set realistic goals that align with my capabilities.

I began to understand maybe halfway through kindergarten that I was not like the other kids – and arguably worse, they did as well. This did not lead to anything good. I was bullied frequently and regularly from then until my senior year in high school, and I attribute the relative peace of that final year mostly to the fact that my peers then were an uncommonly cool group of people.

The *Dick & Jane* books were still in use when I was first learning to read. I was put in the slowest group. Those of us in that slow group were made to read volume one of the series over and over again. Eventually, I complained to my mother and she complained to the school. Soon after, we finally advanced to book two. So, it wasn't only the other kids who saw a difference; it was the teachers as well. Keep in mind that I score very well on aptitude tests and do particularly well in the areas of vocabulary and reading comprehension/qualitative evaluations.

So, what's next for me? Well, I now have a deeper understanding of myself and my limitations. This knowledge has facilitated a level of self-compassion, helping me to forgive myself when I make a mistake or recall past shortcomings.

I don't want to use my Autism as an excuse, but I am starting to accept it as an integral part of my identity. It is real, and it undeniably affects how I experience and navigate the world around me.

Afterword (September 2023)

I struggled trying to find a way to end things in a way that gave some sort of closure. I don't know how successful I was, but now I'm going to risk messing that up by adding a bit more here at the end.

Long before Rea's diagnosis I came to the conclusion that one of the most difficult parts of getting older would be maintaining some sort of balance and optimism. I've seen a lot of people slowly loose themselves to some combination of loneliness, anger, frustration, bitterness and grief as they've aged, and I never want to be one of those people.

Rea set a good example. She was human, and there were times when life challenged her, but she never lost her sense of wonder and joy. That joy lived on up until her final days. All I had to do was put on some Phish, or The Grateful Dead, and a smile would light up her face.

The two of us shared a sense of wonder, and I wouldn't say that I'm a complete stranger to joy, but we were very different people in many ways. I think that is why we worked so well together. For the most part we complimented each other.

I am, and always will be sad and a little mad about the ending to Rea's story. But I am neither bitter nor resentful. I just don't have it in me to be that entitled.

I guess what I'm trying to say is that in spite of what happened with Rea, I feel like I'm doing OK. Which is what I would have wanted for her if our roles had been reversed.

Afterword (November 2024)

I'm about to submit this manuscript for formatting as an actual book, both electronic and print, so I have an opportunity to say a few more words. After I wrote the previous Afterword, I rediscovered the journal that Rea briefly kept just after her diagnosis. She only made a handful of daily entries before stopping. She mentioned around this time that writing was becoming increasingly difficult for her. Writing also meant thinking about her situation, and I know that was hard for her. April 20th, the day after her final entry, was also the first of our initial two-day visits to UCSF, and while the people there were awesome, I suspect that played a part, as again, it made the whole situation that much more immediate and real for her.

I've done as little editing as I could manage. Mostly, I put in paragraph breaks and corrected one or two misspellings.

I remember thinking she'd chosen to write one more time later on, but the only text I could find beyond what is transcribed below was on the final page...

Lockn
Bell Bottom Blues

As for what that final text means, it is most likely a reference to a performance by the Tedeschi Trucks Band at the Lockn' music festival in 2019. Phish's Trey Anastasio accompanied them. An audio-only version can be found on YouTube as I write this.

These are, in a sense, Rea's final words. I think it's appropriate that she is the one who closes out this book. I've included some pictures that were taken on or near the days the entries were made because it just felt like the right thing to do.

Rea's Journal

(April 15-19 2020)

4-15-2020

Thank you Andrea for my beautiful journal and the nudges I needed to get started

We're Currently waiting for info back from the tests @Palo Alto yesterday and info on the study I may get into. Waiting is the hardest!!

I've certainly noticed some recent decline and may be med related, but I don't know.

So far Debbie, Andrea and Julie know all we know, Ken + Carole Know we're seeing Dr. but don't know details.

Writing is getting harder. Mike watched phish with me last night, which was awesome. I hope he will get the support he needs. Debbie is reaching out to him and he is eager for answers so we can plan and move on, whatever that means.

It's another beautiful day and we will need to get out and enjoy the sunshine. I'll see if I keep writing or try typing. This was a good start.

4-16-2020

Heard from UCSF, and we start on Monday. One and a half days to start. I hope we'll be on a monthly schedule or something similar so we can be in Washington most of the time. I'm still loving the Forest book. Buck had to put her Kitty down and she seems to be doing OK. I'll probably fill Ken + Carole in soon.

I'm cutting back on the seizure medicine and I'm hoping this will make me less foggy.

I really like the Wizardry puzzle, but space is a challenge.

Getting medical records is a real pain! We have already been to Valley Care and they say everything is available, but other facilities say they don't have it.

My ears continue to ring. I was hoping med cut back would help. I'll talk to them on Monday about that.

Cloudy today. Mike has talked about getting a dog and we'll have to see how the schedule looks. Also looks like there may not be shows (Phish) until 2021. Well, I've made it to 50!, and hoping for more! I have some visual things going on that I will also talk to them about. If I un focus my eyes, things move down, but it doesn't make me dizzy. I am noticing jumpiness. I hope the new eye prescription works well. Worst case I can have them switched back. Time to go back to tackling the puzzle.

4-17-2020

Had a hard time sleeping, my knee was hurting, not enough walking! Will get back to it today!

Lack of sleep makes memory issues worse I've noticed, and coordination is harder too.

We got the MRI disk from Stanford and hope that will give them what they need. Still trying to decide on getting new glasses or just having them replace the lenses. Will talk to UCSF person and local Opto and decide. Need to thank Andrea for the journal. Not sure if I did.

Decided not to get a hotel. we should sleep better and traffic will be light. Sun is coming out. Yea!

Getting close to the end of the Forest book and I think it will be one of those I won't want to end.

People at Stanford HC were very helpful today. Things are so chaotic for everyone and glad everyone is keeping their cool. They don't seem very busy, which is good and hope it stays that way.

Not too much more to say todays so going to quit now. Need to think of some grateful "I" words.

4-18-2020

Knee has been bothering me, but Aleve and last nights walk helped, more walking today! Also hope allergy med will help clear my head. Ordered new phones yesterday. The red looks cool!

I think we're going to watch a comedy today, maybe the Pixar one.

I'm looking forward to the UCSF appt on Mon + Tue, I expect we will learn more even if it isn't good news, at least we will have some answers.

I should finish the Forest book today and need to pick the next one.

Mike is wanting to head up north soon after UCSF and I'm OK with that. I will need to start getting Mike info like passwords, etc. I am also eager to start dog searching. I expect we will pay Sue to do the training. Actually, I'll start checking that out when I'm done w/this. Which I guess is now. :-)

4-19-2020

Watched our first Disney+ movie last night, "Onward". It was really good and hit the spot given what's going on right now.

A little nervous but also eager for tomorrow. I'm not expecting good news sadly, but need to face reality.

Going to be sunny today and planning to go to Shadow Cliffs on Wed Haven't finished the book yet. It's so good!

Missing contact with w/my friends so much. Hoping another month will be enough and I'll be able to see them again. This is one of the hardest parts!

It's not fair, but it is what it is.

Had an awesome walk on my own last night.

Slow writing day. Maybe more tomorrow.

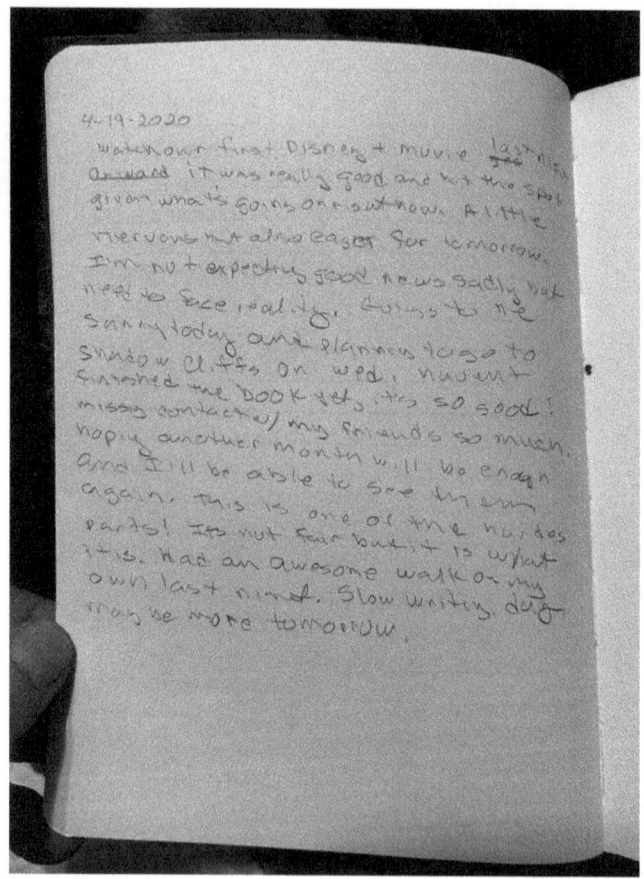

www.ingramcontent.com/pod-product-compliance
Lightning Source LLC
Chambersburg PA
CBHW051606120626

46551CB00014B/1685